DEVELOPMENTS
IN PSYCHO-ANALYSIS

PSYCHOANALYSIS
EXAMINED AND RE-EXAMINED

Consulting Editor: Bernard Friedland, Ph.D.

New York University Post-Doctoral Program in
Psychotherapy and Psychoanalysis

DEVELOPMENTS
IN PSYCHO-ANALYSIS

By

MELANIE KLEIN, PAULA HEIMANN
SUSAN ISAACS and JOAN RIVIERE

Edited by
JOAN RIVIERE

With a Preface by
ERNEST JONES

DA CAPO PRESS • NEW YORK • 1983

Library of Congress Cataloging in Publication Data
Main entry under title:

Developments in psycho-analysis.

  (Psychoanalysis examined and re-examined)
  Reprint. Originally published: London: Hogarth Press, 1952. (The International psycho-analytical library; no. 43)
  Bibliography: p.
  Includes index.
  1. Psychoanalysis — Addresses, essays, lectures. I. Klein, Melanie. II. Riviere, Joan, 1883–   . III. Title: Developments in psychoanalysis. V. Series: International psycho-analytical library; no. 43. [DNLM: 1. Psychoanalysis. WM 460 D489 1952a]
BF173.D457 1983   150.19′5   82-16229
ISBN 0-306-79711-9

This Da Capo Press reprint edition of *Developments in Psychoanalysis* is an unabridged republication of the first edition published in London in 1952. It is reprinted by arrangement with the Hogarth Press Ltd. and Dell Publishing Co., Inc.

Published by Da Capo Press, Inc.
A Subsidiary of Plenum Publishing Corporation
233 Spring Street, New York, N.Y. 10013

THE INTERNATIONAL PSYCHO-ANALYTICAL LIBRARY

EDITED BY ERNEST JONES, M.D.

No. 43

DEVELOPMENTS IN PSYCHO-ANALYSIS

By

MELANIE KLEIN, PAULA HEIMANN
SUSAN ISAACS and JOAN RIVIERE

Edited by
JOAN RIVIERE

With a Preface by
ERNEST JONES

THE HOGARTH PRESS LTD.

40–42 WILLIAM IV STREET, LONDON, W.C.2

AND THE INSTITUTE OF PSYCHO-ANALYSIS

1952

PUBLISHED BY
The Hogarth Press Ltd.
and
The Institute of Psycho-Analysis

LONDON

*

Clarke, Irwin & Co. Ltd.
TORONTO

PREFACE

STUPENDOUS as was his output, both in quantity and in quality, so productive was Freud in original ideas and discoveries that it was not possible for even such a worker as he was to explore all their potential ramifications. Many collaborators have assisted in this gigantic task. A footnote of his was expanded into a book on Hamlet, and many light hints have been developed into essays or even books. This work will continue for many years to come, so fruitful were his inspirations. Furthermore, the use of the methods he devised must in the nature of things lead to fresh discoveries beyond those he made himself and to hypotheses that extend or even rectify his own—a procedure he unhesitatingly applied himself.

There comes a point, however, where such endeavours raise a difficult problem. Bitter experience has taught us that resistance against the unconscious can be so subtle that it may distort the analytic findings and reinterpret them in support of some personal defence. How can this disturbing state of affairs be distinguished from a true development, a deepening of our knowledge of the unconscious? The sole criterion that can legitimately be employed is that valid for all science, a consensus of conclusions reached by *adequately qualified* workers using the same method in similar conditions. What is certainly illegitimate is the Procrustean principle of assessing all conclusions with those reached by Freud, however great our respect for the latter may and should be.

Mrs. Klein's work of the past thirty years, which is the theme of the present volume, illustrates the problem just stated. It has been attacked and defended with almost equal vehemence, but in the long run its value can be satisfactorily estimated only by those who themselves make comparable investigations. Mrs. Riviere in her introductory chapter has dealt very faithfully with the various criticisms and objections that have been expressed by those disagreeing with Mrs. Klein's work, and it would be out of place for me to discuss them further here. I will venture only one personal comment. As is well known, I have from the beginning viewed Mrs. Klein's work with the greatest sympathy, especially as many of the conclusions

v

coincided with those I reached myself; and I have all along been struck by the observation that many of the criticisms have been close echoes of those with which I had been made familiar in the earliest days of psycho-analysis. A good many of her findings and conclusions had been adumbrated in quite early days, by Freud, Rank and others, but what is so distinctive and admirable in her work is the courage and unshakable integrity with which she has quite unsparingly worked out the implications and consequences of those earlier hints, thereby making important fresh discoveries in her course. Her mind is very alien from those who accept the findings of psycho-analysis provided they are not taken too seriously.

ERNEST JONES

CONTENTS

NOTE

A SPECIAL bibliography was appended to Chapter II when originally published in 1936. It is reprinted with the chapter here, since it had the purpose of referring to work done at that date by London psycho-analysts on the topic of this paper.

Chapter Notes, in which more detailed discussion of certain topics or references to them will be found, are appended after certain chapters, in order that the main argument of the chapter should not be overburdened. The letters (Ch. N.) in brackets in the text draw attention to these.

* * *

The authors wish to express their indebtedness to Miss Judith Fay for her arduous and painstaking work in the compilation of the Index.

I

GENERAL INTRODUCTION

By JOAN RIVIERE

'I have made many beginnings and thrown out many suggestions. . . . I can hope that they have opened up a path to an important advance in our knowledge. Something will come of them in the future.'

This passage from Freud's *Autobiography* is only one of many in which he claims that as a science psycho-analysis is fore-ordained to development and expansion. In one of his prefaces he records 'his earnest wish that this book should age rapidly and its deficiencies be replaced by something better'. In 1924, when I was struggling with obscurities in *The Ego and the Id* for the translation, and pestered him to give me a clearer expression of his meaning, he answered me, exasperated, 'The book will be obsolete in thirty years!'

Nearly thirty years have passed since then, and nothing that he wrote is obsolete. There is nothing that he wrote that does not repay intensive study, comparison and reflection. Yet his assumption that his work would grow and develop—and in ways that he himself did not consciously foresee—has been confirmed. As we follow these new paths which lead so deep into the unknown recesses of the mind and at the same time illuminate human behaviour so far and wide, the crowning pleasure of such widening comprehension comes always, as I think, in a recognition that the original seed of our newer gains lay actually embedded in Freud's own thought, unconsidered and undeveloped or almost disowned by him though much of it was.

In saying that the germ of almost all these more recent gains may be found in Freud's own work, I am not undervaluing the original work of the other pioneers, *e.g.* Ferenczi, Ernest Jones and in particular, Abraham, and later the unique share of Melanie Klein, in the body of knowledge and instrument of knowledge that psycho-analysis now is.

This book is a survey of the developments in psycho-analytical

knowledge made by the work of Melanie Klein. Freud discovered the unconscious mind of man; she has explored its
deepest recesses. She has recognized that the world of unconscious feeling and impulse (which we call 'phantasy') is the
effective source of all human actions and reactions, modified
though they are as translated into actual external behaviour or
conscious thought. Although Freud discovered this truth and
applied it in many of his conclusions, there are many problems
to which he did not apply it, and which have been brought
nearer to a solution through Melanie Klein's consistent awareness of the significance of unconscious phantasy. The circumstances under which his work began and was carried through,
i.e. its origin in medicine, no doubt affected his outlook; for
instance, at his starting-point he was greatly occupied with the
differences between 'normal' and 'morbid' mentality, and this
may later to some extent have diverted his attention from the
general laws he had in essence recognized. It may be also that
in some ways he overestimated the force of the reality-principle,
or again did not fully recognize that an interaction of the
external and internal relations of the individual is a duality as
essential and as fundamental in mental functioning as the
other great duality which he discovered.[1]

As it has turned out, however, this other duality, Freud's
theory of the two basic forces—which for the present we have to
call the Life and Death Instincts—eventually made it possible
for Melanie Klein to understand the general law underlying
her findings in her studies of the earliest forms of mental life
in infants and small children. The enormity, to our adult minds,
of the destructiveness and cruelty which any detached enquirer
who follows the paths of her investigations will find in babies
ceases to be such an insoluble mystery when, as she shows,
Freud's hypothesis of a destroying force in our minds, always
in interaction with the life-preserving force, is allowed its due
significance. This concept of a destructive force within every
individual, tending towards the annihilation of life, is naturally

---

[1] For an explanation of the phrase 'the internal relations of an individual',
as contrasted and interacting with his external relations to people, the objects of his love and hate, see Melanie Klein's theory of the inner world of
introjected objects, in particular Chapter IV, Part 2 (*c*), p. 155.

one which arouses extreme emotional resistance; and this, together with the inherent obscurity of its operation, has led to a marked neglect of it by many of Freud's followers, as compared with any other aspect of his work.

Psycho-analysis is a branch of science; it goes its own way, as he knew and expected; 'the possibilities of development inherent in it will withstand all opposition', as he said. It is true that what he left to us has now acquired much that was absent from his explicit formulations—though not much, as I think, of which he had no inkling. Melanie Klein's main discoveries relate to the very early phases of mental life, where she finds in operation mental mechanisms (splitting, projection, etc.) closely similar to those of the psychotic disorders, another aspect of her work which arouses strong emotional resistance. We cannot overlook the fact, however, that when that other unwelcome proposition, the death instinct, previously arrived at by Freud by a different clinical route, is applied to the unwelcome findings revealed by the independent path of her child-analyses, the latter then become capable of explication. It is impossible to ignore the corroboration which the work of each receives from the other on this point. It may be said, moreover, that it is clearly no accident that each of these results in turn have met with disfavour, since they prove to be so closely related. Nevertheless, it was only in the latter years of her own investigations that Melanie Klein could show in detail the inherent connection underlying Freud's duality of instincts and the earliest emotional development of babies, namely, in the relation of persecutory anxiety and the development of guilt-feeling with depressive anxiety to the workings of the death instinct.

Melanie Klein's first book, *The Psycho-Analysis of Children*, is the basis of all her work. Apart from that, her publications have dealt separately and in detail with special aspects of her findings, so that eventually a need was felt for a general survey of her contributions to theory and a correlation of them. The number of those interested in these contributions to psychoanalytical theory has rapidly increased, both among students of psycho-analysis itself and workers in related medical disciplines; while an ever-widening interest in her work is forthcoming in the field of child-psychology, as shown both by members of that profession and by the intelligent lay public. For this reason it was decided to publish in book form a general survey of the developments in psycho-analytical knowledge of which her work consists. The present book is based primarily on four papers which were originally read in a series of Discussions arranged in 1943 in the British Psycho-Analytical Society with the object of enabling members to clarify their views in regard to her work. It is greatly to be regretted that the publication of this survey has been delayed so long after the originals of these chapters were written; and the more so since Susan Isaacs, whose energy had been an essential feature of the original Discussions, was sadly disappointed before her death in 1948 that the book had not appeared. There were various reasons for this delay, ranging from the general difficulties of book publication during and after the war to personal exigencies hampering the contributors, not the least being the great demand for analytic training by applicants after the war. There has been, however, one mitigating circumstance arising from the delay; it has become possible to include in the book some more recent papers by Melanie Klein which did not form part of the Discussions, and which add substantially to the clarification of her views in general.[1] It will be apparent that in

[1] The four papers presented in the Discussions in 1943–4 were: 'The Nature and Function of Phantasy', by Susan Isaacs; 'Some Aspects of the Role of Introjection and Projection', by Paula Heimann; 'Regression', by Susan Isaacs and Paula Heimann; and a paper by Melanie Klein. These papers now form Chapters III, IV, V, parts of VI, VII and VIII and also Chapter X in this book; most of them have been expanded, and difficult points are discussed more fully in the version published here. The fourth paper given in the Discussion series was by Melanie Klein, entitled 'The Emotional Life and Ego-Development of the Infant with Special Reference to the Depressive Position'. This paper was subsequently re-written and expanded into Chapter VI of this book, and some of its material has also been incorporated into Chapter VII, and also into Chapter VIII on 'Anxiety and Guilt'. The four Discussion papers are now supplemented here by Chapter VII, 'On Observing the Behaviour of Young Infants', as well as by Chapter VIII on 'Anxiety and Guilt'. In addition, a more recent paper by Melanie Klein, 'Notes on Some Schizoid Mechanisms', is also included in this book.

All contributions to the Discussions in 1943–4, both the original papers and the replies, were duplicated and circulated to all members during the course of the debates; copies of these are extant in possession of the British Psycho-Analytical Society. Such references as I make in what follows to the

a book of several papers, all but one of which deal directly with a single period of life—the earliest—a certain amount of overlapping and repetition have been unavoidable; the chapters are complementary; aspects of the same phenomena are to some extent artificially isolated and considered from various angles. There is an especially close connection between Chapter VI, 'Theoretical Conclusions on the Emotional Life of the Infant', and Chapter IV, Part 2, 'Early Object Relations'. It is also evident that in a survey such as this, of theory which is largely newly won, it has not been possible to give illustrations or report case-material except in a few instances. Chapter VII entitled 'On Observing the Behaviour of Young Infants' is an exception and therefore of outstanding interest.

In submitting this survey of her work to publication it is relevant at the same time also to give some consideration to the character of the persistent opposition manifested to her views and to the special points upon which it centres. The objections I shall consider are characteristic and are still of significance, although in the course of years they have in general undergone a change, both in content and in form. Before going into any detail in this matter I will discuss first one general characteristic of the opposition which pervades almost every expression of disagreement with her views and requires to be brought into the foreground and examined *per se*. I refer here to the assumption, not always expressed, but always implied and sometimes expressed with vehemence, that her propositions are 'not psycho-analysis'. In some quarters it has been assumed *tout court* that her work is an independent variety of psychological theory, an alternative to psycho-analysis. Opponents who made this assumption have claimed explicitly that they alone represent Freudian psycho-analysis. Yet in fact the main points which play such an important part in her theory of development had been integral features of psycho-analytical theory before her time: *e.g.* introjection and projection, internal objects (as in melancholia), the early pregenital oral- and anal-sadistic primacies. These factors are part and parcel of all her work

criticisms levelled against Melanie Klein's work are partly drawn from this source, though the same views are met with elsewhere, particularly among analysts whose work makes use only of the early concepts of psycho-analysis.

on early development; it is founded on recognized psycho-analytical concepts which owe nothing to her invention, as has been contended by one or two critics.

There is no doubt a difference between psycho-analysis as we understand it at the present time and as we knew it thirty years ago or more; if not, we should not claim that any advances had been made. These papers are an expression of the fact and of our recognition of it; Melanie Klein's work is a development and an extension of the knowledge won by Freud. But a development is not necessarily an incompatibility. In fact it is precisely by the modification of accepted theory and its adjustment to newly recognized data that science proceeds. Freud said, 'The science of physics furnishes an excellent illustration of the way in which even those "basal concepts" which are firmly established in the form of definitions are constantly being altered in their content.'[1] Many new varieties of so-called psycho-analysis have sprung into existence from the earliest days until the present time. It could be said that one feature is common to all these; they have all disputed or denied the basic source and origin of human psychology, as postulated by Freud, in the *instincts with their bodily organs and aims*. Freud's approach was biological from the start: as witness his choice of hunger and love for his starting-point. Melanie Klein's work retains this fundamental relation of psychology to the biological core of the human organism, its function as a vehicle of the instincts, which Freud recognized.

Another assumption often made by those who challenge Melanie Klein's work and the advances in psychological understanding it has brought, as I have said, is that they are the champions and defenders of psycho-analysis proper, and of Freud's views in particular, which must not be challenged. If this were actually true, if it were a fact that our opponents accept and identify themselves with everything Freud put forward, it would still not be scientifically permissible to reject all subsequent modifications of it. Close scrutiny, however, of the detailed arguments used to oppose Melanie Klein's hypotheses shows something different; the tenets of psycho-analysis which are thus defended appear to be of a selected character. Now

[1] 'Instincts and Their Vicissitudes', p. 61.

Freud's statements were not unequivocal; he contradicts himself; he revises a view and then he harks back and restates the original form of it. Freud's own supremely scientific quality of mind is exemplified precisely in these very inconsistencies which he openly displays about certain topics. He cannot bring himself finally to decide between two incompatible alternatives because he recognizes truth in each of them, which to him is more important than immediate consistency. The task of resolving the inconsistency must come later from further work, observations and insight; what is important to him is not to deny an element of truth where he sees it.

Such features of Freud's work are well known: *e.g.* his view of the direct transformation of libido into anxiety, which he subsequently modified to embody the operation of aggression in the process, and later again formulated in the original direct form (see Chapter VIII). Another such indecisive attitude, though less marked, becomes apparent in his views on the formation of the super-ego; he maintains explicitly that its formation arises from the decline of the Oedipus complex. Yet (as shown in Chapter IV 1 (*b*)) he recognized many facts which cannot fail to be connected genetically with its development and lead up to its final establishment at the onset of latency, though he omitted to make these connections. From one angle the most important instance of Freud's own indecisive attitude about his theories is that of his postulation of the life and death instincts. In propounding the theory and in direct discussion of it he was careful not to make it a first principle of psycho-analysis. Nevertheless, in his later work he expresses himself plainly, repeatedly referring quite simply to this instinctual duality as the foundation of intra-psychic conflict.

In several such cases, as in those quoted, Melanie Klein's studies show that many propositions which he threw out as intuitive perceptions, but did not explicitly weave into the main fabric of psycho-analysis, are borne out by her later investigations. In Chapter X, moreover, Paula Heimann is able to show that his two inconsistent expressions of opinion about the origin of anxiety can now be reconciled. This also applies to the question of the super-ego; although he made no explicit reference to any precursory form of it, on the one hand, he yet spoke of early identifications with the parents, occurring long before the super-ego is established, while he explicitly describes parental identification as the sole mechanism of super-ego-formation, although arising at a later date.

Now it is just in this very matter of Freud's own inconsistencies and modifications or later developments in his views—whatever they are to be called—that one of the most conspicuous differences between Melanie Klein and her opponents manifests itself. It becomes clear that those analysts who dispute Melanie Klein's findings most vehemently themselves still stand in the main by Freud's original formulations which were never fully retracted or abandoned; and that where Freud later broke new ground and went ahead, sometimes in more intuitive recognition, they have not followed. It cannot be disputed that this applies in a comprehensive fashion to the theory of the death instinct, which is not merely rejected by many analysts but often treated as if it was no part of his theory and could be detached from his work. They may feel justified in so doing by his express sanction that psycho-analysis is not to stand or fall by this hypothesis, though he can hardly have intended the theory to fall by the wayside and be passed by in oblivion. His own interest in it is fully manifest in his later work, where he relates psychical conflicts and pathological disturbances to this hypothesis of instinctual conflict.

It can be no accident that the problem of anxiety in all its bearings constitutes another fundamental divergence between the work of Melanie Klein and that of her critics. For her it has been throughout the touchstone, the guiding thread which has led her through the maze, and has in the end brought Freud's postulate of a death instinct into logical and intelligible relation with all the other elements of his work. To Freud himself anxiety was of very great significance; it constantly preoccupied him from beginning to end of his work. It is true that his approach to it was to some extent from the physiological angle, as a condition of tension which must be investigated and understood, and that he did not concern himself with the psychological content of the fear (phantasies) to the extent that Melanie Klein has done. Anxiety, with the defences against it, has from the beginning been Melanie Klein's approach to psycho-analytical problems. It was from this angle that she discovered the existence and importance of the aggressive elements in children's emotional life, which led her to her present formulations about persecutory and depressive anxieties and the defences used by the early ego against them. Ultimately it enabled her to bring much of the known phenomena of mental disorders into line with the basic principles of analysis. One interesting point to be mentioned in this connection is the direct link between anxiety and the theory of the life and death instincts.

Melanie Klein's correlation of this theory with the accepted facts of early development, and with her other findings in relation to this period and all their bearing on later life, enabled numerous previously unrelated phenomena to be seen as parts of a coherent whole. Such *applications* of the concept of a death instinct, *i.e.* the ways in which such an instinct operates, or in which the mind is affected by it or reacts to it, are often denied consideration because the death instinct is treated *a priori* as 'a purely biological theory in which psychological conceptions so far have no place', as was said in the Discussions. This is not the question whether or not the death instinct is an acceptable proposition in itself. It is a hypothesis which can claim to be tested by its application, *e.g.* in reference to theories of psychical conflict, or to the psychology of the neuroses, and so on. Freud put forward the duality of the life and death instincts as the fundamental antithesis in the unconscious—to replace the antithesis of ego-instincts and libido which was no longer tenable after the phenomenon of narcissism was recognized— after which he constantly and repeatedly referred to it as the foundation of intra-psychic conflict in his subsequent work. What he wrote about masochism, or about suicidal melancholia, would seem incontestable in itself on this point. One quotation only will suffice to demonstrate Freud's own attitude:

'Defusion and a marked emergence of the death instinct are among the most noteworthy effects of many severe neuroses, *e.g.* the obsessional neuroses. . . . The essence of a regression of libido, *e.g.* from the genital to the sadistic-anal level, would lie in a defusion of instincts, just as the advance from an earlier to the definitive genital phase would be conditioned by an accession of erotic components.'[1]

How is it possible in face of this to maintain that the hypothesis of the death instinct is unrelated to psychical conflict or to the theory of the neuroses? or that it is 'a purely biological theory in which psychological conceptions so far have no place'?

Other instances of the different estimates put by Melanie Klein and analysts of opposing views on some of Freud's work would be his papers on 'Economic Aspects of Masochism' and on 'Negation'. The latter is a striking case in point; it was a rather late and isolated publication of his, and it appears to play no great part in the work of those who dispute Melanie Klein's findings. It is actually one of the richest and most highly condensed productions that he ever composed; short as it is, it contains illumination like a searchlight, ranging from the heights to the depths of mental life. Melanie Klein's theories dovetail with exquisite precision into its tight and rigorous propositions and elucidate them extensively, which in itself is in support of these theories. Again, there are in Freud's writings many remarks made casually, as it were, showing that he was aware of facts which he at no time attempted to work into theory. Melanie Klein has not only shown the validity of these observations or intuitions of his, but also how they actually support and enrich his theory, when it is developed further. Such, for instance, are his references to a little girl's fear of being murdered by her mother, or the connection of the fear of being poisoned by milk or food with experiences at weaning. These interpretations of his are insufficiently explained by psycho-analytical theory as it stands in his work, or by those analysts who reject Melanie Klein's work. (Melanie Klein's interpretations of such phantasies are much more precise in their application and cover the ground more fully, as well as establishing links with other phenomena.) Also in the attitude of these analysts to some of the original formulations of psycho-analytical theory there appears to be an undervaluation of the work of Abraham, Jones and Ferenczi.

In these controversies, therefore, we at times derive an impression which is farcical in effect: each side appearing to

[1] *The Ego and the Id* (1923), p. 57.

claim to be more Freudian than the other, in that each points emphatically to one aspect of Freud's formulations in support: one to the earlier, the other to the modified or later form of his views. Our quotations from Freud, however, are not primarily adduced as evidence that our views are correct, but rather as showing that many of the concepts which have since been developed by Melanie Klein were already inherent in the earliest psycho-analytical theory and observations, and that her work progresses by natural and logical steps from them. The points, however, in which her work has extended beyond Freud's, and has led to findings which diverge from and controvert some of his, are plainly brought into the foreground and openly presented.

These considerations appear to me to define some of the theoretical bases of the differences of opinion between Melanie Klein and her followers and the majority of her opponents. The fact that she can claim much support in Freud's writings—explicit or implied—does not signify that her contributions rest on this foundation. Her results, as distinct from the basic psycho-analytic principles which Freud formulated and which she maintains, stand on their own foundation of independent investigation and unremitting work in their development. She has in fact produced something new in psycho-analysis: namely, an *integrated* theory which, though still in outline, nevertheless takes account of all psychical manifestations, normal and abnormal, from birth to death, and leaves no unbridgeable gulfs and no phenomena outstanding without intelligible relation to the rest. Remembering as we do how little correlation Freud was perforce able to effect between the various fields and subjects of his enquiries and how many problems he broached without pursuing—the two most important being probably the psychotic elements in human psychology and mental development in the earliest period—we are not unaware of the scope of Melanie Klein's achievement, based as it is on his work.

I shall now consider shortly a few specific points of divergence on matters of fact and theory relating to early development. The crux of the matter concerns the course taken by the earliest stages of mental development, virtually within the first months of the first year: the most obscure phase of what Freud called a 'dim and shadowy era'. Melanie Klein's researches have yielded certain findings about the primitive emotional aspects of development in this early period, from birth to six months and onward: namely, early anxieties (of a persecutory type); early love-relation and hate/fear-relation to the primary object (mother); and also a rather later but still very early guilt and grief reaction. These findings are energetically disputed by our opponents, although they also admit that the first months of life are a dark period, and that little is known about the real reactions of the child. One stumbling-block appears to be the nature of the phases of auto-erotism and narcissism preceding object-relation. In the Discussions referred to above, regarding *early object-relations, auto-erotism and narcissism*, Anna Freud states:

'I consider that there is a narcissistic and auto-erotic phase of several months' duration, preceding object-relation in its proper sense, *even though* the beginnings of object-relation are slowly built up during this initial stage.'   (My italics.)

Again, 'Freudian theory allows at this period only for the crudest rudiments of object-relationship and sees life governed by the desire for instinctual gratification, in which perception of the object is only achieved slowly. . . .'

Here she makes a distinction between 'object-relation in its proper sense', on the one hand, and 'the crudest rudiments of object-relationship' or 'the beginnings of object-relation built up during the initial stage', on the other. There can be no such distinction, since the 'beginnings' and so on are the object-relation appropriate and proper to the earliest stage of development. At each stage of instinctual primacy the character or degree of object-relation is proper to that stage. (Only if 'object-relation proper' were understood to mean fully-developed adult object-relation could such a distinction be made.)

It will be seen from Melanie Klein's Chapters VI and VII *et seq.* what kind and degree of object-relation she in fact attributes to the baby in the first months. The existence of the phase called auto-erotism is a fact, not a theory; nor would any analyst wish to deny the existence of a narcissistic condition in the baby. In Chapter IV Paula Heimann shows explicitly that Melanie Klein, so far from denying or discarding these recognized features of early development, is able to explain their genesis. In our view the narcissistic or auto-erotic phase over-laps and co-exists with object-relation, largely owing to the important introjective processes operating at this stage. Every manifestation of development is a link in a chain of processes having a cause and effect relation with other processes: *e.g.* by means of introjection and projection the auto-erotic and nar-cissistic activities and attitudes come into being in relation to instinctual needs, and their defensive function of alleviating instinctual frustration and reducing anxiety must also be appreciated. This theory is supported by certain quotations from Freud. But it appears that to some analysts these passages from Freud mean nothing more than that the child is born with erotogenic zones. It was said in the Discussions that 'the Freudian conception of a narcissistic beginning of life conceives of auto-erotism as an *intrinsic* source of pleasure'. That may be, but even if there is an innate disposition to it, the process of obtaining intrinsic pleasure has a psychological meaning.

The question of the *development of the ego* is a further major issue. Twenty years ago the opposition to Melanie Klein's views was largely concentrated on the dating of the genesis of the super-ego. The question of ego-development has since then come more into the foreground. Latterly the view has been formulated that 'it is a controversial matter whether clashes between opposing instinctual urges of the love-hate, libido-destruction series can come into being before a central ego has been established with power to integrate the mental processes, or only afterwards'.[1]

Melanie Klein's view is that in accordance with the genetic character of development we may postulate an ego which has some rudiments of integration and cohesion from the beginning and which progresses increasingly in that direction; further, that conflict does arise before ego-development is much ad-vanced and power to integrate mental processes is established at all fully. The existence of a synthetic function in relation to

[1] Anna Freud: 'The Significance of the Evolution of Psycho-Analytic Child-Psychology'. *Congrès International de Psychiatrie*, Paris, 1950. Section V: 'Evolution et Tendances Actuelles de la Psychanalyse'. In the discussion following this paper Anna Freud stated that the period before such a central ego has been established extends over roughly the first year of life.

ego-development (*e.g.* sense-perception and reality-testing) is fully demonstrated by Susan Isaacs in Chapter III. We consider that observation supports this view, as also would some theoretical considerations which are common ground among all analysts: such, for instance, as that libido itself (Eros) is defined by Freud as a force serving the purpose of preservation, propagation and unification, *i.e.* its function is a synthetic one; we do not understand the view that at any period of life there could be no synthetic function in operation. In our view struggle and conflict of various kinds, integrating and disintegrating forces, exist and operate from the very beginning in human life; growth and development, and finally involution and dissolution, proceed within the orbit of these forces throughout life.

In discussing the opposition that has now been manifested in the course of some twenty-five years to Melanie Klein's findings and theories, it should be mentioned that the particular objections I have considered here are the present-day representatives, as it were, of other and earlier ones and have been selected for that reason. The form changes somewhat but the significant elements of the dispute remain basically the same. The actual content of the earliest arguments used against Melanie Klein's views differed in many respects from their current content, *e.g.* the existence of powerful sadistic phantasies, primarily oral, at an early age is far less disputed than it was; it is also widely acknowledged that the Oedipus complex and super-ego development start earlier than was formerly assumed. It is also clear that as the appreciation of her work gains ground, the evidence for some of her later propositions, *e.g.* depression in babies, is already beginning to find recognition.

I will conclude this account of the differences and divergencies between Melanie Klein and other analysts by putting on record my own belief that in time to come it will be difficult for trained analysts to appreciate the reality of such a controversy and more especially to imagine how it could have evoked so much time-wasting energy and effort as it did. Nevertheless, human nature being what it is, we can be content that the advances in psycho-analysis made since Freud's work have evinced so much vitality and inherent capacity to find a foothold and generate further progress.

* * * * * *

The present volume was originally intended to contain only the four papers given in the 1943-4 Discussions. It was with some misgivings, therefore, that I then agreed to the inclusion here, as Chapter II, of my 1936 Vienna Lecture, since it antedates the rest of the work more than a little. It has the character of a comparatively short and comprehensive survey, more generally descriptive and less specific and technical than the Discussion papers themselves. Except as a preliminary to them, however, its loose and general formulations are not in character with the book. The main body of the book consists of single papers each dealing with one special aspect of the whole theory of the psychical (emotional) situation in earliest development, say in the first year of life; and it is in them, with their exact and explicit discussions of the detailed operation of these early developmental processes, that the important contributions to our knowledge are made. This preliminary chapter is, moreover, by now to some extent out of date. Specific points in it which we now feel to be actually erroneous, in view of more recent work, have been noted in appended footnotes. One of these is the view that the earliest relation to the external world is a negative and hostile one; it will be seen, from Chapters VI and VII on 'The Emotional Life of the Infant' and 'On Observing the Behaviour of Young Infants', that this is not Melanie Klein's view, and that a love-relation to the external mother exists from the beginning and is shown very early. It develops *pari passu* with the hostile relation to her and to the environment. The other point concerns what I refer to in the paper as 'the narcissistic phase' of development. There I discuss the child's earliest psychical experiences mainly on the basis of Freud's work on the stage of primary identification and show how some of our views about the development of object-relations proceed naturally from this fundamental hypothesis of Freud's. I must, however, draw attention to the great advances that have since been made in the understanding of what constitutes the 'narcissistic phase' and how it develops from primary identification by introjection and projection. (Cf. especially Chapter IV, though the same conclusions are inherent in the work discussed throughout the book.)

The original Discussion papers led off with one on 'The Nature and Function of Phantasy' by Susan Isaacs, in which for the first time a detailed discussion is presented of one aspect of the unconscious mind; it is one which is of the highest significance for the understanding of any psychological problem whatsoever, although it is often overlooked. The mind is a whole, the higher functions do not act independently; the unconscious is not a vestigial or rudimentary part of the mind. It is the active organ in which mental processes function; no mental activity can take place without its operation, although much modification of its primary activities normally ensues before it determines behaviour in an adult. The original primary mental activity which usually remains unconscious we call unconscious 'phantasy'. There is, therefore, an unconscious phantasy behind every thought and every act (except possibly a bodily reflex). Susan Isaacs says: 'Freud's discovery of dynamic psychical reality initiated a new epoch of psychological under-standing. . . . He said: "We suppose that it [the id] is somewhere in direct contact with somatic processes and takes over from them instinctual needs and gives them mental expression." Now in the view of the present writers, this *mental expression is* uncon-scious phantasy. . . . There is no impulse, no instinctual urge or response which is not experienced as unconscious phantasy.' Even if a conscious thought and act be completely rational and appropriate to reality, this is so; not every conscious impulse is at variance with unconscious wishes and not every unconscious wish offends civilized standards or the dictates of necessity.[1]

[1] When Susan Isaacs put forward this proposition in the Discussions (of which the first paper is Chapter III in this book), not only was it disputed that this was Freud's view—every mental process has its origin in the un-conscious—but it was also assumed that it was essentially the contribution of Susan Isaacs and not specifically a fundamental element in Melanie Klein's formulations. This misapprehension needs explicit correction; not only has the truth of the proposition been consistently taken for granted by Melanie Klein throughout her work; but she herself maintains that much of her insight and understanding has been dependent on her undeviating application of this principle. Its truth becomes inescapable during the analysis of small children; there she recognized it and proceeded to apply it.

Although Freud himself made quite specific statements about the unconscious, similar in content to those above, the proposition they contain has been left floating in the air, as it were, and like some other theoretical statements of Freud's, has not been explicitly woven into the texture of theory and technique. It is plain, on the one hand, that this general law has to some extent been intuitively understood by many psychoanalysts, who have acted in accordance with it in always seeking for the unconscious content behind conscious acts and thoughts. One might suppose that to do so would only be carrying Freud's discovery of the unconscious to its logical conclusion; yet in fact many analysts who are not familiar with Melanie Klein's technique do not act upon this conclusion, and when something appears to be rational or 'objective' its connection with the unconscious remains unexplored. This difference in outlook is anything but an academic matter, or a question of alternative 'methods'. The principle at issue is the quite fundamental one of the significance of the unconscious in conscious life. When we realize this fundamental difference in outlook we understand why some analysts see so little in their patients' material, interpret so little, do not even recognize a transference-situation until the patient himself expresses something of it in conscious and direct reference to the analyst, and so on. In that case only a portion of what the patient says or does will be unravelled by analysis.

The analyst's task is to discover and interpret what unconscious content is being expressed at the moment by the patient, here and now, in the session. As we know, his words may or may not be the form chosen by the unconscious for its expression; he will be acting-out in various ways as well as speaking. The phantasy-content behind the acting-out and the speaking can become conscious only after interpretation, so that it may ultimately be expressed fully in words, as it must be. Freud describes the necessity for interpretation and compares the patient with a student who can see nothing at first through a microscope, until he is told what to look for.[1] The analyst has to consider: 'What is it in the patient's unconscious which is coming to expression in all that he is showing me to-day?' The

---

[1] *Introductory Lectures* (1916–17), p. 365.

question whether the form of expression is or would be normal or rational in ordinary life needs to be considered by the analyst; but even if it is, its roots in the unconscious need to be brought into relation with the expression, just as much as where pathological manifestations are concerned, if the patient's personality is ever to become a 'whole' one. It is, however, not merely in its bearing on technique that the importance of this matter lies; but rather for theory and the advance of our general knowledge of the mind, the whole of mental content, not only obviously neurotic manifestions, has to be considered in order to gain a full theoretical understanding of the laws governing the structure and development of the personality as a whole.

In this book the question centres round the earliest phases of mental life—say in the human being's first year—before consciousness in the sense of ideational and conceptual thinking or the capacity to verbalize feelings and thoughts can have been attained. Since, as I say, the understanding of mental functioning and development as a whole is dependent on a recognition of the significance of unconscious phantasy as the source of every mental process, it is evident that this primitive aspect of mental life will be in operation before the higher functions have developed. Susan Isaacs makes very clear that a baby has plenty of 'phantasy' about what is happening to it and inside it. Melanie Klein's work is characterized by the recognition that the mind functions primarily with phantasy, *i.e.* the mental and emotional corollary of impulses relating to bodily objects and actions, which are responses to meaningful experiences of pleasure or pain. It does not seem difficult on reflection to attribute such reactions to a baby's mental capacity. The fact that his sensations and the meaning they have for him have little or no relation to objective external reality is quite irrelevant in this connection, yet it undoubtedly tends to confuse our judgement about his mental (emotional) processes. It seems that the baby and the adult scientific worker are actually at two opposite poles, as it were, of knowledge and experience: the baby to begin with is completely ignorant of the external world, while the scientific worker is aware of nothing else; consequently they have no common ground and cannot communicate. The baby's inborn instincts cause him to impute and derive meaning of some kind to and from every sensation or experience, but the scientific worker is unable to recognize or appreciate such meanings because they have no relation to external or material reality. Only the psycho-analyst can be capable of bridging the gap to some extent, in so far as he or she can assume the baby's condition, infer his reactions, ignore what he ignores, and then test the results by what the baby manifests. We are then faced with the difficult problem of conveying our conclusions to other workers by written words— a difficulty which has beset psycho-analysis from the start, but which may seem to be aggravated by the baby's lack of speech.

The subject-matter of our investigations with infants consists of emotional elements and their relationships, often inextricably bound up and fused with bodily sensations, so that emotion and sensation are indistinguishable and form one experience. A person's feelings are frequently felt in his 'body' as well as his 'mind', which reminds us that fundamentally there is no split or cleavage between the two. But, whereas 'thoughts' can be clothed in words more or less adequately, bodily feelings are much more awkward in this respect; and though we have words for 'emotions', such words are in general invested with a dynamic quality which rouses personal associations and emotions in the hearer or reader and makes them unsuitable for dispassionate scientific usage. In the analytic situation itself this difficulty is hardly at all apparent. Indeed, it is the associated emotional content of ordinary language that qualifies it to be an adequate medium of expression in the analytical room. Abstract unemotional modes of thinking or of expression are concealing a specific anxiety and are defensive. The situation in the analysis of small children is essentially the same, though the proportions of phantasy and feeling may be different. Thoughts or phantasy-content are expressed in play, and feeling is far more directly and intensely manifested than with adults. Nursery language is vivid enough and it suffices for the task. A little child understands much more than he can himself express in words; his form of speech, moreover, is largely acting-out, in play.

It is when we are faced with the presentation of our results to other workers that things are less easy. I sometimes think that an impossible standard is set up by readers of psycho-analysis—not the first particular in which a standard has been demanded of psycho-analysis which would be regarded as preposterous in any other science.[1] On the one hand, readers who are not familiar with the work done and the technical terms in use quarrel with the 'incomprehensible jargon'; on the other hand, whatever is expressed in the ordinary every-day language of human feeling and experience is criticized as unscientific—insufficiently abstract.

As to reporting the evidence for the emotional situations *babies* find themselves in, the difficulty may at first sight appear to be greater even than it is with adults, consequent on their lack of means of expression. Nevertheless, I believe that some day this judgement will prove to have been greatly exaggerated. Babies *have* some means of expression, though by comparison with older beings it appears to us so inadequate; it may be that it is precisely this comparison that blinds us to their sign-language. To my mind, those who say a baby cannot express anything might as well say a foreigner cannot speak if they can't understand him. What is required is sufficient interest in the baby's feelings to enable one to learn his language, and once learnt, it is actually easier and simpler to report it than are the adult's complex and involved emotional processes. It is true that the nature of things is again a handicap in this field, though in a different way from what it is with the adult; nevertheless it has not proved an insuperable obstacle to communicating results to other workers and enabling them to gain thereby. Moreover, such books as *The Nursing Couple*, by M. P. Middlemore, and those of the behaviouristic school, many of which are quoted in Chapter III, have considerable value in this field. A study also of the interpretations of babies' behaviour made by Melanie Klein in Chapter VII will show what an unprecedented contribution to the understanding of it is made by her knowledge of the splitting, projective and introjective processes that she has found to be so characteristic in infancy.

Nevertheless, there are difficulties in reporting the content of unconscious phantasies: they are apt to produce a strong impression of unreality and untruth. Let me take as an instance

[1] Cf. Freud, Preface to *New Introductory Lectures on Psycho-Analysis*.

an internal-object phantasy of a persecutory nature: *e.g.* a woman feels that her mother inside her is in her ears or her stomach, and is angry, is making her deaf or tearing at her intestines; or a man feels that his dangerous jealous father inside him is making the patient impotent or disabling him so that he cannot work. At other times, a patient will unconsciously feel that he has 'good' (idealized) parents inside him, which fill him with a sense of omnipotence, perfection, grandeur and so on. It would seem as if the expression in words of such ideas *in itself* arouses a feeling of unreality and falseness. This would mean that the part played by the observing analyst who has probably supplied the verbalization of these emotional processes is felt to be an alien element which invalidates their authenticity. The phenomenon has been described thus by Freud: 'Something occurs of which we are totally unable to form a conception, but which, if it had entered our consciousness, could only have been described in such a way.'[1] We feel therefore that such phantasies *could* not have been expressed in words; and that in so doing one has destroyed their nature and character. This judgement must obviously arise from a confusion: the verbalization itself is a mental process too adult and too sophisticated to apply to such a content. Again, such statements are not yet sufficiently generalized to be reduced to abstract terms; they are still individual and specific. The highly personal and emotional content overwhelms and invalidates the dispassionate impersonal character of the observer's report in words; this difficulty is otherwise avoided by the use of abstract terms. But there are no abstract terms and they cannot be coined to express particular individual situations such as the examples given. Even more important, too, is the fact that, detached as such statements in a discussion necessarily are from the person and the occasion in which they were experienced, the words used are no longer invested with the appropriate emotions which constitute their reality as experiences in the mind of any individual. On the written page, in the absence of this emotional accompaniment, there is therefore a psychological justification for the unreal and lifeless effect they have.

[1] Freud: *Outline of Psycho-Analysis*, p. 66.

There are manifestly other reasons why statements such as those quoted above are not acceptable to readers. Because such a proposition as that in unconscious phantasy one has loving or hating persons inside one has no physical reality, there is a tendency to reject it as lacking in objectivity—here we meet again the old denial of their own reality to psychical processes (emotional experiences) which Freud had to combat. There is a failure to distinguish between the validity of the statement as an emotional fact and the content of the statement as a matter of material physical fact. Linked with this is the intense psychological resistance against repressed unconscious reality becoming conscious; such propositions offend our standards of morals and of taste, as well as our rational appreciation of what is physically possible, and we tend to denounce their *existence* as impossible. Unconscious phantasies are largely 'unspeakable' and unconscious emotions are often 'ineffable'. But such phantasies are not pathological in infants, though it depends on further development whether a child attains to adult normality or not. The quality of delusion and 'madness' which to our conscious minds appears so strongly to characterize these phantasies derives from the fact that these earliest emotional experiences contain the seeds which later in some cases develop into psychotic disorders. Consequently they stir up in the reader anxieties which all of us experienced in early infancy, dangers which have been averted and overcome with pain and effort in the course of our development. The methods and defences we used in this struggle became an integral and most valued part of our personality, which seems to be menaced again when we are again confronted with these very primitive impulses and dangers.

These may be some reasons why it is that plain statements of things which have probably never been conscious in an individual until his analytic experience, and are never verbalized at all by most people at any age, are not easily tolerated when heard or set down in print; because they often rouse mingled horror and excitement in readers the statements themselves are felt to be lacking in objectivity and dispassionateness. As analysts we are aware of the difficulty of doing justice to our findings with necessarily inadequate means.

The questions relating to the nature and function of phantasy, its unconscious pre-verbal character and the difficulties arising out of this circumstance for the investigator, have led to a digression; I must return to consider the actual contents of this book. The fourth chapter by Paula Heimann on 'Certain Aspects of Introjection and Projection' is the first account of these processes specifically devoted to examining them, their modes of operation and their effects. The existence of the processes was a recognized element in psycho-analytical theory in its early days; projection is also an old psychiatric concept. But, as necessarily happened with most concepts to begin with, the relation of these processes to other recognized mental phenomena was not understood in the early days of psycho-analysis. The part they play in mental functioning throughout life has still not received detailed attention as a topic in itself.

It would seem that we might have guessed at the importance of these processes for primitive mental levels from the body of anthropological knowledge existing before the days of psychoanalysis about the mentality of 'uncivilized' peoples, and later of course much enlarged by the work of Róheim and others. The beliefs, activities and rituals, etc., of primitive tribes appear to be very largely representations both of taking in to the body or expelling from it good and bad objects respectively, and of fears of the converse and defensive measures against that. What to the savage is comparatively conscious, however, and a normal part of life, has become increasingly taboo and repressed to Western civilized man, though it has played a large part in the Christian religion, e.g. in the Communion rite. The psychological need in man to obtain satisfaction and relief by some concrete bodily form of 'taking in goodness' and eliminating bad and dangerous agents from himself is now widely distrusted in educated circles and regarded as deriving from 'superstition'. Paradoxically enough, it still finds an outlet in hypochondriacal terms, e.g. in the prevailing need to imbibe curative goodness by medical attention or drugs, by sunbathing and so on, as well as to eliminate evil by athletics, purgatives, etc. Presumably reliance on the objective nature of medical opinion in these matters disposes of the fear of superstition. But, as Bacon said, 'There is a superstition in avoiding superstition'. However this may be, it would appear remarkable that a characteristic tendency of such intensity, manifested as it is so perpetually in myriad forms—not only bodily—in every type of human being of any age, race or degree of development, should not have been previously recognized as such by any psychologist.[1]

Chapter IV presents a clear account of a complicated subject: the way introjection and projection operate in the earliest stages of development. I shall not attempt to summarize the wealth of detail or the various aspects contained in the chapter, beyond mention of a few of the most important. One section is devoted to the question of the origin of the super-ego; the part played by introjection in the institution of the super-ego is the only instance of its operation, apart from the disorder of melancholia, to be accepted by the opponents of Melanie Klein's views. Another controversial question is that of auto-erotism and narcissism *versus* object-relations in the first months, which has already been mentioned. The internalized objects, which result from the continuous introjection of external objects, are intimately bound up with the satisfaction (organ-pleasure) obtained in the child's own body in auto-erotism; so that to the child (in its phantasy) the part of its body being used for pleasure is a combination of the object and the self.

An important section deals with the relation between inner world and outer world; another with the complications that arise in reference to satisfactions or anxieties when people become recognized as individuals (whole objects, mother, father and so on) and the processes of introjection and projection apply to these relations; finally the onset of the Oedipus feelings is dealt with in this connection. In the section dealing with internal objects, a discussion of hypochondria is used as an illustration of pathological conflicts and phantasies about

---

[1] The explanation of this fact, that the emotional importance of the need to absorb fresh 'goodness' and expel 'badness' has been ignored almost completely by psychologists, lies to my mind in the very close relation it bears to the complex of *depression*, about which also there is clearly an unconscious conspiracy of silence among thinkers. Poets alone seem nowadays able to express the truths of depression in men's minds, and they, alas, now seem able to express nothing else.

internal objects. This is in itself of great interest, especially since there was little or no understanding of this mysterious disorder before Melanie Klein's findings were brought to bear on the problem.

In addition to the presentation of these extremely involved topics which Paula Heimann gives us, the chapter contains many original contributions of her own which throw light on her subject. In several instances these take the form of showing how an apparent incompatibility between Freud's statements and Melanie Klein's findings is to be resolved by closer consideration. This applies, *e.g.*, to the question of object-relations *versus* auto-erotism in the first months, the solution being that auto-erotism is a relation to an object, but an internal one. Again, the conclusions presented about the development of the ego make use of all Freud's own formulations on the subject and go on to show how they are confirmed and at the same time greatly expanded by correlation with Melanie Klein's views. The analysis of hypochondria referred to above expresses her own conclusions in the application of Melanie Klein's theory.

Besides these special contributions, Paula Heimann makes many incidental remarks and asides in this chapter which have the effect of freeing us, as it were, momentarily from the close mesh of the discussion and opening up a wider perspective. She points her conclusions about auto-erotism, for instance, by saying that though it may appear outwardly to constitute a phase of development, it is more properly to be described as a mode of behaviour. This formulation of the problem is highly convincing in my own view, since it at once lights up the connection between auto-erotism and masturbation, clearly two forms of the same process. The latter, which is not limited to any stage of development and may be practised at any age, itself becomes more comprehensible than it has been hitherto when regarded similarly as an activity having a relation to *internal* objects; the hatred and destructive nature of this relation to the internal parents is what produces the characteristic guilt, depression, and phantasies of injury to the self that follow masturbation. Another piece of insight is her saying, in reference to 'taking in and expelling' (introjection and projection) and the manifold phenomena of the kind in life generally, that Nature's patterns appear to be few, but she is inexhaustible in their variation.

The chapter concludes with a Chapter Note on the myth of Narcissus which achieves something new by bringing the best psycho-analytical tradition of myth-interpretation into relation with the 'new' concept of depression—that is, with the age-old human experience of sorrow and despair felt at the loss of the beloved, and followed even by death itself.

It will be seen that this chapter has dealt extensively, among other topics, with the special question of the formation of the inner world of internalized objects, good and bad, by means of introjection and projection; in the subsequent chapters, therefore, this question is less particularly discussed and these mechanisms then come under consideration with special reference to integration and development.

Chapter V on 'Regression' has in my view a special character; it is the simplest, most lucid and easiest to follow in the book. The topic of fixation and regression, moreover, is one which is not especially related to the earliest phases of development. I would suggest that those who are not familiar with Melanie Klein's work might find it helpful to start with this chapter, leaving aside for the moment the detailed discussions of the child's experiences in its earliest months. Every psychotherapist will have had experience of manifestations of fixation and regression; the chapter will not therefore mean exploring unknown territory. The original psycho-analytical view of fixation as caused by a damming-up of libido in consequence of frustration is brought into relation with other factors which are of major importance in Melanie Klein's work: namely, anxiety and the destructive impulses. The discussion of the part played by these factors in reference to the general phenomenon of fixation and regression provides an opportunity for a clear demonstration of the way in which her views supplement the older formulations and present many problems which had previously been far from perspicuous in a more intelligible light. As an example, the typical conflicts and liability to regression which are common at the menopause in women are discussed to illustrate the general proposition that 'it is the recurrence of primitive destructive aims which is the chief causative factor in the outbreak of mental illness'.

There follow two chapters—VI and VII—by Melanie Klein which are complementary, in that the first presents theoretical conclusions from her work and the second serves to illustrate some of these by reference to actual experiences observed in babies. This combined presentation is in the nature of a comprehensive summary of her views at the present time about the earliest stages of development. The picture of the baby which we obtain is based on the biological processes, the operation of the instinctual drives in the young organism, and shows the psychological corollary of them in the form of anxieties more clearly than ever before, and the way in which the processes of splitting and of introjection and projection both serve the operation of the instinctual urges and are used as defences against them. Also the mental corollary of these drives—the beginnings of meaning and phantasy (emotional) content in the dawning mind—takes shape for us in greater detail: it is no longer 'a dim and shadowy era'. We see the beginnings of ego-formation and ego-functioning, as related to the instinctual drives and to the projection-introjection processes, and the beginnings of object-relations running parallel with the early auto-erotic and narcissistic phases of Freud. These very early phases are soon succeeded, though not at the same time abandoned, by object-relations to persons (the whole object) in which typical ambivalence of affects is experienced. This ushers in feelings of guilt, depression and concern for the object, now distinct from the ego. An interesting point is the suggestion that the strength or otherwise of the early splitting mechanisms influences the development of repression. It appears that the high degree of inaccessibility to the unconscious met with in schizoid types derives from the strength of the early splitting processes. In people who have developed more successfully and more nearly reached full maturity, the mind is comparatively 'porous' and there is much more capacity for insight into the unconscious and ability to maintain it when gained; it does not become repeatedly split off again in the same way.

The importance for psychiatry of the understanding of such factors furnished by Melanie Klein's work will be apparent;

I shall refer to this later. Another aspect of the work arises in its application to the practice of psycho-analysis. Melanie Klein's theoretical work has latterly left her little opportunity to digress in her written work into discussions of technique; here she makes an exception. One of the Chapter Notes following Chapter VI points out the necessity to uncover the persecutory aspects of the analyst in the patient's mind, and the serious dangers of allowing the corresponding idealized aspects to mask and obscure the acute anxieties and negative trends which under the surface in the transference nevertheless effectively defeat genuine therapeutic progress. In this chapter Melanie Klein also refers again shortly to the topic of manic defence—another point of great importance for technique; indeed from one angle it constitutes the same technical problem as that just mentioned. The essential feature of the manic defence in earliest development arises from its specific relation to depressive anxieties. It is not so much that a new process or mechanism comes into operation, but that the previous mechanisms of denial, idealization, splitting, and control of objects, external and internal, used in the preceding phase to counteract per-secutory anxiety, are used by the stronger ego against depressive anxieties, *i.e* phantasy-situations in which the loved object is felt to be suffering, injured and in danger; such feelings and phantasies are then by the manic method split off, denied and stifled. Or all feeling may be denied and stifled by this means, all emotional relations suppressed, and at a later phase of development indifference or cynical contempt towards loved persons may supervene. This 'don't care' attitude may thus extend to a complete stifling of all feelings of love, including guilt and concern for the object, and be manifested as an incapacity to love.

The following Chapter VII, 'On Observing the Behaviour of Young Infants', consists of detailed discussion of various types of reaction in babies to post-natal conditions, starting with the earliest, which naturally mainly concern the relation to the breast. Taking various emotional conditions in babies as illustrations, Melanie Klein here shows how the persecutory anxiety of the 'bad' breast comes to expression in the babies' reactions and how by means of satisfaction it is allayed and the good' object (breast, mother) introjected. The same method of demonstrating by illustrations is used in reference to the depressive variety of anxiety, which supervenes after the first three months or so. The incidents reported are most illuminating in their bearing on the theoretical conclusions. It is noteworthy that the situations described and the incidents reported are explained in terms of *object-relations* (external and internal); and this detailed picture of babies' behaviour as seen in this light makes a convincing contribution to Melanie Klein's theory that object-relations are operative and of crucial significance in young infants.

The description of the child's typical experiences deals with instances from the earliest days up to the onset of walking and talking in terms of these emotions, *i.e.* satisfaction and happiness, or of lack and loss (deprivation) with anxiety or terror. The whole effect brings home to the reader the paramount significance at this stage of life of 'obtaining and possessing' or of 'losing and lacking'; emotionally life consists of these two experiences, these two states, and no others. It is clear, too, that obtaining and possessing is reinforced, almost from the start, by seeking, finding, regaining, alternately with repeated losing. This key pattern shows up in vivid outline throughout the progressive stages of the infant's life, first in his relation to the breast or bottle, then to the mother as a person, to his own body, to toys, to the father and other persons, through the weaning stage, again to new foods, new people, new activities—always the one pattern: seeking, finding, obtaining, possessing, with satisfaction, and losing, lacking, missing, with fear and distress. It is borne in upon one that when this fact in all its significance has become part of the accepted body of general knowledge, the conditions affecting the development of infants should be greatly improved, and a corresponding reduction in the intensity of the persecutory and depressive anxieties to which they are subject might be achieved. This would then necessarily result in a much higher incidence of the capacity to avoid and overcome maladjustments and neuroses, and to attain to a greater measure of maturity than is common at the present time.

The examples given light up very clearly the distinction between the two varieties of anxiety (persecutory and depressive) and must be helpful to the reader or student on this point. In her final Chapter Note to this chapter Melanie Klein quotes what Freud wrote about the child's reactions to the mother's absence. In his view a very young child could not feel the loss of the mother as a loss of her love, still less as connoting anger in her; whereas in Melanie Klein's view the child tends rapidly to feel the absent mother as bad (angry, persecuting). However, in this same context (1926) Freud poses the questions, 'When does separation from an object produce anxiety, when does it produce mourning and when does it produce, it may be, only pain? . . . There is no prospect of answering these questions at present.' Nevertheless, an answer has been found to them by Melanie Klein: persecutory anxiety is the ego's *fear for itself*, while damage and destruction to the good object (loss of it) are denied; depression and mourning are predominantly the ego's reaction to its *fear for the loved object* which is destroyed and lost; in this reaction is included the fear for the ego. Pain must surely enter into both these; but if we could conceive of pure pain unmixed with grief or fear, we might say it would arise from the *loss* of a loved object which was still unhurt. This, however, is a highly sophisticated conception which seems not to exist in the primitive levels of our minds; it can probably only be arrived at by various complicated processes of splitting.

Chapter VIII on 'Anxiety and Guilt' provides us with a clarification of the all-important questions relating to anxiety and guilt, which can be said to have been the mainspring of Melanie Klein's work. No problem has ever been dealt with by her apart from its relation to anxiety, but this paper is the first which she has devoted to anxiety as such in its various forms. This aspect of her work is one which meets with the opposition already discussed, since her propositions, although arising essentially out of Freud's work, were in no way adumbrated by him and in some respects directly controvert statements of his. In her view anxiety originates as a direct reaction by the life instinct to the strength of the death instinct in the organism, a supposition which Freud expressly rejected;[1] anxiety takes on

[1] Freud held throughout to the view that there is no fear of death in the unconscious, in fact that the unconscious cannot contemplate any fate

two differentiated forms: the first being persecutory, the second depressive. These views on anxiety derive from her accumulated experience in the analyses of young children. Referring to the hypothesis of the death instinct, she says, 'When the earliest anxiety-situations of young infants are revived and repeated in such analyses, the inherent power of an instinct ultimately directed against the self can be detected in such strength that its existence appears beyond doubt'. The chapter goes on to deal in detail with the differentiation between the two forms of anxiety, persecutory and depressive, showing the relation of guilt to the latter, *i.e.* to love and concern for the injured object. This discussion has a special bearing on psycho-analytic practice; it is an important matter in technique to distinguish clearly between the two varieties of anxiety from which the patient may be suffering at the moment. Melanie Klein mentions in this connection how often the persecutory aspect is brought into the foreground, as a screen and defence against underlying depression and guilt.

This study of the problem of anxiety also throws valuable new light on Freud's hypothesis of the fusion and interaction of the two primary instincts. This concept remains in his presentation very largely theoretical; it is not easy for the student to translate it into terms of experience. In this paper Melanie Klein describes in some detail the role of libido in allaying anxiety and in particular it is shown how the creative and

worse than castration. We must surmise that this view of his was influenced by his discovery of the unconscious primarily as a reservoir of libidinal impulses and by his experience of the beneficial effects of liberating these impulses from repression. From this angle it would appear that castration must represent the worst catastrophe, since it would put an end to all possibilities of libidinal, ultimately beneficial, creative and life-giving activities. Many analysts, however, have found it difficult to subscribe to Freud's view that in the unconscious castration represents the worst catastrophe. Ernest Jones's concept of 'aphanisis'—the total extinction of all and any sexual pleasures and capacities—made a decisive contribution towards widening the concept of apprehended danger ('The Early Development of Female Sexuality', 1927). It could be said to stand midway between the fear of castration (Freud) and the fear of death (Klein); moreover, in Melanie Klein's view depressive anxiety is bound up with fears of death as well as with fears of the extinction of Eros—ultimately one and the same thing.

generative impulses, deriving much impetus from the reparative drives which arise from depressive anxiety, constitute the foundation of a stable and secure mental life.

Chapter IX is of a rather different order from the others. The book as a whole is intended to present a general outline under different headings of Melanie Klein's views on early development; whereas this paper, 'Notes on Some Schizoid Mechanisms', first published in 1946, discusses for the first time new and more recent conclusions of hers, which are not for the most part embodied in the general outline formed by the other chapters. The main topic concerns the splitting mechanisms characteristic of primitive mental levels, which have in fact been considered to some extent in her previous work, but had not received specific attention as such.

The splitting mechanisms are seen mainly as a means by which the earliest types of anxiety are kept at bay. Their prototype may be said to be the splitting of the breast into two, one 'good' and one 'bad', *i.e.* splitting of the object, and the splitting of the ego's affects towards the object, *e.g.* into love and hate. From this original split the two primitive aspects of the object, the idealized and the persecutory, and the two corresponding attitudes towards them develop. Splitting occurs also between internal and external reality, and in relation to emotions, in that some or all may be split off and denied. The anxieties which arise in early infancy and are characteristic of the psychoses in adults drive the ego to develop these defence-mechanisms; the fixation-points of later psychotic disorders are formed in this very early period, and such anxieties and defences are symptomatic of later schizophrenia and paranoia.

The understanding of the projection-introjection mechanisms, especially in reference to the destructive impulses, threw light on the origin of the deepest anxieties of a paranoid-schizoid nature, and the insight into the defensive processes of the splitting mechanisms opens the way to an understanding of confusional, catatonic and other psychotic states. It is as if these forms of mental functioning which are a normal feature of early infancy were a part of our atavistic heritage which has to be repeated ontogenetically on the way to 'higher' development, just as physical development is still in process of recapitulation in the initial period of life. The analogy would not be complete, however, since these stages of development are more than vestigial remains in the full-grown psyche and may be reactivated to some degree even in the most mature adult.

The discussion refers mainly to the concept of splitting occurring in the *ego*. The nature of the early ego is considered, which appears to be largely of an unintegrated character. Under the pressure of intense anxiety (ultimately deriving from the death instinct), the lack of cohesion in the ego would appear to result in a 'falling to pieces' of the ego. This disintegration underlies the later disintegration in schizophrenia. The mechanics of the process are obviously similar to those of dispersal in wartime, to obviate the dangers of concentration and to minimize loss. The effects of these processes on the ego can be detrimental if they are carried too far, *e.g.* when aggressive impulses are too severely split off, denied and so on, there is an impoverishment of the ego, in that many desirable qualities such as potency, strength, knowledge, are closely associated with a measure of aggression.

Another important topic is the concept of 'projective identification', which represents the phantasy of forcing the self in part or as a whole into the inside of the object in order to obtain possession and control of it, whether in love or in hate. This phantasy appears to connect closely with depersonalization phenomena and with claustrophobia.

The exploration of these earliest anxieties and defences has led to a considerable advance in understanding certain psychic processes which, when revived by regression, constitute psychotic disorder, and yet form part of normal early development. This aspect of Melanie Klein's work has provoked much opposition, on the ground that she regards all infants as psychotic. Such an inference actually has no basis; on the contrary, her observations and conclusions have thrown new light for the first time on the processes by which normal development is achieved, as well as on the earliest origins of mental disorders. Her findings, which were made possible by the Play Technique which she invented for analysing small children, have in their turn had an influence on the technique used in adult analyses by her followers as well as by herself. The fuller understanding of the typically psychotic mechanisms has made it possible to recognize and interpret the minor or masked forms of them which are actually present in most if not all neurotics. As Melanie Klein points out, a mechanism such as splitting occurs in the form of transitory dissociations, or of forgetting, even in normal persons. In every analysis, therefore, especially in those of young children in whom these processes are very active and may adversely affect the child's mental and emotional development, as also in people suffering from severe mental disorders, the influence on technique has had invaluable results. The fact that by this means the latter have in many cases become amenable to treatment has a claim on the attention of all psychiatrists.

The paper is highly condensed and in view of the novelty and unfamiliarity of much of its content, it is not easy to assimilate. Study of it is nevertheless most rewarding; every analyst reading it will be reminded of much in his practice and find it exceedingly stimulating.

In Chapter X Paula Heimann puts forward some general reflections on the much-debated hypothesis of the death instinct. It is a topic on which comparatively little has been written in psycho-analytical literature, considering the importance it has in Freud's work. It is a neglected subject; and yet it clearly belongs to the category of propositions which rouse a strong response, either of repulsion or attraction, in the student of psycho-analysis. Perhaps this neglect is partly due to the fact that, as Freud himself avowed, the concept is one which cannot at the present time be regarded as demonstrated and established. Melanie Klein's direct observations of what is felt by children to be an annihilating force in themselves seems to me to contain direct evidence, as far as it goes. Paula Heimann brings together many other interesting considerations bearing on the question, drawn from practice as well as argued on the basis of theory. She emphasizes the exceedingly important fact that the repetition-compulsion, which is an incontestable observation, runs *counter* to the pleasure-principle. She shows how the various theories regarding the nature of anxiety can be reconciled by reference to the concept of a death instinct. The importance in ordinary life of the need to hate, to find or

GENERAL INTRODUCTION

imagine 'bad' persons in the environment, is clarified by the necessity to deflect a measure of the death-dealing force outwards. A very interesting analysis of the possible causation of so-called sexual murders is given. Other points which she considers as well as these all represent an important contribution to this problem—one which is too much ignored. A theory can only be disproved or proved in the process of testing it by applications.

* * * * * *

The development of psycho-analytical knowledge, a large proportion of which forms the matter of this book, like most studies of genetic development, proceeds always backwards in time, *i.e.* in an inverse direction to that of the life of the individual. The first attempts at scientific psychology were concerned only with the superficial, the conscious, the adult forms of mental activity. Even so, the study of hypnotism at the same time was in fact already pointing to the existence of less obvious mental processes. Then Freud's discoveries revealed at one stroke what lies under the adult and the conscious, namely, the forces of unconscious mental activity and their close relation to the psychology of the child. The unconscious mind, operating unknown to him in every adult, is, broadly speaking, still the mentality of the child. The more we progress in knowledge of it and its development, therefore, the farther back in the life of the individual we are led and the more remote and alien our findings become from the conscious, the adult and what are called the rational forms of mental life.

Thus the progress in our knowledge brought about by Melanie Klein's investigations takes us farthest backwards in the life of the individual to a period not previously explored—into what Freud called the 'dim and shadowy era' of the child's mind before it talks or expresses anything in words, *i.e.* its first year or so. To say this is in no way to underestimate the completely novel and revolutionary work on this early period done by Freud himself, or by Abraham, Jones or Ferenczi: the oral phases of libido-development, the theory of projection, cannibalistic and anal phantasies, the existence and significance of introjection. The isolated observations made by these pioneers told us of an unknown territory, yet to be explored; Melanie Klein has surveyed it extensively. Her map is as yet but an outline; details and corrections will follow in abundance. What we have is a coherent picture, nevertheless, in place of isolated and relatively incomprehensible fragments. Nor does this statement undervalue the important and valuable work done on this early period in the child's life by the school of behaviouristic psychology, with its detailed records of the development of the various functions and capacities, at their average date of appearance, and so on. The correlation of these results with physiological development is an equally important branch of study. But such investigations in themselves do little more than enumerate the outward manifestations of mental development and throw no light on the earliest forms of functioning of our mentality as such.

This field of knowledge has hitherto been a closed book to all scientific enquiry; so much so that, as we know, the general assumption of psychologists (and even of some psycho-analysts) has been that the baby *has* no mind and no psychical processes until it begins to express them visibly and audibly in a way adults are accustomed to comprehend. There have always been people, nevertheless, who make precisely the opposite assumption; they, however, are not scientists and are almost as inarticulate as babies themselves; I refer of course particularly to those gifted intuitive mothers and women who nurse children, who have always taken for granted that a baby does feel and 'think' and 'know', and react and respond emotionally, *i.e.* psychically, to whatever happens to him and is done to him. Because their knowledge could not be formulated and reduced to basic principles of a known order, this intuitive recognition of facts by sensitive women has, as I said, even been disputed and denied by science. It is for the first time, therefore, through the work of Melanie Klein, following on Freud's discovery of the unconscious mind and its pre-eminence in childhood, that this world of phenomena, the mind of human beings in their first year or two with all its significance for their subsequent development, becomes open to scientific study.

II

ON THE GENESIS OF PSYCHICAL CONFLICT IN EARLIEST INFANCY [1]

By JOAN RIVIERE

MY object in this paper is to attempt a short general formulation of the earliest psychical developmental processes in the child, that is, of the problems of oral-sadistic impulses and their attendant anxieties, and the fundamental defence-mechanisms against them employed by the ego at this stage of development, with special reference to the defensive functions of projection and introjection.

It would appear that fuller understanding and knowledge of the operation of these factors in the first year or two of life throw considerable light on the whole of early development, and thus clarify some of the obscurity hitherto existing in regard to ego-development and the genetic origin of the super-ego, together with the relation of these to infantile sexuality and libido-development. Any claim that psycho-analysis may make to understand the ego-structure of adults and older children necessarily implies the possibility of tracing its development genetically back to its earliest roots. An understanding of the anxieties and defences which arise in the ego as a result of the child's earliest object-relations must therefore be of special importance for the whole of psycho-analytic work. This orientation of recent work in no way signifies any underestimation of the importance of libido-development or of libidinal processes as such; on the contrary, the significance of the interaction and connections between ego and libido-development only brings out in an even stronger light the crucial importance of infantile libidinal urges in the whole of psychical development.

[1] First published in 1936: *I.J.Ps-A.*, XVII. This paper was read before the Vienna Psycho-Analytical Society, May 5, 1936, and was one of the Exchange Lectures then being arranged by the British and Vienna Societies. The topics of oral sadism, projection and introjection, which I deal with particularly, were especially raised by R. Wälder in his previous lecture before the British Psycho-Analytical Society in November, 1935.

The pioneer work of Melanie Klein has led in particular to a close study of these problems in the British Psycho-Analytical Society and in my view has directly or indirectly influenced most of the work of its members in recent years. I must, however, make it clear that I alone am responsible for the general formulation put forward here. Besides attempting to present as a whole many of the principal theoretical contributions made by our members, my paper is also a personal attempt to co-ordinate newly recognized data into a useful theoretical hypothesis.[1] I must disclaim any intention to prove the views I put forward nor do I personally regard them all as fully established. I can claim that my hypotheses make use of all Freud's findings and do not controvert any of the principles he has laid down; but they extend the application of these principles in some directions where he himself has so far preferred not to pursue them. In *Inhibitions, Symptoms and Anxiety*, in considering the relations between instinct and anxiety, Freud has throughout dealt solely with the demands of Eros, but has not discussed those of the other great primary instinct (the death instinct) and their relations to anxiety. The anxiety-situations which arise from the interplay of aggression and libido form the starting-point of much of the work of English analysts.

We know that no psycho-analytic facts and laws can be proved in any written form. My own work is with adults and I can say it offers strong evidence of the correctness of these assumptions about early stages of development. To us it seems in accordance with all the material to assume that oral and cannibalistic impulses having reference to unmistakable Oedipus situations are formed during the actual exercise of the oral function as an object-relation. The specific content of the analytic material of this kind now available and its wealth have enabled us to form at least experimental hypotheses of what

[1] Owing to the comprehensive and cumulative character of the material upon which the views I express here are based, and the avoidance of detail necessary in such a broad presentation, I have found it impossible, with a few exceptions, to make any specific references to the published work of others. To anyone familiar with the literature forming the Bibliography which concludes my paper my indebtedness to these writers will be very evident, and I wish to express to them my obligation and gratitude for the insight and understanding I have derived from their work.

occurs in the earliest months and years, and of how it may be reconciled with what we know of the mental development of this period. Even the most important part of the Oedipus complex, the gross sexual and aggressive impulses and phantasies, would hardly be regarded as proved or its existence definitely established by extra-analytical observation alone. And it certainly does not follow that, because a baby cannot express feelings in any way we understand, it has none; indeed, that circumstance may be one of the major causes of its special sensitivity to these earliest experiences and their especially significant after-effects. Conclusions about impulses and conflicts arising at a date at which the child has almost no means of *direct* expression must be based on the evidence of repetition in analysis—it is the only source of knowledge of the unconscious mental content existing before consciousness and memory develops fully. I am not expecting therefore immediately to convince you of the validity of our views and our findings, for nothing but analytic experience on the same lines would do so.

The baby's mental life in its first weeks is narcissistic in character and ruled by the pleasure-pain principle, while the ego is primarily a body-ego. This is the stage of primary identification; the dawning psyche is unaware of an external world. Painful stimuli, whether from within or without, impinge upon this pleasure-ego and rouse unpleasure, *e.g.* hunger or bodily pain caused by colic or wind internally, and loud noises or loss of support externally. Imprints of painful experience are formed in the psyche from the experience of birth onward alongside the more continuous experience of satisfaction, and possibly contentment, which is apprehended narcissistically. Freud has described in various works (notably in 'Instincts and Their Vicissitudes') how the primitive ego responds to pleasure and unpleasure. It tries to preserve its pleasure-ego intact by identifying itself with all pleasurable stimuli and dissociating itself from all painful ones. The omnipotence of the psyche in its own domain, the subjective world, enables it to do this.

Freud has given us this broad outline of the origins of mental functioning. But the evolution of the psyche from this stage until the genital libido-organization, the decline of the Oedipus complex and the full development of the super-ego, has not been traced in any detail, and it cannot be said that a satisfying *genetic continuity* between these first and last states is available in psycho-analytical theory.

The work of Melanie Klein and others following her has shown us that the mental processes of projection and introjection are of much greater significance and have a much wider bearing in every stage of ·psychical development than was appreciated.[1] We surmise that Freud's primitive narcissistic stage just described forms the psychic foundation on which these processes develop. Freud himself has connected the abolition of painful stimuli with the process of projection. As soon as pleasurable 'good' states are differentiated from painful 'bad' ones, the good conditions and sensations are referred psychically to the ego and the bad are rejected and expelled. I conclude that this early psychical process is modelled on the pattern of the main physiological functions which preserve life, in fact, on metabolism itself. Freud has connected the narcissistic stage with the function of sleep; I would suggest that psychical introjection is modelled on the function of taking in 'good' nourishment, while projection follows the physiological model of expelling waste products by excretion. One must keep in mind that this narcissistic world of the psyche is one of

[1] For the purpose of this present outline I am mainly concerned to discuss the functions of projection and introjection as defence-mechanisms against instinct and anxiety. As will be seen, however, the exercise of these processes as defences against early object-relations rouses in turn new anxiety-situations, which I go on to consider. Obviously these psychical processes (like all others, in my view) serve a 'multiple function' (Wälder) and, besides operating as defences, promote the gratification of instinct, as well as the growth and development of the individual in general. Although I am here singling out these two early defence-mechanisms for discussion, I in no way intend to underestimate the importance of the numerous others also at work more or less from the beginning, such as above all denial and scotomization, which connect directly with the hallucinatory narcissistic state, and soon also repression proper. Further, I would mention here displacement; turning away from the object; turning towards new objects (as a defence against anxiety relating to a former one); denying and stifling love and intensifying hate of objects in order to diminish (dangerous) desires for them; the striving for control of the object; and so on. Most of these measures, some of which are hardly as yet classified as defence-mechanisms, are referred to in my paper. The view that most defence-mechanisms, including repression, are already at work in the first months of life has been frequently stressed by Melitta Schmideberg, especially in verbal communications to the British Psycho-Analytical Society.

'hallucination', based on sensations and ruled by *feelings* (under the sway of the pleasure-pain principle), entirely autistic, not only lacking in objectivity, but at first without objects[1]; from this omnipotent standpoint, too, all *responsibility* rests on the self and all *causal relations* proceed from within the self.

I said this world was without objectivity; but from the very beginning there exists a core and a foundation in *experience* for objectivity.[2] This foundation can only consist in bodily sensation; an experience of bodily pleasure or pain, even a neutral perception, if intense enough, is presumably registered as such and must infallibly have a reality that nothing can alter or destroy. (Such infallibly and objectively true experiences would form the foundation of the later psychical institution of reality-testing.) I wish especially to point out therefore that from the very beginning of life, on Freud's own hypothesis, the psyche responds to the reality of its experiences by interpreting them— or rather, *mis*interpreting them—in a subjective manner that increases its pleasure and preserves it from pain. This act of a *subjective interpretation of experience*, which it carries out by means of the processes of introjection and projection, is called by Freud hallucination; and it forms the foundation of what we mean by *phantasy-life*. The phantasy-life of the individual is thus the form in which his real internal and external sensations and perceptions are interpreted and represented to himself in his mind under the influence of the pleasure-pain principle. (It seems to me that one has only to consider for a moment to see that, in spite of all the advances man has made in adaptation of a kind to external reality, this primitive and elementary function of his psyche—to misinterpret his perceptions for his own satisfaction—still retains the upper hand in the minds of the great majority even of civilized adults.) To begin with, however, reality is entirely misinterpreted; the perceptions are recognized but they are interpreted falsely.[3] I would draw your attention to the conclusion that phantasy-life is never 'pure phantasy'.

[1] 1950. I should now correct this to: 'at the very first without awareness of external objects'.

[2] E. Glover has emphasized that even babies have a sense of reality of a kind.

[3] Cf. Freud, 'When a perception is reproduced as an ideational concept the reproduction is often not an exact replica of it; it may be modified by omissions, etc.' ('Negation').

It consists of true perceptions and of false interpretations; all phantasies are thus *mixtures* of external and internal reality.

As the child's organs of perception develop, it gradually becomes aware of the external world around it and it begins to *localize stimuli*. (Along with this, the ego proper begins to develop from the body-ego and topographical differentiations in the mental apparatus begin to form.) But the child's psychical response to the external stimuli remains for a time as before; pleasurable external perceptions it misinterprets as part of itself, and whatever it dislikes it rejects and annihilates. And this, I would say, may well be the foundation of the psychical process of *displacement*. For the child's physical sensory apparatus may localize objects correctly, but the psychical apparatus then displaces them in an arbitrary fashion. The displacement of objects stimulating desire or hate, and the allocation of them respectively to the 'me' or 'not-me', would be a corollary to the displacement of affects familiar to us. The first external objects are the breasts and we presume them to be the first things apprehended as external to the 'me', though simultaneously with this recognition they are yet psychically arrogated to the 'me'. I would suggest here that the oral incorporation of milk, and the temporary incorporation of the nipple, are not merely the physical prototypes of introjection, but that the *affective overestimation of this incorporation* has the effect of stimulating and intensifying both the psychical process of absorbing impressions into the self (introjection) and the activity of phantasy-life concerned with the incorporation of objects. And this to my mind points to the explanation of the close connection we invariably find between oral libido and introjection. The nipple with its flow of milk, which satisfies both an external and an internal seat of desire (mouth and stomach) at once, we constantly find as the earliest prototype of every later desired satisfaction, no matter how different in character, in both sexes. Thus all later sources of gratification too would on this same pattern again in phantasy be displaced and internalized into the 'me'—a process that corresponds to 'introjection'.

But we must consider the case of unpleasure severe enough to prevail and defeat narcissistic omnipotence. I will take the case in which pleasure is at a minimum. There is the problem of the baby who will not suck; or there is the extreme instance of the ill baby, perhaps starved or neglected. The condition of such a child is usually one of pining, of depression; it clearly enjoys no satisfaction; moreover, as we say, 'it has no life in it'. It is evidently much nearer to death than a lusty baby that screams. Now my suggestion is that such a child's ego is experiencing the reality of its condition, of its nearness to death and of its danger from the forces of the death instinct operating within it, and that it feels its helplessness against them. Its body has not sufficient life (Eros) to make possible a fusion strong enough to discharge the death instinct outwards in an aggressive act of screaming and by so doing to appeal for help. I suggest that such help-lessness against destructive forces within constitutes the greatest psychical danger-situation known to the human organism; and that this helplessness is the deepest source of anxiety in human beings. This would correspond to the 'traumatic situation' (Freud) and the 'pre-ideational primal anxiety' (Jones).[1] Freud writes (in *Inhibitions, Symptoms and Anxiety*, p. 106) that what the infant experiences as a danger is a 'situation of accumulating tension against which it is helpless'. He connects this danger with later castration-anxiety; and of this he also says 'the ultimate form of this anxiety (and of that relating to the super-ego) appears to me to be the fear of death (anxiety in reference to life)'. In the infant, however, Freud denies an anxiety of death, even at birth. He says, 'We certainly cannot presuppose anything approaching a kind of knowledge in the newborn child of the possibility of its life being extinguished'. I am not suggesting that there is any such 'kind of knowledge' in the child; but I think there is reason to suppose that a child ex-periences *feelings* of the kind, just as any adult can *feel* 'like death', and in a state of great anxiety often does. I admit that my hypothesis is by no means established, but some of us find it in no way incompatible with Freud's other findings, while it proves of the greatest value in elucidating many problems in our practice.

---

[1] We have reason to think, since Melanie Klein's latest work on de-pressive states, that all neuroses are different varieties of defence against this fundamental anxiety, each embodying mechanisms which become successively available to the organism as its development proceeds.

I will take another typical response to an experience of severe unpleasure—this time an acute one, not a constant sub-acute deprivation. The baby's typical response, say to acute hunger, is a reaction in which the whole body is involved: screaming, twitching, twisting, kicking, convulsive breathing, evacuations —all evident signs of overwhelming anxiety. Analytic evidence shows without any doubt that this reaction to the accumulated tension represents and is felt to be an *aggressive* discharge, as we should in any case imagine. If this reaction brings the required satisfaction, narcissistic phantasy can resume its sway. But if the desired breast is not forthcoming and the baby's aggression develops to the limit of its bodily capacities, this discharge, which automatically follows upon a painful sensation, itself produces unpleasure in the highest degree. The child is overwhelmed by choking and suffocating; its eyes are blinded with tears, its ears deafened, its throat sore; its bowels gripe, its evacuations burn it. The aggressive anxiety-reaction is far too strong a weapon in the hands of such a weak ego; it has become uncontrollable and is threatening to destroy its owner. Such a bodily experience is a *real* one and leaves its imprint on the ego, as much analytic material shows. It cannot in fact be undone and obliterated; though the psyche pursues its narcissistic method of instantly projecting all such sensations outside the 'me'.

Moreover, this furious discharge of aggression in the end reduces the child for the time being to the same condition of helpless exhaustion and lifelessness as results from a constant deprivation such as starving (Eros has been temporarily used up). The end-result of aggression directed outward, if it cannot be checked and controlled, is again to produce the worst danger-situation possible, the closest proximity to death. So that, in my view, from the very beginning the internal forces of the death instinct and of aggression are felt to be the cardinal danger threatening the organism.[1] In spite of all later complications and even reversals, I believe anxiety of helplessness in the face of destructive forces within (a severe depletion of Eros within the organism) constitutes the fundamental pattern of all subsequent anxieties. Further, all later psychical developments are

[1] Cf. Melanie Klein, *The Psycho-Analysis of Children*, Chapter 8; also M. N. Searl, 'The Psychology of Screaming'.

built up on this foundation and can be found to contain this situation at their core; *i.e.* they are not merely adaptations to the external world and to the changing needs of the organism but at the same time constitute measures of protection against this primordial danger-situation which is ever present to the ego in the depths. In my view all psychical developments, not merely neurotic symptoms, are compromises and represent the *interplay* of Eros and Thanatos, subserving the demands of the libido but also paying tribute to the demands of the death instinct, while tending to guard against the influence of both instincts in so far as they constitute a danger to the ego.[1]

As long as primary identification persists and the breast is part of the self, such an overwhelming experience of unpleasure must be felt as being experienced by the breast also, as well as by the self, since both are one. At such a level, moreover, the psyche has no experience of space or time by which to correct such alarming impressions. So the breast itself seems also to have been reduced to utter disruption and chaotic disintegration.[2] But I suggest that such a painful experience in itself does much to bring about the recognition of an external object. Not only does the breast in fact frustrate the demands of the 'me' in this situation, and so force a breach in the narcissistic phantasy; but the ego's need to dissociate itself from the unpleasure is so great that it *requires an object* upon which it can expel it, and which it can identify with a bad suffering 'me'. For such an experience of unpleasure is too intense to be merely 'killed', hallucinated as non-existent.

Narcissistic phantasy would thus in itself lead to object-relations,[3] and these object-relations will at first be of a negative order,[4]

[1] Cf. M. N. Searl, 'The essence of the ego is that it knows what it has to do, not in order to live, but to avoid death'. 'The Rôles of the Ego and the Libido in Development.'

[2] W. C. M. Scott, whose experience with psychotic patients supports Melanie Klein's views, has found that the blurring and distortion of the external world by tears in an attack of rage is of great psychical significance as confirming the imagined destruction of the object.

[3] As Freud says, 'Every excess contains within it the germ of its own decay' (*Inhibitions, Symptoms and Anxiety* (1926), p. 65).

[4] 1950. The view that the earliest object-relation is negative and hostile was expressed by Freud. Later work leads to a correction of this hypothesis; it now appears that the beginnings of a good object-relation to the real external mother may be observed very early. Cf. Chapters VI and VII.

since objects are needed to bear the burden of the unpleasure and the aggressive discharges which the psyche of the primitive ego cannot tolerate. This psychical process goes hand in hand, as I see it, with the gradual growth of the physical capacity to *localize* stimuli. As the physical sense-perceptions apprehend objects, the psyche brings these perceived objects into its service by representing them to itself on the basis of narcissistic phantasy as recipients or containers of its own painful experiences. Objective experience, however, leads in the same direction as phantasy; for it is the child's constant *experience* that its satisfactions and its relief from painful stimuli, internal or external, come to it from the external mother, so far as she is apprehended. Thus from the beginning any inexorable internal need is referred as a demand upon the external mother; she and the need are one. (An aggressive anxiety-response also constitutes an appeal to her.) If she does not satisfy it, *she is inexorable in the same way as the internal need; thus she becomes identified with the internal need and pain.*[1] This is, therefore, the deepest level of projection: internal privation and need are always *felt* as external frustration. An internal situation of need and stress is necessarily treated as an external one, partly because help has come and does come (experience), and therefore *must* come (omnipotence), from an external agency. (Another source of this avenue of psychical relief from a painful *internal sensation* is doubtless the experience of relief in anal evacuation by the act of expelling painful faeces.) So the child feels an intolerable helplessness and dependence first in relation to its own internal conditions, then (as a first measure of defence) a dependence in relation to its external conditions, as sources of help in various ways. The dependence on the mother, and fear of loss of her which Freud regards as the deepest source of anxiety, is from one point of view (the self-preservative) already a defence against a greater

---

[1] In an early contribution (*I.J.Ps-A.*, VIII) and in a quite different context, I made the suggestion that the unattainability of a satisfaction (privation) is psychically equivalent to frustration, and is the source of the sense of guilt (super-ego). The light thrown on these problems since those days by the understanding of projection-mechanisms was then lacking. This point of view was worked out further by Ernest Jones in his 'Early Development of Female Sexuality'. In the present context I am indebted to Susan Isaacs for notes supplied me in further amplification of her former paper on 'Privation and Guilt'.

danger (that of helplessness against destruction within). Thus object-relations are sought, as improvements on and protections against the inadequacies and anxieties of a narcissistic state (just as marriage may be sought later as a refuge and defence against masturbation anxieties).

I will refer here once more to the pain and anxiety caused by hunger. Not only do the hunger-pangs feel like foreign agents within one, like biting, gnawing, wasting forces inside one, against which one is helpless; but the intense wishes to seize and devour (the breast) which accompany such hunger at its inception will be identified with these inner devouring agencies or pains.[1] Thus the destructive condition (starvation) becomes equated with the destructive impulses: *'My wishes inside me are devouring and destroying me.'* In these painful and destructive feelings within, which seem like dangerous foreign agencies, we have the deepest root of the phantasied internal bad objects, for which an external (because less dangerous) substitute is needed. And in them too lies the germ of the strict super-ego, in the later development of which these same phantasies of dangerous internal objects play a part (cf. pangs of hunger, gnawing of conscience).

We have the right to assume that a child's aggressive outbursts of anxiety derive in part directly from rage and express its hate and revengeful desires to retaliate. This retaliation too is primarily directed against the pain within and so a child's first hate is directed against itself.[2] All these feelings will be projected on to the breast in phantasy. 'The breasts hate me and deprive me, because I hate them', and conversely; thus a vicious circle is set up. The first apprehension of cause and effect is thus also projected. 'You don't come and help, and you hate me, because I am angry and devour you; yet I *must* hate you and devour you to make you help.' The revengeful hate which cannot be gratified increases tension further; and the thwarting breast is endowed with all the ruthlessness and intemperate absoluteness of the infant's own sensations. Thus 'good' and 'bad'

---

[1] This would be a prototype of all later situations in which a libidinal and aggressive (sadistic) impulse is felt to be at the same time destructive to the ego within (masturbation is the classical example).

[2] Cf. observations of babies scratching, tearing, biting themselves, etc.

internal states become identified in phantasy with a 'good' and a 'bad' external object. The simplest narcissistic position in which the ego arrogates to itself all responsibility, all causal relations, all powers of life or annihilation, while objects are unknown, develops into a narcissistic system (comparable to a paranoia), in which all responsibility and causal relations are referred to an object identified with the self and endowed with similar powers of life and death, etc. Guilt and remorse will also be present to some extent along with these persecutory feelings and will greatly increase the conflict of ambivalence.

The struggle which now begins is that which we connote by the term 'oral-sadistic anxieties'. The drama is played out in terms of good and bad internal conditions, and good and bad external ones; while object-relations arise in part out of the apprehension of such conditions, in part of course from the response to the satisfactions and the love that the child experiences from its mother. It is in this intermediate period (say from a few months to two or three years), between the state of primary identification and that of the full appreciation of real objects and the development of an integrated super-ego, that the child exhibits its major anxieties (phobias of external dangers). The substitution of internal helplessness and pain by an external impotent and cruel breast creates a bad external object, although the image of the good breast exists alongside of it.[1] The aim of psychic phantasy is then *to keep these two images separate and distinct;* if they are allowed to merge, clearly a good breast which is also cruel and vindictive has ceased to be good. But the existence of a bad breast again in itself gives rise to manifold anxieties; *e.g.* fear of its cruelty and retaliation; fear of the aggression aroused in the self against it; and danger to the breast from the aggression of the self, in so far as the bad breast is felt to be identical with the good one. This situation entails the possibility of *both* the external object (breast) and the self being felt as full of destructiveness and danger—it is therefore one of intolerable despair again. This state of mind

[1] In our view this is the root of ambivalence. We believe that already in its first year the child is exposed to conflicting feelings of love and hate, and also of guilt, towards one and the same object.

corresponds to the condition in melancholia and relates essentially to the 'loss of the loved object'. As a defence against such absolute despair the feeling of distrust of the object may now be revived and reinforced; it is one degree less painful than despair. This radical distrust, however, which verges on despair is directly related to persecution-fears and is reproduced in the later paranoia psychosis when further development has not enabled it to be overcome.

Faced with these anxieties of uncontrollable and destructive impulses within and without, the ego resorts to a very intensive use of the defence-methods of projection and introjection so characteristic of this period.[1] Good must be secured within and bad destroyed and expelled. Not only are the bad impulses projected, *i.e.* treated as outside the self; but endeavours are actively made to eliminate and expel them out of the self. Destructive impulses must be got out and be got rid of. Later this develops into the small child's actual destructiveness, which is thus *not merely a discharge* and gratification of impulse. But the suckling who needs to discharge his destructiveness against his only object (the breast) and to gratify his hate (by biting it, etc.) is unable to achieve much of such gratification. This is not only because physically the co-ordinated movements are not yet sufficiently developed, but because the love already felt at this stage for the breast will also inhibit him. Thus phantasy comes again to his aid.

When we speak of 'phantasies' in babies or small children, we do not imply an elaborate *mise en scène* or coherent dramatiza-

---

[1] Freud writes, 'It may well be that before a sharp differentiation between ego and id has arisen, before the development of a super-ego, the psychical apparatus employs other methods of defence from those it uses after these levels have been attained' (*Inhibitions, Symptoms and Anxiety* (1926), p. 157).
It should not be assumed that in general we regard introjection altogether as synonymous with taking in good and projection with eliminating bad. This may be largely true as far as their use as *defences* against these early anxieties is concerned. The terms denote psychical processes which are not restricted to use as defence-mechanisms. From the earliest age, for instance, in regarding the breast as good, the child is also projecting good feelings into the outer world. In later stages of development enormous use is made both of projecting good, as in sublimations, and introjecting bad, as happens in delusions, melancholic and obsessional conditions and in character development generally.

tions in them, nor of course to begin with plastic or verbal representations. We surmise that the child *feels as if* it were carrying out the desired action, and that this affective feeling is accompanied by a corresponding physical excitation in certain organs (*e.g.* mouth or musculature). We conclude that to begin with the child discharges its aggression mainly in the calling up of feelings and sensations of an aggressive order. It is here for instance that in our view the enormously important psychical significance of the excreta as hostile agents and means of discharging aggression arises. Whether training in sphinctercontrol begins early or not, there is no doubt that these physical functions are by nature suited to represent the discharge of 'pain'; and if, as we believe, the psyche needs to localize unpleasure at some definite point outside itself (in an object) the discharge of excreta would in phantasy be *felt* as a transference of the painful excretory substance on to or into that object. (The projectile weapon is the reproduction in objective reality of this primitive phantasy-situation.) Loose motions, flatus and urine are all felt to be burning, corroding and poisoning agents. Not only the excretory but all other physical functions are pressed into the service of the need for aggressive (sadistic) discharge and projection in phantasy. Limbs shall trample, kick and hit; lips, fingers and hands shall suck, twist, pinch; teeth shall bite, gnaw, mangle and cut; mouth shall devour, swallow and 'kill' (annihilate); eyes kill by a look, pierce and penetrate; breath and mouth hurt by noise, as the child's own sensitive ears have experienced. One may suppose that before an infant is many months old it will not only *feel* itself performing these actions, but will have some kind of *ideas* of doing so. All these sadistic activities in phantasy are felt not only to expel the danger from the self but to transfer it into the object (projection). And there follows the anxiety of 'retaliation by the object' (introjection of the bad object).

The fear of retaliation itself surely has a foundation in experience, namely, in that of the continual *recurrence* of internal unpleasure and tension, of need and aggression—the boomerang principle. Projection never succeeds; the feared and hated pain and helplessness always recur, come back. Here would be the core of the idea of talion punishment (a recurrence and repetition of cause and effect in a reversed direction). The persecutors in a paranoia are feared like *revenants* who may appear from nowhere; and we know they derive from faeces. The stools too are always 'still there' although they are constantly expelled. Nor do such phantasy-processes in effect constitute an adequate discharge; the ungratified wishes are by no means satiated. Another vicious circle has arisen. The attempt to externalize the difficulty has to some extent failed, so the original situation of danger within has recurred.

The accompanying process of introjection functions at the same time secondarily as a means of increasing and prolonging 'good' states and conditions within. The process of introjection of course operates continuously from the first dawning perception of 'something' external to 'me', *i.e.* the breast; 'that something is good and I take it into me'. Introjection like projection proceeds parallel with the development of object-relations; each fosters the other. But feelings of helplessness, emptiness (of 'good' sensations) and dependence on the breast all greatly augment and stimulate the desire to take in whatever is perceived as good. These oral cravings thus become the kernel of greed in general. Impulses to accumulate good within are strong, and connect with aggressive impulses to seize (also to steal secretly). The wish to secure the good breast, to have control over it, and be able to keep it for ever, and thus to acquire a perpetual insurance against both lack of satisfaction and the dangers of helplessness and aggression within (and without) leads to a great intensification of introjection. And this process is altogether very closely related to phantasy-building. Both for our theory and our practice, the great significance of introjection lies in the phantasy-systems relating to the internalized objects which develop at this stage. The internalization of all *good* is the paramount need. At first the part-objects, a 'good' breast, good mother's arms and hands, good loving mother's face must be secured within the self and under the control of the self. It is at this stage that a baby 'puts everything into its mouth'. These feelings are paralleled by the earliest experiences of taking in orally, and through eyes and ears, and by grasping things, etc. The absorbing stare with which a six-months baby looks at one plainly demonstrates how he is taking you in.

Surely the child *feels*, if it does not yet *know*, that it is at least 'acquiring knowledge' of new sights and sounds, and so on, every day. We say 'He recognizes me!' and it means 'He has preserved his perception of me intact in his mind since he first took it in'. And I think the baby too knows in his way that *he* is involved in the process; his 'recognition' means to him in feeling that he has preserved his memory of me, as well as that I have appeared again in a concrete form. This impulse to incorporate is another aspect of the developed narcissistic system in which there is complete dependence on a good external object which is identified with the self. For, as a corollary to this, there goes with it the aim of a total absorption of all good objects into the self. These two counterparts represent the aims and significance of the projection and introjection processes, which develop out of primary narcissism as external objects begin to be perceived.[1]

Analytic experience shows very clearly that the strength of this need to internalize all good brings about a mobilization and utilization of erotic impulses in the defensive struggle against sadistic anxieties. The child gratifies and discharges its libido orally on the breast; but since this gratification causes emptiness and helplessness within to disappear, the demand for such 'internalizing' satisfactions is intensified. The physical erotic sensations experienced in reality then increase and 'confirm' the (phantasy) reassurance of having in fact obtained more good into the self. Need for reassurance against anxiety and for erotic satisfaction reinforce each other.[2] Freud has raised the question why a desire should ever become excessive, *i.e.* insatiable, incapable of being gratified. Some analysts assume that libido is only excited biologically, by somatic stimuli. But many psychic manifestations show that a threat from the death instinct produces a strong uprush of Eros, and we may fairly conclude that the aim of this response is to counteract the

[1] 1950. The discussion in this chapter of primary narcissism, the development of introjection and projection processes and their relation to early object-relations, needs to be supplemented by reference to the later chapters, especially to Chapter IV, in which these topics are dealt with far more precisely on the basis of a further ten or fifteen years of research.

[2] Cf. Melitta Schmideberg, 'Some Unconscious Mechanisms in Pathological Sexuality'.

destructive forces felt to be within.[1] The well-known 'avidity of neurotics' in general in my view arises as a response to the constant anxiety of their own internal aggression (sadism, death instinct) which is also the cause of their neurotic symptoms.[2]

The lack of oral satisfaction and the anxieties and conflicts arising out of oral sadism thus seem to lead to the early manifestations of genital excitation in babies. Genital masturbation and erection may be observed in boy babies of a few months, and there is also reason to think that girl babies experience vaginal excitation. One reason for the often traumatic effect of weaning is that the child is left with no opportunity for obtaining erotic satisfaction from any *body* except its own. This stirs up all its anxieties about the existence of good sensations inside itself and its capacity to produce them; and leads to a constant need to test and demonstrate this capacity.[3]

The increase of libido, however, again stimulates a need for objects to be incorporated and this rouses aggressivity again and increases the anxiety of destroying them. And the growing capacity for other activities besides sucking (*e.g.* struggling, biting with teeth, etc.) would give rise to and confirm these apprehensions. Moreover, the good objects within as well as without vanish and are replaced by bad sensations (felt as bad objects), painful faeces, painful effects of screaming, etc. The good breast becomes transformed into a bad thing inside. *The problem of preservation* is the rock on which projection and introjection founder. Emptiness, aggression and sadistic impulses *come back*; just as the good state of well-being after feeding cannot be preserved. The omnipotence of phantasy is a weapon which cuts both ways; it can be used to create goodness, and

[1] This may well be one source of the sexual orgies indulged in at times of war, pestilence, etc.

[2] This represents the situation in melancholia and drug addictions, in which oral cravings are a special feature. The 'pure culture of sadism' in this disorder, as Freud calls it, relates to the conflict between the ego and the phantasied internal objects, each of which is felt to be attacking the other. The cravings to imbibe 'good' substances arise largely because they are needed as a means of assuaging this struggle of two devouring forces.

[3] Analytic experience in our work with children and adults who masturbate compulsively very definitely confirms this view; the compulsion diminishes in direct proportion as the anxieties of aggression and the inaccessible love-impulses towards the phantasied objects are brought to light.

to destroy and expel badness. But what if destructiveness seizes the reins and omnipotently annihilates goodness! The perpetual disappearance of goodness within leads to the anxiety of having 'made it bad' by the action of the organs and poisoning substances in the self. For the destructive apparatus phantasied inside the body is felt as foreign agents, as soon as the ego is not identified with them in actively wishing to destroy, but is hoping to preserve. Here come in the terrors of dangerous retaliating objects within, devouring beasts and monsters, destructive as the child feels it has been to the breast or person it has incorporated. Such retaliating persecutors within are undoubtedly the genetic forerunners of the strict aspect of the super-ego.[1] If nothing good within *lasts*, there can be no confidence and security in oneself. Then only the visible presence of a strong good mother outside can reassure against such fears; hence the dread of darkness, loneliness, etc., which now begins to arise. So again the external situation is used as a defence against and replacement of the internal. An external mother must be (and usually is) strong enough to check and control externally directed sadism; therefore it will be again best to let it out, discharge it externally, and transfer to her (the object) the responsibility of preserving herself and the child.[2]

By the time there is some recognition of real persons externally

---

[1] These phantasies of beasts and destructive influences of all kinds within the self are of course partly formed with the aid of external impressions (*e.g.* pictures and stories of wild beasts, experiences with animals and reptiles, etc.). The phobia or delusion of cancer, for instance—an insidious engulfing creature, ceaselessly advancing its ravages within one—derives directly from this level of phantasy-formation. The understanding we now possess of this type of phantasy seems to throw some light on the general psychical tendency to 'anthropomorphize' any conception of a dynamic force or process within the mind or body which is felt to be independent of the self or not under its control. Horrible though such phantasies may be, it is possible that the anxiety they express may be more tolerable in reference to something with a definite name and shape than otherwise. The other and of course even more significant source of such phantasies of animals and monsters within is the 'totemic' mechanism, the effort to substitute for the parents, as objects of all the aggressive and sadistic impulses, animals whom one may and possibly can legitimately kill (and eat) without the most terrible consequences.

[2] This phantasy-situation is one that unconsciously actuates the asocial character, and in a milder form many childishly 'irresponsible' and dependent people. The complete and secure introjection of a good object has not been achieved in such cases.

there is also some awareness of a 'me' in consciousness: the ego proper has begun to develop. It seems that at first the conscious idea of 'me' is largely coloured by painful associations. Phantasy is then taken up as a refuge from the reality of 'me'. The feeling that 'I am an uncontrolled and uncontrollable bundle of unpleasant and dangerous impulses towards myself and others and therefore they are dangerous to me' leads on to 'I have somebody like my good helping mother inside me, who will watch over me and never allow me to go too far, who will save me and herself (outside me as well as in) from serious danger'. In this feeling of keeping a good helping protecting mother securely inside we undoubtedly have the first rudimentary form of a later helpful and controlling super-ego which one is willing and able to obey. The perceptual recognition of persons in the environment as whole real external objects who produce effects (on the whole, good effects) becomes strengthened and more or less established, even though this objective knowledge is still very much coloured and distorted by the persistence of the narcissistic attitude. A phantasy may then develop of incorporating whole unspoilt (perfect) loved objects, in such a way that they can be preserved successfully in oneself. And that way is, as it were, by segregating them in some deep hidden part of oneself, where the aggression and damaging influences of the 'me' cannot reach them.[1] The physical prototype of this good safe way of incorporating exists in the 'good' sucking activity at the breast, which takes without injuring (in fact produces more milk) and uses the good milk inside for growth and to become a good child to the mother. In sucking too the good substance taken in becomes hidden and irrecoverable, yet is known and felt to be indubitably there; growth and well-being testify to its presence.

How far the full internalization of 'whole' objects,[2] real people

[1] Thinking and ideas later seem to play a special part in this process, and often to represent a 'safe' way of harbouring the good loved ones, in the mind and thoughts; intellectual acquisition is here contrasted with bodily ways of incorporating them: eating, swallowing them, etc. This may lead to the eroticized and compulsive thinking of the obsessional neurosis, if the anxieties connected with such phantasies are too strong.

[2] The phantasies relating to the all-important question of 'whole' objects as contrasted with objects that are in bits, ruined, devastated, etc., are of the utmost significance in practical analytic work. All the most

recognized as such, succeeds is of the greatest importance for development. We find that this stage of object-relations, which corresponds to the genital, is reached to some extent quite early. This does not mean that oral and anal part-object relations are overcome, but that the different positions and feeling-attitudes can be and are alternatively adopted from an early date onwards, in varying degrees. When the loving face of the mother, the hands and arms that nurse and tend, the breast that feeds, become united as one and referred to a definite perception of the mother as a real actively helping person, then love-feelings as distinct from sensual needs arise. So that feelings of love bring about the essential difference between part-object and whole-object relations. Love is a complicated emotional attitude which has many stages and degrees in its development. Obviously the simpler egoistic attitude towards objects, in which they are regarded either as sources of gratification or are feared and hated as enemies, predominates enormously in early stages of development. On this level the child's relation to persons in its environment—whether it feels them as friendly or hostile, whether it desires or hates and fears them —depends to a great extent on whether the child's feelings in itself, its own internal state, is good (satisfying) or bad to itself. The behaviour of the real objects is felt largely as a mirror-reflection of the child's feelings towards them in itself. It is this fact that determines the importance of the child's real experiences and of the environmental factors in its development External love and understanding, patience and good judgement provide a stable world in which the child can feel that the bad or dangerous forces and impulses in himself will be withstood and controlled, and the good and helpful feelings and needs satisfied and encouraged. The storms of desire, hate and terror raging in him can vent themselves there without bringing him face to face with helplessness, despair and destruction again (flight to reality).

difficult resistances connected with the deepest despair and depression centre around this point. The early recognition that persons can and should be 'whole', and the wish that all objects should be unspoilt and 'perfect', leads to the greatest anxieties that one's own aggression may damage and reduce them again to bits (by biting, cutting up, or by parting them from their loved ones, and so on in infinite variety).

If, on the other hand, really harsh treatment or lack of love and helpful understanding is experienced, the child feels its own capacity for good feelings, satisfying to its parents and itself, greatly reduced and its helplessness against its own aggression cannot be overcome. Really strict or cruel parents (or parents on to whom it has projected its own sadism excessively on account of too great anxiety) cannot be endured or internalized—and later on *must not be submitted to* —since they represent the child's own dangerousness (the authority and compulsions of its own uncontrollable impulses).[1] When this relation to external objects is not outweighed by love and belief in them, the incorporation of a whole (loved) object does not succeed. It signifies that the child's trust in its own good feelings towards objects has not been adequately established, and consequently that external objects are not trusted as good and helpful. Little but anxiety of them is genuinely felt, though a superficial adaptation on the lines of placating and secretly circumventing them may be made, if they are not openly defied.[2] But these anxieties seriously interfere with the child's development of independence; preoccupation with the anxiety felt towards all surrounding persons creates an insurmountable, if unconfessed, dependence. These attitudes are then expressed in eating difficulties (concealed fears of poisoning), and in troubles over control of excretory functions generally, and are often aggravated when the mother is pregnant and another child is born.[3] On the other hand, the internalization of good helping persons counteracts these difficulties. And all this will be felt to some extent in the first year, during teething and weaning.

When some appreciation of relativity and of time and space has been gained, things become less absolute than they once were. *Experience* shows that a good external mother is on the

---

[1] This will later on cause the early 'naughtiness' and neurotic difficulties which often arise between two and four years of age.

[2] Such people in later life remain very 'introverted' and independent; they are actually always suspicious of others.

[3] The whole topic of anal and urethral erotism and sadism is too big to be gone into here. It is linked up, on the basis of primary identification and the projection-introjection processes, with all the feelings and impulses towards the inside of the mother's body and its contents.

whole stronger than the child's badness (pain, etc.); while pain can be surmounted and *not* lead to death; waiting a while does *not* mean starvation; the 'lost' mother *does* come back presently, and so on. When walking and talking begin too, they increase the impulses towards control and independence in the self.[1]

The capacity for true love of an object, as distinct from sensual desire, develops on the strength of the identification with such good helping external figures, which results from an internalization of them. The full capacity for love, however, contains many elements and is no simple primary phenomenon. Often enough, as we know, it is not satisfactorily achieved. Love for an object implies the capacity to bear some pain or loss for the object's sake—*i.e.* for the sake of love—without deriving any immediate or concrete return oneself. The simplest and earliest form of love is doubtless a wish in the baby to rediscover his own happiness again in the outer world, in another being. This represents a tendency to project the 'goodness' felt within him, and an impulse to bestow it externally; it implies no loss or renunciation. With advancing recognition of objects it becomes both the wish to satisfy and please his good real objects (mother) and to make some return to them. Tender love-feelings of this kind may be shown on occasions very early. The 'gifts' of urine and faeces made by the baby at the breast can be sacrifices made for love, as we know (though they can also be omnipotent bestowals or hostile weapons). These earliest and simplest impulses to do good to others then become woven in with the fabric of the libidinal object-relations and contribute to the development of anxiety and concern for the well-being and happiness of the loved ones, both internal and external (dread of their destruction). The defensive measures that accompany libidinal development of course also play their part in the process. This leads to regret and remorse and an anxiety to repair harm and restore the damaged goodness both within and without—to bring back good feelings both in self and object. Guilt and a sense of responsibility towards the object develop;

[1] But analytic material suggests that in those small children who live, as it were, on the phantasy of having introjected all needed good, and crave independence as a safeguard against external objects, the new realization of their helplessness and inability to walk and talk comes again as a serious blow to security and satisfaction.

the desires to satisfy it and restore to it increase a hundredfold; and sorrow on *its* behalf can then be felt.[1] All these feelings— some of which are of an exceedingly painful character and give rise to severe conflicts—are contained in the fully-developed emotion of love. The first stirrings of them are present already in the baby's emotional relation to his mother, as soon as he perceives her as a real person and one who helps him. If the young child's ego is able at this early stage to bear the force of these emotions, *i.e.* if it does not have recourse too early and too much to the defence-methods of neutralizing these conflicts (at the same time neutralizing, displacing, or even abolishing all feelings), it will succeed in working over the conflicts and sus- taining these emotional relations. When they can be sustained they imply a definite organization in the object-relations of the ego, and a certain integration of internalized parent-figures, both helping and frustrating, into a super-ego function. Identifications with parent-figures exist on all levels of develop- ment, from the primary narcissistic identification to that of full object-love; the latter cannot be achieved until a 'consolidated' super-ego (Freud) has been established. Thus what distinguishes the first type of identification from the last is the capacity to renounce an instinctual impulse for the object's sake.

It is impossible to do any justice here to the complexity and variety of the anxiety-situations and the defences against them dominating the psyche during these early years. The factors involved are so numerous and the combinations and inter- changes so variable. The internal objects are employed against external, and external against internal, both for satisfaction and for security; desire is employed against hate and destructive- ness; omnipotence against impotence, and even impotence (dependence) against destructive omnipotence; phantasy against reality and reality against phantasy. Moreover, hate and destruction are employed as measures to avert the dangers of desire and even of love. Gradually a progressive development takes place, in some such way as I have tried to sketch here, by means of the interplay of these and other factors, and of them with external influences, out of which the child's ego, his

[1] Melanie Klein, 'A Contribution to the Psychogenesis of Manic-Depressive States' (1934).

object-relations, his sexual development, his super-ego, his character and capacities are formed.

It is the wealth of phantasy-life dealing with wishes and aims to do good to the object for its sake, for its happiness and well-being, found by Melanie Klein and her followers in tiny children, that provides the best evidence for our views. This material brings into our theoretical discussions the huge topic of the attempts at reparation, and their great importance for ego-development. The significance of the phantasies of reparation is perhaps the most essential aspect of Melanie Klein's work; for that reason her contributions to psycho-analysis should not be regarded as limited to the exploration of the aggressive impulses and phantasies. The importance of this aspect is bound up with the theory of the need for defence against aggression. (These impulses, moreover, are one genetic source of the development of creative impulses and sublimations.) For good conditions and good feelings within must be rescued, restored and preserved, if desolation and annihilation of the self and its objects in phantasy are to be averted. The sense of guilt and sorrow produced by the developing love-feelings and super-ego function, in conjunction with the helplessness and uncontrollable aggression which are still so strongly felt, and the anxiety of losing the object, are the factors impelling towards reparation. The objects within, feelings about people, must be put right, for they are part of the self; the self cannot be rescued and preserved without them. And the external objects, real parents, brothers and sisters and so on, must be pleased and made happy, both for their own and the child's sake. Again, if the internal objects are not right, they become both extremely destructive persecutors and unendurably painful accusers, heaping reproaches on the self. And then the child's anxiety and distrust of himself disturbs his relations with the real people round him; they become 'bad' and frightening to him and perhaps actually harsh or unkind as well. A stable peace of mind is dependent on a confidence and security that the good objects are safe and well within and well looked after; hence the efforts to make reparation are an absolutely essential and integral part of development. Even when external factors are in reality hard and difficult, they can be tolerated and improved, but only in so far as this inner stability holds good. Throughout life all psychical capacity to achieve and produce something good—harmony, unity, well-being, new life—rests on this foundation.[1]

Like all other activities, these attempts begin in feelings and phantasy. Just as the infant hallucinates that its physical and libidinal needs are satisfied, so it imagines it can *bring back good feelings* that have been lost. Aggressive greed and revenge are felt to destroy goodness and transform it into bad; so omnipotence shall be used to bring good back, and transform bad feelings into good.[2] As external reality begins to play a part and be drawn into this world of internal values, the compulsion to put and keep things right extends to real things. Washing, eating, playing, must be done in the 'right' way; and those in charge of the child must carry out its need to be right. This connects with the tendencies to *undo harm* and put objects right magically.[3] Gradually, as the undoing and curative actions can be carried out in reality by the growing child itself they give it increasing assurance that it can and will be able to 'do something' itself—to put disaster right in a real and concrete way both in itself and for others. The pebbles and stones it brings to its mother are restorations to her of the babies and her other body-contents it has wanted to rob her of—in its phantasy *has* robbed her of. If the child's anxiety of its bad impulses is still too strong it will feel that the stones may represent fresh attacks on her, and the impossibility of putting right again brings helplessness and despair. Growth and development normally make it possible for the child to satisfy its parents and make them happy more and more in real ways; and this brings satisfaction

---

[1] Even the asocial child and criminal character have these tendencies; but in such cases they are deeply concealed and hidden. Also, since in such types confidence in internal goodness has never become established, the attempts to make good are still confined to a magic world of phantasy and have insufficient relation to objective reality. (Cf. Melanie Klein's discussion of the manic defence-mechanism in 'A Contribution to the Psychogenesis of Manic-Depressive States.)

[2] All the strength and powerful influence for good of religious feelings rests on this type of omnipotence and the identification with a good internal object.

[3] This represents the obsessional attitude often very marked between two and four years of age.

to itself, partly because it signifies compensating and atoning to the parents, both for its destructive phantasies against them and its real naughtiness towards them.

I have tried to show that internal conditions (feelings, sensations) are the earliest forerunners of object-relations. The objects are identified with the internal conditions and so are 'internalized'. Then a good feeling towards an object signifies (in phantasy, creates) a good object; a bad hostile feeling a bad object. (Thus the relation, the attitude to the object, is both the beginning and the ultimate residue of the phantasied object inside.) Projection and introjection are employed in attempts *to keep good and bad separate*, to keep the bad out and the good in. Bad feelings cannot be kept out, however. The oral longings and biting, tearing feelings of fury towards unattainable desired objects are felt as unendurable persecutors within the self, gnawing, devouring and destroying. These 'archaic' feelings are a permanent element in the organization of the super-ego, even though they are certainly not at first (and perhaps never) acknowledged or accepted by the ego. They are denied, and are attributed to foreign agencies within. But in the depths of the unconscious these foreign agencies are one and the same as those objects who were originally desired and incorporated— the real parents. Consciously the hate and rebellion against these inner persecutors are often re-directed against substitutes for the parents (against any authority). Now the full internalization of real persons as helpful loved figures necessitates abandoning this defence-method of splitting feelings and objects into good and bad. It means that all feelings, whether hating or loving, towards the mother really apply to the real person, 'mother herself', and that it is the loved mother who is at the same time hated and whom the child feels is being so terribly attacked by its uncontrollable aggression. And it means that both good and bad feelings have to be tolerated at one and the same time; since love for the object now necessitates that the aggression and pain formerly projected outside the self have to be borne within in the form of guilt. *This merging of the good and bad into one*—the conflict of ambivalence—is what all previous defences have tried to avert, because it meant that the good object would vanish and be transformed into a bad one. It is only if experience has taught sufficiently that love is the stronger that the two feelings can be kept together in relation to a real person and not again be too widely separated in phantasy. But this confidence in love is severely tested, because love for someone who has been injured evokes the pain of guilt, and a child or anyone whose dread of internal pain is too great will be unable to bear the pain of guilt: the pain, that is, of his own aggression towards others turned inward and felt by himself in himself by identification. This is what the self-reproaches coming from the super-ego mean. This pain is so severe that there is a strong temptation to externalize and project the aggression out again on to external authorities. Then the child (masochistically) feels himself injured by them or by his own conscience rather than accept and endure this pain.[1] Love that is felt to a real person evokes guilt and remorse, but also a great longing to undo the harm done and restore to him or her, and to become entirely good oneself. Then again hate and revenge interfere with this, and tendencies to make the *object* responsible for all badness in oneself recur.

These difficulties in development are very complicated and open the way to many more or less neurotic solutions. A normal development and a fully developed super-ego imply a capacity to bear the pain of true guilt-feelings and the ability to make real sacrifices in order to compensate and restore others. This can only be attained: (*a*) if the internal objects are felt to be predominantly good, that is, not too dangerous, so that to submit and identify oneself with them does not mean in phantasy that death itself will be the price exacted in compensation by them; (*b*) if love for them is felt to be stronger than desire or hate, so that robbing and destroying (eating) impulses can be renounced for the sake of love; then love will not be too much identified with eating or too much feared on account of the pain of guilt it entails, and so need not be denied; (*c*) if neither hate nor the responsibility for it need be projected, if these

---

[1] Masochistic suffering offers the ego the advantage of an erotic gratification, which in guilt is absent; and it also provides a considerable measure of aggressive satisfaction in the projection of both guilt and aggression on to the 'persecutor' who inflicts the masochistic suffering on the ego. Guilt offers no outlet for either erotic or aggressive gratification; it entails privation of both the primary instincts.

feelings are not felt to be so dangerous that they must even be exaggerated as a defence against destructive eating impulses; (d) if the pain of guilt can be borne because love for the object outweighs the pain and compensates for it, so that the belief and hope in better things is stronger and more real (less omnipotent and phantastic). When these conditions are present, and the pain of guilt can be borne, it increases love and brings a greater reward in the satisfaction of 'good feelings within', which means unification and reconciliation with the loved ones within and without. When therefore a certain degree of security has been attained that we are capable of feeling and of sustaining a good relation towards the external world, the people and circumstances we are dependent on, this security is equivalent to the love of our internal objects towards us. A very high degree of harmony can then be achieved between all the component parts of the personality: the feelings, memories and experiences which go to make up the ego. These good internal object-relations and feelings are then prized as the most valuable possession of the ego; love and trust is felt towards them (as the ego-ideal) and egoistic impulses which rouse conflict can then be genuinely renounced, or modified and adapted to valuable ends.

BIBLIOGRAPHY

(*N.B.— I.J.Ps-A.* = *International Journal of Psycho-Analysis.*)

BRIERLEY, M. (1932) 'Some Problems of Integration in Women', *I.J.Ps-A.*, XIII.
(1936) 'Specific Determinants in Feminine Development', *I.J.Ps-A.*, XVII.
FIVE PSYCHO-ANALYSTS. (1936) *On the Upbringing of Children.* Kegan Paul.
GLOVER, E. (1932) 'The Aetiology of Drug Addiction', *I.J.Ps-A.* XIII.
(1932) 'A Psycho-Analytic Approach to the Classification of Mental Disorders', *Journal of Mental Science*, October, 1932.
(1933) 'The Relation of Perversion-Formation to the Development of Reality Sense', *I.J.Ps-A.*, XIV.
ISAACS, S. (1929) 'Privation and Guilt', *I.J.Ps-A.*, X.
JONES, E. (1926) 'Origin and Structure of the Super-Ego', *I.J.Ps-A.*, VII.

(1927) 'The Early Development of Female Sexuality', *I.J.Ps-A.*, VIII.

(1929) 'Fear, Guilt and Hate', *I.J.Ps-A.*, X.

(1932) 'The Phallic Phase', *I.J.Ps-A.*, XIII.

(1935) 'Early Female Sexuality', *I.J.Ps-A.*, XVI.

KLEIN, M. (1926) 'Infant Analysis', *I.J.Ps-A.*, VII.

(1927) 'Psychological Principles of Infant Analysis', *I.J.Ps-A.*, VIII.

(1928) 'Early Stages of the Oedipus Conflict', *I.J.Ps-A.*, IX.

(1928) 'Note on a Dream', *I.J.Ps-A.*, IX.

(1929) 'Infantile Anxiety-Situations reflected in a Work of Art and in the Creative Impulse', *I.J.Ps-A.*, X

(1929) 'Personification in the Play of Children', *I.J.Ps-A.*, X.

(1930) 'The Importance of Symbol-Formation in Ego-Development', *I.J.Ps-A.*, XI.

(1931) 'A Contribution to the Theory of Intellectual Inhibition', *I.J.Ps-A.*, XII.

(1932) *The Psycho-Analysis of Children*. Hogarth Press, London.

(1935) 'A Contribution to the Psychogenesis of Manic-Depressive States', *I.J.Ps-A.*, XVI.

PAYNE, S. (1935) 'A Conception of Femininity', *British Journal of Medical Psychology*, XV.

RIVIERE, J. (1936) 'The Negative Therapeutic Reaction', *I.J.Ps-A.*, XVII.

SCHMIDEBERG, M. (1930) 'The Role of Psychotic Mechanisms in Cultural Development', *I.J.Ps-A.*, XI.

(1931) 'A Contribution to the Psychology of Persecutory Ideas', *I.J.Ps-A.*, XII.

(1933) 'Some Unconscious Mechanisms in Pathological Sexuality', *I.J.Ps-A.*, XIV.

(1934) 'The Play-Analysis of a Three-Year-Old Girl', *I.J.Ps-A.*, XV.

(1935) 'The Psycho-Analysis of Asocial Children', *I.J.Ps-A.*, XVI.

SEARL, M. N. (1929) 'The Flight to Reality', *I.J.Ps-A.*, X.

(1929) 'Danger-Situations of the Immature Ego', *I.J.Ps-A.*, X.

(1930) 'The Rôles of Ego and Libido in Development', *I.J.Ps-A.*, XI.

(1932) 'A Note on Depersonalization', *I.J.Ps-A.*, XIII.

(1933) 'The Psychology of Screaming', *I.J.Ps-A.*, XIV.

(1933) 'Play, Reality and Aggression', *I.J.Ps-A.*, XIV.

(1933) 'A Note on Symbols and early Intellectual Inhibition', *I.J.Ps-A.*, XIV.

SHARPE, E. (1930) 'Certain Aspects of Sublimation and Delusion', *I.J.Ps-A.*, XI.
(1935) 'Unconscious Determinants in the Sublimation of Pure Art and Pure Science', *I.J.Ps-A.*, XVI.
STEPHEN, K. (1934) 'Introjection and Projection, Guilt and Rage', *British Journal of Medical Psychology*, XIV.

III

THE NATURE
AND FUNCTION OF PHANTASY

By SUSAN ISAACS

Introduction

I. METHODS OF STUDY

(*a*) *Observational Methods.* (*b*) *The Method of Psycho-Analysis: Transference Situation: Mental Life under Two Years of Age.*

II. THE NATURE AND FUNCTION OF PHANTASY

Common Usages of the Term 'Phantasy': Phantasy as the Primary Content of Unconscious Mental Processes: Hallucination and Primary Introjection: Difficulties in Early Development Arising from Phantasy: Phantasies and Words: Phantasies and Sensory Experience: The Relation of Early Phantasy to the Primary Process: Instinct, Phantasy and Mechanism: Phantasy, Memory-Images and Reality.

Introduction

A SURVEY of contributions to psycho-analytical theory would show that the term 'phantasy' has been used in varying senses by different authors and at different times. Its current usages have widened considerably from its earliest meanings.

Much of this widening of the concept has so far been left implicit. The time is ripe to consider the meaning and definition of the term more explicitly. (CH. N. 1.)

When the meaning of a technical term does become extended in this way, whether deliberately or insensibly, it is usually for a good reason—because the facts and the theoretical formulations they necessitate require it. *It is the relationships between the facts* which need to be looked at more closely and clarified in our thoughts. This chapter is mostly concerned with the definition of 'phantasy'; that is to say, with describing the *series of facts* which the use of the term helps us to identify, to organize and to relate to other significant series of facts. Most of what follows will consist of this more careful study of the relationships between different mental processes.

As the work of psycho-analysis, in particular the analysis of young children, has gone on and our knowledge of early mental life has developed, the relationships which we have come to discern between the earliest mental processes and the later more specialized types of mental functioning commonly called 'phantasies' have led many of us to extend the connotation of the term 'phantasy' in the sense which is now to be developed. (A tendency to widen the significance of the term is already apparent in many of Freud's own writings, including a discussion of unconscious phantasy.[1])

It is to be shown that certain mental phenomena which have been generally described by various authors, not usually in reference to the term 'phantasy', do in fact imply the activity of unconscious phantasies. By correlating these phenomena with the unconscious phantasies with which they are bound up, their true relationships to other mental processes can be better understood, and their function and full importance in the mental life appreciated.

This chapter is not primarily concerned to establish any particular content of phantasy. It will deal with the nature and function of phantasy as a whole, and its place in the mental life. Actual examples of phantasy will be used for illustrative purposes, but it is not suggested that these examples cover the field; nor are they chosen systematically. It is true that the very same evidence which establishes the existence of phantasies even at the earliest ages gives us some indication of their specific charac-

---

[1] In the Discussion on this paper in the British Psycho-Analytic Society in 1943, Dr. Ernest Jones commented with regard to this extension of the meaning of 'phantasy': 'I am reminded of a similar situation years ago with the word "sexuality". The critics complained that Freud was changing the meaning of this word, and Freud himself once or twice seemed to assent to this way of putting it, but I always protested that he made no change in the meaning of the word itself: what he did was to extend the conception and, by giving it a fuller content, to make it more comprehensive. This process would seem to be inevitable in psycho-analytical work, since many conceptions, *e.g.* that of conscience, which were previously known only in their conscious sense, must be widened when we add to this their unconscious significance.'

ter; yet to accept the general evidence for the activity of phantasy from the beginning of life and the place of phantasy in the mental life as a whole does not automatically imply accepting any particular phantasy content at any given age. The relation of content to age may appear to some extent in succeeding chapters, for which this chapter is intended to pave the way by general considerations.

To understand the nature and function of phantasy in the mental life involves the study of the earliest phases of mental development, *i.e.* during the first three years of life. Scepticism is sometimes expressed as to the possibility of understanding psychic life at all in the earliest years—as distinct from observing the sequence and development of behaviour. In fact we are far from having to rely upon mere imagination or blind guesswork, even as regards the first year of life. When all the observable facts of behaviour are considered in the light of *analytic* knowledge gained from adults and from children over two years of age, and are brought into relation with analytic principles, we arrive at many hypotheses carrying a high degree of probability and some certainties regarding early mental processes.

Our views about phantasy in these earliest years are based almost wholly upon inference, but then this is true at any age. Unconscious phantasies are always inferred, not observed as such; the technique of psycho-analysis as a whole is largely based upon inferred knowledge. As has often been pointed out regarding the adult patient too, he does not tell us his unconscious phantasies directly, nor, for that matter, his preconscious resistances. We can often observe quite directly emotions and attitudes of which the patient himself is unaware; these and many other observed data (such as those instanced later, on pp. 100–3) make it possible and necessary for us to infer that such and such resistances or phantasies are operating. This is true of the young child as well as of the adult.

The data to be drawn upon here are of three main sorts, and the conclusions to be put forward are based upon a *convergence* of these lines of evidence.

(*a*) Considerations regarding the relationships between certain established facts and theories, many of which facts and theories, although quite familiar in psycho-analytic thought, have hitherto been dealt with in a relatively isolated way. When considered fully, these relationships require the postulates which will be put forward, and by means of these postulates become better integrated and more adequately understood.

(*b*) Clinical evidence gained by analysts from the actual analysis of adults and children of all ages.

(*c*) Observational data (non-analytic observations and experimental studies) of the infant and young child, by the various means at the disposal of the science of child development.

I   METHODS OF STUDY

(*a*) *Observational Methods*

Before considering our main thesis, it may be useful to survey briefly certain fundamental principles of method which provide us with the material for conclusions as to the nature and function of phantasy, and which are exemplified both in clinical (psycho-analytic) studies and in many of the most fruitful recent researches into the development of behaviour.

A variety of techniques for the study of particular aspects of child development has been evolved in recent years. It is a notable fact that observational researches into the development of personality and social relationships, and especially those which attempt to reach understanding of motives and of mental process generally, tend to pay more and more regard to certain methodological principles, now to be discussed. These principles bring them into closer line with clinical studies and thus form a valuable link between observational methods and analytic technique. They are: (*a*) attention to details; (*b*) observation of context; (*c*) study of genetic continuity.

(*a*) All serious contributions to child psychology in recent years could be instanced as illustrations of the growing appreciation of the need to attend to *the precise details* of the child's behaviour, whatever the field of enquiry may be: emotional, social, intellectual, locomotor or manipulative skills, perception and language. The researches of Gesell, Shirley, Bayley and many others into early mental development exemplify this principle. So do the experimental and observational studies of social development, or the researches into infant behaviour by

D. W. Winnicott and M. P. Middlemore. (CH. N. 2.) Middlemore's research on the behaviour of infants in the feeding situation, for example, demonstrated how varied and complex even the earliest responses of infants turn out to be when noted and compared in close detail, and how intimately the child's experiences, for example, the way he is handled and suckled, influence succeeding phases of feeling and phantasy and his mental processes generally.

Most advances in observational and experimental technique have been devised to facilitate the precise observation and recording of details of behaviour. We shall later refer to the great importance of this principle in psycho-analytic work and the way in which it helps us to discern the content of early phantasies.

(*b*) The principle of noting and recording *the context of observed data* is of the greatest importance, whether in the case of a particular instance or sort of social behaviour, of particular examples of play, questions asked by the child, stages in the development of speech—whatever the data may be. By 'context' is meant, not merely earlier and later examples of the same sort of behaviour, but the whole immediate setting of the behaviour being studied, in its social and emotional situation. With regard to phantasy, for example, we have to note *when* the child says this or that, plays this or that game, performs this or that ritual, masters (or loses) this or that skill, demands or refuses a particular gratification, shows signs of anxiety, distress, triumph, glee, affection or other emotions; who is present—or absent—at the time; what is his general emotional attitude or immediate feeling towards these adults or playmates; what losses, strains, satisfactions have been recently experienced or are being now anticipated? And so on and so forth.

The importance of this principle of studying the psychological context of particular data in the mental life has become increasingly recognized amongst students of children's behaviour, whatever mental process or function of behaviour happens to be the subject of study. Many examples could be given: *e.g.* the study of temper tantrums, by Florence Goodenough; of the innate bases of fear, by C. W. Valentine; of the development of speech in infancy, by M. M. Lewis; of the development of sympathy in young children, by L. B. Murphy. (Сн. N. 2.)

Murphy's work, in especial, has shown how indispensable is this principle in the study of social relationships, and how far more fruitful it proves than any purely quantitative or statistical treatment of types of behaviour or traits of personality, made without reference to context.

One of the outstanding examples of the way in which attention to precise details in their total context may reveal the significance of a piece of behaviour in the inner psychic life of the child is Freud's observation of the play of a boy of eighteen months of age. This boy was a normal child, of average intellectual development, and generally well behaved. Freud writes: 'He did not disturb his parents at night; he scrupulously obeyed orders about not touching various objects and not going into certain rooms; and above all he never cried when his mother went out and left him for hours together, although the tie to his mother was a very close one: she had not only nourished him herself, but had cared for him and brought him up without any outside help. Occasionally, however, this well-behaved child evinced the troublesome habit of flinging into the corner of the room or under the bed all the little things he could lay his hands on, so that to gather up his toys was often no light task. He accompanied this by an expression of interest and gratification, emitting a loud long-drawn-out "o-o-o-oh" which in the judgement of the mother (one that coincided with my own) was not an interjection but meant "gone away" (*fort*). I saw at last that this was a game, and that the child used all his toys only to play "being gone" (*fortsein*) with them. One day I made an observation that confirmed my view. The child had a wooden reel with a piece of string wound round it . . . he kept throwing it with considerable skill, held by the string, over the side of his little draped cot, so that the reel disappeared into it, then said his significant "o-o-o-oh" and drew the reel by the string out of the cot again, greeting its reappearance with a joyful "*Da*" (there). This was therefore the complete game, disappearance and return, the first act being the only one generally observed by the onlookers, and the one untiringly repeated by the child as a game for its own sake, although the greater pleasure unquestionably attached to the second act.

'The meaning of the game was then not far to seek. It was connected with the child's great cultural achievement—the forgoing of the satisfaction of an instinct—as the result of which he could let his mother go away without making any fuss. He compensated himself for this, as it were, by himself enacting the same disappearance and return with the objects within his reach.'[1]

Later on, Freud also noted a further detail in the boy's behaviour: 'One day when the mother had been out for some hours she was greeted on her return by the information "Baby o-o-o-oh" which at first remained unintelligible. It soon proved that during his long lonely hours he had found a method of bringing about his own disappearance. He had discovered his reflection in the long mirror which nearly reached to the ground and had then crouched down in front of it, so that the reflection was *"fort"*.'

The observation of this detail of the sounds with which the boy greeted his mother's return called attention to the further link of the child's delight in making his own image appear and disappear in the mirror, with its confirmatory evidence of his triumph in controlling feelings of loss, by his play, as a consolation for his mother's absence.

Freud also brought to bear upon the boy's play with the wooden reel other and more remote facts which many observers would not have thought had any relation to it, such as the child's general relationship to his mother, his affection and obedience, his capacity to refrain from disturbing her and to allow her to absent herself for hours together without grumbling or protest. Freud thus came to understand much of the significance of the child's play in his social and emotional life, concluding that in the boy's delight in throwing away material objects and then retrieving them, he enjoyed the phantasied satisfaction of controlling his mother's comings and goings. On this basis he could tolerate her leaving him in actuality, and remain loving and obedient.

The principle of observing context, like that of attention to

[1] *Beyond the Pleasure Principle* (1920), pp. 11–13.

detail, is an essential element in the technique of psycho-analysis, whether with adults or children.

(c) The third fundamental principle, of value both in observational and in analytic studies, is that of *genetic continuity*.[1]

Experience has already proved that throughout every aspect of mental (no less than of physical) development, whether in posture, locomotor and manipulative skill, in perception, imagination, language or early logic, any given phase develops by degrees out of preceding phases in a way which can be ascertained both in general outline and in specific detail. This established general truth serves as a guide and pointer in further observations. All studies of developmental status (such as those of Gesell and Shirley) rest upon this principle.

It does not mean that development proceeds at an even pace throughout. There are definite crises in growth, integrations which from their nature bring radical changes in experience and further achievement. *E.g.* learning to walk is such a crisis; but dramatic though it be in the changes it introduces into the child's world, actual walking is but the end phase of a long series of developing co-ordinations. Learning to talk is another such crisis; but again, one prepared for and foreshadowed in every detail before it is achieved. So true is this that the definition of talking is purely a matter of convention. Commonly it is taken to mean the use of two words, an arbitrary standard useful for purposes of comparison, but not intended to blur the continuous course of development. Speech development *begins*, as has often been shown, with the sounds made by the infant when hungry or feeding in the first few weeks of life; and on the other hand, the changes occurring *after* the mastery of the first words are as continuous and as varied and complex as those occurring before this moment.

One aspect of speech development having a special bearing upon our present problems is the fact that *comprehension of words long antedates their use.* The actual length of time during which the child shows that he understands much that is said to him, or spoken in his presence, yet has not come to the point of using any words himself, varies much from child to child. In some highly intelligent children, the interval between comprehension

[1] Cf. Chapter II, p. 40.

and use of words may be as much as one year. This time-lag of use behind comprehension is found generally throughout childhood. Many other intellectual processes, also, are expressed in action long before they can be put into words. (CH. N. 2.) Examples of rudimentary thought emerging in action and in speech from the second year of life are given in the studies of speech development by M. M. Lewis. The experimental studies of the development of logical thinking, by Hazlitt and others, show the same principle at work in later years. (CH. N. 2.)

This general fact of genetic continuity, and its particular exemplifications in speech development, have a specific bearing upon one important question: are phantasies active in the child at the time when the relevant impulses first dominate his behaviour and his experience, or do these become so only in retrospect, when later on he can put his experience into words? The evidence clearly suggests that phantasies are active along with the impulses from which they arise.[1]

Genetic continuity thus characterizes every aspect of development at all ages. There is no reason to doubt that it holds true of phantasy as well as of overt behaviour and of logical thinking. Is it not, indeed, one of the major achievements of psychoanalysis to have shown that the development of the instinctual life, for instance, had a continuity never understood before Freud's work? The essence of Freud's theory of sexuality lies in just this fact of detailed continuity of development.

Probably no psycho-analyst would question the abstract principle, but it is not always appreciated that it is far more than this. *The established principle of genetic continuity is a concrete instrument of knowledge.* It enjoins upon us to accept no particular facts of behaviour or mental processes as *sui generis*, ready-made, or suddenly emerging, but to regard them as items in a developing series. We seek to trace them backwards through earlier and more rudimentary stages to their most germinal forms; similarly, we are required to regard the facts as manifestations of a process of growth, which has to be followed forward to later and more developed forms. Not only is it necessary to study the acorn in order to understand the oak,

---

[1] This question is bound up with the problem of *regression*, which is discussed in Chapter V.

but also to know about the oak in order to understand the acorn. (CH. N. 2.)

(b) The Method of Psycho-Analysis

These three ways of obtaining evidence of mental process from observation of behaviour—that of noting the context, observing details and approaching any particular data as a part of a developmental process—are essential aspects of the work of psycho-analysis, and most fully exemplified there. They are indeed its breath of life. They serve to elucidate the nature and function of phantasy, as well as of other mental phenomena.

The observation of detail and of context are so intimately bound up in analytic work that they may be briefly dealt with together. With adult patients, as well as children, the analyst not only listens to all the details of the actual content of the patient's remarks and associations, including what is not said as well as what is, but notes also where emphasis is put, and whether it seems appropriate. Repetition of what has already been told or remarked, in its immediate affective and associative context; changes occurring in the patient's account of events in his earlier life, and in the picture he presents of people in his environment, as the work goes on; changes in his ways of referring to circumstances and to people (including the names he gives them), from time to time, all serve to indicate the character and activity of the phantasies operating in his mind. So do idiosyncrasies of speech, or phrases and forms of description, metaphors and verbal style generally. Further data are the patient's selection of facts from a total incident, and his denials (e.g. of things he has previously said, of states of mind which would be appropriate to the content of what he is saying, of real objects seen or incidents occurring in the analytic room, of facts in his own life which can certainly be inferred from the other known content of his life or family history, of facts known by the patient about the analyst or of happenings in public affairs, such as war and bombs). The analyst notes the patient's manner and behaviour as he enters and leaves the room, as he greets the analyst or parts from him, and while he is on the couch; including every detail of gesture or tone of voice, pace of speaking and variations in this, idiosyncratic routine or particular changes in mode of expression, changes of mood, every sign of affect or denial of affect, in their particular nature and intensity and their precise associative context. These, and many other such kinds of detail, taken as a context to the patient's dreams and associations, help to reveal his unconscious phantasies (among other mental facts). The particular situation in the internal life of the patient at the moment gradually becomes clear, and the relation of his immediate problem to earlier situations and actual experiences in his history is gradually made plain.

The third principle, that of genetic continuity, is inherent in the whole approach and the moment-by-moment work of psycho-analysis.

Freud's discovery of the successive phases of libidinal development, and the continuity of the various manifestations of the sexual wishes from infancy to maturity, has not only been fully confirmed with every patient analysed, but, as in the case of every sound generalization of observed facts, has proved to be a reliable instrument for further understanding of new data.

Observations in the analytic field of the development of phantasy and of the continuous and developing interplay between psychic reality and knowledge of the external world, are fully in accordance with the data and generalizations regarding development arrived at in other fields, such as bodily skills, perceptions, speech and logical thinking. As with the external facts of behaviour, so with the development of phantasy, we have to regard each manifestation at any given time and in any given situation as a member of a developing series whose rudimentary beginnings can be traced backwards and whose further, more mature, forms can be followed forwards. Awareness of the way in which the content and form of phantasy at any given time are bound up with the successive phases of instinctual development, and of the growth of the ego, is always operating in the analyst's mind. To make this plain (in concrete detail) to the patient is an inherent part of the work.

It was by attending to the details and the context of the patient's speech and manner, as well as of his dreams and associations, that Freud laid bare both the fundamental instinctual drives in the mental life, and the varied processes—the so-called '*mental mechanisms*'—by which impulses and feelings are controlled and expressed, internal equilibrium is maintained and adaptation to the external world achieved. These 'mechanisms' are very varied in type and many of them have received close attention. In the view of the present writers, all these various mechanisms are intimately related to particular sorts of phantasy, and at a later point the character of this relationship will be gone into.

Freud's discoveries were made almost entirely from the analysis of adults, supplemented by certain observations of children. Melanie Klein, in her direct analytic work with children of two years onwards, developed the full resources of analytic technique by using the children's play with material objects, their games and their bodily activities towards the analyst, as well as their talk about what they were doing and feeling, or what had been happening in their external lives. The make-believe and manipulative play of young children exemplify those various mental processes (and therefore, as we shall see, the phantasies) first noted by Freud in the dream-life of adults and in their neurotic symptoms. In the child's relationship to the analyst, as with the adult's, the phantasies arising in the earliest situations of life are repeated and acted out in the clearest and most dramatic manner, with a wealth of vivid detail.

Transference Situation

It is especially in the patient's emotional relation to the analyst that the study of context, of details and of continuity of development proves fruitful for the understanding of phantasy. As is well known, Freud early discovered that patients repeat towards their analyst situations of feeling and impulse, and mental processes generally, which have been experienced earlier on in their relationships to people in their external lives and personal histories. This transference on to the analyst of early wishes, aggressive impulses, fears and other emotions, is confirmed by every analyst.

The personality, the attitudes and intentions, even the external characteristics and the sex of the analyst, *as seen and felt in the patient's mind*, change from day to day (even from moment to moment) according to changes in the inner life of the patient (whether these are brought about by the analyst's comments or by outside happenings). That is to say, *the patient's relation to his analyst is almost entirely one of unconscious phantasy.* Not only is the phenomenon of 'transference' as a whole evidence of the existence and activity of phantasy in every analysand, whether child or adult, ill or healthy; observed in detail, its changes also enable us to decipher the particular character of the phantasies at work in particular situations and their influence upon other mental processes. The 'transference' has turned out to be the chief instrument of learning what is going on in the patient's mind, as well as of discovering or reconstructing his early history; the unfolding of his transference phantasies, and the tracing of their relation to early experiences and present-day situations form the chief agency of the 'cure'.

Repetition of early situations and 'acting-out' in the transference carry us back far beyond the earliest conscious memories; the patient (whether child or adult) often shows us, with the most vivid and dramatic detail, feelings, impulses and attitudes appropriate not only to the situations of childhood but also to those of the earliest months of infancy. In his phantasy towards the analyst, the patient *is* back in his earliest days, and to follow these phantasies in their context and understand them in detail is to gain solid knowledge of what actually went on in his mind as an infant.

Mental Life Under Two Years of Age

For the understanding of phantasy and other mental processes in children from the end of the second year onwards, we thus have not only all the evidence of observed behaviour in ordinary life, but also the full resources of the analytic method used directly.

When we turn to children under two years, we bring certain proved instruments of understanding to the study of their responses to stimuli, their spontaneous activities, their signs of affect, their play with people and with material objects, and all the varied aspects of their behaviour. First, we have those principles of observation already outlined—the value of observing context, of noting precise details, and of regarding the data observed at any one moment as being members of a series which can be traced backwards to their rudimentary beginnings and forwards to their more mature forms. Secondly, we have the insight gained from direct analytic experience into the mental processes so clearly expressed in similar types of behaviour (continuous with these earlier forms) in children of more than two years; above all, the evidence yielded by the repetition of situations, emotions, attitudes and phantasies in the 'transference', during analyses of older children and of adults.

Using these various instruments, it becomes possible to formulate certain hypotheses about the earliest phases of phantasy and of learning, of mental development generally, which can be credited with a considerable degree of probability. There are gaps in our understanding, and from the nature of the case these may take time to remove. Nor are our inferences as certain as those regarding later development. But there is much which is definitely clear, and much more that only awaits further detailed observations, or more patient correlating of the observable facts, to yield a high degree of understanding.

II   THE NATURE AND FUNCTION OF PHANTASY

To turn now to our main thesis:

As has been said, it is on the basis of the convergence of these various lines of evidence that the present-day significance of the concept of phantasy is to be discussed. A consideration of all these sorts of fact and theory calls for a revision of the usages of the term.

Common Usages of the Term 'Phantasy'

Among psycho-analytic writers, the term has sometimes referred (in line with everyday language) only to *conscious* 'fantasies', of the nature of day-dreams. But Freud's discoveries soon led him to recognize the existence of *unconscious* phantasies. This reference of the word is indispensable. The English translators of Freud adopted a special spelling of the word 'phantasy', with the *ph*, in order to differentiate the psycho-analytical significance of the term, *i.e.* predominantly or entirely unconscious phantasies, from the popular word 'fantasy', meaning conscious day-dreams, fictions and so on. The psycho-analytical term 'phantasy' essentially connotes *unconscious* mental content, which may or may not become conscious.

This meaning of the word has assumed a growing significance, particularly in consequence of the work of Melanie Klein on the early stages of development.

Again, the word 'phantasy' has often been used to mark a contrast to 'reality', the latter word being taken as identical with 'external' or 'material' or 'objective' facts. But when external reality is thus called 'objective' reality, this makes an implicit assumption which denies to psychical reality its *own objectivity as a mental fact*. Some analysts tend to contrast 'phantasy' with 'reality' in such a way as to undervalue the dynamic importance of phantasy. A related usage is to think of 'phantasy' as something 'merely' or 'only' imagined, as something unreal, in contrast with what is actual, what *happens* to one. This kind of attitude tends towards a depreciation of psychical reality and of the significance of mental processes *as such*.[1]

Psycho-analysis has shown that the quality of being 'merely' or 'only' imagined is not the most important criterion for the understanding of the human mind. When and under what conditions 'psychical reality' is in harmony with external reality is one special part of the total problem of understanding mental life as a whole: a very important part indeed; but, still, 'only' one part. This will be discussed more fully later.

Freud's discovery of *dynamic psychical reality* initiated a new epoch of psychological understanding.

He showed that the inner world of the mind has a continuous living reality of its own, with its own dynamic laws and characteristics, different from those of the external world. In order

---

[1] Cf. Freud, 'There is a most surprising characteristic of unconscious (repressed) processes to which every investigator accustoms himself only by exercising great self-control; it results from their entire disregard of the reality-test; thought-reality is placed on an equality with external actuality, wishes with fulfilment and occurrences. . . . One must, however, never allow oneself to be misled into applying to the repressed creations of the mind the standards of reality; this might result in undervaluing the importance of phantasies in symptom-formation on the ground that they are not actualities; or in deriving a neurotic sense of guilt from another source because there is no proof of actual committal of any crime.' 'Formulations Regarding the Two Principles in Mental Functioning' (1911).

to understand the dream and the dreamer, his psychological history, his neurotic symptoms or his normal interests and character, we have to give up that prejudice in favour of external reality, and of our conscious orientations to it, that undervaluation of internal reality, which is the attitude of the ego in ordinary civilized life to-day.[1]

A further point, of importance in our general thesis, is that unconscious phantasy is fully active in the normal, no less than in the neurotic mind. It seems sometimes to be assumed that only in the 'neurotic' is psychical reality (*i.e.* unconscious phantasy) of paramount importance, and that with 'normal' people its significance is reduced to vanishing point. This view is not in accordance with the facts, as they are seen in the behaviour of ordinary people in daily life, or as observed through the medium of psycho-analytic work, notably in the transference. The difference between normal and abnormal lies in the way in which the unconscious phantasies are dealt with, the particular mental processes by means of which they are worked over and modified; and the degree of direct or indirect gratification in the real world and adaptation to it, which these favoured mechanisms allow.

Phantasy as the Primary Content of Unconscious Mental Processes

Thus far, we have been upon familiar ground. If, however, we bring recent clinical data into closer relation with certain formulations of Freud's, we take a definite step forward in understanding the function of phantasy.

A study of the conclusions arising from the analysis of young children leads to the view that phantasies are the primary content of unconscious mental processes. Freud did not formulate his views on this point in terms of phantasy, but it can be seen that such a formulation is in essential alignment with his contributions.

Freud has said that '. . . everything conscious has a preliminary unconscious stage. . . .'[2] All mental processes originate

---

[1] An abandonment of the overestimation of the property of consciousness is the indispensable preliminary to any genuine insight into the course of psychic events. . . .' (Freud, *The Interpretation of Dreams* (1900), p. 562.)
[2] *Loc. cit.*, p. 562.

in the unconscious and only under certain conditions become conscious. They arise either directly from instinctual needs or in response to external stimuli acting upon instinctual impulses. 'We suppose that it [the id] is somewhere in direct contact with somatic processes and takes over from them instinctual needs and gives them *mental expression.*'[1] (My italics.)

Now in the view of the present writers, this 'mental expression' of instinct *is* unconscious phantasy. Phantasy is (in the first instance) the mental corollary, the psychic representative, of instinct. There is no impulse, no instinctual urge or response which is not experienced as unconscious phantasy.

In the beginning of his researches, Freud was concerned particularly with libidinal desires, and his 'mental expression of instinctual needs' would refer primarily to libidinal aims. His later studies, however, and those of many other workers, have required us to include destructive impulses as well.

The first mental processes, the psychic representatives of libidinal and destructive instincts, are to be regarded as the earliest beginning of phantasies. In the mental development of the infant, however, phantasy soon becomes also a means of defence against anxieties, a means of inhibiting and controlling instinctual urges and an expression of reparative wishes as well. The relation between phantasy and wish-fulfilment has always been emphasized; but our experience has shown, too, that most phantasies (like symptoms) also serve various other purposes as well as wish-fulfilment; *e.g.* denial, reassurance, omnipotent control, reparation, etc. It is, of course, true that, in a wider sense, all these mental processes which aim at diminishing instinctual tension, anxiety and guilt, also serve the aim of wish-fulfilment; but it is useful to discriminate the specific modes of these different processes and their particular aims.

All impulses, all feelings, all modes of defence are experienced in phantasies which give them *mental* life and show their direction and purpose.

A phantasy represents the particular content of the urges or feelings (for example, wishes, fears, anxieties, triumphs, love or sorrow) dominating the mind at the moment. In early life, there is indeed a wealth of unconscious phantasies which take

[1] *New Introductory Lectures* (1932), p. 98.

specific form in conjunction with the cathexis of particular bodily zones. Moreover, they rise and fall in complicated patterns according to the rise and fall and modulation of the primary instinct-impulses which they express. The world of phantasy shows the same protean and kaleidoscopic changes as the contents of a dream. These changes occur partly in response to external stimulation and partly as a result of the interplay between the primary instinctual urges themselves.

It may be useful at this point to give some examples of specific phantasies, without, however, discussing the particular age or time relations between these actual examples.

In attempting to give such examples of specific phantasies we are naturally obliged to put them into words; we cannot describe or discuss them without doing so. This is clearly not their original character and inevitably introduces a foreign element, one belonging to later phases of development, and to the pre-conscious mind. (Later on we shall discuss more fully the relation between phantasies and their verbal expression.)

On the basis of those principles of observation and interpretation which have already been described and are well established by psycho-analytic work, we are able to conclude that when the child shows his desire for his mother's breast, he *experiences* this desire as a specific phantasy—'I want to suck the nipple'. If desire is very intense (perhaps on account of anxiety), he is likely to feel: 'I want to eat her all up.' Perhaps to avert the repetition of loss of her, or for his pleasure, he may feel: 'I want to keep her inside me.' If he is feeling fond, he may have the phantasy: 'I want to stroke her face, to pat and cuddle her.' At other times, when he is frustrated or provoked, his impulses may be of an aggressive character; he will experience these as, *e.g.*: 'I want to bite the breast; I want to tear her to bits.' Or if, *e.g.*, urinary impulses are dominant, he may feel: 'I want to drown and burn her.' If anxiety is stirred by such aggressive wishes, he may phantasy: 'I myself shall be cut or bitten up by mother'; and when his anxiety refers to his internal object, the breast which has been eaten up and kept inside, he may want to eject her and feel: 'I want to throw her out of me.' When he feels loss and grief, he experiences, as Freud described: 'My mother has gone for ever.' He may feel: 'I want to bring her back, I must have her *now*', and then try to overcome his sense of loss and grief and helplessness by the phantasies expressed in auto-erotic satisfactions, such as thumb-sucking and genital play: 'If I suck my thumb, I feel she *is* back here as part of me, belonging to me and giving me pleasure.' If, after having in his phantasy attacked his mother and hurt and damaged her, libidinal wishes come up again, he may feel he wants to restore his mother and will then phantasy: 'I want to put the bits together again', 'I want to make her better', 'I want to feed her as she has fed me'; and so on and so forth.

Not merely do these phantasies appear and disappear according to changes in the instinctual urges stirred up by outer circumstance, they also exist together, side by side in the mind, even though they be contradictory; just as in a dream, mutually exclusive wishes may exist and be expressed together.

Not only so: these early mental processes have an omnipotent character. Under the pressure of instinct tension, the child in his earliest days not only feels: 'I want to', but implicitly phantasies: 'I am doing' this and that to his mother; 'I *have* her inside me', when he wants to. The wish and impulse, whether it be love or hate, libidinal or destructive, tends to be felt as actually fulfilling itself, whether with an external or an internal object. This is partly because of the overwhelmingness of his desires and feelings. In his earliest days, his own wishes and impulses fill the whole world at the time when they are felt. It is only slowly that he learns to distinguish between the wish and the deed, between external facts and his feelings about them. The degree of differentiation partly depends upon the stage of development reached at the time, and partly upon the momentary intensity of the desire or emotion. This omnipotent character of early wishes and feelings links with Freud's views about hallucinatory satisfaction in the infant.

Hallucination and Primary Introjection

Freud had been led (by his study of unconscious processes in the minds of adults) to assume that, in the beginning of mental life, '. . . whatever was thought of (desired) was simply imagined in an hallucinatory form, as still happens with our dream-thoughts every night'. This he calls the child's 'attempt at satisfaction by hallucination'.[1]

What, then, does the infant hallucinate? We may assume, since it is the oral impulse which is at work, first, the nipple, then the breast, and later, his mother as a whole person; and he hallucinates the nipple or the breast in order to enjoy it. As we can see from his behaviour (sucking movements, sucking his own lip or a little later his fingers, and so on), hallucination does not stop at the mere picture, but carries him on to what he is, in detail, going to do with the desired object which he imagines (phantasies) he has obtained. It seems probable that hallucination works best at times of less intense instinctual tension, perhaps when the infant half awakes and first begins to be hungry, but still lies quiet. As tension increases, hunger and the wish to suck the breast becoming stronger, hallucination is liable to break down. The pain of frustration then stirs up a still stronger desire, viz. the wish to take the whole breast into himself and keep it there, as a source of satisfaction; and this in its turn will for a time omnipotently fulfil itself in belief, in hallucination. We must assume that the incorporation of the breast is bound up with the earliest forms of the phantasy-life. This hallucination of the internal satisfying breast may, however, break down altogether if frustration continues and hunger is not satisfied, instinct tension proving too strong to be denied. Rage and violently aggressive feelings and phantasies will then dominate the mind, and necessitate some adaptation.

Let us consider further what Freud has to say about this situation.

He goes on: 'In so far as it is auto-erotic, the ego has no need of the outside world, but . . . it cannot but for a time perceive instinctual stimuli as painful. Under the sway of the pleasure principle, there now takes place a further development. The objects presenting themselves, in so far as they are sources of pleasure, are absorbed by the ego into itself, "introjected" (according to an expression coined by Ferenczi): while, on the other hand, the ego thrusts forth upon the external world what-

[1] 'Formulations Regarding the Two Principles in Mental Functioning' (1911).

ever within itself gives rise to pain (*v. infra:* the mechanism of projection).'[1]

Although in describing introjection, Freud does not use the phrase 'unconscious phantasy', it is clear that his concept accords with our assumption of the activity of unconscious phantasy in the earliest phase of life.

Difficulties in Early Development Arising from Phantasy

Many of the familiar difficulties of the young infant (*e.g.* in feeding and excreting, or his phobias of strangers and anxiety at being left alone, etc.) can best be integrated with well-established analytic views, and their significance more fully understood, if they are seen as manifestations of early phantasy.

Freud commented on some of these difficulties. *E.g.* he referred to '. . . the situation of the infant when he is presented with a stranger instead of his mother'; and after speaking of the child's anxiety, added: '. . . the expression of his face and his reaction of crying indicate that he is feeling pain as well. . . . As soon as he misses his mother he behaves as if he were never going to see her again'.[2] Freud also referred to 'the infant's misunderstanding of the facts. . . .'

Now, by 'pain' Freud obviously does not here mean bodily, but *mental* pain; and mental pain has a content, a meaning, and implies phantasy. On the view presented here, 'he behaves as if he were never going to see her again' means his phantasy is that his mother has been destroyed by his own hate or greed and altogether lost. His awareness of her absence is profoundly coloured by his feelings towards her—his longing and intolerance of frustration, his hate and consequent anxieties. His 'misunderstanding of the facts' is that same 'subjective interpretation' of his perception of her absence which, as Joan Riviere points out,[3] is a characteristic of phantasy.

On another occasion, when speaking of oral frustrations, Freud says: 'It looks far more as if the desire of the child for its first form of nourishment is altogether insatiable, and as if it never got over the pain of losing the mother's breast. . . . It is

---

[1] 'Instincts and Their Vicissitudes' (1915), p. 78.
[2] *Inhibitions, Symptoms and Anxiety* (1926), p. 167.
[3] Chapter II, p. 41.

probable, too, that the fear of poisoning is connected with weaning. Poison is the nourishment that makes one ill. Perhaps, moreover, the child traces his early illnesses back to this frustration.'[1]

How would it be possible for the child to 'trace his early illnesses back to this frustration' unless at the time of the frustration he experienced it *in his mind*, retained it and later on remembered it unconsciously? At the time when he experiences the frustration, there is not merely a bodily happening but also a mental process, *i.e.* a phantasy—the phantasy of having a bad mother who inflicts pain and loss upon him. Freud says the fear of poisoning is probably connected with weaning. He does not discuss this connection further; but it implies the existence of phantasies about a poisoning breast, such as Melanie Klein's work has shown.

Again, when Freud speaks of the feelings the little girl has about her mother, he refers to the child's 'dread of being killed by the mother'.[2]

Now to speak of a 'dread of being killed by the mother' is obviously a way of describing the child's phantasy of a murderous mother. In our analytic work, we find that the phantasy of the 'murderous' mother supervenes upon that of the mother who is attacked with murderous intent by the child. Sometimes the phantasy of the vengeful mother may come to conscious expression in words later on, as in the small boy, reported by Dr. Ernest Jones, who said of his mother's nipple when he saw her feeding a younger child: 'That's what you bit me with.' As we can confirm by analysis of the transference in every patient, what has happened here is that the child has projected his own oral aggressive wishes on to the object of those wishes, his mother's breast. In his phantasy which accompanies this projection, she (the mother or her breast) is now going to bite him to bits as he wanted to do to her.

---

[1] *New Introductory Lectures* (1932), p. 157.
[2] 'Female Sexuality' (1931). These occasional references by Freud to phantasies in young children, quoted above, are examples of the way in which the intuitive insight of his genius, perforce scientifically unsupported and unexplained at the time, is being confirmed and made intelligible both by the work of certain of his followers, notably Melanie Klein, and by observations of behaviour.

Phantasies and Words

We must now consider very briefly the relation between phantasies and words.

The primary phantasies, the representatives of the earliest impulses of desire and aggressiveness, are expressed in and dealt with by mental processes far removed from words and conscious relational thinking, and determined by the logic of emotion. At a later period they may under certain conditions (sometimes in children's spontaneous play, sometimes only in analysis) become capable of being expressed in words.

There is a wealth of evidence to show that phantasies are active in the mind long before language has developed, and that even in the adult they continue to operate alongside and independently of words. Meanings, like feelings, are far older than speech, alike in racial and in childhood experience.

In childhood and in adult life, we live and feel, we phantasy and act far beyond our verbal meanings. *E.g.* some of our dreams show us what worlds of drama we can live through in visual terms alone. We know from drawing, painting and sculpture and the whole world of art, what a wealth of implicit meaning can reside even in a shape, a colour, a line, a movement, a mass, a composition of form or colour, or of melody and harmony in music. In social life, too, we know from our own ready and intuitive response to other people's facial expression, tones of voice, gestures,[1] etc., how much we appreciate directly without words, how much meaning is implicit in what we perceive, sometimes with never a word uttered, or even in spite of words uttered. These things, perceived and imagined and felt about, are the stuff of experience. Words are a means of *referring* to experience, actual or phantasied, but are not identical with it, not a substitute for it. Words may evoke feelings and images and actions, and point to situations; they do so by virtue of being signs of experience, not of being themselves the main material of experience.

Freud made quite clear, in more than one passage, his own

---

[1] 'When the lady drank to the gentleman only with her eyes, and he pledged with his, was there no conversation because there was neither noun nor verb?'—Samuel Butler.

view that words belong to the conscious mind only and not to the realm of unconscious feelings and phantasies. He spoke, *e.g.*, of the fact that it is real objects and persons which we invest with love and interest, not their names. (CH. N. 3.)

And of visual memory he wrote: '. . . it approximates more closely to unconscious processes than does thinking in words, and it is unquestionably older than the latter, both onto-genetically and phylogenetically'.[1]

Perhaps the most convincing evidence of the activity of phantasy without words is that of hysterical *conversion-symptoms*.[2] In these familiar neurotic symptoms, ill people revert to a primitive pre-verbal language, and make use of sensations, postures, gestures and visceral processes to express emotions and unconscious wishes or beliefs, *i.e.* phantasies. The psychogenic character of such bodily symptoms, first discovered by Freud and followed up by Ferenczi, has been confirmed by every analyst; their elucidation is a commonplace in the work with many types of patient. Each detail of the symptoms turns out to have a specific meaning, *i.e.* to express a specific phantasy; and the various shifts of form and intensity and bodily part affected reflect changes in phantasy, occurring in response to outer events or to inner pressures.

We are not, however, left to depend upon even such convincing general considerations from adults and older children, but can occasionally gather quite direct evidence from a young child that a particular phantasy may dominate his mind long before its content can be put into words.

As an example: a little girl of one year and eight months, with poor speech development, saw a shoe of her mother's from which the sole had come loose and was flapping about. The child was horrified, and screamed with terror. For about a week she would shrink away and scream if she saw her mother wearing any shoes at all, and for some time could only tolerate her mother's wearing a pair of brightly coloured house shoes. The particular offending pair was not worn for several months. The child gradually forgot about the terror, and let her mother

---

[1] *The Ego and the Id* (1923), p. 23.

[2] Dr. Sylvia Payne pointed out this connection in the Discussion on this paper in the British Psycho-Analytical Society, 1943.

wear any sort of shoes. At two years and eleven months, however (fifteen months later), she suddenly said to her mother in a frightened voice, 'Where are Mummy's broken shoes?' Her mother hastily said, fearing another screaming attack, that she had sent them away, and the child then commented, 'They might have eaten me right up'.

The flapping shoe was thus *seen* by the child as a threatening mouth, and responded to as such, at one year and eight months, even though the phantasy could not be put into words till more than a year later. Here, then, we have the clearest possible evidence that a phantasy can be felt, and felt as real, long before it can be expressed in words.

Phantasies and Sensory Experience

Words, then, are a late development in our means of expressing the inner world of our phantasy. By the time a child can use words—even primitive words such as 'Baby o-o-o-oh'—he has already gone through a long and complicated history of psychic experience.

The first phantasied wish-fulfilment, the first 'hallucination', is bound up with *sensation*. Some pleasurable sensation (organ-pleasure) there must be, very early, if the baby is to survive. For instance, if, for one reason or another, the first sucking impulse does not lead to pleasurable satisfaction, acute anxiety is aroused in the infant. The sucking impulse itself may then tend to be inhibited or to be less well co-ordinated than it should. In extreme cases, there may be complete inhibition of feeding, in less marked instances 'pining' and poor development. If, on the other hand, through a natural unity of rhythm between mother and child, or the skilful handling of any difficulties that may arise, the infant is soon able to receive pleasurable satisfaction at the breast, good co-ordination of sucking and a positive attitude to the suckling process is set up which goes on automatically thereafter, and fosters life and health.[1] Changes of contact and temperature, the inrush of sound and light stimulation, etc., are manifestly felt as painful. The inner stimuli of hunger and desire for contact with the mother's body are painful, too. But sensations of warmth, the desired contact,

[1] M. P. Middlemore, *The Nursing Couple* (1941).

satisfaction in sucking, freedom from outer stimulus, etc., soon bring actual experience of pleasurable sensation. At first, the whole weight of wish and phantasy is borne by sensation and affect. The hungry or longing or distressed infant feels actual sensations in his mouth or his limbs or his viscera, which *mean to him* that certain things are being done to him or that he is doing such and such as he wishes, or fears. He *feels as if* he were doing so and so—*e.g.* touching or sucking or biting the breast which is actually out of reach. Or he feels as if he were being forcibly and painfully deprived of the breast, or as if *it* were biting *him*; and this, at first, probably without visual or other plastic images.

Interesting material bearing upon this point is offered by M. P. Middlemore,[1] from the analysis of a girl of two years nine months, who was treated for severe feeding difficulties. In her play, both at home and during her analysis, she was continually biting. 'Among other things she pretended to be a biting dog, a crocodile, a lion, a pair of scissors that could cut up cups, a mincing machine and a machine for grinding cement.' Her unconscious phantasies and conscious imaginative play were thus of an intensely destructive nature. In actuality, she had from birth refused to suck the breast, and her mother had had to give up the attempt to breast-feed her because of the infant's complete lack of interest and response. When she came to analysis, she was eating very little and never without persuasion. She had thus had no experience of actually 'attacking' the breast, not even in sucking, let alone in biting as the animals did whose fierce attacks she played out. Middlemore suggests that the bodily sensations, *i.e.* the pangs of hunger, which disturbed the infant were the source of these fierce phantasies of biting and being bitten.[2] (Ch. N. 4.)

[1] *Loc. cit.*, pp. 189–90.
[2] It was said by Dr. W. C. M. Scott, in the Discussion at the British Psycho-Analytical Society, 1943, that the adult way of regarding the body and the mind as two separate sorts of experience can certainly not hold true of the infant's world. It is easier for adults to observe actual sucking than to remember or understand what the experience of sucking is to the infant, for whom there is no dichotomy of body and mind, but a single, undifferentiated experience of sucking and phantasying. Even those aspects of psychological experience which we later on distinguish as 'sensation', 'feeling', etc., cannot in the early days be distinguished and separated.

The earliest phantasies, then, spring from bodily impulses and are interwoven with bodily sensations and affects. They express primarily an internal and subjective reality, yet from the beginning they are bound up with an actual, however limited and narrow, experience of objective reality.

The first bodily experiences begin to build up the first memories, and external realities are progressively woven into the texture of phantasy. Before long, the child's phantasies are able to draw upon plastic images as well as sensations—visual, auditory, kinaesthetic, touch, taste, smell images, etc. And these plastic images and dramatic representations of phantasy are progressively elaborated along with articulated perceptions of the external world.

Phantasies do not, however, take *origin* in articulated knowledge of the external world; their source is internal, in the instinctual impulses. *E.g.* the inhibitions of feeding sometimes appearing in quite young infants, and very commonly in children after weaning and in the second year, turn out (in later analysis) to arise from the anxieties connected with the primary oral wishes of intense greedy love and hate: the dread of destroying (by tearing to bits and devouring) the very object of love, the breast that is so much valued and desired.[1]

It has sometimes been suggested that unconscious phantasies such as that of 'tearing to bits' would not arise in the child's mind before he had gained the conscious knowledge that tearing a person to bits would mean killing him or her. Such a view does

Sensations, feelings, as such, emerge through development from the primary whole of experience, which is that of sucking—sensing—feeling — phantasying. This total experience becomes gradually differentiated into its various aspects of experience: bodily movements, sensations, imaginings, knowings and so on.

We recall that according to Freud, 'The ego is first and foremost a body-ego' (*The Ego and the Id* (1923), p. 31). As Dr. Scott said, we need to know more about what 'the body' means in unconscious phantasy, and to consider the various studies made by neurologists and general psychologists of the 'body-scheme'. On this view, the unconscious body-scheme or 'phantasy of the body' plays a great part in many neuroses and in all psychoses, particularly in all forms of hypochondriasis.

[1] The aim of oral love is 'incorporating or devouring, a type of love which is compatible with abolition of any separate existence on the part of the object'. Freud, 'Instincts and Their Vicissitudes' (1915), pp. 81–2.

not meet the case. It overlooks the fact that such knowledge is *inherent* in bodily impulses as a vehicle of instinct, in the *aim* of instinct, in the excitation of the organ, *i.e.* in this case, the mouth.

The phantasy that his passionate impulses will destroy the breast does not require the infant to have actually seen objects eaten up and destroyed, and then to have come to the conclusion that he could do it too. This aim, this relation to the object, is inherent in the character and direction of the impulse itself, and in its related affects.

To take another example: the difficulties of children in the control of urination are very familiar. Persistent enuresis is a common symptom even in the middle years of childhood. In the analysis of children and adults it is found that such difficulties arise from particularly powerful phantasies regarding the destructive effect of urine and the dangers connected with the act of urinating. (These phantasies are found in normal people as well, but for particular reasons they have become specially active in incontinent children.) Now the child's difficulty in controlling his urine is connected with phantasies that it is very potent for evil. These anxieties in their turn spring from destructive impulses. It is primarily because he *wants* his urine to be so very harmful that he comes to believe that it is so, not primarily because his mother gets cross when he wets the bed, and certainly not because he has ever observed that his urine is as harmful as in his phantasies he really believes it to be; nor because he has conscious awareness that people may be drowned and burned in external reality.

The situation goes back to early infancy. In the phantasy: 'I want to drown and burn mother with my urine', we have an expression of the infant's fury and aggression, the wish to attack and annihilate mother by means of his urine, partly because of her frustrating him. He wishes to flood her with urine in burning anger. The 'burning' is an expression both of his own bodily sensations and of the intensity of his rage. The 'drowning', too, expresses the *feeling* of his intense hate and of his omnipotence, when he floods his mother's lap. The infant feels: 'I *must* annihilate the bad mother.' He overcomes his feeling of helplessness by the omnipotent phantasy: 'I can and *will* abolish her'—

by whatever means he possesses[1]; and when urinary sadism is at its height, what he feels he can do is to flood and burn her with his urine. Doubtless the 'flooding' and 'burning' also refer to the way in which he feels *he* is overcome, flooded, by his helpless rage, and burnt up by it. The whole world is full of his anger, and he will himself be destroyed by it if he cannot vent it on his mother, discharging it on her with his urine. The rush of water from the tap, the roaring fire, the flooding river or stormy sea, when these are seen or known about as external realities, link up in his mind with his early bodily experiences, instinctual aims and phantasies. And when he is given names for these things, he can *then* sometimes put these phantasies into words.

Similarly with the infant's feelings about his excretions as good things which he wishes to give to his mother. In certain moods and moments he does feel his urine and faeces to be something mother wants and the gift of them is his means of expressing his love and gratitude towards her. Such phantasies of faeces and urine as beneficent are certainly strengthened by the fact that mother is pleased when he gives them at the proper time and place; but his observation of his mother's pleasure is not the primary origin of his feeling of them as good. The source of this lies in his *wish* to give them as good—*e.g.* to feed his mother as she has fed him, to please her and do what she wants; and in his feeling of the goodness of his organs and of his body as a whole, when he is loving her and feeling her good to him. His urine and faeces are then instruments of his potency in love, just as his voice and smile can also be. Since the infant has so few resources at his command for expressing either love or hate, he has to use all his bodily products and activities as means of expressing his profound and overwhelming wishes and emotions. His urine and faeces may be either good or bad in his phantasy, according to his intentions at the moment of voiding and the way (including at a later period the time and place) in which they are produced.

These feelings and fears about his own bodily products link with the so-called 'infantile sexual theories'. Freud first drew attention to the fact, since then very widely observed, that

---

[1] Very often grasping, touching, looking and other activities are felt to be disastrously harmful, as well.

young children, consciously as well as unconsciously, form their own spontaneous theories about the origin of babies and the nature of parental sexual intercourse, based upon their own bodily capacities, *e.g.* babies are made from food, and parental intercourse consists in mutual feeding or eating. Father puts the good food into mother, he feeds her with his genital in return for her feeding him with her breast, and then she has the babies inside her. Or they are made from faeces. Father puts faeces into mother and in so far as the child is loving and able to tolerate the parents' love for each other, he may feel this is good and gives mother life inside her. At other times, when he is feeling full of hate and jealousy and completely intolerant of his parents' intercourse, he wishes father to put bad faeces into mother—dangerous, explosive substances which will destroy her inside, or to urinate into her in a way that will harm her. These infantile sexual theories are obviously not drawn from observation of external events. The infant has never observed that babies are made from food and faeces, nor seen father urinate into mother. His notions of parental intercourse are derived from his own bodily impulses under the pressure of intense feeling. His phantasies express his wishes and his passions, using his bodily impulses, sensations and processes as their material of expression. (Ch. N. 5.)

These and other specific contents of early phantasies, no less than the ways in which they are experienced by the child and their modes of expression, are in accordance with his bodily development and his capacities for feeling and knowing at any given age. They are a *part* of his development, and are expanded and elaborated along with his bodily and mental powers, influencing and being influenced by his slowly maturing ego.

The Relation of Early Phantasy to the Primary Process

The earliest and most rudimentary phantasies, bound up with sensory experience and being affective interpretations of bodily sensations, are naturally characterized by those qualities which Freud described as belonging to the 'primary process': lack of co-ordination of impulse, lack of sense of time, of contradiction and of negation. Furthermore, at this level, there is no discrimination of external reality. Experience is governed by 'all or none' responses and the absence of satisfaction is felt as a positive evil. Loss, dissatisfaction or deprivation are felt in sensation to be positive, painful experiences. We are all familiar with the feeling of being 'full of emptiness'. Emptiness *is* positive, in sensation; just as darkness is an actual thing, not the mere absence of light, whatever we may know. Darkness falls, like a curtain or a blanket. When the light comes it drives away the darkness; and so on.

Thus, when we say (justifiably) that the infant feels a mother who does not remove a source of pain to be a 'bad' mother, we do not mean that he has a clear notion of the negative fact of his mother's not removing the source of pain. That is a later realization. The pain itself is positive; the 'bad' mother is a positive experience, undistinguished at first from the pain. When at six months or so, the infant sits up and *sees* that his mother, as an external object, does not come when he wants her, he may then make the link between what he sees, viz. her not coming, and the pain or dissatisfaction he feels.[1]

When the infant misses his mother and behaves 'as if he were never going to see her again', it does not mean that he then has discriminative notions of time, but that the pain of loss is an absolute experience, with a quality of sheer 'neverness' about it—until mental development and the experience of time, as a slowly built-up external reality, have brought discriminative perceptions and images.

The 'primary process' is, however, not to be regarded as governing the *whole* mental life of the child during any measurable period of development. It might conceivably occupy the main field for the first few days, but we must not overlook the first adaptations of the infant to his external environment, and the fact that both gratification and frustration are experienced from birth onwards. The progressive alterations in the infant's responses during the first few weeks and onwards show that even by the second month there is a very considerable degree of integration in perception and behaviour, with signs of memory and anticipation.

From this time on, the infant spends an increasing amount of

---

[1] This is a highly simplified account of a very complex process, dealt with more fully by Paula Heimann and Melanie Klein in later chapters.

time in experimentative play, which is, at one and the same time, an attempt to adapt to reality and an active means of expressing phantasy (a wish-enactment and a defence against pain and anxiety).

The 'primary process' is in fact a limiting concept only. As Freud said: 'So far as we know, a psychic apparatus possessing only the primary process does not exist, and is to that extent a theoretical fiction.' (CH. N. 6.) Later on, he speaks of the 'belated arrival' of the secondary processes, which seems at first sight somewhat contradictory. The contradiction is resolved if we take the 'belated arrival' to refer not so much to the *onset* of the secondary processes, their rudimentary beginnings, but rather to their full development. Such a view would best accord with what we can see of the infant's actual development, in adaptation to reality, in control and integration.

Instinct, Phantasy and Mechanism

We must now consider another important aspect of our problem, that of the relation between instincts, phantasies and mechanisms. A good deal of difficulty and certain confusions on this matter have appeared in various discussions; one of the aims of this section is to clarify the relations between these different concepts.

The distinction between, *e.g.*, the phantasy of incorporation and the mechanism of introjection has not always been clearly observed. For example, in discussions about specific oral phantasies of devouring or otherwise *incorporating* a concrete object, we often meet with the expression: 'The *introjected* object.' Or people have sometimes spoken of the 'introjected breast', again mixing up the concrete bodily phantasy with the general mental process. It is especially with regard to the mechanisms of introjection and projection that these difficulties seem to have arisen, although the problem of the relation between instincts, phantasies and mechanisms can be considered in a more general way with regard to every variety of mental mechanism.

To consider 'introjection' and 'projection', in particular: these are abstract terms, the names of certain fundamental mechanisms or methods of functioning in the mental life. They refer to such facts as that ideas, impressions and influences are taken into the self and become part of it; or that aspects or elements of the self are often disowned and attributed to some person or group of persons, or some part of the external world. These common mental processes, plainly seen in both children and adults, in ordinary social life as well as in the consulting-room, are 'mechanisms', *i.e.* particular ways in which mental life operates, as a means of dealing with internal tensions and conflicts.

Now these mental mechanisms are intimately related to certain pervasive phantasies. The phantasies of incorporating (devouring, absorbing, etc.) loved and hated objects, persons or parts of persons, into ourselves are amongst the earliest and most deeply unconscious phantasies, fundamentally oral in character since they are the psychic representatives of the oral impulses. Some of these oral phantasies have been described above, for example: 'I want to take and I am taking her (mother or breast) into me.' The distinction should be kept clear between a specific phantasy of incorporating an object and the general mental mechanism of introjection. The latter has a far wider reference than the former, although so intimately related to it. To understand the relationship between phantasies and mechanisms, we must look more closely at the relation of both to instinct. In our view, phantasy is the operative link between instinct and ego-mechanism.

An instinct is conceived as a border-line psycho-somatic process. It has a bodily aim, directed to concrete external objects. It has a representative in the mind which we call a 'phantasy'. Human activities derive from instinctual urges; it is only through the phantasy of what would fulfil our instinctual needs that we are enabled to attempt to realize them in external reality. (CH. N. 7.)

Although themselves psychic phenomena, phantasies are primarily about bodily aims, pains and pleasures, directed to objects of some kind. When contrasted with external and bodily realities, the phantasy, like other mental activities, is a figment, since it cannot be touched or handled or seen; yet it is real in the experience of the subject. It is a true mental function and it has real effects, not only in the inner world of the mind but also in the external world of the subject's bodily development and behaviour, and hence of other people's minds and bodies.

We have already touched incidentally upon many examples of the outcome of particular phantasies; for example, in young children, such difficulties as feeding and excretory troubles and phobias; to these could be added so-called 'bad habits', tics, tantrums, defiance of authority, lying and thieving, etc. We have spoken also of hysterical conversion-symptoms in people of all ages as being the expression of phantasy.[1] Examples are alimentary disturbances, headaches, susceptibility to catarrh, dysmenorrhoea, and many other psycho-somatic changes. But ordinary bodily characteristics, other than illnesses, such as manner and tone of voice in speaking, bodily posture, gait of walking, mode of handshake, facial expression, handwriting and mannerisms generally, also turn out to be determined directly or indirectly by specific phantasies. These are usually highly complex, related both to the internal and the external worlds, and bound up with the psychical history of the individual.

It is noteworthy how often and to what a degree such bodily expressions of individual phantasies may change, whether temporarily or permanently, during the process of analysis. In moments of depression, for instance, the manner of walking and holding the body, the facial expression and voice, the patient's whole bodily response to the physical world as well as to people, will be different from what it is at times of elation, of defiance, of surrender, of determined control of anxiety, etc. These changes during analysis are sometimes quite dramatic.

In outside life, people may have phases of dropping and breaking or losing things, of stumbling and falling, of a tendency to bodily accidents.[2] One has only to look round at people in ordinary life, in the tube train, the bus or restaurant or family life, to see the endless differentiations of bodily characteristics, *e.g.* mannerisms, individualities and idiosyncrasies in dress and speech, etc., through which dominant phantasies and the emotional states bound up with them are expressed.

Analytic work brings the opportunity to understand what

[1] Freud, *New Introductory Lectures* (1932), p. 154. 'Hysterical symptoms spring from phantasies and not from real events.'

[2] 'Accident proneness' has long been recognized among industrial psychologists. The well-known superstition that 'if you break one thing you're sure to break three before you've finished', is a strong confirmation of the view that such tendencies spring from phantasies.

these varied details signify, what particular changing sets of phantasies are at work in the patient's mind—about his own body and its contents, and about other people and his bodily or social relation to them now or in the past. Many such bodily traits become modified and sometimes considerably altered after the analysis of the underlying phantasies.

Similarly, the broader social expressions of character and personality show the potency of phantasies. *E.g.* people's attitudes to such matters as time and money and possessions, to being late or punctual, to giving or receiving, to leading or following, to being 'in the limelight' or content to work among others, and so on and so forth, are always found in analysis to be related to specific sets of varied phantasies. The development of these can be followed out through their various functions of defence in relation to specific situations, back to their origins in primary instinctual sources.

Freud drew attention to a striking example in his study of the 'Exceptions',[1] where he discussed the interesting character-trait exhibited by quite a number of people, that of regarding or even proclaiming themselves as exceptions and behaving as such—exceptions from any demands made by particular persons, such as members of the patient's family or the physician, or by the external world in general. Freud refers to Shakespeare's Richard III as a supreme example of this, and in his discussion he penetrated to some of the phantasies lying behind the apparently simple defiance of Richard on account of his deformity. Freud suggests that Richard's soliloquy[2] is by no means mere defiance,

---

[1] 'Some Character-Types met with in Psycho-Analytic Work' (1915).
[2]   'But I, that am not shaped for sportive tricks,
    Nor made to court an amorous looking-glass;
    I, that am rudely stamp'd, and want love's majesty
    To strut before a wanton ambling nymph;
    I, that am curtail'd of this fair proportion,
    Cheated of feature by dissembling Nature,
    Deform'd, unfinish'd, sent before my time
    Into this breathing world, scarce half made up,
    And that so lamely and unfashionable,
    That dogs bark at me as I halt by them;

    'And therefore, since I cannot prove a lover,
    To entertain these fair well-spoken days,
    I am determined to prove a villain,
    And hate the idle pleasure of these days.'

but signifies an unconscious argument (which we should call a phantasy) as follows: ' "Nature has done me a grievous wrong in denying me that beauty of form which wins human love. Life owes me reparation for this, and I will see that I get it. I have a right to be an exception, to overstep those bounds by which others let themselves be circumscribed. I may do wrong myself, since wrong has been done to me." '

An example which may be quoted from the writer's analytic experience is that of an adolescent boy who came for treatment because of serious difficulties in his home and public school life —*e.g.* very obvious lying of a sort that was certain to be found out, aggressive behaviour, and a wild untidiness in dress. In general the conduct and attitude of this boy of sixteen years of age were entirely out of keeping with his family traditions; they were those of a social outcast. Even when the analysis had brought sufficient improvement for him to join the Air Force, soon after the outbreak of war, he could not follow the normal course of events for those in his social circumstances. He did brilliant work in the Air Force and built up an excellent reputation, but always refused to accept a commission. At the beginning of the analysis he had been lonely and miserable, and entirely without friends. Later he was able to maintain steady friendships, and was very much liked in the Sergeants' Mess, but was quite unable to live up to the social traditions of his family, in which there were distinguished officers.

This boy's illness, as always, was determined by many complex causes of external circumstances and internal response. He had a rich phantasy-life, but dominant amongst all other of his phantasies was that the only way of overcoming his aggressiveness towards his younger brother (ultimately, his father) was to renounce all ambition in their favour. He felt it impossible for both himself and his younger brother (a normal, gifted and happy person) to be loved and admired by his mother and father. In bodily terms, it was impossible for them both, himself and his younger brother (ultimately himself and his father), to be potent; this notion arose in the depths of his mind from the early phantasies of incorporating his father's genital; he felt that if he himself sucked out father's genital from his mother, swallowed it up and possessed it, then the good genital would be destroyed, his younger brother could not have it, would never grow up, never become potent or loving or wise, indeed, never exist! By electing to renounce everything in favour of his younger brother (ultimately, of his father) the boy modified and controlled his aggressive impulses towards both his parents, and his fears of them.

In this boy, many subsidiary internal processes and external circumstances had served to make this particular phantasy dominate his life—the notion that there is only one good thing of a kind—*the* good breast, *the* good mother, *the* good father's penis; and if one person has this ideal object, another must suffer its loss, and thus become dangerous to the possessor. This phantasy is widely found, although in most people it becomes modified and counterbalanced during development, so that it plays a far less dominant part in life.

Similarly, Freud brings out that Richard's claim to be an exception is one which we all of us feel, although in most people it becomes corrected and modified or covered up. Freud remarks: 'Richard is an enormously magnified representation of something we may all discover in ourselves.' (CH. N. 8.) Our view that phantasy plays a fundamental and continuous part, not only in neurotic symptoms but also in normal character and personality, is thus in agreement with Freud's comments.

To return to the particular problem of the phantasy of incorporation; the mental process or unconscious phantasy of incorporating is described in abstract terms as the process of introjection. As we have seen, whichever it be called, its real psychic effects follow. It is not an actual bodily eating up and swallowing, yet it leads to actual alterations in the ego. These 'mere' beliefs about internal objects, such as, 'I have got a good breast inside me', or, it may be, 'I have got a bitten-up, torturing bad breast inside me—I must kill it and get rid of it', and the like, lead to real effects: deep emotions, actual behaviour towards external people, profound changes in the ego, character and personality, symptoms, inhibitions and capacities.

Now the relation between such oral phantasies of incorporation and the earliest processes of introjection has been discussed by Freud in his essay on 'Negation'. Here he not only states that even the intellectual functions of judgement and reality-testing 'are derived from the interplay of the *primary instinctual impulses*' (my italics), and rest upon the *mechanism* of introjection (a point to which we shall return shortly): he also shows us the part played in this derivation by *phantasy*. Referring to that aspect of judgement which asserts or denies that a thing has a particular property, Freud says: 'Expressed in the language of the oldest, that is, of the oral instinctual impulses, the alternative runs thus: "I should like to take this into me and keep that out of me." That is to say, it is to be either *inside me* or outside me.'[1] The wish thus formulated is the same thing as a phantasy.

What Freud picturesquely calls here 'the language of the oral impulse', he elsewhere calls the 'mental expression' of an instinct, *i.e.* the phantasies which are the psychic representatives of a bodily aim. In this actual example, Freud is showing us the phantasy that is the mental equivalent of an *instinct*. But he is at one and the same time formulating the subjective aspect of the *mechanism* of introjection (or projection). Thus *phantasy is the link between the id impulse and the ego mechanism*, the means by which the one is transmuted into the other. 'I want to eat that and therefore I have eaten it' is a phantasy which represents the id impulse in the psychic life; it is at the same time the subjective experiencing of the mechanism or function of introjection.

The problem of how best to describe the process of introjection related to the phantasy of incorporation is often dealt with by saying that what *is* introjected is an image or '*imago*'. This is surely quite correct; but it is too formal and meagre a statement of a complex phenomenon to do justice to the facts. For one thing, this describes only the preconscious processes, not the unconscious.

How does anyone—whether psychologist or other person—come to know this distinction, to realize that what he has actually 'taken inside', his internal object, is an image and not a bodily concrete object? By a long and complex process of development. This, in broad outline, must include the following steps, among others:

(*a*) The earliest phantasies are built mainly upon oral impulses, bound up with taste, smell, touch (of the lips and

[1] 'Negation' (1925).

mouth), kinaesthetic, visceral, and other somatic sensations; these are at first more closely linked with the experience of 'taking things in' (sucking and swallowing) than with anything else. The visual elements are relatively small.

(*b*) These sensations (and images) are a bodily experience, at first scarcely capable of being related to an external, spatial object. (The kinaesthetic, genital and visceral elements are not usually so referred.) They give the phantasy a concrete bodily quality, a 'me-ness', experienced *in* the body. On this level, images are scarcely if at all distinguishable from actual sensations and external perceptions. The skin is not yet felt to be a boundary between inner and outer reality.

(*c*) The visual element in perception slowly increases, becoming suffused with tactile experience and spatially differentiated. The early visual images remain largely 'eidetic' in quality—probably up to three or four years of age. They are intensely vivid, concrete and often confused with perceptions. Moreover, they remain for long intimately associated with somatic responses: they are very closely linked with emotions and tend to immediate action. (Many of the details referred to here so summarily have been well worked out by psychologists.)

(*d*) During the period of development when the visual elements in perception (and in corresponding images) begin to predominate over the somatic, becoming differentiated and spatially integrated, and thus making clearer the distinction between the inner and the outer worlds, the concrete bodily elements in the total experience of perceiving (and phantasying) largely undergo *repression*. The visual, externally referred elements in phantasy become relatively de-emotionalized, desexualized, independent, in consciousness, of bodily ties. They become 'images' in the narrower sense, representations 'in the mind' (but not, consciously, incorporations in the body) of external objects recognized to be such. It is 'realized' that the objects are outside the mind, but their images are 'in the mind'.

(*e*) Such images, however, draw their power to affect the mind by being 'in it', *i.e.* their influence upon feelings, behaviour, character and personality upon the mind as a whole, *from their repressed unconscious somatic associates* in the unconscious world of desire and emotions, which *form the link with the id*; and which do mean, in unconscious phantasy, that the objects to which they refer are believed to be inside the body, to be incorporated.

In psycho-analytic thought, we have heard more of '*imago*' than of 'image'. The distinctions between an '*imago*' and an 'image' might be summarized as: (*a*) '*imago*' refers to an *unconscious* image; (*b*) '*imago*' usually refers to a person or part of a person, the earliest objects, whilst 'image' may be of any object or situation, human or otherwise; and (*c*) '*imago*' includes all the somatic and emotional elements in the subject's relation to the imaged person, the bodily links in unconscious phantasy with the id, the phantasy of incorporation which underlies the process of introjection; whereas in the 'image' the somatic and much of the emotional elements are largely repressed.

If we pay enough attention to the details of the way in which other mental mechanisms operate in the minds of our patients, every variety of mechanism can be seen to be related to specific phantasies or sorts of phantasy. They are always *experienced* as phantasy. For example, the mechanism of *denial* is expressed in the mind of the subject in some such way as: 'If I don't admit it [*i.e.* a painful fact] it isn't true.' Or: 'If I don't admit it, no one else will know that it is true.' And in the last resort this argument can be traced to bodily impulses and phantasies, such as: 'If it doesn't come out of my mouth, that shows it isn't inside me'; or 'I can prevent anyone else *knowing* it is inside me'. Or: 'It is all right if it comes out of my anus as flatus or faeces, but it mustn't come out of my mouth as words.' The mechanism of *scotomization* is experienced in such terms as: 'What I don't see I need not believe'; or 'What I don't see, other people don't, and indeed doesn't exist'.

Again, the mechanism of compulsive confession (which many patients indulge in) also implies such unconscious argument as the following: 'If I say it, no one else will', or 'I can triumph over them by saying it first, or win their love by at least appearing to be a good boy.'[1]

---

[1] In the analysis, a great deal of mocking and triumph and intention to defeat the analyst can often be discerned behind the 'goodness' of such compulsive confessions.

> 'He put in his thumb
> And pulled out a plum,
> And said, "What a good boy am I".'

In general it can be said that ego-mechanisms are all derived ultimately from instincts and innate bodily reactions. 'The ego is a differentiated part of the id.' (CH. N. 9.)

Phantasy, Memory Images and Reality

In quoting just now from Freud's essay on 'Negation', we noted his view that the intellectual functions of judgement and reality-testing 'are derived from the interplay of the primary instinctual impulses'. If, then, phantasy be the 'language' of these primary instinctual impulses, it can be assumed that phantasy enters into the earliest development of the ego in its relation to reality, and supports the testing of reality and the development of knowledge of the external world.

We have already seen that the earliest phantasies are bound up with sensations and affects. These sensations, no matter how selectively overemphasized they may be under the pressure of affect, bring the experiencing mind into contact with external reality, as well as expressing impulses and wishes.[1]

The external world forces itself upon the attention of the child, in one way or another, early and continuously. The first psychical experiences result from the massive and varied stimuli of birth and the first intake and expulsion of breath— followed presently by the first feed. These considerable experiences during the first twenty-four hours must already evoke the first mental activity, and provide material for both phantasy and memory. Phantasy and reality-testing are both in fact present from the earliest days.[2]

External perceptions begin to influence mental processes at

---

[1] Cf. Chapter II.

[2] An appreciation of what external facts, e.g. the way he is fed and handled in the very beginning, and later the emotional attitudes and conduct of both his parents, or his actual experience of loss or change, *mean* to the child in terms of his phantasy-life gives a greater weight to real experiences than would usually be accorded by those who have no understanding of their phantasy-value to the child. Such actual experiences in early life have a profound effect upon the character of his phantasies as they develop, and therefore upon their ultimate outcome in his personality, social relationships, intellectual gifts or inhibitions, neurotic symptoms, etc.

a certain point (actually from birth on, though initially they are not appreciated as external). At first the psyche deals with most external stimuli, as with the instinctual ones, by means of the primitive mechanisms of introjection and projection. Observation of the infant during the first few weeks shows that in so far as the external world does not satisfy our wishes, or frustrates or interferes with us, it is at once hated and rejected. We may then fear it and watch it and attend to it, in order to defend ourselves against it; but not until it is in some degree libidinized through its connections with oral satisfaction, and thus receives some measure of love, can it be played with and learnt about and understood.

We conclude with Freud that the disappointingness of hallucinatory satisfaction is the first spur to some degree of adaptation to reality. Hunger is not satisfied by hallucinating the breast, whether as an external or an internal object, although waiting for satisfaction may be made more tolerable by the phantasy. Sooner or later, hallucination breaks down, and a measure of adaptation to real external conditions (*e.g.* making demands on the external world by crying, seeking movements, restlessness, etc., and by adopting the appropriate posture and movements when the nipple arrives) is turned to instead. Here is the beginning of adjustment to reality and of the development of appropriate skills and of perception of the external world. Disappointment may be the first stimulus to adaptive acceptance of reality, but the postponement of satisfaction and the suspense involved in the complicated learning and thinking about external reality which the child presently accomplishes—and for increasingly remote ends— can only be endured and sustained when it also satisfies instinctual urges, represented in phantasies, as well. Learning depends upon interest, and interest is derived from desire, curiosity and fear—especially desire and curiosity.

In their developed forms, phantasy-thinking and reality-thinking are distinct mental processes, different modes of obtaining satisfaction. The fact that they have a distinct character when fully developed, however, does not necessarily imply that reality-thinking *operates* quite independently of unconscious phantasy. It is not merely that they 'blend and interweave'[1]; their relationship is something less adventitious than this. In our view, *reality-thinking cannot operate without concurrent and supporting unconscious phantasies*[2]; *e.g.* we continue to 'take things in' with our ears, to 'devour' with our eyes, to 'read, mark, learn and inwardly digest', throughout life.

These conscious metaphors represent unconscious psychic reality. It is a familiar fact that all early learning is based upon the oral impulses. The first seeking and mouthing and grasping of the breast is gradually shifted on to other objects, the hand and eye only slowly attaining independence of the mouth, as instruments of exploration and of knowing the outer world.

All through the middle part of his first year, the infant's hand reaches out to everything he sees in order to put it into his mouth, first, to try and eat it, then at least to suck and chew it, and later to feel and explore it. (Only later do his hand and eye become independent of his mouth.) This means that the objects which the infant touches and manipulates and looks at and explores are invested with oral libido. He could not be interested in them if this were not so. If at any stage he were entirely auto-erotic, he could never learn. The instinctual drive towards taking things into his mind through eyes and fingers (and ears, too), towards looking and touching and exploring, satisfies some of the oral wishes frustrated by his original object. Perception and intelligence draw upon this source of libido for their life and growth. Hand and eye retain an oral significance throughout life, in unconscious phantasy and often, as we have seen, in conscious metaphor.

In her papers 'Infant Analysis' and 'The Importance of Symbol-Formation in the Development of the Ego' Melanie Klein took up Ferenczi's view that (primary) identification, which is the forerunner of symbolism, 'arises out of the baby's endeavour to rediscover in every object his own organs and

---

[1] As M. Brierley once put it: 'phantasy-thinking . . . and reality-thinking constantly blend and interweave in the patterns of current mental activity' —in adults as well as children.

W. Stern, too, has written at length (although in reference to the child's conscious fantasies) of 'this mutual, intimate intermingling of reality and imagination', which he says is 'a fundamental fact' (*Psychology of Early Childhood*, p. 277).

[2] Cf. Chapter IV.

their functioning', and also Ernest Jones's[1] view that the pleasure-principle makes it possible for two separate objects to be equated because of an affective bond of interest. She showed, by means of illuminating clinical material, how the primary symbolic function of external objects enables phantasy to be elaborated by the ego, allows sublimations to develop in play and manipulation and builds a bridge from the inner world to interest in the outer world and knowledge of physical objects and events. His pleasurable interest in his body, his discoveries and experiments in this direction, are clearly shown in the play of an infant of three or four months. In this play he manifests (among other mechanisms) this process of symbol-formation, bound up with those phantasies which we later discover in analysis to have been operating at the time. *The external physical world is in fact libidinized largely through the process of symbol-formation.*

Almost every hour of free association in analytic work reveals to us something of the phantasies which have promoted (mainly through symbol-formation) and sustained the development of interest in the external world and the process of learning about it, and from which the power to seek out and organize knowledge about it is drawn. It is a familiar fact that, from one point of view, every instance of concern with reality, whether practical or theoretical, is also a sublimation.[2]

This, in its turn, means that *pari passu* some measure of 'synthetic function' is exercised upon instinctual urges from the beginning. The child could not learn, could not adapt to the external world (human or not) without some sort and degree of control and inhibition, as well as satisfaction, of instinctual urges, progressively developed from birth onwards.

If, then, the intellectual functions are derived from the interplay of the primary instinctual impulses, we need, in order to understand either phantasy or reality-testing and 'intelligence', to look at mental life as a whole and to see the relation between these various functions during the whole process of development. To keep them apart and say 'this is perception and know-

---

[1] 'The Theory of Symbolism' (1916).
[2] See, *e.g.*, E. F. Sharpe, 'Similar and Divergent Unconscious Determinants Underlying the Sublimations of Pure Art and Pure Science' (1935).

ledge, but *that* is something quite different and unrelated, that is mere phantasy', would be to miss the *developmental* significance of both functions. (CH. N. 10.)

Certain aspects of the nexus between thought and phantasy were discussed in the writer's *Intellectual Growth in Young Children*.[1] From direct records of spontaneous make-believe play among a group of children between two and seven years of age, it was possible to show the various ways in which such imaginative play, arising ultimately from unconscious phantasies, wishes and anxieties, creates practical situations which call for knowledge of the external world. These situations may then often be pursued for their own sake, as problems of learning and understanding, and thus lead on to actual discoveries of external fact or to verbal judgement and reasoning. This does not always happen—the play may for periods be purely repetitive; but at any moment a new line of inquiry or argument may flash out, and a new step in understanding be taken by any or all of the children taking part in the play.

In particular, observation made it clear that spontaneous make-believe play creates and fosters the first forms of 'as if' thinking. In such play, the child re-creates selectively those elements in past situations which can embody his emotional or intellectual need of the present, and adapts the details, moment by moment, to the present play situation. This ability to evoke the *past* in imaginative play seems to be closely connected with the growth of the power to evoke *the future* in constructive hypothesis, and to develop the consequences of 'ifs'. The child's make-believe play is thus significant not only for the adaptive and creative intentions which when fully developed mark out the artist, the novelist and the poet, but also for the sense of reality, the scientific attitude and the growth of hypothetical reasoning.

Summary

The argument of this paper may now be summarized:

(1) *The concept of phantasy* has gradually widened in psychoanalytic thought. It now requires clarification and explicit expansion in order to integrate all the relevant facts.

[1] Pp. 99–106.

(2) On the views here developed:

(*a*) Phantasies are the primary content of unconscious mental processes.

(*b*) Unconscious phantasies are primarily about bodies, and represent instinctual aims towards objects.

(*c*) These phantasies are, in the first instance, the psychic representatives of libidinal and destructive instincts; early in development they also become elaborated into defences, as well as wish-fulfilments and anxiety-contents.

(*d*) Freud's postulated 'hallucinatory wish-fulfilment' and his 'primary identification', 'introjection' and 'projection' are the basis of the phantasy-life.

(*e*) Through external experience, phantasies become elaborated and capable of expression, but they do not depend upon such experience for their existence.

(*f*) Phantasies are not dependent upon words, although they may under certain conditions be capable of expression in words.

(*g*) The earliest phantasies are experienced in sensations; later, they take the form of plastic images and dramatic representations.

(*h*) Phantasies have both psychic and bodily effects, *e.g.* in conversion symptoms, bodily qualities, character and personality, neurotic symptoms, inhibitions and sublimations.

(*i*) Unconscious phantasies form the operative link between *instincts* and *mechanisms*. When studied in detail, every variety of ego-mechanism can be seen to arise from specific sorts of phantasy, which in the last resort have their origin in instinctual impulses. 'The ego is a differentiated part of the id.' A mechanism is an abstract general term describing certain mental processes which are experienced by the subject as unconscious phantasies.

(*j*) Adaptation to reality and reality-thinking require the support of concurrent unconscious phantasies. Observation of the ways in which knowledge of the external world develops shows how the child's phantasy contributes to his learning.

(*k*) Unconscious phantasies exert a continuous influence throughout life, both in normal and neurotic people, the differences lying in the specific character of the dominant phantasies, the desire or anxiety associated with them and their interplay with each other and with external reality.

CHAPTER NOTES

Ch. N. 1 (p. 67)

As has often been pointed out, exact definition, urgent though it may be, is only possible in the later phases of a science. It cannot be done in the initial stages. 'The view is often defended that sciences should be built up on clear and sharply defined basal concepts. In actual fact no science, not even the most exact, begins with such definitions. The true beginning of scientific activity consists rather in describing phenomena and then in proceeding to group, classify and correlate them. Even at the stage of description it is not possible to avoid applying certain abstract ideas to the material in hand, ideas derived from various sources and certainly not the fruit of the new experience only. Still more indispensable are such ideas— which will later become the basal concepts of the science—as the material is further elaborated. They must at first necessarily possess some measure of uncertainty; there can be no question of any clear delimitation of their content. So long as they remain in this condition, we come to an understanding about their meaning by repeated references to the material of observation, from which we seem to have deduced our abstract ideas, but which is in point of fact subject to them. Thus, strictly speaking, they are in the nature of conventions; although everything depends on their being chosen in no arbitrary manner, but determined by the important relations they have to the empirical material—relations we seem to divine before we can clearly recognize and demonstrate them. It is only after more searching investigations of the field in question that we are able to formulate with increased clarity the scientific concepts underlying it. . . . The progress of science, however, demands a certain elasticity even in these definitions. The science of physics furnishes an excellent illustration of the way in which even those "basal concepts" that are firmly established in the form of definitions are constantly being altered in their content.' (FREUD, 'Instincts and Their Vicissitudes', pp. 60–1.)

Ch. N. 2 (p. 71)

In this chapter note are included all my references to the literature of early mental development, and to observational studies of infant behaviour, etc., together with comments on some of it, and also some discussion of certain instances of children's behaviour known or reported to me.

A. GESELL, (1) *Infancy and Human Growth*, Macmillan, 1928;

(2) *Biographies of Child Development*, Hamish Hamilton, 1939; (3) *The First Five Years of Life*, Methuen, 1940.

M. SHIRLEY, *The First Two Years*, Vols. I, II and III, University of Minnesota Press, 1933. (A study of the development of twenty-five normal children.)

N. BAYLEY, *The California Infant Scale of Motor Development*, University of California Press, 1936.

D. W. WINNICOTT, 'The Observation of Infants in a Set Situation', *I.J.Ps-A.*, XXII, 1941, pp. 229–49.

MERELL P. MIDDLEMORE, *The Nursing Couple*, Hamish Hamilton, 1941.

FLORENCE GOODENOUGH, *Anger in Young Children*, University of Minnesota Press, 1931. Goodenough trained her observers to record not merely the frequency and time distribution of temper tantrums, but also the context of social and emotional situations and physiological conditions in which they occurred. In this way, she was able to elucidate, to a degree which had not been done before, the nature of the situations which give rise to temper tantrums in young children.

C. W. VALENTINE, 'The Innate Bases of Fear', *Journal of Genetic Psychology*, Vol. XXXVII. Repeating Watson's work on the subject of innate fears, Valentine paid attention to the total situation in which the child was placed as well as to the precise nature of the stimuli applied. He concluded that the setting is always a highly important factor in determining the particular response of the child to a particular stimulus. It is a *whole situation* which affects the child, not a single stimulus. The presence or absence of the mother, for example, may make all the difference to the child's actual response.

M. M. LEWIS, *Infant Speech*, Kegan Paul, 1936. Lewis not only made a complete phonetic record of the development of speech in an infant from birth onwards, but also noted the social and emotional situations in which particular speech sounds and speech forms occurred, enabling us to infer some of the emotional sources of the drive to speech development.

LOIS BARCLAY MURPHY has made a considerable contribution to problems of social development in a series of careful studies of the personalities of young children and their social relationships. *Social Behavior and Child Personality*, Columbia University Press, 1937, p. 191. She showed that it is useless to attempt either ratings of personality as a whole, or of particular traits such as sympathy, without having constant regard to the context of the behaviour studied. The social behaviour and personal characteristics of young children vary according to the specific social context. For example, one boy is excited and aggressive when another particular boy is present, but not so when that boy is absent. Murphy's work gives us many such glimpses of the feelings and motives which enter into the development of the child's traits of personality. She sums up her study of 'sympathetic behaviour' in young children playing in a group: . . . 'the behavior which constitutes this trait is dependent upon the functional relation of the child to each situation, and when shifts in status give a basis for a changed interpretation of the situation in which the child finds himself, changed behavior occurs. A significant proportion of the variations in a child's behavior which we have discussed are related to the child's security, as affected by competitive relations with other children, disapproval by adults, or guilt and self-accusation in relation to injury to another child, . . .' thus emphasizing that sympathetic behaviour (as one aspect of personality) cannot be understood apart from the variations in the context in which it is shown.

An example of the value of observing the context of behaviour has been reported to the writer by a Nursery School Superintendent (Miss D. E. May). She observed in many cases that when a two-year-old child was left in the nursery school for the first time and was feeling lonely and anxious because of the parting with his mother and being in a strange world, the plaything which most readily comforted him was the 'posting box', a box into which he could drop through appropriate holes in the lid a number of small bricks, the lid being then taken off and the lost objects rediscovered inside. The child thus seemed to be able to overcome his feelings of loss about his mother by means of this play, in which he lost and rediscovered objects at his own will—a play on similar lines to that described by Freud.

Another example from the same nursery school is that of a boy of two years and four months, who was terrified and utterly miserable on his second day in the school. He stood by the observer, holding her hand and at first sobbing, occasionally asking, 'Mummy coming, Mummy coming?' A tower of small bricks was placed on a chair near him. At first he ignored the bricks, then when another child had a box of bricks nearby, he quickly carried to this box all but two of the bricks on the chair. The remaining two, a small cube and a larger triangular brick, he placed together on the chair, touching each other, in a position similar to that of himself and the observer who was seated beside him. He then came back and again held the adult's hand. Now he was able to stop crying, and seemed much calmer. When another child came up and removed the bricks, he fetched them back again and put them in position once more, patting the small brick against the triangular one in a gentle and contented way, and then once again held the observer's hand and looked round at the other children quietly.

Here again we see a child comforting himself and overcoming feelings of loss and terror by a symbolic act with the two material objects. He showed that if he were allowed to put two objects (the two bricks) close together, as he wished to be close to his mother, he could control his distress and feel contented and trustful with another adult, believing she would enable him to find his mother again.

These instances illustrate the fact that some degree of insight into the child's feelings and phantasies can be gained from observation in ordinary life, provided we pay attention to details and to the social and emotional context of the particular data.

HAZLITT, in her chapter on 'Retention, Continuity, Recognition and Memory', in *The Psychology of Infancy* (p. 78), says: 'The favourite game of "peep-bo" which the child may enjoy in an appropriate form from about the third month gives proof of the continuity and retentiveness of the mind of the very young child. If impressions died away immediately and the child's conscious life were made up of a number of totally disconnected moments this game could have no charm for him. But we have ample evidence that at one moment he is conscious of the change in experience, and we can see him looking for what has just been present and is now gone.'

Hazlitt's whole treatment of those problems takes the line that explicit memory grows out of early recognition, *i.e.* 'any process of perceiving which gives rise to a feeling of familiarity'. She goes on: 'In speaking of the month-old child's sucking reaction to the sound of the human voice it has not been assumed that the child recognizes the voices, that there is a conscious experience corresponding to the idea "voices again". There may or may not be such conscious experience. . . . As the weeks go by, however, numberless instances of recognition occur in which the child's expression and general behaviour form a picture so like that which accompanies conscious experience of recognition at the later stages that it is difficult to resist the inference that the child is recognizing in the true sense of the word. Records tell of children from eight weeks onwards appearing to be distressed by strange and reassured by familiar faces.'

Hazlitt also takes the view that even judgement is present from a very early time, *e.g.* in the child's adaptive responses, in the third and fourth months. Hazlitt has no doubt that the very earliest responses of the infant show the rudimentary qualities from which memory, imagination, thinking, etc., develop. She says: 'Another argument for the view here taken that judgement is present from a very early time is that the expression of surprise at stimuli which are not surprising through their intensity, but from being changed in some way from their usual appearance, is quite common by six months and shows itself every now and then much earlier than this.'

Another important field in which this law of genetic continuity operates is that of logical relations. The experimental studies of Hazlitt ('Children's Thinking' (1930)) and others have shown that the child can understand and act upon certain logical relations (such as identity, exception, generalization, etc.) long before he can express these relations in words. And he can understand them in simple concrete terms before he can appreciate them in a more abstract form. E.g. he can act upon the words 'all . . . but not . . .' when he cannot yet understand the word 'except'; again, he can comprehend and act upon 'except' before he can use the word himself.

M. M. LEWIS, 'The Beginning of Reference to Past and Future in a Child's Speech', *B.J.Ed.Psy.*, VII, 1937 and 'The Beginning and Early Functions of Questions in a Child's Speech', *B.J.Ed.Psy.*, VIII, 1938.

BALDWIN, 'Canons of Genetic Logic', *Thought and Things, or Genetic Logic*.

CH. N. 3 (p. 90)

'The system Ucs contains the thing-cathexes of the object, the first and true object-cathexes; the system Pcs originates in a hyper-cathexis of this concrete idea by a linking up of it with the verbal ideas of the words corresponding to it. It is such hyper-cathexes, we may suppose, that bring about higher organization in the mind and make it possible for the primary process to be succeeded by the secondary process which dominates Pcs.' ('The Unconscious' (1915), *Collected Papers*, IV, pp. 133-4.)

CH. N. 4 (p. 92)

'A girl of two years and nine months was treated for feeding difficulties. She ate very little—never without being persuaded by her parents—but in her games and fantasies during analysis and at home she was continually biting. Among other things she pretended to be a biting dog, a crocodile, a lion, a pair of scissors that could cut up cups, a mincing machine and a machine for grinding cement. The history of her feeding was peculiar. She was weaned during the first fortnight because she showed no interest in the breast and would not feed. She slept during sucking and refused the nipple repeatedly, not with much ado, but by quietly turning the head away. The difficulty in feeding seemed to have originated entirely in the child, for the mother secreted a fair amount of milk to begin with; moreover, she had suckled an elder child successfully and wanted to feed this one. As I did not watch the attempts at breast-feeding I cannot say whether the inertia was a simple one or whether, as I presume, it masked irritability. What was clear was that the baby was unwilling to suck, while difficulties which began at the breast continued steadily through all kinds of feeding from bottle, spoon and cup. Until she came for treatment she had never put a spoonful of food into her own mouth. The point is that although she had never sucked the breast properly, still less "attacked" it, she entertained very fierce fantasies of biting. What was their physical foundation, unless it was the feelings which disturbed her during hunger?' (M. P. MIDDLEMORE, *The Nursing Couple,* pp. 189–90, Hamish Hamilton, 1941.)

CH. N. 5 (p. 96)
Scupin records an instance (of his own boy of eleven and half months) which illustrates the interpretation of an observed reality in terms of phantasy arising from the infant's own primary instinctual life. 'When we [his parents] were fighting in fun, he suddenly uttered a wild scream. To try if it was the noise we made that had frightened him, we repeated the scene in silence; the child looked at his father in horror, then stretched his arms out longingly to his mother and snuggled affectionately up against her. It quite gave the impression that the boy believed his mother was being hurt, and his scream was only an expression of sympathetic fear.' (Quoted by W. STERN in *Psychology of Early Childhood*, p. 138.)

An example of a child in the second year being comforted by ocular proof that his parents were not fighting was noted by a colleague of the writer's. His boy suffered from frequent attacks of anxiety, the cause of which was not understood, and he could take comfort from neither parent. Their caresses and soothing voices did not relieve his anxiety. But they found, at first by accident, that when he was in these moods, if they kissed *each other* (not him) in his presence, his anxiety was immediately relieved. It is thus to be inferred that the anxiety was connected with his fear of his parents quarrelling, and his phantasy of their intercourse being mutually destructive, the anxiety being relieved and the child reassured by the visible demonstration that they could love each other and be gentle together in his presence.

Ch. N. 6 (p. 98)

More fully FREUD writes: 'When I termed one of the psychic processes in the psychic apparatus the *primary* process, I did so not only in consideration of its status and function, but was also able to take account of the temporal relationship actually involved. So far as we know, a psychic apparatus possessing only the primary process does not exist, and is to that extent a theoretical fiction; but this at least is a fact: that the primary processes are present in the apparatus from the beginning, while the secondary processes only take shape gradually during the course of life, inhibiting and overlaying the primary, whilst gaining complete control over them perhaps only in the prime of life. Owing to this belated arrival of the secondary processes, the essence of our being, consisting of unconscious wish-impulses, remains something which cannot be grasped or inhibited by the preconscious; and its part is once and for all restricted to indicating the most appropriate paths for the wish-impulses originating in the unconscious. . . .' (*The Interpretation of Dreams*, p. 555.)

Ch. N. 7 (p. 99)

As Dr. Adrian Stephen said, in the Discussion on this paper in the British Psycho-Analytical Society, 1943:

'To go back to Freud's writings: at the very beginning of his *Three Essays on the Theory of Sexuality* he describes instincts as having aims and objects. Aim is the word for the behaviour which an instinct impels us to take, for instance sexual intercourse, and object is the word for the person with whom the intercourse is to take place; or eating, I take it, may be the aim of an instinct and food the object. Freud in this passage was obviously thinking of cases in which the object is a concrete object, but he would certainly have agreed, as I suppose we all should, that the object may be imaginary or, if you like, phantastic. . . .

'Of course we all know that phantasies are built up on the basis of memories, memories of satisfaction and frustration and so on, and as we grow older and as our instincts evolve and our store of memories becomes greater and more varied no doubt our phantasies change considerably in the complexity and variety of their content; but it is difficult to suppose that instinctual impulses, even in a small baby, are not accompanied by some sort of phantasies of their fulfilment. To suppose this would be really to suppose that a baby can have a wish without wishing for anything—and to my thinking wishing for something implies phantasying the fulfilment of that wish. . . .

'We all of us know what it is to be thirsty. In this condition we mostly try to get hold of something to drink and we probably have conscious and unconscious phantasies both about the drink we want and about how to obtain it. We can then describe our psychic processes in two ways. We can say that we want a drink or that we want to quench our thirst. In the one case we are describing a phantasy about the object, in the other we are describing our aim of reducing instinctual tension. In actual fact though we are employing different words and different concepts the facts we are trying to describe are really the same. What we want is not merely the drink and not merely the satisfaction of quenching our thirst. What we want is the thirst-satisfying drink—and our phantasy is that we get this drink and to say this is certainly not to deny the importance of the pleasure.

'The phantasy and the impulse to get pleasure are not two separate psychic entities, though it may be useful sometimes to separate them conceptually; they are two aspects of one psychic process. . . .'

Ch. N. 8 (p. 103)
FREUD writes: '. . . now we feel that we ourselves could be like Richard, nay, that we are already a little like him. Richard is an enormously magnified representation of something we can all discover in ourselves. We all think we have reason to reproach nature and our destiny for congenital and infantile disadvantages; we all demand reparation for early wounds to our narcissism, our self-love. Why did not nature give us the golden curls of Balder or the strength of Siegfried or the lofty brow of genius or the noble profile of aristocracy? Why were we born in a middle-class dwelling instead of in a royal palace? We could as well carry off beauty and distinction as any of those whom now we cannot but envy.' ('Some Character-Types met with in Psycho-Analytic Work' (1915), Collected Papers, IV, pp. 318–44.)

Ch. N. 9 (p. 107)
'. . . one must not take the difference between ego and id in too hard-and-fast a sense, nor forget that the ego is a part of the id which has been specially modified.' (The Ego and the Id, pp. 51–2.) Again, '. . . Originally, of course, everything was id; the ego was developed out of the id by the continual influence of the external world. In the course of this slow development certain material in the id was transformed into the preconscious state and was thus taken into the ego.' (Outline of Psycho-Analysis, p. 43.)

CH. N. 10 (p. 111)

M. BRIERLEY has also written:

'. . . the existence of "internalized object" phantasies would not contravene the memory-trace hypothesis since memories and phantasies have a common trace origin. All images are memory-images, reactivations of past experience. It was suggested that, artificially simplified, the concept of an "internalized good object" is the concept of an unconscious phantasy gratifying the wish for the constant presence of the mother in the form of a belief that she is literally inside the child. Such an unconscious phantasy would help the child to retain conscious memory of its mother during temporary absences though it might fail to bridge a prolonged absence. A two-year-old child's memory of its mother will not be a simple system but the resultant of two years of life with her. The conscious memory will be the accessible part of a far more extensive unconscious mother-system having its roots in earliest infancy.' ('Notes on Metapsychology as Process Theory', pp. 103–4.)

IV

CERTAIN FUNCTIONS OF INTROJECTION AND PROJECTION IN EARLY INFANCY

By PAULA HEIMANN

PART 1

THE RELATION TO THE MENTAL STRUCTURE

IN Freud's theory the structure of the mind is composed of three main parts differentiated by their functions. The id, most closely related to the body, is the reservoir of the instincts and thus the source of energy for all mental activities. This means that it is the dynamic matrix from which the other systems, ego and super-ego, derive. The id represents a person's unconscious, most primitive and elemental urges, which are dictatorial and do not know compromise or renunciation. The ego is the interpreter and intermediary between the various parts of the mind and the outside world. The super-ego is the internalized representative of the person's most important objects, his parents, the internal residue of his earliest and most intense emotional ties. It is the system of all morality, conscious and unconscious.

These differentiations are brought about by the fact that the individual exists in a world on which he is dependent by virtue of his instincts: his wish to keep alive, his desire for pleasure and his fear of destruction.

It seems evident that an organism which depends to a vast extent on other organisms and powers outside itself, for attaining its purposes, must become influenced and changed by such contacts. Now what are the processes by which these alterations (differentiations of the original substance) are brought about? I intend to show in this section the role which the mechanisms of introjection and projection play in relation to these changes.

(a) The Ego

In Freud's scheme the ego is 'the surface part of the id'. Its position determines its functions: it has to mediate between inside and outside happenings. This means that it has to recognize and become familiar with the events and objects in the outer world, *i.e.* to perceive them, and to judge their suitability or otherwise for the satisfaction of the needs of the id. The role of the ego in reconnaissance and judgement extends further to these internal needs and to the commands and prohibitions issued from the super-ego. It has to judge also their suitability with regard to the given conditions in the outer world. The ego is not only the liaison officer between id, super-ego and outside world, it is also the officer in command of the operations to be carried out by motor activity.

It discharges painful inner tensions and obtains gratification or allays anxiety by objective or subjective means, that is, by actions with an external source of pleasure or by imagining or hallucinating the satisfactory experience. At times it allows free passage to the claims of the id, at other times it enforces modifications of these claims which may result in sublimation or inhibition. In mediating between the mental systems and the outer world it develops various functions and techniques (defence-mechanisms). Since sense-organs and the approaches to motility are in its operational sphere, it controls afferent and efferent processes.

All these activities of the ego (which have here been listed summarily) are derived from its primary function of perception. '. . . [the ego] clearly starts out from its nucleus, the system Pcpt. . . .'[1] 'In the ego perception plays the part which in the id devolves upon instinct.'[2]

The surface part of the id on which the outer stimuli impinge learns to perceive them, that is, to receive or to reject them. Perception is not a passive experience for the ego, but involves various interrelated activities. With attention, which is necessary for perception (a part of perception), the ego brings something of itself which we may call interest or curiosity to the outer stimuli. It searches the outer world for stimuli; as Freud

[1] Freud, *The Ego and the Id* (1923), p. 27.   [2] *Loc. cit.*, p. 30.

puts it, it meets them half-way. It is further active in storing what it has taken notice of and received in the memory system, and in utilizing it in further perceptive acts. In this way the ego becomes aware of the outer world and increasingly familiar with it. Thus perception leads to consciousness and in further practice one increases the other. Although not the whole of it is conscious, as follows from its connection with the unconscious id, the ego becomes the seat of consciousness, of the sense of time and space, of reason and logic, and of the tendency towards synthesis and coherence in functioning. In all these respects it differs from the id and these differentiations are brought about ultimately through its capacity of perception.

So far we have connected perception with the reception of stimuli. This seems quite natural—the very words we use show that we tend to regard these two processes as belonging closely together; they have the same root (cf. also the German word '*wahrnehmen*', or words like 'comprehend' and 'apprehend' which describe a result of perception).

However, perception is also connected with the rejection of stimuli, and the ego is not only the organ for the reception of stimuli, it also functions as a barrier against them. Whether it acts in one capacity or the other, depends on its judgement of the incoming stimuli. Freud described the process of judgement as follows:

'Originally the property to be decided about might be either good or bad, useful or harmful. Expressed in the language of the oldest, that is, of the oral instinctual impulses, the alternative runs thus: "I should like to eat that, or I should like to spit it out"; or, carried a stage further: "I should like to take this into me and keep that out of me." '[1]

He commented on the fact that, when judgement is thus traced to its origin, it can be taken as an example of the development of intellectual functions from the interplay between the primary instincts.

As the surface part of the id, the ego is directed by the instincts, the needs of the id, and the complex process of perception serves the purpose of mediating between the id and the outer world. It is essential that the ego should admit entry only

[1] 'Negation' (1925), p. 183.

to those stimuli which are suitable and bar off those which are dangerous. In both parts of perception introjection and projection are operative. When the ego receives stimuli from outside, it absorbs them and makes them part of itself, it introjects them. When it bars them off, it projects them, because the decision of their harmfulness is subsequent to a trial introjection. Selection, discrimination, etc., are based on introjection and projection. (Only after a certain amount of experience, at a fairly advanced stage of development, can the ego dispense with its original method of testing by first taking in the stimulus.)

It is not only in expelling an unsuitable external stimulus, which it proved a mistake, as it were, to take in, that the ego uses projection. When it discharges inner tensions, it projects something of its own. Thus projection relates to what was originally part of the self as well as to what was originally part of the outer world. Moreover, whilst the projection of what is bad and useless is more striking and was discovered early in psycho-analytic work, more recent observations have shown that the ego also projects what is good and useful. In fact it might be said that this notion is implied in Freud's statement that it projects—'thrusts forth whatever within itself gives rise to pain'[1]—because the inner tensions felt as pain must be traced ultimately to the co-existence of the two opposite instincts of life and death, the impulses for self-preservation and pleasure and the dangerous destructive impulses. That the ego thrusts forth libidinal impulses and brings about a libidinal object cathexis is a familiar psycho-analytic notion. In the view expressed here this represents a projection of what is good and useful, since the libidinal impulses derive from the force of life. In meeting the external stimuli half-way, the ego meets them with both aggression and libido, though the proportions vary on different occasions. On this conception introjection, too, does not exclusively relate to what is part of the outer world, because introjection can be secondary to projection. An

---

[1] 'The objects presenting themselves, in so far as they are sources of pleasure, are absorbed by the ego into itself, 'introjected' (according to an expression coined by Ferenczi); while, on the other hand, the ego thrusts forth upon the external world whatever within itself gives rise to pain (v. infra, the mechanism of projection).' 'Instincts and Their Vicissitudes' (1915), p. 78.

object can become good and desirable precisely in consequence of an earlier projection of what was good, and when in its further contact with such an object the ego introjects from it, it receives back what was in part originally its own, it 're-introjects'.[1] Introjection and projection interact in various ways.

The statement that the ego becomes differentiated from the id through perception does not merely mean that it develops the capacity to perceive and in consequence achieves consciousness and awareness of reality. Perception and its component operations (attention, taking notice of, storing in memory, judging, etc.) are bound up with introjection and projection, and it is these processes of adding something new to the self or ridding it of something of its own which have an inestimable share in the modification of the original id into the ego. This is the point which I wish to stress in the present discussion. These mechanisms of introjection and projection represent not only an essential part of the function of the ego, they are the roots of the ego, the instruments for its very formation. To appreciate the role which introjection and projection play in early development in the function of perception leads us to realize that perception cannot be divorced from object-relation. It is clear then why perception is the 'nucleus' of the ego, and why this function of the organism results in the vast change in the human being from an instinct-driven creature to a social being with reason and control. At this point we may well reconsider ego-development from another angle.

In my view the use of the term 'stimulus', which derives from physiology, tends to obscure the issue. Objectively the stimuli which impinge upon the id and enforce perception and ego-formation come from physical (animate or inanimate) nature and from human beings, the persons surrounding the infant. But in subjective experience, which to begin with is bodily sensation, the world and its stimuli mean the feeding mother, because it is in contact with her that the infant has his most important sensations. (For a long time the child takes things 'personally',

---

[1] This process—re-introjection—is more fully described in Chapter VI. Object-relations in which this kind of projection and re-introjection predominate are characterized by compulsive idealization of the object, combined with a peculiar dependence on it which, if it is not actually slavish, borders on it.

he regards his parents as omnipotent and makes them responsible for all his experiences.) Phenomena which are in fact caused by natural events, and are perceived by the infant as sensations fusing with or interfering with his instinctual needs, are by him attributed to his feeding mother and interpreted in oral terms.

Thus the perception of the outer world, with all the activities implied in perception, can be traced to the infant's first contacts with another human being and within these to his experiences at his mother's breast. This is his most important external source of sensations, of satisfaction or dissatisfaction, pleasure or pain. The first perception of importance must be essentially the sensations[1] of receiving by mouth, sucking, swallowing, spewing.

Further, since instinctual development begins under oral primacy, oral experiences set their stamp on all sensations and experiences, so that at the beginning all experiences include oral elements: mouthing and swallowing and spitting (introjecting and projecting) recur. This is not to deny the multitude of infantile impulses and needs; it is merely seeing them in proportion to the dominant oral instincts, which is in keeping with the established view of oral primacy. In this sense it is justified to regard the oral sensation of feeding as the first perception.

Beginning with the introjection of the breast the infant proceeds to introject all his objects. Since these themselves are psychological entities, it is not surprising that introjection and projection lead to an interplay between psychological forces with dynamic results: the development of the ego and the super-ego, the formation of character.[2]

To some extent, that is with infants of a few months of age, these conclusions can be confirmed by studying their behaviour. The baby comes to know the outer world by 'taking everything into his mouth'. He also devotes an intense attention to the objects around him and becomes familiar with them step by step and bit by bit by staring, sucking, grasping. Mouth and hands and eyes and ears take in and absorb the object of his curiosity. When muscular control permits, he imitates the

---

[1] Cf. Freud, 'The ego is first and foremost a body ego' (*The Ego and the Id*, p. 33).

[2] The question of constitution and heredity is not touched upon in these considerations. It lies outside the scope of this section, which is only concerned with the development of the ego from individual experience.

object, represents by his own body what he has 'noticed' about the person he is concerned with, thus showing that he has absorbed, 'introjected' him (or her). Some psychological schools postulate an instinct of imitation. In the view presented here, imitation is not a special instinct, but part of the complex process of perception and object-relation.

The question may be asked when exactly then does the ego, the differentiation from the amorphous id, begin? Can we identify the first step? It is obvious that the ego does not come into being all of a sudden as a well-established entity. It develops gradually, by repetition of experience, and unequally as regards its various functions. In Freud's analogy, the crust is not equally firm in all its parts at once. Consciousness, to take one of the ego functions, will be fleeting and momentary to begin with, and only gradually become permanent in certain respects. Whilst we may not be able to determine practically the beginning of the ego (but with sharpened perception we may become able to do this), we can be clear about our concepts, and within our conceptual frame we can define the beginning of the ego with the first introjections of another psychological entity.

By virtue of his needs and his utter helplessness, guided by his oral instincts, the infant turns to the outer world and makes contact with another human being. He sucks at his mother's breast. This simple process can be defined in several ways: as a direct expression of instinctual needs, that is an id-activity (since by definition the id is the seat of the instincts); or, since, again by definition, it is the surface part of the id, *i.e.* the ego which performs the contacts with the outer world, as an activity of the ego. Now this is not a play with words. The burden of the argument is this: when we consider the earliest processes we cannot make a sharp distinction between the id and the ego, because in our view the ego is formed from experiences with the outer world. The earliest contacts (introjections and projections) start this process. The infant's first sucking is then neither an id-activity nor an ego-activity; it is both, it is an activity of the incipient ego.

Freud compared the working of the mind, the most complicated organ, with the working of the simplest organism, the amoeba. Life is maintained through an organism's intake of foreign but useful matter and discharge of its own, but harmful, matter. Intake and discharge are the most fundamental processes of any living organism. The mind, also a part of a living organism, is no exception to this rule: it achieves adaptation and progress by employing throughout its existence the fundamental processes of introjection and projection. The experiences of introducing something into the self and expelling something from it are psychic events of the first magnitude. They are the basic processes, not only for maintaining life (as in physical metabolism), but for all differentiations and modifications in any given organism. Such taking in and expelling consists of an active interplay between the organism and the outer world; on this primordial pattern rests all intercourse between subject and object, no matter how complex and sophisticated such intercourse appears. (I believe that in the last analysis we may find it at bottom of all our complicated dealings with one another.) The patterns Nature uses seem to be few, but she is inexhaustible in their variation.

The combined action of introjection and projection accounts for the change of a part of the id into an ego; disturbances in this interplay lead to failure in development. A child who is 'too good' indiscriminately absorbs his objects; he remains a shell of impersonations and imitations and does not develop into a 'character'. He lacks 'personality'. We may parallel this observation with one from the field of psychotherapy. In hypnosis and similar techniques, symptoms disappear by the patient's passive and undiscerning acceptance of suggestion, but his personality remains unaltered. Psycho-analysis affects the personality structure and thus goes to the core of the symptoms, by working with the patient's resistances, *i.e.* the patient's active and critical co-operation involves the combined use of the basic functions of introjection and projection.

The view that introjection and projection are the architects of the mental structure and that they build up the ego from the beginning of life is not held universally among psycho-analysts. It is mainly Melanie Klein's researches which have yielded the data enabling us to appreciate this role of introjection and projection. Ferenczi introduced the concept of introjection into psycho-analysis; Freud, although he traced judgement 'in the oldest, that is, the oral language' to introjection and projection, explicitly acknowledged the influence of introjection on the formation of the character (*i.e.* the ego) only after the decline of the Oedipus complex. As we show here, Melanie Klein's findings concerning ego-formation are fully in line with Freud's work, although there is at present no general acceptance of this fact. When we consider super-ego formation, it will be seen that her work has also led to important divergences from some of Freud's views.

Introjection and projection occur throughout life, but like all other processes they are subject to development, and influenced by the expanding functions of the ego. Their main purpose, viz. obtaining pleasure and avoiding pain, remains the same, but what constitutes pleasure and pain changes in accordance with the person's total progression. The mechanisms of introjection and projection start under the predominance of the oral instincts, but from the primitive and self-centred bodily aim of seizing or ejecting ('eating or spitting out') there develops the give and take in mature relationships, the super-personal function of procreation in adult sexuality, as well as the sublimated exchange of concrete or abstract creativeness.

(b)   The Super-Ego

The view that introjection leads to the formation of the super-ego is fully accepted in psycho-analytic thought, whereas it is not generally recognized that introjection plays an identical part in the building up of the ego.

There are various reasons for this. Research into ego-development has on the whole been later in date, while the conflicts between the ego and the super-ego (not at first called by this name) arrested the psycho-analyst's attention from the very beginning, owing to their conspicuous nature. Moreover, Freud's patients were adults and thus presented the conflicts of a developed ego. Although Freud came to reconstruct the development of the ego by discovering the element of regression in mental illness, he had not that opportunity of seeing the processes of growth from such a close range as the analysis of young children affords. When Melanie Klein discovered the appropriate approach to young children by her Play Technique, her observations gave a new impetus to research into ego-formation, and the problems of the developing ego came much more into the focus of psycho-analytic investigation.

One might wonder why, once the structural effect of intro-jection was established in the field of super-ego research, theoretical considerations alone did not direct psycho-analysts to apply to the ego what had been found about the super-ego. But psycho-analysis has always been an empirical science and has never been based on theoretical conclusions.

Ferenczi, when introducing the concept of introjection, was concerned with showing that introjection is the means by which the widening of the child's interests proceeds. In his view (which the authors of this book share) all mental progress is effected by the child's introjecting more and more from his surroundings. Taking up this concept from Ferenczi, Freud went on to further discoveries, and in his later work introjection became the key to the understanding of melancholia (1917) as well as of the general structure of the mind (1923). When in his final formulation about a moral institution in the mind he coined the term 'super-ego', he said[1]:

'. . . and here we have that higher nature, in this ego-ideal or super-ego, the representative of our relation to our parents. When we were little children we knew these higher natures, we admired them and feared them; and later we *took them into ourselves*. . . .' (My italics.)

This unequivocal statement, which is frequently repeated and elaborated in his later writings, left no doubt as to his view about the decisive role which introjection plays in super-ego formation, and it has found the fullest confirmation in sub-sequent psycho-analytic work. But certain conclusions which follow from Freud's exposition of the formation of the super-ego have not been generally drawn.

Freud correlated the origin of the super-ego with the disso-lution of the Oedipus complex.[2] When the child (more or less successfully) outgrows the Oedipus complex, he establishes his

---

[1] *The Ego and the Id* (1923), p. 47.

[2] In this connection the problem of the dissolution of the Oedipus complex is not discussed.

parents inside himself, builds up this 'higher nature' in himself. Identification with the parents, acceptance of their demands, takes the place of the Oedipus wishes. But the identification resulting from introjection is not a complete one, since in some very essential respects the child must *not* be like the parents.

'The super-ego is, however, not merely a deposit left by the earliest object-choices of the id; it also represents an energetic reaction-formation against these choices. Its relation to the ego is not exhausted by the precept: "You *ought to be* such and such (like your father)"; it also comprises the prohibition: "You *must not be* such and such (like your father); that is, you may not do all he does; many things are his prerogative." . . .'[1]

The introjection of the parents is a selective process, certain aspects of the parents being excluded. The ego 'samples' the objects of the external world, introjects certain of their aspects and projects others, and it follows this fundamental pattern also with regard to the parents at the Oedipus stage. Thus it is not only introjection which leads to super-ego formation. Projection has a share in it as well. Indeed the process of super-ego formation would entirely miscarry if such projection did not occur. It is by virtue of the combination of these two mechanisms that the child achieves an identification with his parents which is capable of exerting pressure against the Oedipus desires and establishing the 'energetic reaction-formation'. Super-ego formation also is a structural result of the combined action of introjection and projection.

According to Freud the super-ego is the 'heir' or successor of the Oedipus complex. The Oedipus complex represents the culmination of the child's sexual development; it marks the end of its first onset. The latency period follows its decline, until with puberty the second onset of sexual development occurs, resulting in the establishment of adult sexuality. The close of the Oedipus complex, the beginning of the latency period and the formation of the super-ego are interrelated processes. Freud thought that the super-ego, which steps into the place of the Oedipus complex, contributes to its very decline. This seems a difficult proposition. If the super-ego is the successor of the Oedipus complex and owes its origin to its destruction, it seems

---

[1] *Loc. cit.*, pp. 44–5.

difficult to understand how it can help to bring about its decline. The solution of this problem, however, can be found if we interpret the factors leading up to this point in a different way.

Freud advances several reasons for the dissolution of the Oedipus complex. It may be that it comes to an end because the biologically predestined course of the libido passes on beyond it and dooms it to disappear, as the first teeth are doomed to fall out. It may be that the persistent frustration of his wishes makes the child abandon his painful position. These two explanations are complementary, combining as they do a biological with a psychological approach. The latter, however, gives rise to the question of the psychological mechanism by means of which a desired and frustrating object is given up. What enables the child to give up his Oedipus wishes, to give up his parents as the objects of his passionate desires? Freud's research into the processes of melancholia has provided the answer. He discovered that in melancholia, which is the pathological response to the experience of losing a loved object (be it through death or a change of heart), the ego, while abandoning the object in the real world, establishes it inside itself; it introjects the lost loved object.

As Freud mentions,[1] at the date when he explained melancholia by connecting it with the mechanism of introjection, it was not known how frequent and how typical this process of introjection is; he had described the introjection which takes place in melancholia as a 'kind of regression to the mechanism of the oral phase'.[2] In other words, melancholia is merely the most severe example of the principle which governs psychological processes in the situation when a loved object is lost.

Such a loss is experienced by the child at the decline of the Oedipus complex, when he has to give up his parents as sexual objects. The mechanism of introjection comes into play with the result that the super-ego, formed by the internalized parents, replaces the former Oedipus constellation.

Any mental process must be regarded from at least three aspects. It aims at obtaining satisfaction of libidinal or destructive impulses and is therefore a derivative of the instinctual urges. It aims at avoiding pain and anxiety, and in so far it

---

[1] *Loc. cit.*, p. 35.　　　　[2] 'Mourning and Melancholia' (1917).

represents a mechanism of defence. It increases and exercises mental functions and thus it has a developmental character. In any given case the relative significance of these three facets may vary. Introjection of the parents at the dissolution of the Oedipus complex serves predominantly the dual purpose of defence (against the pain of object-loss) and of mental growth.

But, again, if introjection occurs whenever the lost-object situation arises, there are many occasions earlier in date than the dissolution of the Oedipus complex for introjection of a lost love-object to occur; indeed, psycho-analytic observation of young children, corroborated by study of their behaviour, leaves no doubt about this. Early childhood is fraught with the danger of loss of the object (subjectively felt). The subjective experience of losing the mother occurs repeatedly for the infant, since 'as soon as he misses his mother, he behaves as if he were never going to see her again'.[1]

Freud assigns super-ego formation roughly to the fifth year of life, while he places ego-formation very much earlier (the ego being already in existence at the second oral, the narcissistic stage, *i.e.* in early infancy). In this view of Freud's, therefore, there would appear to be a gap in the structural development of the child's mind. Yet the abundant references in Freud's writings to the earlier phenomena of introjection and projection tell another story, the truth of which is demonstrated by observations made first by Melanie Klein in early analyses and confirmed later by several analysts in work with adults as well. The conclusion (which is in line with the principle of the gradual evolution of all human functions) is that the super-ego as described by Freud is the *end-result* of a long process which goes through different stages in close relation with the successive phases of instinctual and ego-development.

Here, then, is the answer to the apparent contradiction in Freud's statement that the super-ego arises from the ruins of the Oedipus complex and is yet instrumental for its breaking up. With the decline of the Oedipus complex super-ego formation reaches a new and highly important level, whilst the earlier introjections (and projections) provide its foundations.

There is no doubt that Freud gave these earlier introjections

[1] *Inhibition, Symptoms and Anxiety* (1926), p. 167.

a certain role in the formation of the super-ego, since he spoke of the child's identifications with his parents (which result from introjection) as having 'probably long been present'. After dealing with introjection as a defence against losing an object and pointing out that the child experiences such a loss at the decline of the Oedipus complex, Freud said: '. . . to compensate for this loss of objects, identifications with the parents, which have probably long been present, become greatly intensified. . . .'[1]

To-day we can no longer question the fact of the child's earlier identifications with his parents, and these, we maintain, constitute the super-ego in the earlier phases as much as at the decline of the Oedipus complex.

Introjection and projection are amongst the earliest mental mechanisms. But the same mechanism used at different stages of maturity will have different effects. The early introjected objects differ greatly from the later super-ego, yet they have certain features in common with it. The climax of a process differs from the preceding stages, but the preceding stages belong together and to the climax. There is a genetic continuity between the persecutory fears of the infant, roused initially by his cannibalistic impulses, the anxiety of the latency child in connection with the disapproving internal voice of his parents, and the sense of guilt, mortification and remorse of the adult who has failed to act in accordance with his ideals.

The primitive stages of the super-ego are formed during phases in which primitive phantasy determines the infant's relation with his objects, and consequently his concepts of his parents are grossly distorted. Introjection begins at the part-object stage, with the introjection of the mother's breast, to which the infant attributes extreme powers of good and evil, of giving pleasure and security or of causing pain and persecution. Gradually the infant's emotional and intellectual orbit widens. This development interacts with the gradual shifting of the instinctual primacies, and reflects the result of the mechanisms of introjection and projection. The internal figures correspond to some extent to his objects in the outer world, although they are far from correct portraits of the real people in the child's environment. The infant proceeds from the part-object

[1] *New Introductory Lectures* (1932), p. 87

stage to the stage of whole objects, *i.e.* of individual persons, and advance in perception means also a movement towards more realistic concepts. This process is mirrored in the child's world of inner objects, which are to begin with exceedingly phantastic 'parts' (corresponding to his primitive notions about his parents) and gradually approach more and more to the likeness of the real parents until they appear in the way described by Freud as the super-ego. This super-ego forms the peak of a system which develops *pari passu* and under mutual influence with the developing ego. It is the super-ego of the genital stage, hence it represents a great advance on the earlier introjections. It is a more mature formation than the phantastic internal objects of the primitive periods, more integrated and stable and more conducive towards a realistic social morality.

Tensions between ego and super-ego (introjected objects) vary in content with the current stage of development. The prohibitions and commands issued by the super-ego correspond to the impulses dominant at a given time, *e.g.* in the fully developed 'classical' Oedipus complex the prohibitions are directed against passionate desires for the one parent and murderous rivalry against the other, as first discovered by Freud; in the anal phase the anal-sadistic, in the oral phase the oral-sadistic impulses are forbidden by the current type of super-ego. It may be remembered in this connection that Abraham drew attention to the inhibition of greed in early infancy and that Ferenczi presented the notion of a 'sphincter-morality'.

Although Freud showed that introjection occurs in earliest infancy, that is long before the time to which he allotted the Oedipus complex, and although he recognized the structural results of this mechanism, he was quite definite in tracing the super-ego to the decline of the Oedipus complex. Moreover, he considered that later introjections of the parents or parent-substitutes merely affect the character of the ego, not of the super-ego. The view then that the formation of both ego and super-ego begins in early infancy and proceeds in an inter-acting fashion diverges from Freud's views and presents some new problems. If, as we maintain, the introjected objects throughout childhood build up both the child's ego and his super-ego, we have to find the factor which determines the outcome of introjection and projection. When does an act of introjection contribute to ego-formation, when to the formation of the super-ego? I would suggest that this discriminating factor lies in the attributes of the introjected parent with which the child is *predominantly* concerned at the moment. The emotional situation in which the child performs the act of introjection decides its result. The whole play of affects, of instinctual urges and the prevailing contents of anxiety have to be considered. In other words, what decides the issue of an act of introjection is the dominant motive on the part of the child when introjecting his object. If his main interest in the act of introjection is focussed on his parent's intelligence, skill, manipulation of things—functions belonging to the intellectual and motor sphere of the ego—the introjected object is mainly taken up into the child's ego.[1] If the child introjects his object in an actual conflict between love and hate, and is particularly concerned with his object's ethical attributes, then the introjected object contributes to the formation of the super-ego. The child who introjects his mother while she is carrying out a certain action, say washing him, learns in this way how to wash himself (or an object), *i.e.* a skill. This would be an example of introjection furthering ego-development.

In unconscious phantasy, however, washing may have a moral meaning, like restoring an object harmed by soiling, and this meaning may be actually of predominant significance. In this case the introjection of the mother whilst she washes the child would also strongly add to the super-ego system. When we thus analyse actual instances of introjection, we come to see that ego and super-ego formation can be closely linked with each other, and we shall be warned against a too rigid demarcation between the two. At this point we are again in agreement with Freud's view that the three systems, whilst they enjoy a certain

---

[1] This is not to say that the ego comprises nothing but intellectual and motor functions. It will be remembered that I am not dealing in this chapter with the ego or super-ego systems in their totality, but am concerned only with the problem of introjection and projection in relation to these systems. I also wish to stress that the description of the influence of introjected objects on ego and super-ego formation does not exhaust the theme of the vicissitudes of the introjected objects. These are dealt with in various connections in this book, *e.g.* in 'Inner World and Outer World', p. 155.

individuality and independence, are not autarchic, and can still fuse with one another. Though differentiated, the mind is one. Ego and super-ego are yet parts of the id.

The broader concept of the super-ego which follows from Melanie Klein's work also covers better those aspects of the super-ego system in which protection and encouragement rather than fear and inhibition prevail. If we do not confine ourselves to the super-ego formed by the introjection of the parents of the fully developed Oedipus complex, but regard it as a structure built up throughout childhood and beginning with the introjection of the nursing mother (breast), we understand those conditions, both normal and pathological, in which the super-ego/ego relationship is predominantly of the mother/infant type, as well as those in which the scope of the ego is widened and its activities stimulated. The kind super-ego (the benign internal objects) acts as a spur for ego-development and enables the ego to expand and venture forth no less than the threatening super-ego (the strict internal father) prohibits activities. In many instances the young child dares to undertake something new because his parents encourage him to do so, and when he trusts them his self-confidence is greater. These experiences too are internalized and form a pattern for the super-ego. Moreover, on the first of any such occasions, an introjection occurs resulting in the child's greater courage at the actual time. When the benign super-ego causes an expansion of the ego, it does so because in the individual's internal world his relationship with his kind parents is preserved and continued, that is, the ego has assimilated its good objects and grows as a result of such assimilation.[1]

These parts of the super-ego, its maternal and its friendly components, do not easily harmonize with the super-ego as described by Freud. In his concept, the father's strictness appears as the main constituent of the super-ego—except (and this is perhaps the single exception) in his essay on 'Humour', in which Freud explicitly pictures the kindness and succour of the super-ego and declares that these features are in full agreement with its origin from the parents.

[1] Cf. Paula Heimann, 'Sublimation and its Relation to Processes of Internalization'.

The question may be asked whether in view of these differences it would not be wiser to reserve Freud's term for the super-ego he described, that is, for the introjections of the parents at the decline of the Oedipus complex. Such a decision obviously could only be made as a result of very thorough investigation—the more difficult because, as in the essay just mentioned, Freud's descriptions are not unequivocal. Moreover, it is our general experience in psycho-analytic research that the widening of our knowledge has led to a widening of our terms, the most famous example being the extension of the concept of sexuality which Freud introduced early in his work. Clarity is better served by keeping the same name for processes which are inherently of the same nature and developmentally connected—as is the case with regard to the early introjections and those occurring during the decline of the Oedipus phase. Notwithstanding this consideration it is sometimes more descriptive to speak of 'internal objects' rather than of the 'super-ego'.

PART 2

EARLY OBJECT-RELATIONS

(a) The Concept of Primitive Objects

In this section my aim is to show how introjection and projection affect the child's relationships, primarily with his mother and father.

The problem of infantile object-relations has often been considered amongst psycho-analysts, but a consensus of opinion has not been reached.[1] Freud's statements on this issue are not

[1] Ferenczi and the Hungarian school of psycho-analysts acknowledged the existence of early infantile object-relations. A representative exposition of their views can be found in *I.J.Ps-A.*, XXX, 1949, 4 (Ferenczi Number) which contains contributions by Ferenczi, Alice Balint, Michael Balint and Endre Petö. Cf. also the relevant bibliography given by the authors. Michael Balint's paper in this journal 'Early Developmental Stages of the Ego. Primary Object Love' advances many arguments against the assumption of an objectless primary narcissistic stage which are in full agreement with the views presented by the authors of this book. There are, however, some differences of opinion between Balint and the present writers regarding the assessment of the nature of the destructive impulses and the role of introjection and projection in early infancy.

unequivocal and are open to different interpretations. In his early work he was almost exclusively concerned with the libidinal side of infantile experiences and described his observations in terms of movements of the libido rather than in terms of the infant's feelings and phantasies. He stressed the paramount significance of the infant's libidinal experiences at his mother's breast, his first object, yet he did not enter into an analysis of their content, the emotions and phantasies involved in these early experiences. Indeed the bulk of Freud's writings, though rich in hints to the contrary, suggests that Freud did not think that the infant forms object-relations at an early age. He described identification with an object as the earliest form of a tie, but he differentiated this from object-relation. On the other hand, he often connected identification with the establishment of the object within the ego (introjection).

The following passage from his Encyclopaedia Articles (1922) illustrates his view of the libidinal processes in early infancy (p. 119):

'In the first instance the oral component instinct finds satisfaction "anaclitically" by attaching itself to the sating of the desire for nourishment; and its object is the mother's breast. It then detaches itself, becomes independent and at the same time *auto-erotic*, that is, it finds an object in the child's own body. Others of the component instincts also start by being auto-erotic and are not until later diverted on to an external object. . . .'

Thus Freud laid more stress on the auto-erotic than the allo-erotic aspect of early infantile life. Melanie Klein's work, on the other hand, has dealt extensively with early object-relations; her researches and those of her collaborators show auto-erotism in a different light.

According to Freud's libido-theory infantile sexual life starts with auto-erotism and narcissism (in this order); in these phases the infant's libido is directed to his own body. The implication of this view seems to be that the infant does not know or wish for a libidinal object other than himself. At the time at which the libido-theory was formed, the destructive impulses were regarded as component instincts of the libido, and not as representatives of a primary instinct. Thus libidinal attachment to an object and object-relation were at that time synonymous, and the theory that the infant has no object for his libido is tantamount to a negation of any kind of infantile object-relation.

Before dealing more fully with auto-erotism and narcissism I will state briefly the views on infantile object-relations held by the authors of this book.

Every capacity or function develops through a series of steps, although the individual stages may show striking differences. It is here that, as Susan Isaacs[1] has pointed out, the principle of genetic continuity serves as an 'instrument of discovery'. Progress and changes in any single capacity are bound to have repercussions on the whole personality. These principles are particularly significant when considering the early phases of development.

The capacity for object-relation too is subject to the process of development, and accordingly the child's relation to another person varies considerably at different stages. To begin with, his attitude to his objects is entirely determined by his physical needs, his impulses and phantasies. It is predominantly through the medium of his sensations that he experiences his objects, and sensory experience forms the matrix of both unconscious phantasy and conscious perception.[2] Since the elementary categories of sensory experience are pleasurable or painful, these are also the primary characters of the infant's object-relation.

It takes the whole long course of emotional and mental progression for a person to arrive at mature object-relations, in which the object is acknowledged as an individual in its own right, an entity whose character is independent of the subject's wishes and needs. Many people do not ever achieve this 'objective' appreciation of another person, or they do not achieve it in relations of high emotional significance; others lose it in states of emotional tension. The development of a reality-sense in personal relations is concurrent with and interdependent on the growth of the ego, which in turn depends on the maturing of the instinctual impulses.

We cannot hope to understand early object-relations without

[1] Chapter III, p. 75.
[2] *Loc. cit.*, pp. 91–5. Cf. also Part 1 above, 'The Mental Structure,' pp. 126–7.

the fullest appreciation of the role which phantasy plays in mental life. In addition we have to be aware of the principle of genetic continuity and of the fact that, whilst we, for our convenience, follow in our investigation a certain thread at a time, mental life is a whole, a complex pattern, of which these threads form coherent and interacting parts, though they are by no means inherently consistent or harmonious.

The essential difference between infantile and mature object-relations is that, whereas the adult conceives of the object as existing independently of himself, for the infant it *always refers in some way to himself*.[1] It exists only by virtue of its function for the infant, and only in the world bounded by his own experiences. Whilst in reality the infant is utterly helpless and depends for the maintenance of his life completely on his mother (or her substitute), in phantasy he assumes an omnipotent position to his objects; they belong to him, are part of him, live only through and for him—he continues the pre-natal oneness with his mother.

Since at the beginning of life the oral instincts reign supreme over all other instinctual urges (oral primacy), the infant approaches his objects first of all as something for his mouth. That is to say, an object for the infant is what either tastes and feels pleasant in his mouth and during swallowing, and is therefore good, or something that tastes nasty, hurts the mouth and throat, cannot be swallowed or cannot be got into the mouth (*i.e.* frustrates[2]), and is therefore bad. If it is good, it is swallowed; if it is bad, it is spat out.[3] Unconscious phantasy is a dynamic

---

[1] I would here mention the 'ideas of reference' which occur in pre-psychotic and psychotic states, *i.e.* in connection with far-reaching regression, impairment of the reality-sense and paranoid tendencies.

[2] Frustration and gratification can be defined in terms of separation and union. The simplest pattern of gratification is represented by the 'hungry mouth'/'feeding breast' entity, a pattern of experience which is not conducive to a clear differentiation between subject and object. This concept of frustration as the experience of separation from the object which fulfils the subject's needs is implicit in many presentations of human development. In psycho-analytic literature the basic frustration lies in the 'birth trauma', in biblical mythology it is in the expulsion from paradise. It is clear that regarded from this aspect frustration is a factor of first magnitude for development. The need to adjust to separation leads to the development of capacities and behaviour appropriate to reality and independence.

[3] Freud, 'Instincts and Their Vicissitudes' (1915), p. 78; also 'Negation' (1925), p. 183.

process. The oral object is not only held in the mouth, but either swallowed and incorporated, or spat out and expelled, and the mechanisms of introjection and projection are bound up with the sensations and phantasies experienced in the contact with the object. Owing to these mechanisms the infant's object can further be defined as what is inside or outside his own body, but even while outside, it still is part of himself and refers to himself, since 'outside' results from being ejected, 'spat out'; thus the body boundaries are blurred. This might also be put the other way round: because the object outside the body is 'spat out', and still relates to the infant's body, there is no sharp distinction between his body and what is outside.

Two main patterns follow from the operation of introjection and projection in early object-relations, and their interaction leads to confusing and unstable situations.

(1) The infant's feelings about his objects essentially revolve round their being 'good' or 'bad', 'inside' or 'outside' (and they are closely knit with his sensations).

(2) Within the fusion between self and object the infant tends to usurp the object's 'good', i.e. pleasurable qualities, and treat them as belonging to the self, and to disown his 'bad' painful qualities and treat them as belonging to the object. In other words there is a tendency to introject what is pleasurable and to split off and project what is painful. The connection between projection and badness is of particular significance for the understanding of infantile anxiety.[1]

Infantile object-relations are fluid and oscillate between extremes. There is a tendency to massive reactions. Feelings are all good or all bad, and so is the object for the infant. Intermediate tones are absent. What in fact is only an aspect of the object is treated as all of it at the given time, and the aspect selected corresponds with the infant's predominant urge. The object is treated as both inside, 'me', and outside, 'not-me', yet if outside as concerning the self and depending on it. But in the same way in which unconscious phantasy is in general the

[1] Cf. Chapters V and VIII; also Part 1, 'The Mental Structure', above; also in Chapter III the example of the little boy who, seeing his baby sister sucking at his mother's breast, pointed to it and said to his mother: 'That is what you bit me with.'

forerunner of logical thinking, so this arbitrary, phantastic relation to objects is the basis for realistic and mature object-relations; it is one type of object-relationship.

The capacity to differentiate, which tends to mitigate the intensity of emotional reactions and which is an important step towards clearer thinking, develops on this primitive foundation, which for a long time remains dominant. I am inclined to see one reason for the universal phenomenon of infantile amnesia in the fact that early infantile feeling-thinking is so confused and that the light of consciousness is maintained only for moments—parts of the developing ego sink back into the id.[1]

When we analyse states of severe depression (which, as we know, involves regression to the oral phase of development), we can see how the phantasies about the introjected object yet comprise an element of the 'me', and how fluid the feelings are about what is 'me' and what is the object. The analysis of such states gives indeed a very impressive picture of oscillations between the self and objects, internal and external. We have to recognize a dual nature in these early object-relations: the object is both perceived and ignored, accepted and denied. This dual process occurs either simultaneously or in such rapid sequence as to be practically simultaneous. (The very obscure problem of time-concepts in early life cannot be entered into here.) This dualism can also be described in terms of limitations set by physiological and by psychological factors: in part the infant does not yet recognize objects because his capacity for perception develops only gradually, but partly from psychological motives he denies, by means of omnipotence and magic, what he has perceived.

(b) Auto-Erotism, Narcissism and the Early Relation to Objects

The fact that the infant obtains pleasure by sucking his thumb or another part of his body has, of course, been noted since time immemorial; it was Freud,[2] however, drawing upon Lindner's conclusions, who recognized its implications and connected it systematically with the complex process of sexual development. On his analysis of the infant's behaviour his libido-theory was

[1] Cf. Part 1, 'The Mental Structure', above.
[2] *Three Essays on the Theory of Sexuality* (1905).

built up, and for a time the phenomena of auto-erotism stood in the foreground of psycho-analytical theory.

Further observations of adults who had given up sexual interest in other persons, whether completely, in certain forms of schizophrenia, or temporarily in neurotic hypochondria and in organic illness, led Freud to conclude that narcissism is a regular constituent in sexual development.[1] Narcissism is the state in which the ego directs its libido upon itself. The difference between auto crotism and narcissism, according to Freud, is that in the earlier condition there is not yet an ego (which has to be formed); the auto-erotic impulses are primordial, and ante-date the formation of the ego. It is evident, however, that since ego-formation is a gradual process the two phases are bound to merge into one another.

In Freud's libido-theory, then, auto-erotism and narcissism represent the earliest form taken by the libido and precede object-libidinal phases. With further progress in psycho-analytic work this view has come to be reconsidered.

When analysing the infant's auto-erotic sucking Freud pointed out that it rests upon an experience with an object, the mother's breast, which has acquainted the infant with a pleasure which he later reproduces auto-erotically. At first, according to Freud, infantile libido is attached to an object and amalgamated with feeding; later it becomes detached both from this self-preservative function and from the object. Freud did not here enter into the question of what happens in the infant's mind when he abandons the object.

In other connections, however, Freud showed what follows when an object is given up; the abandoned object is established within the ego, introjected. He suggested that such introjection may be the 'sole condition on which an object can be given up',[2] and connected introjection with identification, i.e. the process by which one ego 'becomes like' another ego. He also referred to oral cannibalistic incorporation as an element in this type of identification.

Freud did not apply his discoveries about the vicissitudes of

---

[1] 'On Narcissism: an Introduction' (1914).

[2] 'Mourning and Melancholia' (1917), *The Ego and the Id* (1923), *New Introductory Lectures* (1932) and in other papers.

the lost object to the first instance of such an experience, *i.e.* the development of auto-erotic gratification in the infant. At this point he singled out the role memory plays in it and stated that in his auto-erotic sucking the infant remembers the breast. Melanie Klein's work has widened our understanding of the infant's remembering the breast by connecting it with his phantasies and with the effects of introjection and projection.

When an adult turns to memories to console himself about an unpleasant actuality, he is aware of having these past experiences *within himself*. When the infant in his thumb-sucking 'remembers' his past pleasures of sucking at the mother's breast, he is not aware of remembering the past, of reviving a memory within himself, but feels himself in actual contact with the desired breast, although in reality he merely sucks his own finger. His phantasies of incorporating the breast, which form part of his oral experiences and impulses, lead him to identify 'his finger with the incorporated breast. He can independently produce his own gratification, because in his phantasy a part of his own body represents the object which in reality he lacks. In his auto-erotic activity he turns to his internalized good breast, and organ pleasure is connected with pleasure from an imagined object.

If these factors are taken into consideration, it cannot be maintained that auto-erotic activities are without an object. Whilst the external source of gratification is absent, there is in phantasy an internal gratifying object which makes it possible to do without or to abandon the external one.

In describing infantile modes of mental functioning, Freud suggested that under the dominance of the pleasure principle 'whatever was thought of (desired) was simply imagined in an hallucinatory form'.[1] He coined the term 'hallucinatory gratification'. Remembering and hallucinating are related, in that both conditions make use of a previously experienced situation. According to Freud hallucination is the result of the cathexis passing over entirely from the memory-system to the perception-system.[2] In other words, the reactivation of a remembered situation is not experienced as such in hallucination, but as the *perception* of something that is in fact a memory. It seems

[1] 'Formulations Regarding the Two Principles of Mental Functioning' (1911); see also Chapter IX.   [2] *The Ego and the Id* (1923).

plausible that this can occur, because originally perception goes along with incorporation phantasies and the perceived object is then felt to be within the body-boundary. In hallucinatory gratification the infant utilizes his incorporation phantasies. Since he possesses the good breast within himself, he has it at his beck and call, can omnipotently manipulate it, and deny the actual condition of frustration and pain. The inner 'good' object has such strong psychic reality that for the time being the need for the feeding breast can be stifled, overpowered, successfully denied and projected outside, whilst the sucked part of his body is identified with the introjected breast, the desired object. Introjection and projection account for the infant's independence in his auto-erotism.

I would say that in general the phenomenon of hallucination loses much of its strangeness when we see its connection with introjection and projection. A person who is hallucinating has regressed to the primitive mode of perception which involves introjection, and by using several primitive mechanisms (magic, omnipotence and denial) he conjures up the image of his internalized object and projects it into the outside world. In his conscious conviction the object then exists in tangible reality, and this conviction may serve as a defence against frustration. What is hallucinated may be a visual image, or it may be auditory, or a bodily sensation, according to which elements of the relation with the internal object predominate at the time. The value of this defence against frustration varies; an hallucination may be the gratifying Fata Morgana of a loved and lost person or a dreaded persecutor. (There is some gain even in the latter case, since it is easier to defend oneself against an external enemy than an internal one.[1])

To repeat: in our view auto-erotism is based on phantasies

---

[1] As an example: a patient of mine was certain that on entering my room he had seen a pool of blood in a corner, and he avoided looking in that direction. He thought that I had been murdered by the patient who preceded him. In the course of the analytic session it turned out that he himself had felt murderous rage and jealousy, while he had been waiting. In projecting his murderous wishes on to the previous patient, the hated rival, he became convinced that this patient had murdered me, and he came to see a pool of blood in the corner. This incident involves a great number of factors which need not be discussed here. It illustrates how the projection of inner processes leads to hallucination.

concerning an inner gratifying 'good' breast (nipple, mother) which is projected on to, and thus represented by, a part of the infant's own body. This process is, as it were, met half-way by the erotogenic quality of the child's organs and the plastic character of his libido. Owing to this plasticity, one kind of pleasure (sucking) can replace the other (feeding) which is missing, the mouth pleasure being supplemented by pleasurable sensations in the finger which represents the feeding breast. The introjective and projective mechanisms serve here as a defence against frustration and protect the infant from being flooded by rage and aggression. Therefore he is able to turn to and accept the real, external breast when it reappears. The phantasies about the internal object thus pave the way back to the external one, whilst conversely the external object provides the experience from which the internal object is constructed. The internal object thus functions in this vital way as a core for the growth and development of object-relations. These considerations constitute a re-formulation of the original theory of auto-erotism. When we take into account the infant's oscillation between his internal and external object (breast), we can no longer regard auto-erotism as a definite 'phase of development' which extends over a certain period. We regard auto-erotic activities rather as a mode of behaviour, coincident with allo-erotic activities, or as transitory states within a period which is rich in experiences with objects; and this not only because auto-erotism is bound up with phantasies about an internal object, but because the actual relation with the breast (and other objects) is of a progressive character. Feeding at the mother's breast throughout this auto-erotic phase is an object-libidinal experience of the highest order. Freud called it the 'unattainable prototype of every later sexual satisfaction'.[1] We may also remember that normally eating never, in full adult life, loses its libidinal complexion; and Freud's final theory of the primary instincts takes full account of this fact by placing the self-preservative and the sexual impulses closely together as the carriers of the primary life instinct.

Although the infant is capable of intense auto-erotic gratifications, at the same time he experiences and even strengthens his

[1] *Introductory Lectures* (1915–16), p. 264.

erotic ties with his external objects. The oscillation between auto-erotic behaviour and object-erotic experiences constitutes one of those interacting processes which characterize early emotional life.

I have said above that in our view auto-erotism and narcissism cannot be regarded as sharply differentiated from each other. On the other hand, since narcissism is considered to occur somewhat later, it is coincident with a more advanced ego; so that the two conditions differ in those respects which are related to the stage of ego-development. It follows that in the narcissistic phase perception is more advanced and the reality-principle more operative. This is specially significant with regard to inner reality, e.g. frustration from *inner* sources. Unpleasant inner stimuli cannot be so easily denied and projected outside as in the earlier phase. The capacity for hallucinatory gratification is lessened and frustration more felt than before when the mechanism of hallucination had easier play. This, I believe, would support the impression that there is a difference between auto-erotism and narcissism, and account for the observation that the narcissistic condition contains a stronger element of aggression than the auto-erotic condition.

The fact that through the advance in ego-formation perception is functioning better, and hallucinatory gratification is less easily brought about, cannot be without influence on the infant's attitude to the experience of frustration and on the distribution of libidinal and aggressive tendencies. Since the infant is more strongly exposed to frustration (by the lessening of defensive hallucination), hostility against the object which is felt to cause his painful condition is aroused; and when he turns to his internal object, he does so under the pressure of hostility against the external one. One might say that in this respect the difference between simple auto-erotic gratification and narcissistic behaviour is that in the first case the turning *to* the internal good breast is the determining emotion, and in the latter it is the turning *away* from the external bad breast. This tallies with certain observations; in the first case the return to the external object would occur more easily than in the second instance.[1]

---

[1] Instances of marked refusal in infants under one year to accept the mother on her return after absence are often observed.

This view would also explain difficulties encountered in the analysis of narcissistic patients. Freud spoke of the limit to analytic influence which seemed to be set by narcissistic behaviour.[1] The understanding of the interplay between internal and external objects, of the complicated emotional attitudes of hatred and anxiety towards the external object and of the precarious relation to the internal one, when it is sought predominantly in hate against the external object, opens up an avenue of approach to narcissistic conditions.

The fact that in narcissism the relation to the internal object is precarious is of importance. As was pointed out above, in narcissism the movement towards the internal breast is predominantly a movement away from the external one. Since, however, the mechanisms of denial and splitting are less effective at this stage of a more advanced ego and more advanced reality-sense, some of the hate and fear stirred by frustration from the external object are carried over into the relation to the internal one, and necessitate compensatory processes in reference to it—a reactive over-strengthening of its libidinal cathexis.

To illustrate these views we may digress to a discussion of narcissism in adult life, as revealed by analysis. In hypochondriacal states the patient's whole interest is consumed by his concern for a particular part of his body. In pronounced cases the patient is unable to take his place in his family and continue with his ordinary activities. His interest in his surroundings and in people is subordinated to that of processes in his body, and events count only in so far as they affect the organ(s) imagined to be ill. The relation to this part of his body is very complicated. The intense observation given to the various sensations felt in his body betrays to the analyst the strong libidinal element and pleasure in the condition which is entirely unconscious, whilst in consciousness pain, anxiety and worry are registered. There is a similar double attitude to his doctors (and there are always several doctors being consulted) in that they are both distrusted and objects of complaint for not helping, and also continuously sought and treated as authorities. Thus the relation to people in the external world and belief in their goodness are not entirely given up; on the other hand, the

[1] 'On Narcissism: an Introduction' (1914).

patient abandons his ordinary interests and activities in favour of his interest in his body and his various symptoms. He perseveres with this preoccupation and clings tenaciously to his symptoms.

The behaviour of the adult hypochondriac suggests a type of narcissism in which the internal object, represented by the particular part of his body about which he is concerned, is preferred to external objects, and is in so far loved; but since this internal object is felt to be injured and therefore not gratifying, it is also hated and feared, so that on this account again it requires attention and must be watched carefully and with suspicion all the time.

The patient's conscious feeling that on account of his illness he cannot work or be concerned with people proves on analysis to cover a very complex situation; there is a hatred towards the people nearest to him (parents or parent-substitutes) which is a potent cause for finding any work impossible and for making excessive demands; this hostility is repressed and converted into the particular organ-sensations which absorb the patient's interest. These organ-sensations, moreover, tell a specific story of the patient's phantasies referring to the objects of his hostility, that is to say, his relations with the people who are important in his life are carried on in the field of these bodily sensations. The absence of conscious guilt for abstaining from work (which is felt ultimately to be work for these objects) and for being a burden to his family finds its explanation in the fact that the guilt also is converted and appears as the conscious suffering, anxiety and depression caused by the 'ill' organ. Looked at from another aspect, the guilt for his unconscious hostile impulses towards his nearest objects, usually the members of his family, is appeased by the suffering caused by the various painful sensations from the 'ill' organ. We know that unconscious guilt can be represented by a need for punishment, and this need is indeed fulfilled by the intense suffering connected with hypochondriacal fears. Thus the conscious absorption of interest by his own body and the manifest lack of ordinary interests and concerns covers an unconscious relation, rich in content, to his external objects, which are converted into internal ones and represented by the patient's own body. It can further be seen on analysis that the patient's unconscious hostility is bound up with frustrations attributed by him to his objects, and the whole hypochondriacal system seems to have emanated from such frustrations to which the patient could not adjust.

This summary description refers to analytic observations with adult patients, and the question arises whether these observations can be taken as true replicas of infantile narcissism or whether they represent a secondary elaboration of an original state. If the latter is the case, the question is which features belong to the original and which to later phases.

When we analyse other forms of mental illness, *e.g.* paranoia and delusional behaviour, such as delusional jealousy, we find again this kernel of an interplay between the relation to external, real people and to internal, phantasied objects, whereas otherwise the psychical material is very different. It should be justifiable to regard the common elements in different mental illnesses as deriving from the primitive, infantile stages of mental life to which regression has taken place, and the differences as determined by the varying advances made by the ego in its development.

This consideration holds for all mental illness, which, as Freud has pointed out, always involves regression, but the contribution to illness by the dysfunction of the advanced ego is not so far sufficiently investigated. It is, however, safe to assume that the root principles of the adult condition are the same as in the infantile condition, and that the additions by the later ego-stages concern rather the ramifications, the variations of the pattern, the use of the current settings of experience and the rationalizations.

This sequence: frustration by the external object (breast), real or imagined, and most frequently a mixture of both; hatred, persecutory fear of the hated and hence dangerous object; the turning away from it and the seeking of pleasure from sources within the self (bodily organs), is in my view to be regarded as the nucleus of hypochondriacal states. I would also conclude that in the infantile condition there is an equivalent to the pain and anxiety related to the organ in adult hypochondria, *i.e.* that in the infantile condition also there is some degree of limitation of the gratification obtained. This, I believe, leads to a compensatory hyper-cathexis of the organ (internal object) with libido and an excessive rejection of the external object.

The goodness of the internal object, which is treated as 'me' and represented by a part of the subject's body, feeds, as it were, on the badness of the external object. In other words, in order to maintain the self as good and the internalized object (which fuses with the self) as benevolent and helpful, the subject in the narcissistic condition hates and rejects the object in the external world. Thus hate and rejection form an important part of this defence against frustration, which is based on the technique of splitting the emotions of love and hate, with the corresponding splitting and doubling of the object into good/internal and bad/external. The tenacity with which the hypochondriac patient clings to his symptoms, and goes on consulting doctors and rejecting them, shows this technique of splitting and doubling, which in the complex setting of adult life can assume very confusing forms.

In this connection I wish to refer very briefly to another pathological condition in adult life, in which the patient uses the mechanisms of splitting in order to secure his belief that he himself is good, whilst the other person is bad. The delusional aspects of paranoid conditions show clearly the role played by denial. As is well known, delusional jealousy and fear of persecution are based on denial and projection. It appears that in these conditions it is above all the sense of guilt which the patient cannot tolerate and against which he sets going the defences of denial, splitting and projecting. Without attempting to deal here with the very intricate problem of guilt,[1] I wish to stress the observation that a person's intolerance of the sense of guilt is essentially his intolerance of admitting, even to himself, that there is something bad in himself, *i.e.* that something of *him* is bad, which he cannot disown by treating it as a foreign object inside himself. The result of the technique of delusional projection is twofold: fear of persecution by the person who is chosen for such projection and a conviction of the goodness of what is felt to be the self. It might be said that the individual pays the penalty of persecution for self-complacency.

The hypothesis, then, is that in the narcissistic condition the

[1] See Chapter VIII.

external object is hated and rejected, so that one loves the internal object which is fused with the self and experiences pleasure from it. (CH. N. 1.) The external object and its inner representation (gained through introjection) are thus sharply divided. However, the technique of splitting the object into two derives from and presupposes the fundamental premise that somewhere the two are only one. The technique is only partly successful, and the pleasure in narcissism is incomplete, more so than in simple wish-fulfilling auto-erotism. (The fact that at some point or other the infant does register the unsatisfactoriness of the phantasied internal breast is of vital significance, in that it compels him to turn again to the real breast in the outer world.)

Auto-erotism and narcissism are modes employed by the infantile ego of dealing with frustration (and regressively reached again in certain psycho-pathological states in later years). Essentially they employ the mechanisms of introjection and projection by which the infantile ego becomes endowed with a good object inside the infant's body, represented by some part of his body. Both conditions involve phantasies originally experienced in contact with an object.

The phantasy-object to which the infant is at any time related differs in accordance with the stages in his ego-development. In the earlier phase, characterized by simple wish-fulfilling, auto-erotic activities, the object is virtually a 'part-object', whilst in later phases, when narcissistic states play a greater role, objects are already recognized as persons ('whole object' stage).[1] In this connection we have to consider an economic factor. It seems plausible to assume that hallucinatory gratification can occur more easily when its object is a part, *i.e.* the nipple, than when it is a person; for the memory which underlies hallucination, if it concerns the nipple, is bound up with the full sensation of the mouth/nipple contact: the nipple really was 'inside' the infant, enclosed by his lips, gums and tongue. It may well be that in the earlier phase, the part-object relation, a greater quantity of libido is concentrated on the object than in the later phase, whereas sensations and emotions may occur in a less concentrated form if the object is felt as a person.

[1] Cf. Part 1 above, 'The Mental Structure'.

(c) Inner World and Outer World

Introjection sets processes going which involve all spheres of psychic life and often, too, have a not inconsiderable influence on physical life. Less, perhaps, than any other developmental mechanism is it an event that is over and done with, once it has taken place. An inner world comes into being. The infant feels that there are objects, parts of people and people, inside his body, that they are alive and active, affect him and are affected by him. This inner world of life and events is a creation of the infant's unconscious phantasy, his private replica of the world and objects around him. Thus it forms part of his relation to his environment, and he is no less affected by the condition and activities and feelings—imagined by himself, though they are—of his self-created inner objects than by the real people outside himself. Sensations, feelings, moods and modes of behaviour are largely determined by such phantasies about people inside the body and events in the inner world. These events reflect the outer world in a phantastically elaborated and distorted way, yet at the same time they can make the outer world appear as only a reflection of themselves. All the feelings the infant is capable of he experiences also in relation to his inner objects, and all his mental functions, emotional and intellectual, his relations with people and things, are decisively influenced by this system of phantasies. He may feel protected or persecuted, elated or depressed, by his internal objects, or he may feel himself their benefactor or their persecutor.

It must be understood that a description of these most primitive psychic processes, these unconscious phantasies, can be no more than an approximation. In a sense all our descriptions are artificial, because we have to use words for experiences which take place at a more primitive level before verbalization (which probably involves a progressive modification) has been achieved. The most primitive psychic processes are bound up with sensation. The original experience, of which we can render the content only by using words, is certainly in the form of sensation, and it might be said that (to begin with) the infant has only his body with which to express his mental processes. Analytic work uncovers these unconscious contents as basic formations in the psyche, and within the analytic situation words seem a sufficient means for understanding. When, however, these phantasies are spontaneously expressed outside the analytic situation in language, that is, by the insane or by the poet, it is clear that words are handled as a material with sensual qualities. In the one case we observe a process of far-reaching regression and deterioration, in the other one of special creativeness; yet they have in common this sensual, material quality of their language.

The phantasies about the inner world are inseparable from the infant's relation with the outer world and real people. It is only a limitation in our means of description which makes it appear as if there were two distinct entities which influence one another, instead of one whole, one multi-faceted interacting experience.

In a similar way it is a descriptive artefact to distinguish instinctual impulses and unconscious phantasy.[1] We must be aware that we are merely following another aspect of the same experience when we now turn to a discussion of instinctual impulses.

Freud suggested that the child's libido has a 'polymorph-perverse' character, until the establishment of the genital phase unites the divergent trends and subordinates them to the genital aim.[2] Later knowledge about a primary source of the destructive impulses leads to an extension of the libido-theory and affects our understanding of the vicissitudes of phantasy. Infantile phantasy reflects the immature, 'polymorph', libidinal and destructive nature of infantile instinctual impulses; the phantasies about internalized objects are unco-ordinated, full of contradictions and of changes from one extreme of feeling to another, and highly unstable. Experiences with the outer world, with real people, are taken over and continued, partly with great distortions, under the sway of the instinctual urges. In accordance with the modification of instinctual aims which represents instinctual development and interacts with the progressive organization of the ego, the infant's phantasies about his internal objects also change. The process can be described in

[1] Cf. Susan Isaacs: Chapter III.
[2] *Three Essays on the Theory of Sexuality* (1905).

terms of unification, consistency and stability; gradually the 'internal objects' assume an abstract character. Phantasies about living entities within the self develop into ideas and mental work with concepts, a process which begins in quite young children. At the height of maturity this system of phantasies is resolved in the formation of an integrated ego and a uniform super-ego. That this, however, is achieved only in varying degrees, and may be again disrupted under conditions of strain, with the result that the primitive phantasies reappear, is a daily observation for the analyst.[1]

In auto-erotism it is predominantly a 'good' inner breast to which the infant takes refuge when the external 'real' breast frustrates him. But this victory of mind over body, of a pleasurable phantasy over a painful reality, is only short-lived; the painful reality reasserts itself. It seems probable that when this happens, when the gratifying phantasy (or hallucination) comes to an end and the ego is compelled to perceive the painful inner need, frightening phantasies (or hallucinations) begin. In other words in the infant's experience his internal breast changes from good to bad, from loving to hating, from pleasurable to dangerous; and the infant turns in distress to the outer world, seeking and demanding a 'good' breast there. Good breast and bad breast, the breast within reach and satisfying—be this objectively or only subjectively—or frustrating, this on the most primitive stage is his whole concern and on this basis object-relations are built up.[2]

Quick alternations from good to bad feelings and objects, both of an absolute order, seem specific for early infantile life; but the transition from a bad inner to a good outer breast may not be quick. Our knowledge about these early processes is still incomplete, but it seems that the capacity to accept a gratifying object after frustration in part depends on a favourable combination of projection and introjection, i.e. the ego expels the bad inner breast and incorporates the good breast from outside. A smooth operation of this type of the introjective and projective mechanisms in early infancy, which presupposes an

---

[1] Cf. the system of bad-good internal objects, 'the devils' and 'the design', in the analysis of a painter. (Paula Heimann, *loc. cit.*)

[2] Cf. the 'sequence' described above, p. 152.

affectionate and helpful environment, may be at the bottom of a person's confidence that bad things go and good things come.

This favourable pattern, where the feelings about a persecuting inner breast stimulate the wish to expel it and take in a good breast, promotes the infant's contact with the outer world. But it does not always prevail. There are conditions in which the infant feels that his body is filled with bad objects, too powerful for him to do anything about them, and this may inhibit the mechanism of projection and subsequently interfere with introjection. (In so far as the inhibition of projection represents a failure to turn aggression outwards in self-defence, it would ultimately suggest a failure of the life instinct in its fight against the death instinct within.) Again, the fear that everything within is bad and dangerous may lead to the despair that there is nowhere anything good, or that, although there may still be something good outside, it cannot be taken in, as it would only turn bad through contact with the powerful bad objects and forces within. Phantasies of this kind create a vicious circle; the inner situation gets worse, because it cannot be relieved by introjecting a good object, but the worse it gets, the more introjection becomes inhibited. It is a state of mounting anxiety and distress.

Another type of disturbance in introjection and projection is brought about by the inability to project any goodness, preparatory to introjecting goodness from the object; such projection would promote trust in the object.

Processes of this kind, disturbances in the use of the mechanisms of introjection and projection, underlie the early infantile neurotic symptoms: the phobias, feeding difficulties such as feeble, listless sucking, incapacity to hold the nipple, rejection of the breast, exaggerated responses to slight obstacles,[1] or troubles in sleeping, difficulties in the excretory functions, etc.

It can happen that such disturbances continue almost without interruption or modification, and affect the whole mental life of the child. An extreme case of this kind has been described by Melanie Klein.[2] In this child there was an excessive inhibition

[1] Cf. M. P. Middlemore, The Nursing Couple; also Chapter VII.
[2] 'The Importance of Symbol-Formation in the Development of the Ego.'

of emotional and intellectual development which could be traced to severe disturbances in the functioning of introjection and projection. They had first been manifested in a striking manner in the infant's attitude to the breast (and to food) and had persisted in his contact with people up to the beginning of analysis, when he was four years old.

I have said that to begin with objects do not exist independently for the infant, but are always in some way referred to himself. Conversely, he refers his own experiences to his objects so that processes in the 'me' are felt to be connected with objects. As long as his phantasies centre upon the one object, his mother's breast, he ascribes any sensation of pain to persecution by this breast, *i.e.* he is bitten, or poisoned, or starved by it; when he feels pleasure and comfort, he is fed and nursed by it. This attitude represents an early example of animistic thinking which Freud described as characteristic for primitive man and infants.[1] There is an important link between animism on the one hand and idealization or persecution on the other; we see remnants of these daily in superstitions and obsessional rituals.

I would suggest that we can also trace other primitive convictions to infantile object-relationships, *e.g.* belief in the omnipotence of feelings, thoughts or wishes, and in the talion principle. Phantasies about objects residing in oneself lead to an equation between inner mental processes and activities carried out in the external world. The inner objects, the citizens of the inner world, are felt to be as much aware of and affected by the subject's feelings, wishes and thoughts as are people in the outer world by words and actions. In subjective experience, therefore, it is true that feelings are all-powerful, *e.g.* hostile impulses are an attack on the inner object, which is thereupon expected to punish.[2] That punishment by an internal object is a retaliation in kind also follows from the character of the infantile object-relation, the fusion between the self and the internal object. Since the child projects his own impulses on to his objects (wherever he places them, internal and external),

[1] *Totem and Taboo* (1912–13), p. 75 ff.
[2] Perhaps one has to look for the power of such conviction in order to account for the mysterious deaths recorded of savages who felt they had committed a supreme crime and who had not been subjected to punishment by any external agency.

he expects his objects to do to him what he has done (or imagines he has done) to them. The internal object, attacked and injured by the aggressive wish, returns the attack immediately. Further, fear of retaliation by the internal object is transferred back (projected) on to the external object, on to the real people in the external world. We often see in analysis that a patient cannot give up a hostile attitude, say the impulse to dominate others, because he is convinced that the moment he stops ruling his family, he will become their slave. This attitude —'either I or the other must be in power'—ignores the object's individuality, and betrays the infantile way of conceiving of the other in the image of the self (projection). Such a person is unable to concede that another person may be an *other* being, different from himself.

(d) Introjection and Projection in Reference to Whole Objects

With the progress in the functions of the ego[1] (perception, memory, synthesis, etc.) which leads to the 'whole object' type of relationship, infantile emotional life becomes far more complex. In the earlier phase, owing to the inefficiency of his intellectual powers and the use of primitive defences like magic, denial, omnipotence and splitting,[2] the infant conceives of his objects (or part-objects) in a simple and uniform way: when he feels gratified, his object is good and loved, when he is frustrated, the same object is bad and hated; he does not realize that he treats two aspects of one and the same object as if there were two different and unconnected objects. Whenever, as a result of development, this technique of 'not associating' or splitting is not available, the infant is exposed to the conflict of ambivalence, of simultaneous love and hate, attraction and rejection towards the same object, and this conflict leads to certain anxiety-situations.

Although the infant loves the good part-object, his love for his mother once he recognizes her as a person is a deeper, richer and more precious experience; disturbances in his love-feelings now mean more to him than at the stage of the primitive love for the breast. At the same time, the earlier fears of

[1] Cf. Part I above, 'The Mental Structure', p. 126.
[2] Cf. Chapter IX, p. 293.

injuring the good breast and of being persecuted by the bad breast develop into the far more complex guilt/anxiety of destroying and losing the loved mother, and give rise to the crucial condition which Melanie Klein has discovered and described as the *Infantile Depressive Position*.[1]

At this point introjection and projection, which in the earlier phase, in auto-erotic and narcissistic states, have been the predominant defence against frustration and object-loss, lead to severe anxieties. Since the infant's instinctual life is still under oral primacy, incorporation and expulsion phantasies are still exceedingly strong. The mouth, the main instrument of early love which has the aim of incorporating the loved object, is also the main organ of expressing the hostile aggressive impulses and of rejecting the object. When the splitting mechanisms diminish, the dangerous qualities of the oral activities are felt along with the desires dictated by love. Thus the fear arises of destroying the loved mother in the very act of expressing love for her, and the fear of losing her in the very process designed to secure her possession. These anxieties are multiplied by the dual aspect of the loved object, again the result of the greater coherence and integration of the ego, since the loved and gratifying mother is now also the dangerous frustrating person. To yield to the desire to incorporate the good object is fraught with the danger of taking in its badness, and conversely the expulsion of the bad inner object threatens the loss of its goodness. (The cul-de-sac into which these feelings and phantasies lead can be seen clearly in the tantrums of the older child, who by his simultaneous craving for love and inability to accept it may be well-nigh inaccessible to all attempts to comfort him. In analytic work certain transference crises repeat this state of mind.) In response to anxieties of this kind the infant may become inhibited in the use of the mechanisms of introjection and projection and retarded in his development (as described in an earlier passage of this chapter); or there may be a rapid alternation between introjection and projection, a frantic taking in and expelling of objects, resulting in instability, moodiness and failure to develop the capacity to become attached to objects.

---

[1] 'A Contribution to the Psychogenesis of Manic-Depressive States' (1935); 'Mourning and its Relation to Manic-Depressive States' (1940).

Looked at from another angle, such anxieties may conduce towards abandoning the advances made—the growing pains are too intolerable—and regressing to the earlier, more primitive phase (paranoid-schizoid position).[1] At this point we encounter the problem of the negative aspect of progression, which will be discussed further in the next chapter. It may be pointed out that such dualism is not confined to the mechanisms of intro-jection and projection.

It is in general true that a mental process which allays con-flicts and anxieties of a certain kind rouses others, so that only a relative freedom from anxiety, a relative peace of mind, is achieved. Such is mental life; there is no standstill for any length of time, especially during the period of growth and develop-ment. Serenity, the prerogative of the old and wise, often goes together with a halt in progression. Even satisfaction of impulse, often considered the best defence against tension, is only tem-porarily successful; frequently it fails altogether and constitutes in itself a source of most intense conflict.

(e) *The Origin of the Oedipus Complex*

The progress in ego-functions which results in the capacity to recognize individual persons decisively widens the infant's world. When he arrives at integrating the multiple impressions, previously largely isolated and dissociated, into the concept of a person, he in fact meets with *two* persons, mother *and* father, and this situation includes their interrelationship. The field of his emotional experiences is not only increased quantitatively, but changed in quality as well, in that he enters upon the triangular type of object-relation, which, as we know, has always a special significance.

This early triangular setting represents the origin of the Oedipus complex. It differs from the developed—now often called 'classical'—Oedipus complex in all those respects which are determined by the primitive character of the infant's mental condition at this stage.

Whilst with the recognition of persons more channels of gratification are opened for the infant, whilst the father more and more plays a role in his life and represents an object of love,

[1] Cf. Chapter IX.

interest and pleasure, the infant has now to deal with all the stimulations, excitations and conflicts which are inherent in a relationship between three persons.

The new and most important factor, which represents a problem of the first magnitude for the infant, lies in the parents' interrelationship. He divines that there are physical intimacies between his parents—and in so far recognizes a reality; but he conceives of these intimacies in terms of his own impulses, in other words, his notions are determined by projection and by so much are a gross distortion of reality. The parents do to one another what he himself would like to do.

At this primitive stage, at the beginning of the Oedipus complex, the infant's instinctual impulses are 'polymorphously perverse'. Oral, urethral, anal and genital stirrings co-exist and form a chaotic, overlapping, criss-cross pattern, a condition of rivalling claims, inherently frustrating, and frustrated by the outside world. Libidinal aims blend with destructive ones, and hostile tendencies are roused all the more owing to frustration and jealousy. Helplessness and omnipotence, the predominance of phantasy over reality lead to confusion between impulses and objects. What is desired or feared is treated as happening, and anxiety and frustration are felt as persecution by objects.

In infantile feeling/thinking instinctual stirrings mean so many specific activities. Thus oral impulses go together with phantasies of sucking, squeezing, biting, tearing, cutting, emptying and exhausting, swallowing, devouring and incorporating the object; the urethral/anal aims concern burning, flooding, drowning, expelling and exploding, or sitting upon and dominating the object. Owing to the unconscious equations between various organs and functions, their difference can be obliterated; every organ can be felt as a means of acquiring the desired object and of attacking in hate. The aim of squeezing and cutting out in particular is allocated to mouth, urethra and anus alike, and the object can be annihilated both by eating[1] and excreting. The impulse of poisoning and soiling the object occupies as it were a middle position between the oral and the

---

[1] One of Freud's earliest discoveries, which led him to most important conclusions, concerns the existence of cannibalistic impulses at the beginning of development.

urethral/anal drives. On these pre-genital aims are super-imposed those which have their source in genital stirrings, so that at their inception the true genital aims of penetrating or receiving, connected with the wish of creating and possessing children, have to struggle against the influence of the pre-genital phantasies, which lack a stable borderline between the libidinal and the destructive and rouse intense fears.

This bewildering condition of the infant's own instinctual drives and phantasies represents the material, the resources from which he draws, when occupied with his parents' interrelation-ship. The result is that he forms notions of something exceed-ingly dangerous and frightening; the 'primal scene' (Freud) has its roots in the infant's phantasies as they operate at the very beginning of the Oedipus complex.

Another aspect of the highly complex condition of the early infantile Oedipus complex is due to the incorporation-phan-tasies. Although the instinctual drives from all bodily sources operate in a rivalling way, as described above, the oral aims and mechanisms predominate at the beginning in a *primus inter pares* constellation (oral primacy). This means that incorporation-phantasies prevail in the infant's relation with his parents. They are internalized, not only as single individuals, but also in their aspect as a couple, the 'combined parental figure',[1] whose dangerous activities take place within the infant's self and body. All the anxieties about internal persecution, which in the earlier phase related to part-objects, are now aroused and intensified by being experienced towards the combined parents.

Incorporation further enters into the infant's phantasies about the parents' intimacies, so that he believes they incorporate each other and from each other. It would appear as if it is pre-cisely these notions which account for his intolerance towards their union, in that the cannibalistic interpretation of the primal scene leads to the fear of the parents' death, and this would mean his own death. Next to this maximal fear there are many other libidinal and frightening phantasies, of which only one needs to be mentioned here. It arises from the infant's desire for the father's genital.

How the infant arrives at any notion of the father's penis may

[1] Melanie Klein, *Psycho-Analysis of Children* (1932).

still be regarded as an open question. Phylogenetic factors as well as ontogenetic ones have to be considered, amongst the latter the infant's own genital stirrings. Here it may suffice to state that desires and phantasies centring on the father's penis occur in infants of either sex, and that to begin with the penis is largely equated with the breast; in the outcome, the predominant aims are of an oral character, to suck, eat and incorporate it.

Attributing his own impulses to his parents (projection) the infant imagines that in their sexual union the mother incorporates the father's penis and carries it hidden in her body (and that the father does the same with the mother's breast).[1] This mother with an internal penis plays a formidable role in the infant's phantasies. She appears to possess everything that the infant desires, she gives far too little, and she is his rival where the father is concerned. Resentment is intensified if weaning is actually in progress. Frustration, envy and rage give rise to violent impulses, such as breaking into her body and robbing from it what she withholds.

In this mother with the hidden internal penis we recognize the forerunner of the 'phallic woman', a female figure with a male genital. According to Freud this image occurs during the 'phallic phase' of the child's development and essentially represents a defence against the fear of castration. Melanie Klein's work has traced the origin of the phallic woman to the mother at the beginning of the Oedipus complex when, in accordance with the primacy of the oral instinctual impulses, incorporation-phantasies reign supreme and lead to the notion of an internal penis which the mother keeps within her body.

Whilst the boy in his genital sensations experiences masculine penetrative impulses towards the mother (direct Oedipus complex), he also feels her as a rival with regard to his receptive feminine aims, directed both towards the father and the mother with the father's penis. Thus his 'feminine position'[2] derived

[1] A complete description of the early infantile Oedipus complex would have to deal with many more feelings and phantasies operative at this period, e.g. those which concern the mother's genital and those which are derived from the infant's excretory sensations and images. The above presentation follows only certain aspects of an extremely complex process.

[2] Melanie Klein, *Psycho-Analysis of Children*.

from his oral incorporative impulses conflicts with his developing masculinity; the inverted Oedipus complex is an important part of the chaotic polymorphous condition at the outset of this nuclear conflict.

Identification with the first love-object, the mother, resulting from introjection, intensifies the girl's hetero-sexual and the boy's homo-sexual components of inborn bi-sexuality.

Many of the infant's desires are inherently unfulfillable. To the individual shortcomings of his environment which cause frustration, there are added the general causes of frustration which follow from the infant's insatiability for libidinal gratification and from the destructive components of his instinctual strivings. There are thus many sources for hatred against his parents and such hatred is focussed particularly on their union. Hatred determines the character in which the object is perceived. The early notions about the parents' physical intimacies abound in hateful and destructive elements, some of which reach consciousness in later periods. The concept of sexual intercourse as a rape, in which the woman is the victim of male violence, or of a mutually loathsome and destructive act; the notion of the vampire woman who sucks her partner to death; the monsters of folklore and mythology, which are partly male and partly female, or half-human, half-animal; these are some examples which testify to the horror roused by the deepest and earliest phantasies about the parents' union.

Gradually the child's capacity for realistic perceptions develops, and concurrently he progresses towards the establishment of the genital zone. This process implies the overcoming of the pre-genital aims, a clarification of many concepts, *e.g.* the recognition of the differences between the various bodily parts and functions, and the taming of the destructive impulses. Out of the chaotic pattern of instinctual aims of the early infantile Oedipus complex there crystallizes the child's heterosexual object-choice and the wish for loving genital relations, including the wish to give or receive a child (no longer equated with food or faeces) with the parent of the opposite sex, whilst rival-hatred against the parent of the same sex is limited to the genital sphere.

In this process of growth, unification and clarification which extends over the first childhood years, introjection and projection make important contributions towards modifying the inner and the outer worlds, and lessening both persecution and its counterpart, idealization. The child loses more and more of his helplessness and omnipotence, and the parents of their characters as gods or monsters. This goes together with a change in the child's phantasies about his internal parents. He comes to feel them less and less as physical objects within his own body, and more and more as ideas and principles to guide and warn him in his dealings with the world. Thus from the primitive notions about incorporated parts and persons the system of the super-ego is gradually built up.

CHAPTER NOTE

Ch. N. 1 (p. 154)

The term 'narcissism' is derived from the Greek myth of Narcissus, who fell in love with his own image in a fountain. This incident, however, should be considered within the full context of the story. The myth (of which several variations have been transmitted) essentially runs as follows: A nymph (later immortalized as Echo, a subtle point, for it combines reward with punishment since she had been so talkative) fell in love with Narcissus, but he rejected her. She implored Aphrodite to avenge her, and Aphrodite answered her prayer by making Narcissus mistake his own reflection in the water for a water-nymph. He fell violently in love with the beautiful creature he saw in the water, and he tried to embrace her. The frustration he experienced from his unsuccessful attempts ever to come close to his beloved was reflected in the face he saw. Narcissus mistook this to mean that his beloved nymph was in distress and it roused in him the wish to save and succour her. He suffered not only the pain of unfulfilled erotic desires, but the despair of being unable to remove the beloved object's suffering. In the end he pined away and died. He was changed into the flower which bears his name.

According to this myth the Greeks did not believe in self-love as a primary condition and attributed to it the complex character of object-love. It is indeed this fact, that Narcissus experienced all the emotions which belong to love for an object, from erotic desire to concern for the suffering object and the impulse to help and restore its happiness, which constitutes his punishment for having caused Echo the pain of unrequited love. Whilst objectively he loves himself (his own image reflected in the water), subjectively he loves another person. As a consequence of his guilt for rejecting Echo, he must mourn for an unattainable (lost) object and succumb to a suicidal depression.

Whilst I do not attempt to give a full analysis of this myth, I will add one remark concerning the detail of Narcissus' looking into the water and beholding his reflection which he treats as an object. A deeper meaning of this detail comes to light if we apply the familiar rule of interpretation by inferring the opposite of what is described. Narcissus looks into the outside world, the water, but the unconscious meaning suggested is the opposite: he looks inside himself. This element would then describe the unconscious phantasy of a (loved) object residing within the subject, and this is the basis for the identification of the subject with the object, which in the manifest content of the myth is represented by the mirror reflection of the subject mistakenly regarded as an object. That Narcissus was the son of a water-nymph adds poignancy to his experience.

It seems noteworthy that the Greek concept of narcissism comes so close to the findings of Melanie Klein, at which she arrived empirically, by following without a preconceived theory the phantasies presented by children in their analyses.

V

REGRESSION

By PAULA HEIMANN and SUSAN ISAACS

PART I

INTRODUCTION

THE term *regression* has been used by Freud and other writers in various senses.

In the sense which we shall here discuss, Freud uses it to refer to the backward movement of the libido which retraces its former path of development back to a certain point—a process which occurs in characteristic forms in particular types of mental illness. This concept of the *regression of the libido* is intimately bound up with his conclusions about the forward course of development of the libido and its 'fixation-points', conclusions which are complementary to the notion of regression and were formulated *pari passu* with it.

.As we know, Freud discovered that the sexual instinct as met with in the adult is a complex set of component impulses and sensations, involving various membranes and organs of the body and having a complicated developmental history from the earliest days. Psycho-analytic work has shown that these impulses and sensations are bound up with specific feelings and phantasies, and this concept of 'psycho-sexuality' has proved indispensable for understanding the sexual life of human beings. Sexuality passes through various phases (oral, anal and genital), in each of which one of the chief erotogenic zones is predominant in aim. The earlier phases do not pass away altogether, they become more or less subordinated to the later aims. In the normal person, the libidinal life as a whole is eventually integrated under the primacy of the genital organ and its aims and satisfactions.

The order and essential character of this development of the libido is biologically determined, and springs from organic sources. It is not inherently dependent upon circumstance or experience. Yet it is at every phase of its history profoundly sensitive to psychical events, and responds to external and internal influences, both quantitative and qualitative.

These internal or external factors may halt the forward movement of some part of the libido at any point of development, to which this part then remains bound to a greater or lesser degree. Under certain conditions, the libido is liable to flow back to earlier stages of development and to such 'fixation-points', which exert a pull on the forward-reaching libido.

Freud defines 'fixation' as 'a particularly close attachment of the instinct to its object'. (The object may be an external object or part of the subject's own body.) He says that such fixation 'frequently occurs in very early stages of the instinct's development and so puts an end to its mobility, through the vigorous resistance it sets up against detachment'.[1]

Fixations not only hamper sexual development as such, by preventing the normal advance of libido from one erotogenic zone to another, and from the earliest to later objects. They *may* also limit the capacity of the subject to achieve sublimation; since sublimation depends upon the relinquishing of the primary objects and modes of instinctual satisfaction in some degree for substitute objects and derived (symbolic) forms of activity. Fixation may lead to inhibition of ego-development, too, the ego renouncing those functions which are too closely bound up with early fixations.

Every mental illness involves some degree and some form of regression of the libido to early fixation-points. Regression is a phenomenon of the utmost importance in the etiology of neurosis, psychosis and the involution of character. In hysteria, the libido regresses with regard to its objects, seeking again the earliest incestuous loves, whilst its aims remain (chiefly) genital. In obsessional neurosis (and certain forms of character deterioration), 'regression of the libido to an antecedent stage of the sadistic-anal organization is the most conspicuous factor and determines the form taken by the symptoms'.[2]

In *Inhibitions, Symptoms and Anxiety*, Freud refers also to the effect of the regression of the libido upon the super-ego in obsessional neurosis: 'In order to effect the destruction of the

---

[1] 'Instincts and Their Vicissitudes' (1915), p. 65.
[2] *Introductory Lectures on Psycho-Analysis* (1916–17), p. 288.

Oedipus complex, a regressive degradation of the libido takes place as well, the super-ego becomes exceptionally severe and unkind, and the ego, in obedience to the super-ego, produces strong reaction-formations in the shape of conscientiousness, pity and cleanliness . . .' (p. 64).

These regressive changes thus involve not only the sexual life itself; they affect the sublimations, the emotions and the whole personality of the subject. The whole complex interplay and balance of the various mechanisms at work in the mental life are altered when regression occurs. This is patent in obsessional neurosis and the psychoses, but it is also true in hysteria, although less dramatically.

Freud's observations of these facts in adult mental life were confirmed by analysts who worked directly with young children. Every analyst rediscovers their truth in every patient, and many authors have amplified and extended the details of our knowledge. Abraham's contributions in this field were outstanding, and will be discussed in a later section. Ernest Jones's pioneer study of the effect of anal fixation upon the character influenced all later opinion. Space will not allow us to mention valuable additions to our knowledge made by many other analysts.

The classic view as to the *causes* of regression laid stress upon the damming-up of the libido. This damming-up might arise (according to this view) either from external factors (frustration) or internal ones (fixation, inhibition in development, biological accessions of libido at puberty and menopause). Both sets of influences give rise to an increase in libido which cannot be satisfied or disposed of, and which consequently disturbs the balance within the psyche and sets up an intolerable stress. The quantitative factor is considered to be of great importance.

These earlier formulations as to the *causes* of regression now require to be reconsidered in the light of Freud's own further work on the death instinct, and also of the added knowledge about early mental development which has been gained through the analysis of young children. Freud's theories were framed upon material obtained chiefly from the analysis of adults, supplemented by a brief study of a five-year-old and some observations of infants and young children. The work of Melanie

Klein, in her much more extensive observations and analyses of very young children, has amplified the well-known facts of regression and thrown new light upon their inter-connections. The outcome of these fuller observations conforms with the changes in our views about the causes of regression which are required by Freud's own later work.

PART 2

DATA FROM INFANTS AND YOUNG CHILDREN

In working directly with young children, whether in analysis or when observing them with an analytic eye, the opportunity is given of studying the experiences of the child in his earliest phases of libidinal development, *at the time when fixations occur*, and thus of seeing the relation of libidinal wishes to impulses of aggression, the anxiety stirred by different impulses in various circumstances, and the earliest defences against anxiety and ways of controlling impulse. The child's relations to his objects in particular situations of feeling and impulse, and the varied and changing expressions of his phantasies about his objects, together with early processes of symbol-formation and displacement, the first sublimations, as well as fixations, can be directly observed. Moreover, the setting of all these processes in their context of feeling can be noted, as the child's varied emotions—love, hate, fear, anger and guilt, joy and sorrow—come up in changing situations. Such contemporary studies of the changes in feeling, impulse and phantasy bring valuable confirmations to the views about fixations which are arrived at when working back from the memories of adult life or later childhood. They yield also a juster perspective as to the relative emphasis which should be placed on different elements in the situation and a better sense of the complex interplay of factors.

As a brief illustration, we may consider an example of a child's play. A girl of sixteen months often plays her favourite game with her parents. She picks small imaginary bits off a brown embossed leather screen in the dining-room, carrying these pretended bits of food across the room in her finger and thumb and putting them into the mouth of father and mother alternately. She chooses the brown screen, with small raised lumps on it, from among all the other objects of varying colour and shape in the room, to represent the 'food' she wishes to give her parents. On the most familiar analytic lines, we are justified in concluding that these small brown lumps represent faeces, and can thus link this play of feeding her parents with symbolic faeces with an earlier experience of the child's. Several times earlier (between twelve and sixteen months) the child had smeared herself with her faeces when lying in her cot in the early mornings, and put them into her mouth. She had been scolded and reproached by her parents at the time for doing this. Here, then, she is making a pleasurable game out of the situation of anxiety and guilt. The experience of eating and smearing her faeces is still at work in her mind: her libido is fixated. The reproaches of her parents are still causing her distress. When she is with her parents, she fears they will frown and scold again—as shown by her uneasiness if they will not play this game with her. Not only does the memory of their actual reproaches disturb her, however, but also the anxiety arising from the aggressive impulses expressed in the original smearing, which (she feels) may have done them harm and turned them into enemies.[1]

In her play now which, as can be seen in the child's manner, brings her great pleasure and libidinal satisfaction of various kinds—handling faeces again in symbolic form, winning the smiles of her parents, playing the part of the mother who feeds—she is overcoming the anxiety and guilt which bind her libido to the original smearing and eating. She is making an effort to sublimate her oral-sadistic and anal-sadistic impulses. She shows her reparation-wishes in her endeavour to 'feed' her parents: but in feeding them with 'faeces' she also makes them share her guilt and tries to prove that eating faeces does not poison and destroy.

Taking the occasions when the child actually ate and smeared her faeces together with this frequent and pleasurable game

---

[1] In *Civilization and its Discontents* (1929), p. 116, Freud expressed his agreement with Melanie Klein's view that, as Freud puts it, 'the original severity of the super-ego does not—or not so much—represent the severity which has been experienced or anticipated from the object, but expresses the child's own aggressiveness towards the latter'.

which soon followed, we can say that the game itself may be regarded as the birth of a sublimation: and yet, at the same time, it expresses a strong fixation. And we can see how the libidinal pleasure in fixation is used to overcome feelings of anxiety and guilt. (How intense and definite this particular fixation may turn out to be—which would doubtless be affected by later experiences as well—we cannot say without knowing more about the later history of the child.)

The original smearing and eating of faeces by the child was probably also an instance of the overcoming of aggressive impulses and anxiety by libidinal pleasure. It occurred when the child was alone in her cot in the early mornings, as such smearing and eating of faeces nearly always do occur. By doing this, the child was enabled to refrain from screaming and disturbing her parents—as the boy of eighteen months described by Freud was enabled to let his mother leave him without protest by his repetitive game with the cotton-reel. It seems likely that in this way she kept at bay the fear of starvation and the dread of losing her parents, as well as the screaming attacks upon them, with all the anxiety these arouse.[1]

We shall now formulate briefly certain general conclusions about the causes of fixation and regression to which we are brought by the closer study of infants and young children, conclusions which fill the gaps in earlier views and correct their perspective.

Causative Factors in Fixation and Regression

The history of the libido has long been appreciated as a focal aspect of development. As we have seen, it has to be brought into relation with all other mental phenomena at every stage. Its successive phases affect not only the characteristic mechanisms at the time, but also other sources of instinctual energy, and every sort of emotion and intellectual activity; indeed, they shape the whole of the mental life at each phase.

(a) The quality and intensity of *feelings* are profoundly affected by the stage of libidinal development; and in their turn emotions help to determine fixations and the further history of the libido. We would emphasize that feelings and the vicissitudes

[1] Cf. Searl, 'The Psychology of Screaming' (1933).

of feelings are always essential data for the understanding of any phase of libidinal development, or of development as a whole. In especial, we have learnt that the development of the libido cannot be understood without reference to *feelings of anxiety* and the situations and impulses which give rise to anxiety.

(*b*) The influence of *anxiety* upon libidinal development is highly complex, varying with the interplay of the child's psychical constitution and his circumstances at each crisis of his life; but, one way or another, it is always a potent factor.

When stirred too intensely (by whatever situation), anxiety contributes to a fixation of the libido at that point, and may check further development. A fixation is thus partly to be understood as a *defence against anxiety*. It is a familiar observation that libidinal pleasure—whether oral, anal or genital—may be used as such a defence; it has, for instance, often been noted that children may masturbate in school under the stress of some fear or anxiety.

On the other hand, if in more favourable circumstances anxiety is aroused, but not overpoweringly, it serves to increase desire and acts as a spur to libidinal development. In many of her case studies, Melanie Klein has given evidence for these conclusions and surveyed the role of anxiety in the sexual development of both male and female. She has shown that specific anxieties not only contribute in both sexes to fixations and regressions, but also play an essential part in stimulating the libido to move forward from pre-genital positions to the genital one. In our view neither fixation nor normal libidinal development can be understood without taking these facts into consideration.[1]

(*c*) Anxiety thus influences libidinal development. Anxiety itself, however, arises from *aggression*. It is evoked by the aggressive components in the pre-genital stages of development. It is the destructive impulses of the child in the oral and anal phases (discovered by Freud, described more fully by Abraham and later by Melanie Klein) which are, through the anxiety they stir up, the prime causes of the fixation of the libido. These destructive

---

[1] In his study of 'Early Female Sexuality' (1935), Ernest Jones also has shown the influence of anxiety in helping to determine both fixations and normal development.

components in the pre-genital impulses have to be overcome and neutralized by the libido, which, in so far as it is thus occupied, cannot move freely forward to new aims and genital primacy. The amount of libido which has to be held back at the oral and anal levels in order to counter these aggressive elements (according to their intensity, whether this be due to innate strength or to adverse circumstances) makes so much the less available for genitality. This renders the genital aim so much the more precarious, and regression so much the more likely an event if further anxiety be evoked by frustration on the genital level with consequent further aggression and hate.

As Freud showed, it is frustration which initiates regression. But, in our view, it does so not only by a simple 'damming-up' of libido, but also by evoking hate and aggression and consequent anxiety. The newly evoked hate and aggression reactivate the hardly overcome pre-genital sadism, and this in its turn pulls back the libido to its earlier forms, in order to neutralize the destructive forces once again at work in the mind. Freud classed regression as a defence. We understand more fully now what it is a defence against. (We shall consider this matter again in a later section.)

(*d*) The way in which impulses and feelings work to induce fixation and regression cannot be understood without appreciating the part played by *phantasies*. How do the libidinal and aggressive instincts operate *in the mind*? Through unconscious phantasy, which is their psychic representative—as has been argued in Chapter III. Freud stated that hysterical symptoms spring from reminiscences,[1] and for a time he believed that such reminiscences are related to traumatic sexual experiences in childhood. In his first theories on the etiology of the psychoneuroses sexual seduction by an adult, experienced passively by the child, was specific for hysteria; whereas an active part in sexual experiences taken by the child was pathognomonic

---

[1] 'On the Psychical Mechanism of Hysterical Phenomena' (1893); 'The Origin of Psycho-Analysis' (1909), First Lecture. And in 'Negation', he spoke of 'the *language* of the oldest, that is, of the oral instinctual impulses . . .' (our italics). The whole essay on 'Negation' shows that, in his view, phantasy is not only the mental expression of instinct, but is the link between an instinct and the psychic mechanisms specifically related to that instinct.

for obsessional neurosis.[1] As is well known from his own impressive descriptions,[2] Freud could not maintain these views when further work convinced him that the reminiscences of the hysterical patient, the reproduction of seduction scenes in childhood, were based not on actual experience, but on phantasy. In fact it is this realization, crystallizing in Freud's concept of *psychic reality* as distinct from external or material reality, which marks a decisive turning-point in psycho-analytical theory.

It is the *phantasies* of loss and destruction arising from the sadism of the pre-genital levels which stir anxiety—phantasies of the destruction of the desired object by devouring, expelling, poisoning, burning and so on, with the ensuing dread of total loss of the source of life and love, of the 'good' object, as well as the dread of retaliation, persecution and threat to the subject's own body from the destroyed and dangerous 'bad' object.

It is well known that phobias, night-terrors and sleeping difficulties occur at a very early age, and that even at the breast some infants show neurotic feeding disturbances, whilst these are frequent during and after the period of weaning. Obviously, etiological theories about such disturbances occurring in later childhood and adult life cannot be considered complete or adequate unless and until they embrace those earliest symptoms as well.[3] In our view, these early phobias are an attempt to deal, by the projection of internal dangers on to the outer world, with the anxieties arising primarily from the cannibalistic phantasies characteristic of the oral-sadistic stage, phantasies which Freud himself discovered, although he did not bring them into relation with the early phobias.

The significance of animal phobias was discussed by Melanie Klein in *The Psycho-Analysis of Children*, pp. 219, *et seq.* In her view, they are a mode of defence involving projection against anxieties relating to the cannibalistic phantasies, and provide a

[1] 'Heredity and the Aetiology of the Neuroses' (1896); 'The Aetiology of Hysteria' (1896).

[2] 'My Views on the Part played by Sexuality in the Aetiology of the Neuroses' (1905); 'Hysterical Phantasies and Their Relation to Bisexuality' (1908); 'An Autobiographical Study' (1935).

[3] In *Inhibitions, Symptoms and Anxiety* (1926), Freud said that the earliest phobias of infancy 'so far have not been explained' (p. 105), and added that 'it is not at all clear what their relation is to the undoubted neuroses that appear later on in childhood'.

means for modifying the child's fears of his threatening super-ego as well as of his dangerous id. 'The first move is to thrust out these two institutions into the external world and assimilate the super-ego to the real object. The second move is familiar to us as the displacement on to an animal of the fear felt of the real father. . . . Regarded in this light, an animal phobia would be much more than a distortion of the idea of being castrated by the father into one of being bitten by a horse or eaten by a wolf. Underlying it would be not only the fear of being castrated but a still earlier fear of being devoured by the super-ego, so that the phobia would actually be a modification of anxiety belonging to the earlier stages.'

Melanie Klein then goes on to discuss Freud's two cases of Little Hans and the Wolf-Man.[1] Little Hans had overcome his earliest anxieties with considerable success. The object of his phobia—a horse—was not a very terrifying representative of his father—as compared with the wolf in the case of the Wolf-Man. The fact that his father could be represented by a horse meant that his fear of his father was not extreme; moreover, he could actually play at horses with his father, which confirms that the anxiety persisting in the form of the phobia was not overwhelming. In the Wolf-Man, primitive anxieties were far more intense and unmodified. Melanie Klein takes the view that the passive feminine side which, as Freud described, was 'strongly accentuated', the tender passive attitude, covered up an overwhelming dread of the father. She points out that Freud's data show that the patient's whole development was abnormal and was governed by the dread of the wolf-father. The early and rapidly developing obsessional neurosis which the patient had shown was evidence of very serious disturbances. And the later history of this patient—as described by Ruth Mack Brunswick—confirmed Melanie Klein's estimate of the nature and degree of the early cannibalistic anxieties lying behind the wolf-phobia.

These primary anxieties are at one and the same time the source of the paranoid symptoms and of the homosexual emphasis in paranoia. 'Against a dangerous devouring father of

[1] 'A Phobia in a Five-year-old Boy' (1909); 'The History of an Infantile Neurosis' (1918).

this sort, they [such boys] could not engage in the struggle which would naturally result from a direct Oedipus attitude and so they had to abandon their heterosexual position' (p. 224). The primary oral and anal anxieties are the chief factors in the homosexual fixation, and hence the main sources of the tendency to regress to the paranoid mechanisms.

It is the anxiety stimulated by cannibalistic phantasies which is the most potent factor in oral fixations. We find in adults as well that these phantasies operate powerfully behind the various forms of oral and anal fixations: perversions, drug addictions, etc. The dread of the destroyed internal object (devoured and therefore inside) can only be allayed by continual oral pleasure, by constantly imbibing more good, in order to counteract the bad already inside, and in this way also proving that the external sources of good have not been destroyed or lost irretrievably. It is this insatiable need which binds the libido to oral and anal forms.

We know that such fixations of the oral phase, with all its phantasies and anxieties, lead to profound disturbances of the genital function.[1] Yet this is far from being the whole story. The early phantasies by no means play a wholly retarding and fixating part in libidinal development. We pointed out above that when it is not too intense anxiety acts as a spur to libidinal development. (This depends, however, not only on the degree of anxiety, but also upon the specific nature of the phantasies involved—which, in their turn, are influenced by actual experiences as well as by primary impulses.)

It is now widely recognized that the earlier stages have definite and positive contributions to make to the genital phase. For example, in certain respects, successful genitality in men and women alike is actually dependent upon specific impulses, feelings and phantasies belonging to the oral phase. When the genital life is satisfactory in the man, the specific genital phantasies include an oral element, e.g. the phantasy of the penis as a giving and feeding organ, identified with the breast, whilst the female genital is felt to be safe and attractive because the tender impulses of suckling are attributed to it. In this way,

[1] Among many other studies, M. Brierley's paper, 'Some Problems of Integration in Women' (1932), is to be noted.

contributions from the oral phase strengthen genital impulses, and do not interfere with the mobility of the libido. Similarly, the woman's genital impulses and phantasies take over her happy experiences at the breast. Her pleasure in actively encompassing the penis, her freedom from the dread of engulfing it and destroying it and castrating her partner, is in part drawn from the unconscious memories of having loved and cherished and safely enjoyed the nipple in active sucking. These memories also enable her to feel that the penis itself is a good and not a threatening object.[1]

These are, of course, only selected aspects of the highly complicated relationship between pre-genital and genital sexuality, but they may serve to illustrate our general point: namely, with regard to those positive contributions of the oral phase to the genital function, it is not enough to say that there is a displacement of certain elements in the oral phase to the genital. This is true, but it is an incomplete statement. Those oral phantasies and aims have remained *uninterruptedly active* in the unconscious mind exerting a favourable influence and promoting genitality. The oral libido has remained labile enough to be transferred to the genital and satisfied there.

This transfer comes about—and this is a most important point in reference to the theory of libidinal development and regression—partly because the earliest onset of genital impulses appears whilst the oral stage is still active. There is actually much more overlap between various stages of libidinal development than was formerly realized. The genital *phase*, as such, is not present in the earliest days; but genital *trends* certainly begin to make their appearance whilst the child is still predominantly in the oral phase. It is, for example, an observable fact that erections occur from time to time during the suckling period; and we do not regard the 'reflex' explanation as adequate and convincing.

The fully integrated genital phase, with the primacy of the genital, is bound up with the full development of the Oedipus complex, but both have their first rudimentary beginnings in

[1] Ernest Jones's 'Early Female Sexuality' (1935) should be read in this connection. Cf. also Ferenczi's concept of amphimixis in his 'Thalassa' (1924).

the oral phase.[1] The differences between earlier and later genital erotism correspond to the differences between earlier and later stages in all fields of mental development. The fundamental difference is that in the earliest phase the oral libido has the primacy[2] and genital erotism is sporadic and subordinate, whilst in the later full genital phase, the aims and pleasures of the other erotogenic zones are subordinated to the primacy of the genital and integrated into its service. This primacy carries with it great changes in the balance of the libidinal and aggressive instincts, as well as qualitative differences in their specific aims. There are, moreover, also profound changes in the object-relationships with which these aims are connected.

Not only is there an overlap between the various phases of libidinal development; there is also a movement backwards and forwards between the various phases within those particular periods when one or other phase can be said to be predominant.

(c) The contribution of the oral phase to successful genitality cannot, however, be fully understood without reference to *phantasies of incorporation and the mechanism of introjection*. As has been shown in Chapter IV on 'Introjection and Projection', early oral satisfactions lead to the incorporation of a 'good' breast, as well as to a good relationship with the external mother. This good internal object (nipple, breast, mother) helps the child to find a good external object once again in the genital phase, and to feel that his impulses towards it cherish and feed and give life to it.

Bound up with these phantasies, moreover, are the reparative wishes. Genitality can be maintained when the reparative

---

[1] In various passages, particularly in the *Introductory Lectures* (1915) and in the *Three Essays on the Theory of Sexuality* (1905), Freud warns us against exaggerating the differences between the infant and the adult.

[2] Experimental studies by non-analytic investigators have demonstrated that during the first ten days of life the sensitivity of the skin is subordinated to oral activity. The sucking reflex can be evoked by gentle touches on the skin of the cheek and by other stimuli. 'Stimulation of the lips of a newborn infant is followed by the sucking reaction in over ninety per cent. of the infants of a given age, but a stimulation of the cheeks, eyes, temperature, taste, smell, and so forth, will also produce it. That is to say, sucking is a specific reaction to stimulation of the lips, but it is a reaction to many other stimuli also.' (*The Behavior of the Newborn Infant*, by Karl Chapman Pratt, p. 210.) These experimental facts confirm Freud's theory of the early *primacy* of oral libido.

wishes can operate securely. Genitality breaks down and regression comes about when the reparative tendencies are disturbed (often by frustration and the ensuing hatred and aggression), since the genital is then felt to have proved destructive and dangerous.

This brings into operation not only the fear of hurting and damaging the external loved object, but also the dread of the 'bad' internal object, or the super-ego. In *Inhibitions, Symptoms and Anxiety* (quoted earlier), Freud referred to the severe and implacable super-ego of the obsessional neurotic. He expresses his sense of the intimate interplay between the level of regression reached and the kind of super-ego when he says: '. . . the super-ego, originating as it does in the id, cannot dissociate itself from the regression and defusion of instinct which have taken place here' (p. 66). We should fill this out by adding that the hate and aggression aroused by the frustration which starts the regressive process at once evokes the dread of the super-ego, the hating and vengeful internal object; and this in its turn stimulates the need to hate and fight again with all the weapons of pre-genital sadism. In our view, the part played by internal objects and the super-ego is an essential factor in the regressive process.

Another important advance in the understanding of regression, gained chiefly from Melanie Klein's work with young children, together with the closer study of psychotic states largely stimulated by such work, is that fixation and other pathological states can be fruitfully approached from the angle of *progression*, as well as that of regression.

In his study of paranoia[1] Freud suggested that the paranoid symptoms are not to be regarded only as regressive, but also as having a restitutive aspect. *The delusion-formation which we take to be a pathological product is in reality an attempt at recovery*, a process of reconstruction (p. 457). He describes how Schreber, the subject of this study, has withdrawn libidinal cathexis from the persons in his environment and from the external world generally, all things having become indifferent and irrelevant to him. This is rationalized as a world catastrophe: 'The end of the world is the projection of this internal catastrophe; for his subjective world has come to an end, since he has withdrawn his

---

[1] 'An Autobiographical Account of a Case of Paranoia' (1911).

love from it' (pp. 456–7). He builds it up again 'so that he can once more live in it' by the work of his delusions. '. . . the man has recaptured a relation, and often a very intense one, to the people and things in the world, although the relation may now be a hostile one where formerly it was sympathetic and affectionate.' The symptoms of the illness are but a sign of the process of recovery which then 'forces itself so noisily upon our attention'.

Later in the same essay, Freud speaks of the 'agitated hallucinations in dementia praecox as being a struggle between regression and an attempt at recovery' (p. 463).

Various workers have carried further these suggestions of Freud's with regard to the progressive and restitutive elements in pathological states and symptoms; in particular Melanie Klein has shown how at successive stages of development the child deals in different ways with his earliest anxiety-situations. She says: 'Let us briefly summarize what has been said about the evolution of phobias. In the suckling the earliest anxiety-situations find expression in certain phobias. In the earlier anal stage, with its animal phobias, objects of an intensely terrifying nature are still involved. In the later anal stage, and still more in the genital stage, these anxiety-objects are greatly modified.

'The process of modification of a phobia is, I believe, linked with those mechanisms upon which the obsessional neuroses are based and which begin to be active in the later anal stage. It seems to me that obsessional neurosis is an attempt to cure the psychotic conditions which underlie it, and that in infantile neuroses both obsessional mechanisms and mechanisms belonging to a previous stage of development are already operative' (*The Psycho-Analysis of Children*, p. 226).

Again, in Chapter XII of the same book, she discusses other methods of cure attempted by the ego to overcome early infantile anxieties with a psychotic content, and shows how each of the fixations and pathological symptoms apt to appear at successive stages of development have both a retrospective and a prospective function, binding anxiety and thus making further development possible. Therapeutically, obsessional symptoms often lose their hold upon the patient when the underlying paranoid anxieties are resolved, thus making the obsessional technique less necessary for psychic equilibrium.

From the study of young children, we should say that these opposite tendencies, progression and regression, are at work all the time in mental life. There is a constant ebb and flow between them during the whole period of development and at all times of mental stress. Any point of relative stability is actually a compromise between the two tendencies, depending upon the specific phantasies which are at work. Similarly, there is a constant movement of the mind between the various mechanisms which are available for disposing of anxiety and mastering instinct (splitting, introjection, projection, displacement, distribution, repression, isolation, undoing and the rest). Eventually a certain compromise between these various mechanisms is reached, acceptable to the ego and yielding a measure of control of anxiety, and between the forward and backward movements of the libido, together with the destructive components with which it is always more or less fused: a compromise optimal for each individual personality.

Certain of these points we shall now consider in more detail, particularly with reference to Freud's later work.

PART 3

CONSIDERATIONS ARISING FROM FREUD'S CONCLUSIONS AS TO LIFE AND DEATH INSTINCTS

Regression, Fixation and the Destructive Instincts

The phenomena of progression and regression provide further evidence of the duality which underlies human life. They have ultimately to be traced to the life and death instincts. As has been pointed out in Chapter IV, psycho-analytic investigation was at first almost exclusively occupied with the manifestations of the life instinct and the libido. The study of regression was for many years almost entirely concerned with its libidinal aspect. It was Abraham especially who made a systematic study of the part played by the destructive instincts. He demonstrated that they also have a development, as shown in the successive changes in their aims. Building on Freud's theory of the three main libidinal phases, Abraham examined the phenomena of aggression in certain mental illnesses and arrived at the conclusion that the destructive no less than the libidinal impulses undergo a change of aim in relation to objects.

Freud saw the first destructive aim arising during the primacy of the oral zone, namely cannibalism. Abraham[1] subdivided the oral phase into oral-sucking and oral-biting stages. He pointed out the force of the destructive impulses during the onset of teething, but he held that the first oral stage was free from aggressive impulses. (In this we do not follow him, since we hold that there is evidence of some destructive aims already during the sucking stage. Abraham himself, when discussing the oral character, attributes an element of cruelty to the sucking stage, which makes people who have regressed to that stage 'something like vampires to other people'.) He described devouring by biting as the first destructive aim. This is followed at the first anal stage by the aim of destroying by expulsion. During the second anal stage, an important modification of the destructive instincts takes place, their aim being changed into that of control by retention. Though there is still a strong aggressive cathexis of the object, a mitigation of the destructive impulses is shown by the desire to preserve it. It is spared the full destruction of the earlier phases, on condition of being subject to control. At the final stage of instinctual development, the genital phase, the libido carries the field and—according to Abraham—there is full object-love without ambivalence (post-ambivalence). Freud's theory of a primary instinct of destruction was published in 1920 (*Beyond the Pleasure Principle*), and was thus available to Abraham. Abraham must have known it when he wrote his 'Development of the Libido' in 1924. He did not link his own new findings with the theory of the death instinct, although to us it appears that they are in line with it.

Bringing together what we have learnt from Freud, Abraham and from Melanie Klein's work with young children regarding the instinctual aims of the pre-genital stages, we can now discern in detail the ways in which these libidinal and destructive aims are together expressed in bodily impulses. The libidinal desire

[1] 'A Short Study of the Development of the Libido' (1924).

to suck is accompanied by the destructive aim of sucking out, scooping out, emptying, exhausting. The libidinal pleasure in biting is experienced along with the destructive impulse of devouring. To the pleasure of expelling corresponds the destructive aim of annihilating, whilst the pleasure of retaining coincides with the impulse to control and dominate. These considerations have an important bearing on the discussion of the role which the derivatives of the death instinct play in regression. Whilst some analysts think of regression predominantly in terms of the libido, we see *concurrent* changes in the destructive impulses as well, *i.e.* their return to earlier, archaic aims. We hold that it is this *recurrence of primitive destructive aims which is the chief causative factor in the outbreak of mental illness.*

A precondition of regression is the formation of fixation-points. On the basis of Abraham's findings referred to above, and Melanie Klein's extensive researches, we consider that a fixation-point has not only a libidinal, but a destructive charge as well. Both become again operative when in regression the instinctual and emotional life of an earlier phase once more becomes dominant.

In this situation, violent anxiety is experienced which derives from several sources: (*a*) The present-day frustration which initiates the regression. It is accepted that frustration stimulates hatred and anxiety. (*b*) The specific anxieties (paranoid, depressive and super-ego types of anxiety) which are revived by the return to primitive instinctual impulses (fixation-points). Freud says[1]: 'Every stage of development has its own particular conditions for anxiety; that is to say, a danger-situation appropriate to it. . . . As development proceeds, the old conditions for anxiety should vanish, since the danger-situations which correspond to them have lost their force owing to the strengthening of the ego. But this only happens to a very incomplete degree.' We have already mentioned Freud's reference to the extreme severity of the super-ego in regressive conditions. (*c*) The horror with which the ego reacts to being faced with the impulses and phantasies of a phase from which it had already removed itself. In describing the effect of regression at puberty in obsessional neurosis, Freud says: 'The ego will recoil with astonishment

[1] *New Introductory Lectures* (1932), p. 116.

from promptings to cruelty and violence which enter consciousness from the id. . . .'[1]

In our view, thus, the facts just summarized, which include
the breaking down of the sublimations and the modifications
to which the destructive instincts were subjected in the course
of development, have to be seen in operation together with the
vicissitudes of the libido.

There is another point at which our conclusions diverge from
Freud's view of regression, in so far as this was still based on the
earlier forms taken by his theory. Freud emphasized the damming-up of the libido as the cause of regression and of neurotic
illness. Owing to the frustration which renders the discharge
and satisfaction of the libido impossible, the libido becomes
dammed up and this ushers in regression. 'The dissatisfied and
dammed-up libido may now open the path to regression. . . .'[2]

But if we accept Freud's theory of the life and death instincts,
formulated in *Beyond the Pleasure Principle*, we are no longer
justified in singling out the libido when considering regression
and psycho-pathological conditions. The question now arises
whether regression is not the outcome of a failure of the libido
to master the destructive impulses and anxiety aroused by
frustration. We believe that this is so: that the pathological
condition of dammed-up libido occurs only when the libido—
in spite of its increase or apparent increase—proves unable to
counter the destructive impulses which are evoked by the same
factors which caused the damming-up of the libido, namely, the
frustration.

As an example, we may briefly consider the problem of the
menopause.

We know that many women fail to cope with the conflicts of
the menopause and break down into illnesses of varying persistence and seriousness. This tendency to mental disturbance
at the time of the menopause raises many theoretical problems.
We know that important physiological changes, *e.g.* in the
hormonic balance, occur, but we still have to consider the
psychological processes connected with this physical factor.

Here, as always, in our endeavour to understand neurotic

[1] *Inhibitions, Symptoms and Anxiety* (1926), p. 68.
[2] 'Types of Neurotic Nosogenesis' (1912), p. 119.

conflict, or for that matter normal mental development and normal personality, we are concerned with the mind-body entity. The prime movers of all mental life are the instincts, those borderland dynamic processes which relate both to body and to mind. It is quite possible that the internal secretions of our glands come very close to being the material vehicle of the instincts. They certainly are a vital part of those bodily processes which underlie and give rise to instinctual phenomena. We know that changes in the endocrine balance affect moods and impulses and phantasies. We also know that things may act the other way round, that emotional conflict may disturb the endocrine balance and that strictly psychological treatment, the solving of emotional conflict by psycho-analysis, can itself act favourably upon the balance of the hormones.

Our problem thus lies in understanding the ways in which a woman deals with the changes in stimulation arising from the hormonic imbalance. How does she deal with these changes in internal stimuli and with the actual responses of her husband or other people to the alteration in her appearance and personality which may occur at this period? What are the psychological factors which help one woman to overcome these difficulties—which to some extent are bound to arise—and those which lead another woman to fall a victim to her difficulties? We cannot doubt that the degree and the manner in which every woman meets the problems of the menopause depend in part upon her previous psychological history: for example, the extent to which she has overcome her Oedipus complex and her castration phantasies, and the ways in which she dealt with her earliest anxieties, as well as the width and stability of her sublimations.

Many women regress at the point of menopausal conflict because the decline of sexual productivity deprives them not only of direct instinctual gratification but also of a reassuring factor of the first magnitude. It is not only in devout Catholics that we meet with the feeling that sexual intercourse is something bad and guilty for which only procreation can make amends. This attitude to sexuality arising from the Oedipus complex and earlier anxieties exists, as is well known, in the unconscious of many women who believe themselves free of religious or ethical scruples about sexuality. Once this redeeming factor disappears, unabated guilt may flood a woman's mind. The knowledge that she can no longer bear children may open the door to severe anxieties, particularly those centring upon a destroyed and barren inside, for which in unconscious phantasy a persecuting mother is made responsible. Not to produce a live child is felt to be the same as to contain dead bodies inside (a phantasy which derives ultimately from the cannibalistic and destructive impulses of early instinctual life). These feelings stir up the fear of her own death. In the wake of these anxieties penis-envy is stimulated, the possession of the penis becoming again so desired and needed since the feminine privilege of bearing children has come to an end. Guilt towards the husband, partly for her impulse to castrate him, partly because now she deprives him of fatherhood, enter into the complicated picture. Moreover, the husband from whom she no longer receives a child assumes the role of the father who never satisfied her desire for a child, and thus the incestuous phantasies are revived which make sexual intercourse the primary crime. In consciousness these anxieties and conflicts may appear under the guise of being haunted by the fear of becoming unattractive and old. Women in the menopause often develop an increased demand for sexual intercourse, sexual gratification and success, affection and love. They are in the 'dangerous age'. Analytic investigation of such cases makes it evident that libidinal desires are vastly increased through anxiety and guilt.

In more normal women the anxieties about the barren inside are dealt with and overcome in a great variety of ways: for example, through the sublimations and the reassurances provided by good social and sexual relationships.

Many other factors as well enter into the problem of the menopause, but these may suffice here, since we are concerned to show our approach to the problem of dammed-up libido rather than to investigate the psychology of the menopause as such.

Actual analyses of menopausal breakdowns are sometimes like a text-book of psycho-pathology, showing most clearly how regression has revived the unsolved conflicts of every stage of development, including the earliest stages. One gains the impression that the menopause represents a demand note for all the psychological debts incurred before—debts which did not matter as long as biological prosperity seemed secure.

In the situation in which the ego is confronted by the task of mastering the dammed-up libido, it is also faced with that of mastering destructive impulses and anxieties. These considerations are derived from clinical observations. In our view, their theoretical basis is to be found in Freud's theory regarding the fusion of the two opposed instincts, e.g. '. . . the fact that what we are concerned with are scarcely ever pure instinctual impulses, but mixtures in varying proportions of the two groups of instincts. . . .'[1]

To sum up our conclusions on this matter: At the fixation-point, not only is libido immobilized, but the destructive impulses and anxieties specific for that period of development, which form the background of unsolved conflicts, also remain potentially active and threaten to interfere with a firm establishment of the genital phase. The maintenance of pre-genital instinctual modes of behaviour and phantasies is not as such a pathological factor. We have referred above to their significance as stepping-stones in the mastering of anxiety. Pre-genital aggressive and libidinal aims may contribute to genital ones and colour and enrich the genital activities, provided they are capable of subordination under the primacy of the genital. This, however, depends upon the balance between libido and destructive impulses, determining the type of phantasy which accompanies genital activity.

The breakdown of the genital phase involves the libido, the destructive instincts and the ego-achievements alike. As is well known, deterioration in character and impairment of sublimations form part of the regressive process.

Another element in regression is that the *reparative aims* may be interfered with. As already pointed out, we lay great stress upon the role which reparation and sublimation play in maintaining mental health. The instinctual processes of the pre-genital phases give rise to specific anxieties. The ego, built up by introjection and projection, is endangered in various ways by the fears of loss or destruction of its objects. Their restoration is a most urgent aim, giving impetus to sublimation.

[1] *Inhibitions, Symptoms and Anxiety* (1926), p. 82.

These ego-achievements, thus, in addition to the gratifications which they provide, are prime factors in the fight against anxiety and guilt.[1] A certain degree and quality of guilt and anxiety stimulate reparation and thus encourage sublimation. An excess of these emotions, however, has a paralysing effect on sublimations. As long as the individual feels that his destructive impulses are kept in check or that harm done by him is being repaired, he can maintain the genital level, because he can then tolerate actual frustration and his libido can be re-directed on to other objects. And in so far as sublimation can be maintained and gratifications from other objects be sought, this in its turn helps him to bear frustration. Here we have a benign circle. But if reparation and sublimation break down, the ego's defences are overrun, gratifications of the aim-inhibited libido are lost, the strength of the destructive impulses is intensified and pregenital anxiety-situations are revived. Persecution fears and despair make the actual frustration unbearable, partly because it has been augmented by these processes. Here there is a vicious circle involving both the re-emergence of archaic impulses with their associated anxieties, and the breakdown of sublimation and reparation—a circle which reflects the mutual influence of fixation and regression.

Regression and Inhibition

Regression may result in symptom-formation or in inhibition, or in both. Freud held that the ego-function of an organ becomes inhibited if the sexual significance of that function, the erotogenicity of the organ in question, becomes too great. He says: 'As soon as writing, which entails making a liquid substance flow on to a piece of white paper, assumes the significance of copulation, or as soon as walking becomes a symbolic substitute for treading[2] upon the body of mother earth, both writing and walking are stopped because they represent the performance of a forbidden sexual act. The ego renounces those functions, which are within its sphere, in order not to have to

[1] In his paper 'Fear, Guilt and Hate' (1929), Ernest Jones made a comprehensive study of the interaction between these emotions.
[2] *Inhibitions, Symptoms and Anxiety* (1926), pp. 16–17. In the original the word used by Freud was '*stampfen*', which should be translated by 'trampling'; it conveys more violence and hostility than is expressed by 'treading'.

undertake fresh measures of repression—in order to avoid coming into conflict with the id.'

In the light of the theory of the fusion between libido and destructive impulses the processes of inhibition come once more under discussion. We do not propose to deal with this problem thoroughly, but wish to show in broad lines our approach to it. The two examples mentioned in the quotation above (writing assuming the significance of copulation, and walking that of trampling upon the mother's body) are not on the same level. The latter obviously contains a considerable measure of cruelty, and we venture to think that it is precisely this, the phantasy of violence, derived from the admixture of destructiveness, which causes anxiety and guilt and enforces—by the intervention of the super-ego—an inhibition of that activity. If in his phantasies the subject feels he would trample on his mother's body, he comes to be afraid that he would destroy her, and it is his depressive and persecutory anxieties which bring about the inhibition of walking. In a similar way writing will be inhibited if its anal- and urethral-sadistic meanings predominate over the reparative and genital phantasies and for this reason call forth defensive mechanisms by the ego.

Regression and Defusion

Turning now to the metapsychological aspect of regression, we find ourselves confronted with a great number of problems which cannot be regarded as finally settled, although Freud brought forward certain essential considerations. He put the phenomena of fusion and defusion into the focus of the problem and linked regression with defusion. Regression and defusion are to be regarded as different aspects of the same highly complex phenomenon. 'Making a swift generalization, we might conjecture that the essence of a regression of libido, e.g. from the genital to the sadistic-anal level, would lie in a defusion of instincts, just as, conversely, the advance from an earlier to the definitive genital phase would be conditioned by an accession of erotic components.'[1] And again: 'As regards the metapsychological explanation of regression, I am inclined to find it in a "defusion of instinct", in a detachment of the erotic com-

[1] *The Ego and the Id* (1923), pp. 57–8.

ponents which at the beginning of the genital stage had become joined to the destructive cathexes belonging to the sadistic phase.'[1]

These statements could be taken to imply that the fusion of the instincts is broken up when regression takes place, and that there is no fusion at the pre-genital stages which are re-occupied in the backward flow of the instincts. This implication could, however, scarcely be correct. Freud repeatedly emphasized that the two opposed instincts always occur in a state of fusion, and direct analytic observations fully bear out this view. We quote two passages from Freud. 'As a result of theoretical considerations, supported by biology, we assumed the existence of a death instinct. . . . This hypothesis throws no light whatever upon the manner in which the two classes of instinct are fused, blended and mingled with each other, but that this takes place regularly and very extensively is an assumption indispensable to our conception.'[2] And: '. . . what we are concerned with are scarcely ever pure instinctual impulses but mixtures in varying proportions of the two groups of instincts. . . .'[3]

These passages clearly exclude the idea of there being no fusion at the pre-genital stages. It seems rather that Freud did not envisage a complete, but only a partial detachment of the erotic components. Such partial detachment would suffice to bring about regression and a strengthening of the destructive impulses, although there is still a fusion of the instincts at the lower level to which regression proceeds. This view would be in accordance with Freud's statement about the varying proportions in the ever-present mixture of the two instincts, and with his differentiation of the pre-genital and genital phases with regard to the proportion of the two instincts. The salient point in the processes described as defusion lies, in our view, in an effective strengthening of the destructive component, whether this be due to a quantitative or a constellative factor.

It may be useful to state again briefly our views about the interaction of regression and fixation. We know Freud's view that regression becomes possible by virtue of the formation of

[1] *Inhibitions, Symptoms and Anxiety* (1926), p. 63.
[2] *The Ego and the Id* (1923), p. 56.
[3] *Inhibitions, Symptoms and Anxiety* (1926), p. 84.

fixation-points. On the journey to genital sexuality, we pass through various points, stations, as it were, in development; and since some part of the libido—together with some part of the aggressive impulses, in our view—is left at those 'stations', we may return to them, may regress. It is worth while reminding ourselves that this journey is an *internal* process and that the stations are inside ourselves. The impulses 'left behind' are actually within ourselves—just as our memories are; and those, we know, are never lost by the psyche which has once experienced them, although they may appear to be. Thus, whilst we are maintaining our libido at the genital level, the earlier 'points' are still uninterruptedly active *in the unconscious*. The manner and the degree in which the pre-genital impulses and phantasies influence our lives depend partly upon the strength of the libido. In the example of menopausal conflicts, the situation is not simply that there is a regression to the anal-sadistic stage. Under the stress of the many conflicts involved in the loss of procreation, all the earlier impulses and phantasies may become active. This creates a hard task of psychical adjustment for every woman; yet she may pull through without definitely regressing. This process of combating the freshly stimulated activities of the pre-genital elements is a temporary and fluid condition which is not in itself a regression. The existence of the struggle and the need for a readjustment is a proof of the dynamic potentialities of the fixation-points.

This helps us over one difficulty, but still others have to be faced. The problem of the quantity of the libido and the destructive instincts, for instance, must be considered. Does the absolute amount of instinctual energy remain the same throughout life? Does the energy of one instinct, say that of the libido, increase, and that of the other decrease? Are such quantitative changes responsible for the prescribed order of instinctual phases? Or does the total amount of both instincts remain unaltered and have we to explain the changes in the primacy of the phases merely by the successive cathexis of one zone after another?

Some observations speak for the assumption of quantitative changes in the course of life. It would appear that Freud was inclined to this view. He says: 'As a result of reaching a certain

period in life, and in accordance with regular biological
processes, the quantity of libido in the mental economy has
increased to an extent which by itself suffices to upset the
balance of health and establish the conditions for neurosis. As
is well known, such rather sudden intensifications in libido are
regularly connected with puberty and the menopause, with the
reaching of a certain age in women; in many people they may
in addition manifest themselves in periodicities as yet un-
recognized.'[1]

On the other hand, there are considerations which would be
in favour of another view, also expressed by Freud, that libidinal
satisfaction is highest at the breast, and never again attained,
and that the child's first, most primal impulses 'have an intensity of their own which is greater than anything that comes
later'.[2] These impressions do not suggest a weak instinctual life
at the beginning, which becomes stronger in the course of
development. It still might be possible that periodic increases
occur, however, as for instance when the capacity for procreation is attained. This view may have to be balanced against
a number of other considerations: e.g. naivety *versus* sophistica-
tion, on the one hand, and on the other, the contribution of
earlier to later experiences, as already discussed. The peculiar
intensity of naïve, primal impulse is implicit in the height of
adult mature libidinal experience, *i.e.* genital orgasm.

These are speculations to which we are tempted by the
'indefinite' character of the instincts. After all, Freud calls the
instincts 'mythological beings, superb in their indefiniteness'
(*New Introductory Lectures*, p. 124). We may remember that the
instincts belong to the borderland between soma and psyche,
and that our field is that of the psyche, whilst we look to the
physiologist to provide us with the complementary data. We
may speculate about the instincts, but our convictions are
derived from psychological observation, from the investigation
of behaviour, feelings, emotions, phantasies. It may be that not
absolute quantities of instinctual energy, but specific features,

---

[1] 'Types of Neurotic Nosogenesis' (1912), p. 118.
[2] 'Female Sexuality' (1931), p. 297. Also cf. *Introductory Lectures* (1916–17),
p. 264: 'Satisfaction at the breast is the unattainable prototype of every
later satisfaction.'

inherent in the organ which has the lead, decide the issue between the fused instincts; and that the function of the organ stamps its character on the instinctual stage reached. By virtue of its super-personal function of procreation, the genital would be best endowed to serve the purposes of the life instinct, so that by its operation a condition is brought about which amounts to an 'accession of erotic components'. But we cannot consider only the biological function of the organ which has the primacy. The *phantasies* associated with the various organs and their functions decide the issue psychologically. The first zones of instinctual experience are charged with phantasies of a strongly aggressive order. In advancing to the primacy of the genital, the primitive destructive impulses become modified and worked over, and the destructive phantasies become milder. Those phantasies associated with procreation are naturally and inevitably of a creative and reparative type.

Freud was inclined to the view that quantitative factors decide progression and regression, but he was also convinced of the significance of 'the manner in which the two classes of instinct are fused, blended, mingled with each other'. We have tried to show how oral elements may enrich genital experiences, in that the penis, in addition to its genital function as such, may also in phantasy take over functions of feeding and comforting. Some of the pre-genital elements are, however, not suitable to enter genitality.

It is probable that one of the functions of the libido is to bind the destructive instincts, to drain the sources of destructive impulses and thus to master them. The libido would succeed best at the genital stage in utilizing the destructive impulses for its own purposes, thus attaining the overlordship in the fusion. That there is a fusion of the instincts even at the genital phase is clearly demonstrated to us by the analysis of impotence and frigidity, in which the fear of aggression leads to inhibition of the sexual act. As is well known, a certain degree and mode of aggressive elements, or to put it more specifically, a certain contribution from the derivatives of the destructive instinct, are indispensable for the functioning of genitality. But the ego can allow the destructive impulses to enter into the genital act only if the mastery of the libido is assured; that is to say, if a far-reaching modification of their aims under the influence of the libido has already been attained.

To summarize: it cannot be doubted that there is a fusion of the opposed instincts at every stage of development. The character of that fusion, however, varies with the stages, but we are not yet in a position to say precisely in what this character consists. The safest hypothesis seems to be that it is not determined only by quantitative factors. As is suggested in Chapter X, the predominance of the life instinct cannot be understood in quantitative terms only. The interrelation between the instincts, the manner of their 'blending and mingling', is at least as important, and may turn out to be the essence of the matter.

Defusion would then mean a breaking up of that particular admixture, the overthrow of the rule of the libido in that form and not merely a detachment of the libidinal components or a diminution of their quantity.

If such detachment does take place, however, we have to account for the detached amount of libido. We know that Freud held that libido which becomes detached from objects is transferred into ego-libido and augments the primary narcissism. If we apply this conclusion to the defusion in regression, narcissism and regression have thus to be brought into relation with each other. As was pointed out in Chapter IV on 'Introjection and Projection', narcissism is in our view bound up with the subject's relation to his internal objects. Regression would thus involve the internal-object system of phantasies and feelings. We cannot however attempt to deal with this important problem within the framework of this chapter. (We have drawn attention above to the role of the super-ego in regression.)

The phenomena comprised in regression are thus, in our view, highly complex and fluid, involving a shifting equilibrium —and loss of equilibrium—on all sides of the mental life. As we suggested, the backward flow of libido and destructive instincts requires to be considered within the context of emotional experience and phantasy-life.

VI

SOME THEORETICAL CONCLUSIONS REGARDING THE EMOTIONAL LIFE OF THE INFANT[1]

By MELANIE KLEIN

M Y study of the infant's mind has made me more and more aware of the bewildering complexity of the processes which operate, to a large extent simultaneously, in the early stages of development. In writing this chapter I have therefore attempted to elucidate some aspects only of the infant's emotional life during his first year, and have selected these with particular emphasis on anxieties, defences and object-relations.

The First Three or Four Months of Life
(The Paranoid-Schizoid Position)[2]

I

At the beginning of post-natal life the infant experiences anxiety from internal and external sources. I have for many years held the view that the working of the death instinct within gives rise to the fear of annihilation and that this is the primary cause of persecutory anxiety. The first external source of anxiety can be found in the experience of birth. This experience, which, according to Freud, provides the pattern for all later anxiety-situations, is bound to influence the infant's first relations with the external world.[3] It would appear that

---

[1] I have received valuable assistance in my contributions to this volume from my friend, Lola Brook, who went carefully over my manuscripts and made a number of helpful suggestions, both as regards formulations and the arrangement of the material. I am much indebted to her for her unfailing interest in my work.

[2] In Chapter IX, 'Notes on Some Schizoid Mechanisms', which deals in more detail with this subject, I mention that I have adopted Fairbairn's term 'schizoid' in addition to my own term 'paranoid position'.

[3] In *Inhibitions, Symptoms and Anxiety* (1926), p. 109, Freud states that 'there is much more continuity between intra-uterine life and the earliest infancy than the impressive caesura of the act of birth allows us to believe'.

the pain and discomfort he has suffered, as well as the loss of the intra-uterine state, are felt by him as an attack by hostile forces, *i.e.* as persecution.[1] Persecutory anxiety, therefore, enters from the beginning into his relation to objects in so far as he is exposed to privations.

The hypothesis that the infant's first experiences of feeding and of his mother's presence initiate an object-relation to her is one of the basic concepts put forward in this book.[2] This relation is at first a relation to a part-object, for both oral-libidinal and oral-destructive impulses from the beginning of life are directed towards the mother's breast in particular. We assume that there is always an interaction, although in varying proportions, between libidinal and aggressive impulses, corresponding to the fusion between life and death instincts. It could be conceived that in periods of freedom from hunger and tension there is an optimal balance between libidinal and aggressive impulses. This equilibrium is disturbed whenever, owing to privations from internal or external sources, aggressive impulses are reinforced. I suggest that such an alteration in the balance between libido and aggression gives rise to the emotion called greed, which is first and foremost of an oral nature. Any increase in greed strengthens feelings of frustration and in turn the aggressive impulses. In those children in whom the innate aggressive component is strong, persecutory anxiety, frustration and greed are easily aroused and this contributes to the infant's difficulty in tolerating privation and in dealing with anxiety. Accordingly, the strength of the destructive impulses in their interaction with libidinal impulses would provide the constitutional basis for the intensity of greed. However, while in some cases persecutory anxiety may increase greed, in others (as I suggested in *The Psycho-Analysis of Children*) it may become the cause of the earliest feeding inhibitions.

The recurrent experiences of gratification and frustration are powerful stimuli for libidinal and destructive impulses, for love and hatred. As a result, the breast, inasmuch as it is gratifying,

---

[1] I have suggested that the struggle between the life and death instincts already enters into the painful experience of birth and adds to the persecutory anxiety aroused by it. Cf. Chapter VIII.

[2] Cf. Chapters III, IV and VII.

is loved and felt to be 'good'; in so far as it is a source of frustration, it is hated and felt to be 'bad'. This strong antithesis between the good breast and the bad breast is largely due to lack of integration of the ego, as well as to splitting processes within the ego and in relation to the object. There are, however, grounds for assuming that even during the first three or four months of life the good and the bad object are not wholly distinct from one another in the infant's mind. The mother's breast, both in its good and bad aspects, also seems to merge for him with her bodily presence; and the relation to her as a person is thus gradually built up from the earliest stage onwards.

In addition to the experiences of gratification and frustration derived from external factors, a variety of endopsychic processes—primarily introjection and projection—contribute to the twofold relation to the first object. The infant projects his love impulses and attributes them to the gratifying (good) breast; just as he projects his destructive impulses outwards and attributes them to the frustrating (bad) breast. Simultaneously, by introjection, a good breast and a bad breast are established inside.[1] Thus the picture of the object, external and internalized, is distorted in the infant's mind by his phantasies, which are bound up with the projection of his impulses on to the object. The good breast—external and internal—becomes the prototype of all helpful and gratifying objects, the bad breast the prototype of all external and internal persecutory objects. The various factors which enter into the infant's feeling of being gratified, such as the alleviation of hunger, the pleasure of sucking, the freedom from discomfort and tension, i.e. from privations, and the experience of being loved—all these are attributed to the good breast. Conversely, every frustration and discomfort are attributed to the bad (persecuting) breast.

I shall first describe the ramifications of the infant's relation to the bad breast. If we consider the picture which exists in the infant's mind—as we can see it retrospectively in the analyses of children and adults—we find that the hated breast has

---

[1] These first introjected objects form the core of the super-ego. In my view the super-ego starts with the earliest introjection processes and builds itself up from the good and bad figures which are internalized in love and hatred in various stages of development and are gradually assimilated and integrated by the ego. Cf. Chapter IV.

acquired the oral-destructive qualities of the infant's own impulses when he is in states of frustration and hatred. In his
destructive phantasies he bites and tears up the breast, devours
it, annihilates it; and he feels that the breast will attack him in
the same way. As urethral- and anal-sadistic impulses gain in
strength, the infant in his mind attacks the breast with poisonous
urine and explosive faeces, and therefore expects it to be
poisonous and explosive towards him. The details of his sadistic
phantasies determine the content of his fear of internal and external persecutors, primarily of the retaliating (bad) breast.[1]

Since the phantasied attacks on the object are fundamentally
influenced by greed, the fear of the object's greed, owing to
projection, is an essential element in persecutory anxiety: the
bad breast will devour him in the same greedy way as he desires
to devour it.

Even during the earliest stage, however, persecutory anxiety
is to some extent counteracted by the infant's relation to the
good breast. I have indicated above that although his feelings
focus on the feeding relationship with the mother, represented
by her breast, other aspects of the mother enter already into the
earliest relation to her; for even the very young infant responds
to his mother's smile, her hands, her voice, her holding him and
attending to his needs. The gratification and love which the
infant experiences in these situations all help to counteract persecutory anxiety, even the feelings of loss and persecution
aroused by the experience of birth. His physical nearness to his
mother during feeding—essentially his relation to the good
breast—recurrently helps him to overcome the longing for a
former lost state, alleviates persecutory anxiety and increases
the trust in the good object. (Ch. N. 1.)

II

It is characteristic of the emotions of the very young infant
that they are of an extreme and powerful nature. The frustrating

[1] The anxiety relating to attacks by internalized objects—first of all part-
objects—is in my view the basis of hypochondria. I put forward this hypothesis in my book *The Psycho-Analysis of Children*, pp. 204, 350, 362, and also
expounded there my view that the early infantile anxieties are psychotic in
nature and the basis for later psychoses.

(bad) object is felt to be a terrifying persecutor, the good breast tends to turn into the 'ideal' breast which should fulfil the greedy desire for unlimited, immediate and everlasting gratification. Thus feelings arise about a perfect and inexhaustible breast, always available, always gratifying. Another factor which makes for idealization of the good breast is the strength of the infant's persecutory fear, which creates the need to be protected from persecutors and therefore goes to increase the power of an all-gratifying object. The idealized breast forms the corollary of the persecuting breast; and in so far as idealization is derived from the need to be protected from persecuting objects, it is a method of defence against anxiety.

The instance of hallucinatory gratification may help us to understand the ways in which the process of idealization comes about. In this state, frustration and anxiety derived from various sources are done away with, the lost external breast is regained and the feeling of having the ideal breast inside (possessing it) is reactivated. We may also assume that the infant hallucinates the longed-for pre-natal state. Because the hallucinated breast is inexhaustible, greed is momentarily satisfied. (But sooner or later, the feeling of hunger turns the child back to the external world and then frustration, with all the emotions to which it gives rise, is again experienced.) In wish-fulfilling hallucination, a number of fundamental mechanisms and defences come into play. One of them is the omnipotent control of the internal and external object, for the ego assumes complete possession of both the external and internal breast. Furthermore, in hallucination the persecuting breast is kept widely apart from the ideal breast, and the experience of being frustrated from the experience of being gratified. It seems that such a cleavage, which amounts to a splitting of the object and of the feelings towards it, is linked with the process of denial. Denial in its most extreme form—as we find it in hallucinatory gratification—amounts to an annihilation of any frustrating object or situation, and is thus bound up with the strong feeling of omnipotence which obtains in the early stages of life. The situation of being frustrated, the object which causes it, the bad feelings to which frustration gives rise (as well as split-off parts of the ego) are felt to have gone out of existence, to have been annihilated, and by these means gratification and relief from persecutory anxiety are obtained. Annihilation of the persecutory object and of a persecutory situation is bound up with omnipotent control of the object in its most extreme form. I would suggest that in some measure these processes are operative in idealization as well.

It would appear that the early ego also employs the mechanism of annihilation of one split-off aspect of the object and situation in states other than wish-fulfilling hallucinations. For instance, in hallucinations of persecution, the *frightening* aspect of the object and situation seems to prevail to such an extent that the good aspect is felt to have been utterly destroyed—a process which I cannot discuss here. It seems that the extent to which the ego keeps the two aspects apart varies considerably in different states and on this may depend whether or not the aspect which is denied is felt to have gone completely out of existence.

Persecutory anxiety essentially influences these processes. We may assume that when persecutory anxiety is less strong, splitting is less far-reaching and the ego is therefore able to integrate itself and to synthesize in some measure the feelings towards the object. It might well be that any such step in integration can only come about if, at that moment, love towards the object predominates over the destructive impulses (ultimately the life instinct over the death instinct). The ego's tendency to integrate itself can, therefore, I think, be considered as an expression of the life instinct.

Synthesis between feelings of love and destructive impulses towards one and the same object—the breast—gives rise to depressive anxiety, guilt and the urge to make reparation to the injured loved object, the good breast. This implies that ambivalence is at times experienced in relation to a part-object—the mother's breast.[1] During the first few months of life, such states of integration are short-lived. At this stage the ego's capacity to achieve integration is naturally still very limited and to this contributes the strength of persecutory anxiety and of

---

[1] In my paper 'A Contribution to the Genesis of Manic-Depressive States', I suggested that ambivalence is first experienced in relation to the complete object during the depressive position. In keeping with the modification of my view regarding the onset of depressive anxiety (cf. Chapter VIII) I now consider that ambivalence, too, is already experienced in relation to part-objects.

the splitting processes which are at their height. It seems that, as development proceeds, experiences of synthesis and, in consequence, of depressive anxiety, become more frequent and last longer; all this forms part of the growth of integration. With progress in integration and synthesis of the contrasting emotions towards the object, mitigation of destructive impulses by libido becomes possible.[1] This however leads to an *actual diminution* of anxiety which is a fundamental condition for normal development.

As I suggested, there are great variations in the strength, frequency and duration of splitting processes (not only between individuals but also in the same infant at different times). It is part of the complexity of early emotional life that a multitude of processes operate in swiftest alternation, or even, it seems, simultaneously. For instance, it appears that together with splitting the breast into two aspects, loved and hated (good and bad), splitting of a different nature exists which gives rise to the feeling that the ego, as well as its object, is in pieces; these processes underlie states of disintegration.[2] Such states, as I pointed out above, alternate with others in which a measure of integration of the ego and synthesis of the object increasingly comes about.

The early methods of splitting fundamentally influence the ways in which, at a somewhat later stage, repression is carried out and this in turn determines the degree of interaction between conscious and unconscious. In other words, the extent to which the various parts of the mind remain 'porous' in relation to one another is determined largely by the strength or weakness of the early schizoid mechanisms.[3] External factors

---

[1] This form of interaction between libido and aggression would correspond to a particular state of fusion between the two instincts.

[2] Cf. Chapter IX.

[3] I found that with patients of a schizoid type, the strength of their infantile schizoid mechanisms ultimately accounts for the difficulty of getting access to the unconscious. In such patients, the progress towards synthesis is hampered by the fact that under the pressure of anxiety they become again and again unable to maintain the links, which have been strengthened in the course of the analysis, between different parts of the self. In patients of a depressive type, the division between unconscious and conscious is less pronounced and therefore such patients are much more capable of insight. In my view they have overcome more successfully their schizoid mechanisms in early infancy.

play a vital part from the beginning; for we have reason to assume that every stimulus to persecutory fear reinforces the schizoid mechanisms, *i.e.* the tendency of the ego to split itself and the object; while every good experience strengthens the trust in the good object and makes for integration of the ego and synthesis of the object.

III

Some of Freud's conclusions imply that the ego develops by introjecting objects. As regards the earliest phase, the good breast, introjected in situations of gratification and happiness, becomes in my view a vital part of the ego and strengthens its capacity for integration. For this internal good breast—forming also the helpful and benign aspect of the early super-ego—strengthens the infant's capacity to love and trust his objects, heightens the stimulus for introjection of good objects and situations, and is therefore an essential source of reassurance against anxiety ; it becomes the representative of the life instinct within. The good object can, however, only fulfil these functions if it is felt to be in an undamaged state, which implies that it has been internalized predominantly with feelings of gratification and love. Such feelings presuppose that gratification by sucking has been relatively undisturbed by external or internal factors. The main source of internal disturbance lies in excessive aggressive impulses, which increase greed and diminish the capacity to bear frustration. In other terms, when, in the fusion of the two instincts, the life instinct predominates over the death instinct—and correspondingly libido over aggression—the good breast can be more securely established in the infant's mind.

However, the infant's oral-sadistic desires, which are active from the beginning of life and are easily stirred by frustration from external and internal sources, inevitably again and again give rise to a feeling that the breast is destroyed and in bits inside him, as a result of his greedy devouring attacks upon it. These two aspects of introjection exist side by side.

Whether feelings of frustration or gratification predominate in the infant's relation to the breast is no doubt largely influenced by external circumstances but there is little doubt that constitutional factors, influencing from the beginning the strength of the ego, have to be taken into account. I formerly made the suggestion that the ego's capacity to bear tension and anxiety, and therefore in some measure to tolerate frustration, is a constitutional factor.[1] This greater inborn capacity to bear anxiety seems ultimately to depend on the prevalence of libido over aggressive impulses, that is to say, on the part which the life instinct plays from the outset in the fusion of the two instincts.

My hypothesis that the oral libido expressed in the sucking function enables the infant to introject the breast (and nipple) as a relatively undestroyed object does not run counter to the assumption that destructive impulses are most powerful in the earliest stages. The factors which influence the fusion and defusion of the two instincts are still obscure, but there is little reason to doubt that in the relation to the first object—the breast—the ego is at times able, by means of splitting, to keep libido apart from aggression.[2]

I shall now turn to the part which projection plays in the vicissitudes of persecutory anxiety. I have described elsewhere[3] how the oral-sadistic impulses to devour and scoop out the mother's breast become elaborated into the phantasies of devouring and scooping out the mother's body. Attacks derived from all other sources of sadism soon become linked with these oral attacks and two main lines of sadistic phantasies develop. One form—mainly oral-sadistic and bound up with greed—is to empty the mother's body of everything good and desirable. The other form of phantasied attack—predominantly anal—is to fill her body with the bad substances and parts of the self which are split off and projected into her. These are mainly

---

[1] Cf. *Psycho-Analysis of Children*, Chapter 3, p. 83, n.

[2] It is implicit in my argument (as presented here and in former writings) that I do not agree with Abraham's concept of a pre-ambivalent stage in so far as it implies that destructive (oral-sadistic) impulses first arise with the onset of teething. We have to remember, though, that Abraham has also pointed out the sadism inherent in 'vampire-like' sucking. There is no doubt that the onset of teething and the physiological processes which affect the gums are a strong stimulus for cannibalistic impulses and phantasies; but aggression forms part of the infant's earliest relation to the breast, though it is not usually expressed in biting at this stage.

[3] Cf. *Psycho-Analysis of Children*, p. 185.

represented by excrements which become the means of damaging, destroying or controlling the attacked object. Or the whole self—felt to be the 'bad' self—enters the mother's body and takes control of it. In these various phantasies, the ego takes possession by projection of an external object—first of all the mother—and makes it into an extension of the self. The object becomes to some extent a representative of the ego, and these processes are in my view the basis for identification by projection or 'projective identification'.[1] Identification by introjection and identification by projection appear to be complementary processes. It seems that the processes underlying projective identification operate already in the earliest relation to the breast. The 'vampire-like' sucking, the scooping out of the breast, develop in the infant's phantasy into making his way into the breast and further into the mother's body. Accordingly, projective identification would start simultaneously with the greedy oral-sadistic introjection of the breast. This hypothesis is in keeping with the view often expressed by the writer that introjection and projection interact from the beginning of life. The introjection of a persecutory object is, as we have seen, to some extent determined by the projection of destructive impulses on to the object. The drive to project (expel) badness is increased by fear of internal persecutors. When projection is dominated by persecutory fear, the object into whom badness (the bad self) has been projected becomes the persecutor *par excellence*, because it has been endowed with all the bad qualities of the subject. The re-introjection of this object reinforces acutely the fear of internal and external persecutors. (The death instinct, or rather, the dangers attaching to it, has again been turned inwards.) There is thus a constant interaction between persecutory fear relating to the internal and external worlds, an interaction in which the processes involved in projective identification play a vital part.

The projection of love-feelings—underlying the process of attaching libido to the object—is, as I suggested, a precondition for finding a good object. The introjection of a good object stimulates the projection of good feelings outwards and this in turn by re-introjection strengthens the feeling of possessing a

[1] Cf. Chapter IX.

good internal object. To the projection of the bad self into the object and the external world corresponds the projection of good parts of the self, or of the whole good self. Re-introjection of the good object and of the good self reduces persecutory anxiety. Thus the relation to both the internal and external world improves simultaneously and the ego gains in strength and in integration.

Progress in integration which, as I suggested in an earlier section, depends on love-impulses predominating temporarily over destructive impulses, leads to transitory states in which the ego synthesizes feelings of love and destructive impulses towards one object (first the mother's breast). This synthetic process initiates further important steps in development (which may well occur simultaneously): the painful emotions of depressive anxiety and guilt arise; aggression is mitigated by libido; in consequence, persecutory anxiety is diminished; anxiety relating to the fate of the endangered external and internal object leads to a stronger identification with it; the ego therefore strives to make reparation and also inhibits aggressive impulses felt to be dangerous to the loved object.[1]

With growing integration of the ego, experiences of depressive anxiety increase in frequency and duration. Simultaneously, as the range of perception increases, in the infant's mind the concept of the mother as a whole and unique person develops out of a relation to parts of her body and to various aspects of her personality (such as her smell, touch, voice, smile, the sound of her footsteps, etc.). Depressive anxiety and guilt gradually focus on the mother as a person and increase in intensity; the depressive position comes to the fore.

---

[1] Abraham refers to instinctual inhibition appearing first at '. . . the stage of narcissism with a cannibalistic sexual aim' ('A Short Study of the Development of the Libido', p. 496). Since inhibition of aggressive impulses and of greed tends to involve libidinal desires as well, depressive anxiety becomes the cause for those difficulties in accepting food which occur in infants at a few months of age and increase at weaning time. As regards the earliest feeding difficulties, which arise with some infants from the first few days onwards, they are caused, in my view, by persecutory anxiety. (Cf. *Psycho-Analysis of Children*, pp. 219–20.)

IV

I have so far described some aspects of mental life during the first three or four months. (It must be kept in mind, though, that only a rough estimate can be given of the duration of stages of development, as there are great individual variations.) In the picture of this stage, as I presented it, certain features stand out as characteristic. The paranoid-schizoid position is dominant. The interaction between the processes of introjection and projection—re-introjection and re-projection—determines ego-development. The relation to the loved and hated—good and bad—breast is the infant's first object-relation. Destructive impulses and persecutory anxiety are at their height. The desire for unlimited gratification, as well as persecutory anxiety, contribute to the infant's feeling that both an ideal breast and a dangerous devouring breast exist, which are largely kept apart from each other in the infant's mind. These two aspects of the mother's breast are introjected and form the core of the super-ego. Splitting, omnipotence, idealization, denial and control of internal and external objects are dominant at that stage. These first methods of defence are of an extreme nature, in keeping with the intensity of early emotions and the limited capacity of the ego to bear acute anxiety. While in some ways these defences impede the path of integration, they are essential for the whole development of the ego, for they again and again relieve the young infant's anxieties. This relative and temporary security is achieved predominantly by the persecutory object being kept apart from the good one. The presence in the mind of the good (ideal) object enables the ego to maintain at times strong feelings of love and gratification. The good object also affords protection against the persecuting object because it is felt to have replaced it (as instanced by wish-fulfilling hallucination). These processes underlie, I think, the observable fact that young infants alternate so swiftly between states of complete gratification and of great distress. At this early stage the ego's ability to deal with anxiety by allowing the contrasting emotions towards the mother, and accordingly the two aspects of her, to come together is still very limited. This implies that a mitigation of the fear of the bad object by the trust in the good one and depressive anxiety only arise in fleeting experiences. Out of the alternating processes of disintegration and integration develops gradually a more integrated ego, with an increased capacity to deal with persecutory anxiety. The infant's relation to parts of his mother's body, focussing on her breast, gradually changes into a relation to her as a person.

These processes present in earliest infancy may be considered under a few headings:

(a) An ego which has some rudiments of integration and cohesion, and progresses increasingly in that direction. It also performs from the beginning of post-natal life some fundamental functions; thus it uses splitting processes and the inhibition of instinctual desires as some of the defences against persecutory anxiety, which is experienced by the ego from birth onwards.

(b) Object-relations, which are shaped by libido and aggression, by love and hatred, and permeated on the one hand by persecutory anxiety, on the other by its corollary, the omnipotent reassurance derived from the idealization of the object.

(c) Introjection and projection, bound up with the phantasy-life of the infant and all his emotions, and consequently internalized objects of a good and bad nature, which initiate super-ego development.

As the ego becomes increasingly able to sustain anxiety, the methods of defence alter correspondingly. To this contributes the growing sense of reality and the widening range of gratification, interests and object-relations. Destructive impulses and persecutory anxiety decrease in power; depressive anxiety gains in strength and comes to a climax at the period which I shall describe in the next section.

The Infantile Depressive Position

I

During the second quarter of the first year certain changes in the infant's intellectual and emotional development become marked. His relation to the external world, to people as well as to things, grows more differentiated. The range of his gratifications and interests widens, and his power of expressing his emotions and communicating with people increases. These observable changes are evidence of the gradual development of the ego. Integration, consciousness, intellectual capacities, the relation to the external world and other functions of the ego are steadily developing. At the same time the infant's sexual organization is progressing; urethral, anal and genital trends increase in strength, though oral impulses and desires still predominate. There is thus a confluence of different sources of libido and aggression, which colours the infant's emotional life and brings into prominence various new anxiety-situations; the range of phantasies is widening, they become more elaborated and differentiated. Correspondingly there are important changes in the nature of defences.

All these developments are reflected in the infant's relation to his mother (and to some extent to his father and to other people). The relation to the mother as a person, which has been gradually developing while the breast still figured as the main object, becomes more fully established and the identification with her gains in strength when the infant can perceive and introject the mother as a person (or, in other words, as a 'complete object').

While some measure of integration is a precondition for the ego's capacity to introject the mother and the father as whole persons, further development on the line of integration and synthesis is initiated when the depressive position comes to the fore. The various aspects—loved and hated, good and bad—of the objects come closer together, and these objects are now whole persons. The processes of synthesis operate over the whole field of external and internal object-relations. They comprise the contrasting aspects of the internalized objects (the early super-ego) on the one hand and of the external objects on the other; but the ego is also driven to diminish the discrepancy between the external and internal world, or rather, the discrepancy between external and internal figures. Together with these synthetic processes go further steps in integration of the ego, which result in a greater coherence between the split-off parts of the ego. All these processes of integration and synthesis cause the conflict between love and hatred to come out in full force. The ensuing depressive anxiety and feelings of guilt alter not only in quantity but also in quality. Ambivalence is now experienced predominantly towards a complete object. Love and hatred have come much closer together and the 'good' and 'bad' breast, 'good' and 'bad' mother, cannot be kept as widely separated as in the earlier stage. Although the power of destructive impulses diminishes, these impulses are felt to be a great danger to the loved object, now perceived as a person. Greed and the defences against it play a significant part at this stage, for the anxiety of losing irretrievably the loved and indispensable object tends to increase greed. Greed, however, is felt to be uncontrollable and destructive and to endanger the loved external and internal objects. The ego therefore increasingly inhibits instinctual desires and this may lead to severe difficulties in the infant's enjoying or accepting food,[1] and later to serious inhibitions in establishing both affectionate and erotic relations.

The steps in integration and synthesis described above result in a greater capacity of the ego to acknowledge the increasingly poignant psychic reality. The anxiety relating to the internalized mother who is felt to be injured, suffering, in danger of being annihilated or already annihilated and lost for ever, leads to a stronger identification with the injured object. This identification reinforces both the drive to make reparation and the ego's attempts to inhibit aggressive impulses. The ego also again and again makes use of the manic defence. As we have seen already, denial, idealization, splitting and control of internal and external objects are used by the ego in order to counteract persecutory anxiety. These omnipotent methods are, in some measure, maintained when the depressive position arises but they are now predominantly used in order to counteract depressive anxiety. They also undergo changes, in keeping with the steps in integration and synthesis, that is to say they become less extreme and correspond more to the growing capacity of the ego to face psychic reality. With this altered form and aim, these early methods now constitute the manic defence.

---

[1] Such difficulties, which can be frequently observed in infants particularly at weaning (*i.e.* during the change-over from breast- to bottle-feeding or when new foods are added to bottle-feeding, etc.) can be regarded as a depressive symptom well known in the symptomatology of depressive states. This point is dealt with in some detail in Chapter VII. Cf. also footnote on p. 208 above.

Faced with a multitude of anxiety-situations, the ego tends to deny them and, when anxiety is paramount, the ego even denies the fact that it loves the object at all. The result may be a lasting stifling of love and turning away from the primary objects and an increase in persecutory anxiety, *i.e.* regression to the paranoid-schizoid position.[1]

The ego's attempts to control external and internal objects— a method which, during the paranoid-schizoid position, is mainly directed against persecutory anxiety—also undergo changes. When depressive anxiety has the ascendancy, control of objects and impulses is mainly used by the ego in order to prevent frustration, to forestall aggression and the ensuing danger to the loved objects—that is to say, to keep depressive anxiety at bay.

There is also a difference in the use of splitting the object and the self. The ego, although earlier methods of splitting continue in some degree, now divides the complete object into an uninjured live object and an injured and endangered one (perhaps dying or dead); splitting thus becomes largely a defence against depressive anxiety.

At the same time, important steps in ego-development take place, which not only enable the ego to evolve more adequate defences against anxiety but also eventually result in an actual diminution of anxiety. The continued experience of facing psychic reality, implied in the working through of the depressive position, increases the infant's understanding of the external world. Accordingly the picture of his parents, which was at first distorted into idealized and terrifying figures, comes gradually nearer to reality.

As has been discussed earlier in this chapter, when the infant introjects a more reassuring external reality, his internal world improves; and this by projection in turn benefits his picture of the external world. Gradually, therefore, as the infant re-introjects

---

[1] This early regression may cause severe disturbances in early development, *e.g.* mental deficiency (cf. Chapter IX); it may become the foundation for some form of schizophrenic illness. Another possible outcome of the failure in working through the infantile depressive position is manic-depressive illness; or a severe neurosis may ensue. I therefore hold that the infantile depressive position is of central importance in the development of the first year.

again and again a more realistic and reassuring external world and also in some measure establishes within himself complete and uninjured objects, essential developments in the super-ego organization take place. As, however, good and bad internal objects come closer together—the bad aspects being mitigated by the good ones—the relation between the ego and super-ego alters, that is to say, a progressive assimilation of the super-ego by the ego takes place. (Ch. N. 2.)

At this stage the drive to make reparation to the injured object comes into full play. This tendency, as we have seen earlier, is inextricably linked with feelings of guilt. When the infant feels that his destructive impulses and phantasies are directed against the complete person of his loved object, guilt arises in full strength and, together with it, the over-riding urge to repair, preserve or revive the loved injured object. These emotions in my view amount to states of mourning, and the defences operating to attempts on the part of the ego to overcome mourning.

Since the tendency to make reparation ultimately derives from the life instinct, it draws on libidinal phantasies and desires. This tendency enters into all sublimations, and remains from that stage onwards the great means by which depression is kept at bay and diminished.

It appears that there is no aspect of mental life which is not, in the early stages, used by the ego in defence against anxiety. The reparative tendency, too, first employed in an omnipotent way, becomes an important defence. The infant's feelings (phantasy) might be described as follows: 'My mother is disappearing, she may never return, she is suffering, she is dead. No, this can't be, for I can revive her.'

Omnipotence decreases as the infant gradually gains a greater confidence both in his objects and in his reparative powers.[1] He feels that all steps in development, all new achievements are giving pleasure to the people around him and that in this way he expresses his love, counter-balances or undoes the

---

[1] It can be observed in the analyses both of adults and children that, together with a full experience of depression, feelings of hope emerge. In early development, this is one of the factors which helps the infant to overcome the depressive position.

harm done by his aggressive impulses and makes reparation to his injured loved objects.

Thus the foundations for normal development are laid: relations to people develop, persecutory anxiety relating to internal and external objects diminishes, the good internal objects become more firmly established, a feeling of greater security ensues, and all this strengthens and enriches the ego. The stronger and more coherent ego, although it makes much use of the manic defence, again and again brings together and synthesizes the split-off aspects of the object and of the self. Gradually the processes of splitting and synthesizing are applied to aspects kept apart less widely from one another; perception of reality increases and objects appear in a more realistic light. All these developments lead to a growing adaptation to external and internal reality.[1]

There is a corresponding change in the infant's attitude towards frustration. As we have seen, in the earliest stage the bad persecutory aspect of the mother (her breast) came to stand in the child's mind for everything frustrating and evil, internal as well as external. When the infant's sense of reality in relation to his objects and trust in them increases, he becomes more capable of distinguishing between frustration imposed from without and phantastic internal dangers. Accordingly hatred and aggression become more closely related to the actual frustration or harm derived from external factors. This is a step towards a more realistic and objective method of dealing with his own aggression, which rouses less guilt and ultimately enables the child to experience, as well as to sublimate, his aggression in a more ego-syntonic way.

In addition, this more realistic attitude towards frustration—which implies that persecutory fear relating to internal and external objects has diminished—leads to a greater capacity in the infant to re-establish the good relation to his mother and to other people when the frustrating experience no longer operates. In other words, the growing adaptation to reality—bound up with changes in the working of introjection and projection—

---

[1] As we know, splitting under the stress of ambivalence to some extent persists throughout life and plays an important part in normal mental economy.

results in a more secure relation to the external and internal world. This leads to a lessening of ambivalence and aggression, which makes it possible for the drive for reparation to play its full part. In these ways the process of mourning arising from the depressive position is gradually worked through.

When the infant reaches the crucial stage of about three to six months and is faced with the conflicts, guilt and sorrow inherent in the depressive position, his capacity for dealing with his anxiety is to some degree determined by his earlier development; that is to say, by the extent to which during the first three or four months of life he has been able to take in and establish his good object which forms the core of his ego. If this process has been successful—and this implies that persecutory anxiety and splitting processes are not excessive and that a measure of integration has come about—persecutory anxiety and schizoid mechanisms gradually lose in strength, the ego is able to introject and establish the complete object and to go through the depressive position. If, however, the ego is unable to deal with the many severe anxiety-situations arising at this stage—a failure determined by fundamental internal factors as well as by external experiences—a strong regression from the depressive position to the earlier paranoid-schizoid position may take place. This would also impede the processes of introjection of the complete object and strongly affect the development during the first year of life and throughout childhood.

II

My hypothesis of the infantile depressive position is based on fundamental psycho-analytic concepts regarding the early stages of life; that is to say, primary introjection and the preponderance of oral libido and cannibalistic impulses in young infants. These discoveries by Freud and Abraham have materially contributed to the understanding of the etiology of mental illnesses. By developing these concepts and relating them to the understanding of infants, as it emerged from the analyses of young children, I came to realize the complexity of early processes and experiences and their effect on the infant's emotional life; and this in turn was bound to throw more light on the etiology of mental disturbances. One of my conclusions was that there exists a particularly close link between the infantile depressive position and the phenomena of mourning and melancholia.[1]

Continuing Freud's work on melancholia, Abraham pointed out one of the fundamental differences between normal mourning on the one hand and abnormal mourning on the other. (CH. N. 3.) In normal mourning the individual succeeds in establishing the lost loved person within his ego, whereas in melancholia and abnormal mourning this process is not successful. Abraham also described some of the fundamental factors upon which that success or failure depends. If cannibalistic impulses are excessive, the introjection of the lost loved object miscarries, and this leads to illness. In normal mourning, too, the subject is driven to reinstate the lost loved person within the ego; but this process succeeds. Not only are the cathexes attached to the lost loved object withdrawn and re-invested, as Freud put it, but during this process the lost object is established within.

In my paper on 'Mourning and its Relation to Manic-Depressive States', I expressed the following view: 'My experience leads me to conclude that, while it is true that the characteristic feature of normal mourning is the individual's setting up the lost loved object inside himself, he is not doing so for the first time but, through the work of mourning, is reinstating that object as well as all his loved *internal* objects which he feels he has lost.' Whenever grief arises, it undermines the feeling of secure possession of the loved internal objects, for it revives the early anxieties about injured and destroyed objects—about a shattered inner world. Feelings of guilt and persecutory anxieties—the infantile depressive position—are reactivated in full strength. A successful reinstating of the *external* loved object which is being mourned, and whose introjection is intensified through the process of mourning, implies that the loved *internal* objects are restored and regained. Therefore the testing of

---

[1] For the relation of the infantile depressive position to manic-depressive states on the one hand and to normal grief on the other, cf. my 'A Contribution to the Psychogenesis of Manic-Depressive States' and 'Mourning and its Relation to Manic-Depressive States'.

reality characteristic of the process of mourning is not only a means of renewing the links to the external world but of *re-establishing the disrupted inner world*. Mourning thus involves a repetition of the emotional situation the infant experiences during the depressive position. For under the stress of fear of loss of the loved mother, the infant struggles with the task of establishing and integrating his inner world, of building up securely the good objects within himself.

One of the fundamental factors in determining whether or not the loss of a loved object (through death or other causes) will lead to manic-depressive illness or will be normally overcome is, in my experience, the extent to which, in the first year of life, the depressive position has been successfully worked through and the loved introjected objects securely established within.

The depressive position is bound up with fundamental changes in the infant's libidinal organization, for during this period—about the middle of the first year—the infant enters upon the early stages of the direct and inverted Oedipus complex. I shall restrict myself here to the broadest outline only in giving an account of the early stages of the Oedipus complex.[1] These early stages are characterized by the important role which part-objects still play in the infant's mind while the relation to complete objects is being established. Also, though genital desires are coming strongly to the fore, the oral libido is still leading. Powerful oral desires, increased by the frustration experienced in relation to the mother, are transferred from the mother's breast to the father's penis.[2] Genital desires in the infant of either sex coalesce with oral desires and therefore an oral, as well as a genital, relation to the father's penis ensues. Genital desires are also directed towards the mother. The infant's desires for the father's penis are bound up with jealousy

[1] See Chapter IV, Part 2. I have given detailed accounts of the Oedipus development in my *Psycho-Analysis of Children* (particularly Chapter 8); also in my papers 'Early Stages of the Oedipus Conflict' and 'The Oedipus Complex in the Light of Early Anxieties'.

[2] Abraham writes, in 'A Short Study of the Development of the Libido' (1924), p. 490: 'Another point to be noted in regard to the part of the body that has been introjected is that the penis is regularly assimilated to the female breast, and that other parts of the body, such as the finger, the foot, hair, faeces and buttocks, can be made to stand for those two organs in a secondary way. . . .'

of the mother because he feels she receives this desired object. These manifold emotions and wishes in either sex underlie both the inverted and the direct Oedipus complex.

Another aspect of the early Oedipus stages is bound up with the essential part which the mother's 'inside', and his own 'inside', play in the young infant's mind. During the preceding period, when destructive impulses prevail (paranoid-schizoid position), the infant's urge to enter his mother's body, and take possession of its contents, is predominantly of an oral and anal nature. This urge is still active in the following stage (depressive position), but when genital desires increase it is directed more towards the father's penis (equated to babies and faeces) which, he feels, the mother's body contains. Simultaneously the oral desires for the father's penis lead to its internalization, and this internalized penis—both as a good and bad object—comes to play an important part in the infant's internal object world.

The early stages of the Oedipus development are of the greatest complexity: desires from various sources converge; these desires are directed towards part-objects as well as towards whole objects; the father's penis, both desired and hated, exists not only as a part of the father's body, but is also simultaneously felt by the infant to be inside himself and inside the mother's body.

Envy appears to be inherent in oral greed. My analytic work has shown me that envy (alternating with feelings of love and gratification) is first directed towards the feeding breast. To this primary envy jealousy is added when the Oedipus situation arises. The infant's feelings in relation to both parents seem to run like this: when he is frustrated, father or mother enjoys the desired object of which he is deprived—mother's breast, father's penis—and enjoys it constantly. It is characteristic of the young infant's intense emotions and greed that he should attribute to the parents a constant state of mutual gratification of an oral, anal and genital nature.

These sexual theories are the foundation for combined parent figures such as: the mother containing the father's penis or the whole father; the father containing the mother's breast or the whole mother; the parents fused inseparably in sexual intercourse.[1] Phantasies of this nature also contribute to the notion of 'the woman with a penis'. Furthermore, owing to internalization, the infant establishes such combined parent figures within himself, and this proves fundamental for many anxiety-situations of a psychotic nature.

As, gradually, a more realistic relation to the parents develops, the infant comes to consider them as separate individuals, that is to say, the primitive combined parent figures lose in strength.[2]

These developments are interlinked with the depressive position. In both sexes, the fear of the loss of the mother, the primary loved object—that is to say, depressive anxiety—contributes to the need for substitutes; and the infant first turns to the father, who at this stage is also introjected as a complete person, to fulfil this need.

In these ways, libido and depressive anxiety are deflected to some extent from the mother, and this process of distribution stimulates object-relations as well as diminishes the intensity of depressive feelings. The early stages of the direct and inverted Oedipus complex thus bring relief to the anxieties of the child and help him to overcome the depressive position. At the same time, however, new conflicts and anxieties arise, since the Oedipus wishes towards the parents imply that envy, rivalry and jealousy—at this stage still powerfully stirred by oral-sadistic impulses—are now experienced towards two people who are both hated and loved. The working through of these conflicts, first arising in the early stages of the Oedipus complex, is part of the process of modification of anxiety which extends beyond babyhood into the first years of childhood.

To sum up: the depressive position plays a vital part in the

---

[1] Cf. the concept of the combined parent figure in *Psycho-Analysis of Children*, particularly Chapter 8.

[2] The infant's capacity to enjoy at the same time the relation to *both* parents, which is an important feature in his mental life and conflicts with his desires, prompted by jealousy and anxiety, to separate them, depends on his feeling that they are separate individuals. This more integrated relation to the parents (which is distinct from the compulsive need to keep the parents apart from one another and to prevent their sexual intercourse) implies a greater understanding of their relation to one another and is a precondition for the infant's hope that he can bring them together and unite them in a happy way.

child's early development and normally, when the infantile neurosis comes to an end at about five years of age, persecutory and depressive anxieties have undergone modification. The fundamental steps in working through the depressive position are, however, made when the infant is establishing the complete object—that is to say, during the second half of the first year— and one might contend that if these processes are successful, one of the preconditions for normal development is fulfilled. During this period persecutory and depressive anxiety are again and again activated, as for instance in the experiences of teething and weaning. This interaction between anxiety and physical factors is one aspect of the complex processes of development (involving all the infant's emotions and phantasies) during the first year; to some extent indeed this applies to the whole of life.

I have emphasized throughout this chapter that the changes in the emotional development and object-relations of the infant are of a gradual nature. The fact that the depressive position develops gradually explains why, usually, its effect on the infant does not appear in a sudden way.[1] Also we have to keep in mind that while depressive feelings are experienced, the ego simultaneously develops methods of counteracting them. This, in my view, is one of the fundamental differences between the infant who is experiencing anxieties of a psychotic nature and the psychotic adult; for, at the same time as the infant goes through these anxieties, the processes leading to their modification are already at work. (CH. N. 4.)

Further Development and the Modification of Anxiety

I

The infantile neurosis can be regarded as a combination of processes by which anxieties of a psychotic nature are bound, worked through and modified. Fundamental steps in the modification of persecutory and depressive anxiety are part of the development during the first year. The infantile neurosis, as I

---

[1] Nevertheless, signs of recurrent depressive feelings can, with close observation, be detected in normal infants. Severe symptoms of depression occur quite strikingly in young infants in certain circumstances, such as illness, sudden separation from the mother or nurse, or change of food.

see it, therefore begins within the first year of life and comes to an end when, with the onset of the latency period, modification of early anxieties has been achieved.

All aspects of development contribute towards the process of modifying anxiety and, therefore, the vicissitudes of anxiety can only be understood in their interaction with all developmental factors. For instance, acquiring physical skills; play activities; the development of speech and intellectual progress in general; habits of cleanliness; the growth of sublimations; the widening of the range of object-relations; the progress in the child's libidinal organization—all these achievements are inextricably interwoven with aspects of the infantile neurosis, ultimately with the vicissitudes of anxiety and the defences evolved against it. Here I can only single out a few of these interacting factors and indicate how they contribute to the modification of anxiety.

The first persecutory objects, external and internal, are—as discussed already—the mother's bad breast and the father's bad penis; and persecutory fears relating to internal and external objects interact. These anxieties, focussing first on the parents, find expression in the early phobias and greatly affect the relation of the child to his parents. Both persecutory and depressive anxiety contribute fundamentally to the conflicts arising in the Oedipus situation[1] and influence libidinal development.

The genital desires towards both parents, which initiate the early stages of the Oedipus complex (at about the middle of the first year), are at first interwoven with oral, anal and urethral desires and phantasies, both of a libidinal and aggressive nature. The anxieties of a psychotic nature, to which destructive impulses from all these sources give rise, tend to reinforce these impulses and, if excessive, make for strong fixations to the pre-genital stages.[2]

The libidinal development is thus at every step influenced by anxiety. For anxiety leads to fixation to pre-genital stages and

---

[1] The interrelation between persecutory and depressive anxieties on the one hand and castration fear on the other is discussed in detail in my paper 'The Oedipus Complex in the Light of Early Anxieties'.

[2] Cf. Chapter V.

again and again to regression to them. On the other hand, anxiety and guilt and the ensuing reparative tendency add impetus to libidinal desires and stimulate the forward trend of the libido; for giving and experiencing libidinal gratification alleviate anxiety and also satisfy the urge to make reparation. Anxiety and guilt, therefore, at times check, and at other times enhance the libidinal development. This varies not only between one individual and another but may vary in one and the same individual, according to the intricate interaction between internal and external factors at any given time.

In the fluctuating positions of the direct and inverted Oedipus complex, all the early anxieties are experienced; for jealousy, rivalry and hatred in these positions again and again stir up persecutory and depressive anxiety. Anxieties focussing on the parents as internal objects, however, are gradually worked through and diminished as the infant derives an increasing feeling of security from the relation to the external parents.

In the interplay between progression and regression, which is strongly influenced by anxiety, genital trends gradually gain the ascendant. As a result the capacity for reparation increases, its range widens and sublimations gain in strength and stability; for on the genital level they are bound up with the most creative urge of man. Genital sublimations in the feminine position are linked with fertility—the power to give life—and thus also to re-create lost or injured objects. In the male position, the element of life-giving is reinforced by the phantasies of fertilizing and thus restoring or reviving the injured or destroyed mother. The genital, therefore, represents not only the organ of procreation but also the means of repairing and creating anew.

The ascendancy of genital trends implies a great progress in ego-integration, for these trends take over libidinal and reparative desires of a pre-genital nature and thus a synthesis between pre-genital and genital reparative tendencies comes about. For instance, the capacity to receive 'goodness', in the first place the desired food and love from the mother, and the urge to feed her in return, and thus to restore her—the basis for oral sublimations—are a precondition for a successful genital development.

The growing strength of the genital libido, which includes progress in the capacity to make reparation, goes side by side with a gradual lessening of the anxiety and guilt aroused by destructive tendencies, notwithstanding that in the Oedipal situation genital desires are the cause of conflict and guilt. It follows that genital primacy implies a diminution of oral, urethral and anal trends and anxieties. In the process of working through the Oedipus conflicts and achieving genital primacy, the child becomes able to establish his good objects securely in his inner world and to develop a stable relation to his parents. All this means that he is gradually working through and modifying persecutory and depressive anxiety.

There are grounds to assume that as soon as the infant turns his interest towards objects other than the mother's breast— such as parts of her body, other objects around him, parts of his own body, etc.—a process starts which is fundamental for the growth of sublimations and object-relations. Love, desires (both aggressive and libidinal) and anxieties are transferred from the first and unique object, the mother, to other objects; and new interests develop which become substitutes for the relation to the primary object. This primary object is, however, not only the external but also the internalized good breast; and this deflection of the emotions and creative feelings, which become related to the external world, is bound up with projection. In all these processes, the function of symbol-formation and phantasy activity is of great significance.[1] When depressive anxiety arises, and particularly with the onset of the depressive position, the ego feels driven to project, deflect and distribute desires and emotions, as well as guilt and the urge to make reparation, on to new objects and interests. These processes, in my view, are a mainspring for sublimations throughout life. It is, however, a precondition for a successful development of sublimations (as well as of object-relations and of the libidinal organization), that love for the first objects can be maintained

---

[1] I have to refrain here from describing in detail the ways in which symbol-formation from the beginning is inextricably bound up with the phantasy-life of the child and with the vicissitudes of anxiety. I refer here to Chapters III and VII; also to some of my former writings, 'Infant Analysis' (1926) and 'The Importance of Symbol-Formation in the Development of the Ego' (1930).

while desires and anxieties are deflected and distributed. For, if grievance and hatred towards the first objects predominate, they tend to endanger sublimations and the relation to substitute objects.

Another disturbance of the capacity for reparation and consequently for sublimations arises if, owing to a failure in overcoming the depressive position, the hope of making reparation is impeded or, to put it otherwise, if there is despair about the destruction wrought on loved objects.

II

As suggested above, all aspects of development are bound up with the infantile neurosis. A characteristic feature of the infantile neurosis is the early phobias which begin during the first year of life and, changing in form and content, appear and reappear throughout the years of childhood. Both persecutory and depressive anxieties underlie the early phobias, which include difficulties with food, *pavor nocturnus*, anxiety relating to the mother's absence, fear of strangers, disturbances in relations with the parents and object-relations in general. The need to externalize persecutory objects is an intrinsic element in the mechanism of phobias.[1] This need derives from persecutory anxiety (relating to the ego) as well as from depressive anxiety (centring on the dangers threatening the good internal objects from internal persecutors). Fears of internal persecution also find expression in hypochondriacal anxieties. They also contribute to a variety of physical illnesses, *e.g.* the frequent colds of young children.[2]

Oral, urethral and anal anxieties (which enter both into the acquiring and inhibiting of habits of cleanliness) are basic

---

[1] Cf. *Psycho-Analysis of Children*, pp. 182, 219–26.

[2] My experience has shown me that those anxieties which underlie hypochondriasis are also at the root of hysterical conversion symptoms. The fundamental factor common to both is the fear relating to persecution within the body (attacks by internalized persecutory objects, or to the harm done to internal objects by the subject's sadism, such as attacks by his dangerous excrements)—all of which is felt as physical damage inflicted on the ego. The elucidation of the processes underlying the transformation of these persecutory anxieties into physical symptoms might throw further light on the problems of hysteria.

features in the symptomatology of the infantile neurosis. It is also a characteristic feature of infantile neurosis that during the first years of life relapses of various kinds occur. As we have seen above, if anxiety of a persecutory and depressive nature is reinforced, a regression to the earlier stages and to the corresponding anxiety-situations takes place. Such regression manifests itself for instance in the breaking down of already established habits of cleanliness; or phobias apparently overcome may reappear in slightly changed forms.

During the second year, obsessional trends come to the fore; they both express and bind oral, urethral and anal anxieties. Obsessional features can be observed in bed-time rituals, rituals to do with cleanliness or food and so on, and in a general need for repetition (*e.g.* the desire to be told again and again the same stories, even with the same expressions, or to play the same games over and over again). These phenomena, though part of the child's normal development, can be described as neurotic symptoms. The lessening or overcoming of these symptoms amounts to a modification of oral, urethral and anal anxieties; this, in turn, implies a modification of persecutory and depressive anxieties.

The capacity of the ego step by step to evolve defences which enable it in some measure to work through anxieties is an essential part of the process of modification of anxiety. In the earliest stage (paranoid-schizoid), anxiety is counteracted by extreme and powerful defences, such as splitting, omnipotence and denial.[1] In the following stage (depressive position), the defences undergo, as we have seen, significant changes which are characterized by the ego's greater capacity to sustain anxiety. As in the second year further progress in ego-development takes place, the infant makes use of his growing adaptation to external reality and of his growing control of bodily functions in the testing of internal dangers by external reality.

All these changes are characteristic of the obsessional mechanisms which can also be regarded as a very important

[1] If these defences persist excessively beyond the early stage to which they are appropriate, development may suffer in various ways; integration is impeded, phantasy-life and libidinal desires are hampered; in consequence the reparative tendency, sublimations, object-relations and the relation to reality may be impaired.

defence. For instance, by acquiring habits of cleanliness, the infant's anxieties about his dangerous faeces (*i.e.* his destructiveness), his bad internalized objects and internal chaos are again and again temporarily diminished. Control of the sphincter proves to him that he can control inner dangers and his internal objects. Furthermore, the actual excrements serve as evidence against his phantastic fears of their destructive quality. They can now be ejected in conformity with the demands of mother or nurse who, by showing approval of the conditions under which the excrements are produced, also seem to approve of the nature of the faeces, and this makes the faeces 'good'.[1] As a result, the infant might feel that the harm which, in his aggressive phantasies, was done by his excrements to his internal and external objects can be undone. The acquiring of habits of cleanliness, therefore, also diminishes guilt and satisfies the drive to make reparation.[2]

Obsessional mechanisms form an important part of ego-development. They enable the ego to keep anxiety temporarily at bay. This in turn helps the ego to achieve greater integration and strength; thereby the gradual working through, diminishing and modifying of anxiety become possible. However, obsessional mechanisms are only one of the defences at this stage. If they are excessive and become the main defence, this can be taken as an indication that the ego cannot effectively deal with anxiety of a psychotic nature and that a severe obsessional neurosis is developing in the child.

Another fundamental change in defences characterizes the stage at which the genital libido gains in strength. When this happens, as we have seen, the ego is more integrated; the

[1] The recognition that there is a need in the child to acquire habits of cleanliness, a need which is bound up with anxiety and guilt and the defences against it, leads to the following conclusion. Training in cleanliness, if applied without pressure and at a stage when the urge for it becomes apparent (which is usually in the course of the second year) is helpful for the child's development. If imposed on the child at an earlier stage, it may be harmful. Furthermore, at any stage the child should only be encouraged but not forced to acquire habits of cleanliness. This is necessarily a very incomplete reference to an important problem of upbringing.

[2] Freud's view on reaction-formations and 'undoing' in the process of obsessional neurosis underlies my concept of reparation, which in addition embraces the various processes by which the ego feels it undoes harm done in phantasy, restores, preserves and revives the object.

adaptation to external reality has improved; the function of consciousness has expanded; the super-ego is also more integrated; a fuller synthesis of unconscious processes, that is to say within the unconscious parts of the ego and super-ego, has come about; the demarcation between conscious and unconscious is more distinct. These developments make it possible for repression to take a leading part among the defences.[1] An essential factor in repression is the reprimanding and prohibiting aspect of the super-ego, an aspect which as a result of progress in the super-ego organization gains in strength. The demands of the super-ego to keep out of consciousness certain impulses and phantasies, both of an aggressive and libidinal nature, are more easily met by the ego because it has progressed both in integration and in assimilation of the super-ego.

I have described in a former section that even during the first months of life the ego inhibits instinctual desires, initially under pressure of persecutory and, somewhat later, of depressive anxieties. A further step in the development of instinctual inhibitions comes about when the ego can make use of repression.

We have seen the ways in which the ego uses splitting during the paranoid-schizoid phase.[2] The mechanism of splitting underlies repression (as is implied in Freud's concept); but in contrast to the earliest forms of splitting which lead to states of disintegration, repression does not normally result in a disintegration of the self. Since at this stage there is greater integration, both within the conscious and the unconscious parts of the mind, and since in repression the splitting predominantly effects a division between conscious and unconscious, neither part of the self is exposed to the degree of disintegration which may arise in previous stages. However, the extent to which splitting processes are resorted to in the first few months of life vitally influences the use of repression at a later stage. For if early schizoid mechanisms and anxieties have not been sufficiently overcome, the result may be that instead of a fluid

[1] Cf. Freud, '. . . we shall bear in mind for future consideration the possibility that repression is a process which has a special relation to the genital organization of the libido and that the ego resorts to other methods of defence when it has to secure itself against the libido on other levels of organization.' (*Inhibitions, Symptoms and Anxiety* (1926), pp. 84-5.)
[2] Cf. Chapter IX.

boundary between the conscious and unconscious, a rigid barrier between them arises; this indicates that repression is excessive and that, in consequence, development is disturbed. With moderate repression, on the other hand, the unconscious and conscious are more likely to remain 'porous' to one another and therefore impulses and their derivatives are, in some measure, allowed to come up again and again from the unconscious and are subjected by the ego to a procedure of selection and rejection. The choice of the impulses, phantasies and thoughts which are to be repressed depends on the increased capacity of the ego to accept the standards of the external objects. This capacity is linked with the greater synthesis within the super-ego and the growing assimilation of the super-ego by the ego.

The changes in the structure of the super-ego, which come about gradually, and are throughout linked with the Oedipal development, contribute to the decline of the Oedipus complex at the onset of the latency period. In other words, the progress in the libidinal organization and the various adjustments of which the ego becomes capable at this stage are bound up with the modification of persecutory and depressive anxieties relating to the internalized parents, which implies greater security in the inner world.

Viewed in the light of the vicissitudes of anxiety, the changes characteristic of the onset of the latency period could be summarized as follows: the relation with the parents is more secure; the introjected parents approximate more closely to the picture of the real parents; their standards, their admonitions and prohibitions are accepted and internalized and therefore the repression of the Oedipus desires is more effective. All this represents a climax of the super-ego development which is the result of a process extending over the first years of life.

Conclusion

I have discussed in detail the first steps in overcoming the depressive position which characterize the latter half of the first year of life. We have seen that in the earliest stages, when persecutory anxiety predominates, the infant's objects are of a primitive and persecutory nature; they devour, tear up, poison, flood, etc., that is to say, the variety of oral, urethral and anal desires and phantasies are projected on to the external as well as on to the internalized objects. The picture of these objects alters step by step in the infant's mind as the libidinal organization progresses and anxiety becomes modified.

His relations both to his internal and external world improve simultaneously; the interdependence between these relations implies changes in the processes of introjection and projection which are an essential factor in diminishing persecutory and depressive anxieties. All this results in a greater capacity of the ego to assimilate the super-ego, and in this way the strength of the ego increases.

When stabilization is achieved, some fundamental factors have undergone alteration. I am not concerned at this point with the progress of the ego—which, as I have tried to show, is at every step bound up with the emotional development and the modification of anxiety—it is the *changes in unconscious* processes which I wish to underline. These changes become, I think, more understandable if we link them with the origin of anxiety. Here I refer back to my contention that destructive impulses (the death instinct) are the primary factor in the causation of anxiety.[1] Greed is increased by grievances and hatred, that is to say, by manifestations of the destructive instinct; but these manifestations are in turn reinforced by persecutory anxiety. When, in the course of development, anxiety both diminishes and is more securely kept at bay, grievances and hatred as well as greed diminish, and this ultimately leads to a lessening of ambivalence. To express this in terms of instincts: when the infantile neurosis has run its course, that is to say, when persecutory and depressive anxieties have been diminished and modified, the balance in the fusion of the life and death instincts (and thus between libido and aggression) has in some ways altered. This implies important changes in unconscious processes, that is to say, in the structure of the super-ego and in the structure and domain of the unconscious (as well as conscious) parts of the ego.

We have seen that the fluctuations between libidinal positions

[1] Cf. Chapter VIII.

and between progression and regression which characterize the first years of childhood are inextricably linked with the vicissitudes of the persecutory and depressive anxieties arising in early infancy. These anxieties are thus not only an essential factor in fixation and regression but also perpetually influence the course of development.

It is a precondition for normal development that in the interplay between regression and progression fundamental aspects of the progress already achieved are maintained. In other words, that the process of integration and synthesis is not fundamentally and permanently disturbed. If anxiety is gradually modified, progression is bound to dominate over regression and, in the course of the infantile neurosis, the basis for mental stability is established.

CHAPTER NOTES

Ch. N. 1 (p. 201)

Margaret A. Ribble has reported observations on 500 infants ('Infantile Experience in Relation to Personality Development', 1944), and expressed views, some of which are complementary to conclusions I reached through the analysis of young children.

Thus, regarding the relation to the mother from the beginning of life, she stresses the infant's need to be 'mothered' which goes beyond the gratification by sucking; e.g. on p. 631, she says:

'Much of the quality and the cohesiveness of a child's personality depends upon an emotional attachment to the mother. This attachment or, to use the psycho-analytic term, cathexis for the mother grows gradually out of the satisfaction it derives from her. We have studied the nature of this developing attachment which is so elusive yet so essential in considerable detail. Three types of sensory experience, namely, tactile, kinaesthetic, or the sense of body position, and sound, contribute primarily to its formation. The development of these sensory capacities has been mentioned by nearly all observers of infantile behavior . . . but their particular importance for the personal relation between mother and child has not been emphasized.'

The importance of this personal relation for the physical development of the child is stressed by her in various places; e.g. on p. 630 she says:

'. . . the most trivial irregularities in the personal care and handling of any baby, such as too little contact with the mother, too little handling, or changes of nurses or in general routine, frequently result in such disturbances as pallor, irregular breathing, and feeding disturbances. In infants who are constitutionally sensitive or poorly organized, these disturbances, if they are too frequent, may permanently alter the organic and psychic development, and not infrequently they threaten life itself.'

In another passage the author summarizes these disturbances as follows (p. 630):

'The infant is, by its very incompleteness of brain and nervous system, continuously in potential danger of functional disorganization. Outwardly the danger is that of sudden separation from the mother who either intuitively or knowingly must sustain this functional balance. Actual neglect or lack of love may be equally disastrous. Inwardly the danger appears to be the mounting of tension from biological needs and the inability of the organism to maintain its inner energy or metabolic equilibrium and reflex excitability. The *need for oxygen* may become acute because the young infant's breathing mechanisms are not well enough developed to work adequately with the increasing inner demand caused by rapid forebrain development.'

These functional disturbances which, according to M. Ribble's observation, may amount to a danger to life, could be interpreted as an expression of the death instinct which, according to Freud, is primarily directed against the organism itself (*Beyond the Pleasure Principle*). I have contended that this danger which stirs up the fear of annihilation, of death, is the primary cause of anxiety. The fact that the biological, physiological and psychological factors are bound up from the beginning of post-natal life is illustrated by M. Ribble's observations. I would draw the further conclusion that the mother's consistent and loving care of the baby, which strengthens his libidinal relation to her (and which, with infants who are 'constitutionally sensitive or poorly organized', is even essential for keeping them alive), supports the life instinct in its struggle against the death instinct. In the present chapter and in Chapter VIII I discuss this point more fully.

Another issue on which Dr. Ribble's conclusions coincide with mine relates to the changes which she describes as occurring approximately by the third month. These changes can be regarded as the physiological counterpart to the features of emotional life which I describe as the onset of the depressive position. She says (p. 643):

'By this time, the organic activities of breathing, of digesting, and of circulating blood have begun to show considerable stability, indicating that the autonomic nervous system has taken over its specific functions. We know from anatomical studies that the foetal system of circulation is usually obliterated by this time. . . . At about this time, typical adult patterns of brain waves begin to appear in the electro-encephalogram . . . and they probably indicate a more mature form of cerebral activity. Outbursts of emotional reaction, not always well differentiated but obviously expressing positive or negative direction, are seen to involve the entire motor system. . . . The eyes focus well and can follow the mother about, the ears function well and can differentiate the sounds she makes. Sound or sight of her produces the positive emotional responses formerly obtained only from contact, and consist of appropriate smiling and even genuine outbursts of joy.'

These changes are, I think, bound up with the diminution of splitting processes and with progress in ego-integration and object-relations, particularly with the capacity of the infant to perceive and to introject the mother as a whole person—all of which I have described as happening in the second quarter of the first year with the onset of the depressive position.

Cʜ. N. 2 (p. 214)

If these fundamental adjustments in the relation between the ego and the super-ego have not sufficiently come about in early development, it is one of the essential tasks of the psycho-analytic procedure to enable the patient to make them retrospectively. This is only possible by the analysis of the earliest stages of development (as well as of later ones), and by a thorough analysis of the negative as well as of the positive transference. In the fluctuating transference situation, the external and internal figures—good and bad—which primarily shape the super-ego development and object-relations, are transferred on to the psycho-analyst. Therefore at times he is bound to stand for frightening figures, and only in this way can the infantile persecutory anxieties be fully experienced, worked through and diminished. If the psycho-analyst is inclined to reinforce the positive transference, he avoids playing in the patient's mind the part of bad figures and is predominantly introjected as a good object. Then, in some cases, belief in good objects may be strengthened; but such a gain may be far from stable, for the patient has not been enabled to experience the hatred, anxiety and suspicion which in the early stages of life were related to the frightening and dangerous aspects of the parents. It is only by analysing the negative as well as the positive transference that the psycho-analyst appears alternately in the role of good and bad objects, is alternately loved and hated, admired and dreaded. The patient is thus enabled to work through, and therefore to modify, early anxiety-situations; the splitting between the good and bad figures decreases; they become more synthesized, that is to say, aggression becomes mitigated by libido. In other words, persecutory and depressive anxieties are diminished, as one might say, at the root.

Cн. N. 3 (p. 217)

Abraham referred to the fixation of libido at the oral level as one of the fundamental etiological factors in melancholia. He described this fixation in a particular case as follows: 'In his depressive states he would be overcome by longing for his mother's breast, a longing that was indescribably powerful and different from anything else. If the libido still remains fixated on this point when the individual is grown up, then one of the most important conditions for the appearance of a melancholic depression is fulfilled.' (*Selected Papers*, p. 458.)

Abraham substantiated his conclusions, which threw new light on the connection between melancholia and normal mourning, by extracts from two case-histories. These were actually the first two cases of manic-depression to undergo a thorough analysis—a new venture in the development of psycho-analysis. Up to that time not much clinical material had been published in support of Freud's discovery regarding melancholia. As Abraham said (*loc. cit.*, pp. 433-4): 'Freud described in general outlines the psychosexual processes that take place in the melancholic. He was able to obtain an intuitive idea of them from the occasional treatment of depressive patients; but not very much clinical material has been published up till now in the literature of psycho-analysis in support of this theory.'

But even from these few cases Abraham had come to understand that already in childhood (at the age of five) there had been an actual state of melancholia. He said he would be inclined to speak of 'a "primal parathymia" ensuing from the boy's Oedipus complex' and concluded this description as follows: 'It is this state of mind that we call melancholia' (p. 469).

Sandor Radó, in his paper 'The Problem of Melancholia' (1928) went further and considered that the root of melancholia can be found in the hunger situation of the suckling baby. He said: 'The deepest fixation-point in the depressive disposition is to be found in the situation of threatened loss of love (Freud), more especially in the hunger situation of the suckling baby.' Referring to Freud's statement that in mania the ego is once more merged with the super-ego in unity, Radó inferred that 'this process is the faithful intra-psychic repetition of the experience of that fusing with the mother that takes place during drinking at her breast'. Nevertheless, Radó did not apply this conclusion to the emotional life of the infant; he referred only to the etiology of melancholia.

Ch. N. 4 (p. 221)

The picture of the first six months of life which I have outlined in these two sections implies a modification of some concepts presented in my *Psycho-Analysis of Children*. I there described the confluence of aggressive impulses from all sources as the 'phase of maximal sadism'. I still believe that aggressive impulses are at their height during the stage in which persecutory anxiety predominates; or, in other words, that persecutory anxiety is stirred up by the destructive instinct and is constantly fed by the projection of destructive impulses on to objects. For it is inherent in the nature of persecutory anxiety that it increases hatred and attacks against the object who is felt to be persecutory, and this in turn reinforces the feeling of persecution.

Some time after the *Psycho-Analysis of Children* was published I worked out my concept of the depressive position. As I now see it, with the advance in object-relations between three to six months of age, both destructive impulses and persecutory anxiety diminish and the depressive position arises. While, therefore, my views have not altered regarding the close connection between persecutory anxiety and the predominance of sadism, I have to make an alteration as far as dating is concerned. Formerly I suggested that the phase of maximal sadism is at its height about the middle of the first year; now I would say that it extends over the first three months of life and corresponds to the paranoid-schizoid position described in the first section of this chapter. If we were to assume a certain individually varying sum-total of aggression in the young infant, this amount, I think, would be no less at the beginning of post-natal life than at the stage when cannibalistic, urethral and anal impulses and phantasies operate in full strength. Considered in terms of quantity only (a point of view which, however, does not take into account the various other factors determining the operation of the two instincts) it could be said that, as more sources of aggression are tapped and more manifestations of aggression become possible, a process of distribution takes place. It is inherent in development that an increasing number of aptitudes, both physical and mental, gradually come into play; and the fact that impulses and phantasies from various sources overlap, interact and reinforce one another can also be considered as expressing progress in integration and synthesis. Furthermore, to the confluence of aggressive impulses and phantasies corresponds the confluence of oral, urethral and anal phantasies of a libidinal nature. This means that the struggle between libido and aggression is carried out over a wider field. As I said in my *Psycho-Analysis of Children*, p. 212:

'The emergence of the stages of organization with which we are acquainted corresponds, I should say, not only to the positions which the libido has won and established in its struggle with the destructive instinct, but, since these two components are for ever united as well as opposed, to a growing adjustment between them.'

The infant's capacity to enter into the depressive position and to establish the complete object within himself implies that he is not as strongly ruled by destructive impulses and persecutory anxiety as at an earlier stage. Increasing integration brings about changes in the nature of his anxiety, for when love and hatred become more synthesized in relation to the object this gives rise, as we have seen, to great mental pain—to depressive feelings and guilt. Hatred becomes to some extent mitigated by love, whereas feelings of love are to some extent affected by hatred, the result being that the infant's emotions towards his objects change in quality. At the same time the progress in integration and in object-relations enables the ego to develop more effective ways of dealing with the destructive impulses and the anxiety to which they give rise. However, we must not lose sight of the fact that sadistic impulses, particularly since they are operative at various zones, are a most potent factor in the infant's conflicts arising at this stage; for the essence of the depressive position consists of the infant's anxiety lest his loved object be harmed or destroyed by his sadism.

The emotional and mental processes during the first year of life (and recurring throughout the first five or six years) could be defined in terms of success or failure in the struggle between aggression and libido; and the working through of the depressive position implies that in this struggle (which is renewed at every mental or physical crisis) the ego is able to develop adequate methods of dealing with and modifying persecutory and depressive anxieties— ultimately of diminishing and keeping at bay aggression directed against loved objects.

I chose the term 'position' in regard to the paranoid and depressive phases because these groupings of anxieties and defences, although arising first during the earliest stages, are not restricted to them but occur and recur during the first years of childhood and under certain circumstances in later life.

VII

ON OBSERVING THE BEHAVIOUR OF YOUNG INFANTS

By MELANIE KLEIN

I

THE theoretical conclusions presented in the previous chapter are derived from psycho-analytic work with young children.[1] We should expect such conclusions to be substantiated by observations of infants' behaviour during the first year of life. This corroborative evidence, however, has its limitations, for, as we know, unconscious processes are only partly revealed in behaviour, whether of infants or adults. Keeping this reservation in mind, we are able to gain some confirmation of psychoanalytic findings in our study of babies.

Many details of infants' behaviour, which formerly escaped attention or remained enigmatic, have become more understandable and significant through our increased knowledge of early unconscious processes; in other words, our faculty for observation in this particular field has been sharpened. We are, no doubt, hampered in our study of young infants by their inability to talk, but there are many details of early emotional development which we can gather by means other than language. If we are to understand the young infant, though, we need not only greater knowledge but also a full sympathy with him, based on our unconscious being in close touch with his unconscious.

I now propose to consider a few details of infant behaviour in the light of the theoretical conclusions put forward in various chapters of the present book. Since I shall take little account here of the many variations which exist within the range of fundamental attitudes, my description is bound to be rather over-simplified. Also, all inferences which I shall draw as to

---

[1] The analysis of adults, too, if carried to deep layers of the mind, affords similar material and provides convincing proof regarding the earliest as well as later stages of development.

further development must be qualified by the following consideration. From the beginning of post-natal life and at every stage of development, external factors affect the outcome. Even with adults, as we know, attitudes and character may be favourably or unfavourably influenced by environment and circumstances, and this applies to a far greater extent to children. Therefore, in relating conclusions drawn from my psycho-analytic experience to the study of young infants, I am only suggesting possible, or, one might say, probable lines of development.

The new-born infant suffers from persecutory anxiety aroused by the process of birth and by the loss of the intra-uterine situation. A prolonged or difficult delivery is bound to intensify this anxiety. Another aspect of this anxiety-situation is the necessity forced on the infant to adapt himself to entirely new conditions.

These feelings are in some degree relieved by the various measures taken to give him warmth, support and comfort, and particularly by the gratification he feels in receiving food and in sucking the breast. These experiences, culminating in the first experience of sucking, initiate, as we may assume, the relation to the 'good' mother. It appears that these gratifications in some way also go towards making up for the loss of the intra-uterine state. From the first feeding experience onwards, losing and regaining the loved object (the good breast) become an essential part of infantile emotional life.

The infant's relations to his first object, the mother, and towards food are bound up with each other from the beginning. Therefore the study of fundamental patterns of attitudes towards food seems the best approach to the understanding of young infants.[1]

The initial attitude towards food ranges from an apparent absence of greed to great avidity. At this point I shall, therefore, briefly recapitulate some of my conclusions regarding greed: I suggested in the previous chapter that greed arises when, in the interaction between libidinal and aggressive impulses, the

---

[1] As regards the fundamental importance of oral traits for character-formation, cf. Abraham, 'Character-formation on the Genital Level of the Libido', *Selected Papers* (1925), Chapter 25.

latter are reinforced; greed may be increased from the outset by persecutory anxiety. On the other hand, as I pointed out, the infant's earliest feeding inhibitions can also be attributed to persecutory anxiety; this means that persecutory anxiety in some cases increases greed and in others inhibits it. Since greed is inherent in the first desires directed towards the breast, it vitally influences the relation to the mother and object-relations in general.

II

Considerable differences in the attitude towards sucking are noticeable in babies even during the first few days of life,[1] and become more pronounced as time goes on. We have, of course, to take into full consideration every detail in the way the infant is fed and handled by his mother. It can be observed that an initially promising attitude towards food may be disrupted by adverse feeding conditions; whereas difficulties in sucking can sometimes be mitigated by the mother's love and patience.[2] Some children who, although good feeders, are not markedly greedy, show unmistakable signs of love and of a developing interest in the mother at a very early stage—an attitude which contains some of the essential elements of an object-relation. I have seen babies as young as three weeks interrupt their sucking for a short time to play with the mother's breast or to look towards her face. I have also observed that young infants—even as early as in the second month—would in wakeful periods after feeding lie on the mother's lap, look up at her, listen to her voice and respond to it by their facial expression; it was like a

[1] Michael Balint (in 'Individual Differences in Early Infancy', pp. 57–79, 81–117) concluded from observations of 100 infants ranging in age from five days to eight months that the sucking rhythm varies from one infant to another, each infant having his individual rhythm or rhythms.

[2] We must keep in mind, though, that however important these first influences are, the impact of the environment is of major importance *at every stage* of the child's development. Even the good effect of the earliest upbringing can be to some extent undone through later harmful experiences, just as difficulties arising in early life may be diminished through subsequent beneficial influences. At the same time we have to remember that some children seem to bear unsatisfactory external conditions without severe harm to their character and mental stability, whereas with others, in spite of favourable surroundings, serious difficulties arise and persist.

loving conversation between mother and baby. Such behaviour implies that gratification is as much related to the object which gives the food as to the food itself. Marked indications of an object-relation at an early stage, together with pleasure in food, augur well, I think, both for future relations with people and for emotional development as a whole. We might conclude that in these children anxiety is not excessive in proportion to the strength of the ego, *i.e.* that the ego is already in some measure able to sustain frustration and anxiety and to deal with them. At the same time we are bound to assume that the innate capacity for love which shows itself in an early object-relation can only develop freely because anxiety is not excessive.

It is interesting to consider from this angle the behaviour of some infants in their first few days of life, as described by Middlemore under the heading of 'sleepy satisfied sucklings'.[1] She accounts for their behaviour in the following terms: 'Because their sucking reflex was not immediately elicited, they were free to approach the breast in various ways.' These infants by the fourth day fed steadily and were very gentle in the approach to the breast. '. . . they seemed to like licking and mouthing the nipple as much as they liked sucking. An interesting outcome of the forward distribution of pleasant feeling was the habit of play. One sleepy child began each feed by playing with the nipple in preference to sucking. During the third week, the mother contrived to shift the accustomed play to the end of the feed, and this persisted throughout ten months of breast-feeding, to the delight of mother and child' (*loc. cit.*). Since the 'sleepy satisfied sucklings' both developed into good feeders and continued the play at the breast, I would assume that with them the relation to the first object (the breast) was from the beginning as important as the gratification derived from sucking and from food. One could go still further. It may be due to somatic factors that in some babies the sucking reflex is not immediately elicited, but there is good reason to believe that mental processes are also involved. I would suggest that the gentle approach to the breast preceding the pleasure in sucking may also in some measure result from anxiety.

I have referred in the previous chapter to my hypothesis that

[1] *The Nursing Couple*, pp. 49–50.

difficulties in sucking occurring at the beginning of life are bound up with persecutory anxiety. The infant's aggressive impulses towards the breast tend to turn it in his mind into a vampire-like or devouring object, and this anxiety could inhibit greed and in consequence the desire to suck. I would therefore suggest that the 'sleepy satisfied suckling' might deal with this anxiety by restraining the desire to suck until he has established a safe libidinal relation to the breast by licking and mouthing it. This would imply that from the beginning of post-natal life some infants attempt to counteract the persecutory anxiety about the 'bad' breast by establishing a 'good' relation to the breast. Those infants who are already able at such an early stage to turn markedly to the object appear to have, as suggested above, a strong capacity for love.

Let us consider from this angle another group Middlemore describes. She observed that four out of seven 'active satisfied sucklings' were biting the nipple and that these babies did not 'bite the nipple in trying to get a better hold on it; the two babies who bit most frequently had easy access to the breast'. Furthermore, 'the active babies who bit the nipple most often seemed somewhat to enjoy biting; their biting was leisurely and quite unlike the uneasy chewing and gnawing of unsatisfied babies. . . .'[1] This early expression of pleasure in biting might lead us to conclude that destructive impulses were unrestrained in these children and therefore that greed and the libidinal desire to suck were unimpaired. However, even these babies were not as unrestrained as might appear, for three out of seven 'refused a few of their earlier feeds with struggles and screaming protests. Sometimes they screamed at the gentlest handling and contact with the nipple while evacuation occurred at the same time; but at the next feed they were sometimes intent upon sucking'.[2] This, I think, indicates that greed may

[1] Middlemore suggests that impulses to bite enter into the infant's aggressive behaviour towards the nipple long before he has any teeth and even though he rarely grips the breast with his gums. In this connection (*loc. cit.*, pp. 58–9) she refers to Waller (section 'Breast Feeding' in *The Practitioner's Encyclopaedia of Midwifery and the Diseases of Women*), who 'speaks of excited babies biting angrily at the breast, and attacking it with painful vigour'.

[2] *Loc. cit.*, pp. 47–8.

be reinforced by anxiety in contrast to the 'sleepy satisfied sucklings' in whom anxiety causes greed to be restrained.

Middlemore mentioned that of the seven 'sleepy satisfied' infants she observed, six were handled very gently by their mothers, whereas with some 'unsatisfied sucklings' the mother's anxiety was aroused and she became impatient. Such an attitude is bound to increase anxiety in the child and thus a vicious circle is established.

As regards the 'sleepy satisfied sucklings', if, as I suggested, the relation to the first object is used as a fundamental method of counteracting anxiety, any disturbance in the relation to the mother is bound to stir up anxiety and may lead to severe difficulties in taking food. The mother's attitude seems to matter less in the case of the 'active satisfied sucklings', but this may be misleading. As I see it, with these infants the danger does not lie so much in the disturbance in feeding (although even with very greedy children, feeding inhibitions occur) as in the impairment of the object-relation.

The conclusion is that with all children the mother's patient and understanding handling from the earliest days onwards is of the greatest moment. This is seen more clearly as a result of our increased knowledge of early emotional life. As I have pointed out, 'The fact that a good relation to its mother and to the external world helps the baby to overcome its early paranoid anxieties throws a new light on the importance of the earliest experiences. From its inception analysis has always laid stress on the importance of the child's early experiences, but it seems to me that only since we know more about the nature and contents of its early anxieties, and the continuous interplay between its actual experiences and its phantasy-life, are we able fully to understand *why* the external factor is so important.'[1]

At every step, persecutory and depressive anxieties may be reduced, or, for that matter, increased by the mother's attitude; and the extent to which helpful or persecutory figures will prevail in the infant's unconscious is strongly influenced by his actual experiences, primarily with his mother, but also soon with the father and other members of the family.

[1] Cf. 'A Contribution to the Psychogenesis of Manic-Depressive States' (1934).

III

The close bond between a young infant and his mother centres on the relation to her breast. Although, from the earliest days onwards, the infant also responds to other features of the mother—her voice, her face, her hands—the fundamental experiences of happiness and love, of frustration and hatred, are inextricably linked with the mother's breast. This early bond with the mother, which is strengthened as the breast is being securely established in the inner world, basically influences all other relationships, in the first place with the father; it underlies the capacity to form any deep and strong attachment to one person.

With bottle-fed babies the bottle can take the place of the breast if it is given in a situation approximating to breast-feeding, *i.e.* if there is close physical nearness to the mother and the infant is handled and fed in a loving way. Under such conditions the infant may be able to establish within himself an object felt to be the primary source of goodness. In this sense he takes into himself the good breast, a process which underlies a secure relation to the mother. It would appear, however, that the introjection of the good breast (the good mother) differs in some ways between children who are breast-fed and those who are not. It is beyond the frame of the present chapter to elaborate on these differences and their effect on mental life. (CH. N. 1.)

In my description of very early object-relations I have referred to children who are good feeders but do not show excessive greed. Some very greedy infants also give early signs of a developing interest in people in which, however, a similarity to their greedy attitude towards food can be detected. For instance, an impetuous need for the presence of people often seems to relate less to the person than to the attention desired. Such children can hardly bear to be left alone and appear to require constantly either gratification by food or by attention. This would indicate that greed is reinforced by anxiety and that there is a failure both in establishing securely the good object in the inner world and in building up trust in the mother as a good external object. This failure may foreshadow future difficulties: for instance, a greedy and anxious need for company, which often goes with the fear of being alone, and may result in unstable and transitory object-relations which could be described as 'promiscuous'.

IV

To turn now to the bad feeders. A very slow taking of food often implies lack of enjoyment, *i.e.* of libidinal gratification; this, if coupled with an early and marked interest in the mother and in other people, suggests that object-relations are partly used as an escape from persecutory anxiety attaching to food. Although good relations to people may develop in such children, the excessive anxiety which manifests itself in this attitude to food remains a danger to emotional stability. One of the various difficulties which may arise later is an inhibition in taking in sublimated food, *i.e.* a disturbance in intellectual development.

A marked refusal of food (as compared with slow feeding) is clearly an indication of a severe disturbance, although with some children this difficulty diminishes when new foods are introduced, *e.g.* bottle instead of breast, or solid food instead of liquid.

A lack of enjoyment of food or complete refusal of it, if combined with a deficiency in developing object-relations, indicates that the paranoid and schizoid mechanisms, which are at their height during the first three to four months of life, are excessive or not being adequately dealt with by the ego. This in turn suggests that destructive impulses and persecutory anxiety are prevalent, ego-defences inadequate and modification of anxiety insufficient.

Another type of deficient object-relation is characteristic of some over-greedy children. With them food becomes almost the exclusive source of gratification and little interest in people develops. I would conclude that they, too, do not successfully work through the paranoid-schizoid position.

V

The young infant's attitude towards frustration is revealing. Some infants—among them good feeders—may refuse food when a meal is delayed, or give other signs of a disturbance in the relation to the mother. Infants who show both pleasure in food and love for the mother bear frustration over food more easily, the ensuing disturbance in the relation to the mother is less severe and its effects do not last so long. This is an indication that trust in the mother and love for her are relatively well established.

These fundamental attitudes also influence the way bottle-feeding (supplementing breast-feeding or as a substitute for it) is accepted even by very young infants. Some babies experience a strong sense of grievance when the bottle is introduced; they feel it to be a loss of the primary good object and a deprivation imposed by the 'bad' mother. Such feelings do not necessarily manifest themselves in the repudiation of the new food; but the persecutory anxiety and distrust stirred up by this experience may disturb the relation to the mother and therefore increase phobic anxieties, such as fear of strangers (at this early stage new food is in a sense a stranger); or difficulties over food may appear later on, or the acceptance of food in sublimated forms, *e.g.* knowledge, may be impeded.

Other babies accept the new food with less resentment. This implies a greater actual tolerance of deprivation, which is different from an apparent submission to it and derives from a relatively secure relation to the mother, enabling the infant to turn to a new food (and object) while maintaining love for her.

The following instance illustrates the way in which a baby came to accept bottles supplementing breast-feeding. The infant girl *A* was a good feeder (but not excessively greedy) and soon gave those indications of a developing object-relation which I have described above. These good relations to food and to the mother were shown in the leisurely way in which she took her food, coupled with evident enjoyment of it; in her occasional interruption of her feed, when only a few weeks old, to look up at the mother's face or at her breast; a little later on, in even taking friendly notice of the family during her feed. In the sixth week a bottle had to be introduced following the evening feed, because the breast milk was insufficient. *A* took the bottle without difficulty. In the tenth week, however, she showed on two evenings signs of reluctance while drinking from the bottle, but finished it. On the third evening she refused it altogether. There seemed no physical nor mental disturbance at the time, sleep and appetite were normal. The mother, not wishing to force her, put her into the cot after the breast feed, thinking she might go to sleep. The child cried with hunger, so the mother, without picking her up, gave her the bottle which she now emptied eagerly. The same thing happened on the subsequent evenings: when on the mother's lap, the infant refused the bottle, but took it at once when she was put into her cot. After a few days the baby accepted the bottle while she was still in her mother's arms and sucked readily this time; there was no more difficulty when other bottles were introduced.

I would assume that depressive anxiety had been increasing and had, at this point, led to the baby's revulsion against the bottle given immediately after breast-feeding. This would suggest a relatively early onset of depressive anxiety[1] which, however, is in keeping with the fact that in this baby the relation to her mother developed very early and markedly; changes in this relation had been quite noticeable during the few weeks preceding the refusal of the bottle. I would conclude that because of the increase in depressive anxiety the nearness to the mother's breast and its smell heightened both the infant's desire to be fed by it and the frustration caused by the breast being empty. When she was lying in her cot A accepted the bottle because, as I would suggest, in this situation the new food was kept apart from the desired breast which, at that moment, had turned into the frustrating and injured breast. In this way she may have found it easier to keep the relation to the mother unimpaired by the hatred stirred up by frustration, that is to say, to keep the good mother (the good breast) intact.

We have still to explain why after a few days the baby accepted the bottle on her mother's lap and subsequently had no more difficulties over bottles. I think that during these days she had succeeded in dealing with her anxiety sufficiently to accept with less resentment the substitute object together with the primary one; this would imply an early step towards a dis-

---

[1] In my view, as stated in the preceding chapter, depressive anxiety already operates to some extent during the first three months of life and comes to a head during the second quarter of the first year.

tinction between food and the mother, a distinction which in general proves of fundamental importance for development.

I shall now quote an instance in which a disturbance in the relation with the mother arose without being immediately connected with frustration over food. A mother told me that when her infant *B* was five months old she had been left crying longer than usual. When at last the mother came to pick up the child, she found her in a 'hysterical' state; the baby looked terrified, was evidently frightened of her, and did not seem to recognize her. Only after some time did she fully re-establish contact with her mother. It is significant that this happened in day-time, when the child was awake and not long after a meal. This child usually slept well, but from time to time woke up crying for no apparent reason. There are good grounds for the assumption that the same anxiety which was underlying the day-time crying was also the cause for the disturbed sleep. I would suggest that because the mother did not come when she was longed for, she turned in the child's mind into the bad (persecuting) mother, and that for this reason the child did not seem to recognize her and was frightened of her.

The following instance is also revealing. A twelve-week-old infant girl *C* was left sleeping in the garden. She woke and cried for her mother, but her crying was not heard because a strong wind was blowing. When the mother at last came to pick her up, the baby had obviously been crying for a long time, her face was bathed in tears, and her ordinarily plaintive cry had turned into uncontrollable screaming. She was carried indoors, still screaming, and her mother's attempts to soothe her came to nothing. Eventually, though it was nearly an hour before her next feed was due, the mother resorted to offering her the breast —a remedy which had never failed when the child had been upset on previous occasions (though she had never screamed so persistently and violently before). The baby took the breast and began sucking lustily, but after a few sucks she rejected the breast and resumed her screaming. This continued until she put her fingers into her mouth and began sucking them. She often sucked her fingers, and on many occasions put them into her mouth when offered the breast. As a rule, the mother had only gently to remove the fingers and substitute the nipple and the baby would begin feeding. This time, however, she refused the breast and again screamed loudly. It took a few moments before she sucked her fingers again; her mother allowed her to suck them for some minutes, rocking and soothing her at the same time, till the baby was sufficiently calm to take the breast and sucked herself to sleep. It would appear that with this baby, for the same reasons as in the previous instance, the mother (and her breast) had turned bad and persecuting, and therefore the breast could not be accepted. After an attempt to suck, she found that she could not re-establish the relation to the good breast. She resorted to sucking her fingers, that is to say to an auto-erotic pleasure (Freud). I would, however, add that in this instance the narcissistic withdrawal was caused by the disturbance in the relation to the mother, and that the infant refused to give up sucking her fingers because they were more trustworthy than the breast. By sucking them she re-established the relation to the internal breast and thus regained enough security to renew the good relation to the external breast and mother.[1] Both these instances also add, I think, to our understanding of the mechanism of early phobias, e.g. the fear stirred by the mother's absence (Freud).[2] I would suggest that the phobias which arise during the first months of life are caused by persecutory anxiety which disturbs the relation to the internalized and the external mother.[3]

The division between the good and bad mother and the strong (phobic) anxiety relating to the bad one are also illustrated by the following instance. A ten-month-old boy D was held up to the window by his grandmother and watched the street with great interest. When he looked round, he suddenly saw very close to him the unfamiliar face of a visitor, an elderly woman, who had just come in and was standing beside the grandmother. He had an anxiety-attack which only subsided when the grandmother took him out of the room. My conclusion is that at this moment the child felt that the 'good' grandmother had disappeared and that the stranger represented the 'bad' grandmother (a division based on the splitting of the

---

[1] See Chapter IV, Part 2, section (b), 'Auto-Erotism, Narcissism and the Earliest Relations to Objects'.
[2] *Inhibitions, Symptoms and Anxiety*, pp. 167, 168.
[3] See Chapters VI and VIII.

mother into a good and bad object). I shall return to this instance later on.

This explanation of early anxieties also throws a new light on the phobia of strangers (Freud). In my view the persecutory aspect of the mother (or the father), which largely derives from destructive impulses towards them, is transferred on to strangers.

VI

Disturbances of the kind I have described in the young infant's relation to his mother are already observable during the first three or four months of life. If these disturbances are very frequent and last long they can be taken as an indication that the paranoid-schizoid position is not being dealt with effectively.

A persistent lack of interest in the mother even at this early stage, to which a little later on is added an indifference towards people in general and towards toys, suggests a more severe disturbance of the same order. This attitude can also be observed in young infants who are not bad feeders. To the superficial observer these children, who do not cry much, may appear as contented and 'good'. From the analysis of adults and children, whose severe difficulties I could trace back to babyhood, I concluded that many such infants are in fact mentally ill and withdrawn from the external world owing to strong persecutory anxiety and excessive use of schizoid mechanisms. In consequence depressive anxiety cannot be successfully overcome; the capacity for love and object-relations, as well as phantasy-life, is inhibited; the process of symbol-formation is impeded, resulting in an inhibition of interests and sublimations.

Such an attitude which could be described as apathetic is distinct from the behaviour of a really contented infant who at times demands attention, cries when he feels frustrated, gives various signs of his interest in people and pleasure in their company, and is yet at other times quite happy by himself. This indicates a feeling of security about his internal and external objects; he can bear the temporary absence of the mother without anxiety because the good mother is relatively secure in his mind.

VII

In other chapters I have described the depressive position from various angles. To consider here the effect of depressive anxiety first of all in connection with phobias: so far I have related them to persecutory anxiety only and illustrated this point of view by some instances. Thus I assumed that the five-month-old baby girl *B* was frightened of her mother who in her mind had changed from the good into the bad mother, and that this persecutory anxiety also disturbed her sleep. I would now suggest that the disturbance in the relation to the mother was caused by depressive anxiety as well. When the mother did not return, the anxiety lest the good mother was lost because greed and aggressive impulses had destroyed her came to the fore; this depressive anxiety was bound up with the persecutory fear that the good mother had changed into the bad one.

In the following instance depressive anxiety was also stirred up by the infant missing the mother. From the age of six or seven weeks, the infant girl *C* had been accustomed to play on her mother's lap during the hour preceding her evening feed. One day, when the baby was five months and one week old, the mother had visitors and was too busy to play with the baby who, however, received a good deal of attention from the family and the visitors. Her mother gave her the evening feed, put her to bed as usual, and the infant soon dropped off to sleep. Two hours later she woke and cried persistently; she refused milk (which at this stage was already occasionally given by spoon as a supplement and was usually accepted) and went on crying. Her mother gave up the attempt to feed her, and the baby settled down contentedly on her lap for an hour, playing with the mother's fingers, was then given her night feed at the usual time and quickly fell asleep. This disturbance was most unusual; she may have woken up on other occasions after the evening feed, but it was only once when she was ill (about two months previously) that she had woken up and cried. Except for the omission of the play with the mother there had been no break in the normal routine to account for the baby waking up and crying. There was no sign of hunger or physical discomfort;

she had been happy all day and slept well during the night following the incident.

I would suggest that the baby's crying was caused by her having missed the playtime with her mother. *C* had a very strong personal relation with her and always thoroughly enjoyed this particular hour. While at other waking periods she was quite content by herself, at this time of the day she would get restless and obviously expected her mother to play with her until the evening feed. If having missed this gratification caused the disturbance in her sleep, we are led to further conclusions. We should have to assume that the baby had a memory of the experience of this particular enjoyment at this particular time of the day; that the playtime was for the baby not only a strong satisfaction of libidinal desires but was also felt to be a proof of the loving relationship with the mother—ultimately of the secure possession of the good mother; and that this gave her a feeling of security before falling asleep, bound up with the memory of the playtime. Her sleep was disturbed not only because she missed this libidinal gratification but also because this frustration stirred up in the infant both forms of anxiety: depressive anxiety lest she should have lost the good mother through her aggressive impulses and, consequently, feelings of guilt[1]; also persecutory anxiety lest the mother should have turned bad and destructive. My general conclusion is that from about three or four months onwards both forms of anxiety underlie phobias.

The depressive position is bound up with some of the important changes which can be observed in young infants towards the middle of the first year (although they begin somewhat earlier and develop gradually). Persecutory and depressive anxieties at this stage express themselves in various ways, *e.g.* an increased fretfulness, a greater need for attention, or temporary turning away from the mother, sudden attacks of temper, and a greater fear of strangers; also children who normally sleep well sometimes sob in their sleep or suddenly wake up crying

---

[1] With somewhat older infants it can easily be observed that if they are not given the particular signs of affection expected by them at bedtime their sleep is likely to be disturbed; and that this intensification of the need for love at the moment of parting is bound up with feelings of guilt and the wish to be forgiven and to be reconciled with the mother.

with distinct signs of fear or sadness. At this stage the facial expression changes considerably; the greater capacity for perception, the greater interest in people and things and the ready response to human contacts are all reflected in the child's appearance. On the other hand, there are signs of sadness and suffering which, although transient, contribute to the face becoming more expressive of emotions, both of a deeper nature and a wider range.

VIII

The depressive position comes to a head at the time of weaning. While, as described in earlier passages, progress in integration and the corresponding synthetic processes in relation to the object give rise to depressive feelings, these feelings are further intensified by the experience of weaning.[1] At this stage the infant has already undergone earlier experiences of loss, *e.g.* when the intensely desired breast (or bottle) does not immediately reappear and the infant feels that it will never come back. The loss of the breast (or bottle), however, occurring at weaning is of a different order. This loss of the first loved object is felt to confirm all the infant's anxieties of a persecutory and depressive nature. (CH. N. 2.)

The following instance will serve as an illustration. The infant

[1] S. Bernfeld in his *Psychology of the Infant* (1929) came to the important conclusion that weaning is bound up with depressive feelings. He describes the varied behaviour of infants at the time of weaning, ranging from hardly noticeable longing and sorrow to actual apathy and complete refusal of nourishment, and compares the states of anxiety and restlessness, irritability and a certain apathy which may take possession of an adult with a similar condition in the infant. Among the methods of overcoming the frustration of weaning he mentions the withdrawal of the libido from the disappointing object through projection and repression. He qualifies the use of the term 'repression' as 'borrowed from the developed state of the adult'. But he nevertheless concludes that '. . . its essential properties exist in these processes' (in the infant) (p. 296). Bernfeld suggests that weaning is the first obvious cause from which pathological mental development branches off and that the nutritional neuroses of infants are contributory factors to the predisposition to neurosis. One of his conclusions is that, since some of the processes by which the infant overcomes his sorrow and feeling of loss at weaning work noiselessly, a conclusion about 'the effects of weaning will have to be drawn from an intimate knowledge of the child's reaction to its world and its activities, *which are the expression of its phantasy-life*, or *at least are the nucleus of it*'. (*Loc. cit.*, p. 259, my italics.)

E, weaned from his last breast feed at nine months, showed no particular disturbance in his attitude to food. He had by that time already accepted other foods and throve on them. But he showed an increased need for the mother's presence and in general for attention and company. One week after the last breast feed, he sobbed in his sleep, woke up with signs of anxiety and unhappiness and could not be comforted. The mother resorted to letting him suck the breast once more. He sucked both breasts for about the usual time, and although there was obviously little milk he seemed completely satisfied, went happily to sleep and the symptoms described above were much reduced after this experience. This would go to show that depressive anxiety relating to the loss of the good object, the breast, had been allayed by the very fact that it re-appeared.

At the time of weaning some infants show less appetite, some an increased greed, while others oscillate between these two responses. Such changes occur at every step in weaning. There are babies who enjoy the bottle much more than being suckled even though some of them have been satisfactorily breast-fed; with others appetite much improves when solid foods are introduced, and again there are infants who at this point develop difficulties over eating which persist in some form or other throughout the early years of childhood.[1] Many infants find only certain tastes, certain textures of solid food acceptable and repudiate others. When we analyse children we learn a good deal about the motives for such 'fads' and come to recognize as their deepest root the earliest anxieties in relation to the mother. I shall illustrate this conclusion by an instance of the behaviour of a five-month-old baby girl *F* who had been breast-fed but who had also had bottles from the beginning. She refused with violent anger solid food such as vegetables when given them by her mother, and accepted them quite calmly when her father fed her. After a fortnight she accepted the new foods from her mother. According to a reliable report,

[1] In her *Social Development in Young Children*, particularly Chapter 3, Section II.A.i., Susan Isaacs gave instances of feeding difficulties and discussed them in connection with anxieties arising from oral sadism. There are also some interesting observations in D. W. Winnicott's *Disorders of Childhood*, particularly pp. 16 and 17.

the child, who is now six years old, has a good relation with both parents as well as with her brother, but shows consistently little appetite.

We are reminded here of the baby girl *A* and the way she accepted supplementary bottles. With baby *F*, too, some time elapsed before she could adapt herself sufficiently to the new food to take it from her mother.

Throughout this chapter I have attempted to show that the attitude towards food is fundamentally bound up with the relation to the mother and involves the whole of the infant's emotional life. The experience of weaning stirs up the infant's deepest emotions and anxieties, and the more integrated ego develops strong defences against them; both anxieties and defences enter into the infant's attitudes towards food. Here I must confine myself to a few generalizations about changes in attitudes towards food at the time of weaning. At the root of many difficulties over new food is the persecutory fear of being devoured and poisoned by the mother's bad breast, a fear which derives from the infant's phantasies of devouring and poisoning the breast.[1] To persecutory anxiety, at a somewhat later stage,

[1] I suggested formerly that the young infant's phantasies of attacking the mother's body with poisonous (explosive and burning) excrements are a fundamental cause of his fear of being poisoned by her and lie at the root of paranoia; similarly, that the impulses to devour the mother (and her breast) turn her in the young infant's mind into a devouring and dangerous object. ('Early Stages of the Oedipus Conflict'; 'The Importance of Symbol-Formation in the Development of the Ego'; also *The Psycho-Analysis of Children*, particularly Chapter 8.)

Freud, too, refers to the little girl's fear of being murdered or poisoned by her mother; a fear of which he says '. . . it may later on form the nucleus of a paranoic disorder' (*New Introductory Lectures on Psycho-Analysis*, p. 154). Further: 'It is probable, too, that the fear of poisoning is connected with weaning. Poison is the nourishment that makes one ill.' (*Loc. cit.*, p. 157.) In his earlier paper, 'Female Sexuality', Freud also refers to the girl's dread in the pre-Oedipal stage 'of being killed (devoured?) by the mother'. He suggests that '. . . this anxiety corresponds to the hostility which the child develops towards her mother because of the manifold restrictions imposed by the latter in the process of training and physical care, and that the immaturity of the child's psychic organization favours the mechanism of projection'. He also concludes '. . . that in this dependence on the mother we have the germ of later paranoia in women'. In this context he refers to the case reported in 1928 by Ruth Mack-Brunswick ('Die Analyse eines Eifersuchtswahnes') 'in which the direct source of the disorder was the patient's pre-Oedipal (sister) fixation' (p. 254, n.).

is added (though in varying degrees) the depressive anxiety lest greed and aggressive impulses should destroy the loved object. During and after the process of being weaned this anxiety may have the effect of increasing or inhibiting the desire for new food.[1] As we have seen earlier, anxiety may have varying effects on greed: it may reinforce it or may lead to strong inhibitions of greed and of the pleasure in taking nourishment.

An increase in appetite at the time of weaning would in some cases suggest that during the period of being suckled the bad (persecutory) aspect of the breast had predominated over the good one; furthermore, depressive anxiety about the apprehended danger to the loved breast would contribute to inhibiting the desire for food (that is to say, that both persecutory and depressive anxieties are operative in varying proportions). Therefore the bottle, which is in some measure removed in the infant's mind from the first object, the breast—while also symbolizing it—can be taken with less anxiety and more pleasure than the mother's breast. Some infants, however, do not succeed in the symbolic substitution of the bottle for the breast, and if they enjoy their meals at all it is when they are given solid foods.

A decrease in appetite when breast- or bottle-feeding is first withdrawn is a frequent occurrence and clearly indicates depressive anxiety relating to the loss of the primary loved object. But persecutory anxiety, I think, always contributes to the dislike of the new food. The bad (devouring and poisonous) aspect of the breast which, while the infant was being suckled, was counteracted by the relation to the good breast, is reinforced by the deprivation of being weaned, and is transferred on to the new food.

As I indicated above, during the process of being weaned both persecutory and depressive anxieties strongly affect the relation to the mother and food. It is, however, the intricate interaction of a variety of factors (internal and external) which

[1] We may draw a comparison here with the attitude of manic-depressive patients towards food. As we know, some patients refuse food; others show temporarily an increase of greed; again others oscillate between these two responses.

at this stage determines the issue; by which I mean, not only the individual variations in the attitudes towards objects and food, but over and above this, the success or failure in working through and in some measure overcoming the depressive position. Much depends on how far in the earlier stage the breast has been securely established within, and consequently how far love for the mother can be maintained in spite of deprivations—all of which partly depends on the relation between mother and child. As I suggested, even very young infants can accept a new food (the bottle) with comparatively little grievance (instance *A*). This better inner adaptation towards frustration, which develops from the first days of life onwards, is bound up with steps towards the distinction between mother and food. These fundamental attitudes largely determine, particularly during the process of being weaned, the infant's capacity to accept, in the full sense of the word, substitutes for the primary object. Here again the mother's behaviour and feelings towards the child are of major importance; the loving attention and the time she devotes to him help him with his depressive feelings. The good relationship with the mother may in some measure counteract the loss of his primary loved object, the breast, and thus favourably influence the working through of the depressive position.

The anxiety about the loss of the good object, coming to a head at weaning time, is also stirred up by other experiences such as physical discomfort, illnesses and in particular teething. These experiences are bound to reinforce persecutory and depressive anxieties in the infant. In other words, the physical factor can never solely account for the emotional disturbance to which illnesses or teething give rise at this stage.

IX

Among the important developments we find towards the middle of the first year is the widening of the range of object-relations and in particular the increasing importance of the father for the young infant. I have shown in other contexts that depressive feelings and the fear of losing the mother, in addition to other developmental factors, add impetus to the infant's turning to the father. The early stages of the Oedipus complex and the depressive position are closely linked and develop simultaneously. I shall mention only one instance, the little girl *B* already referred to.

From the age of about four months onwards, the relation with her brother, several years her senior, played a prominent and noticeable part in her life; it differed, as could easily be seen in various ways from her relation with the mother. She admired everything her brother said and did, and persistently wooed him. She used all her little tricks to ingratiate herself, to win his attention and displayed a conspicuously feminine attitude towards him. At that time the father was absent, except for very short periods, and it was not until she was ten months old that she saw him more often and from that time onwards developed a very close and loving relation with him, which in some essentials paralleled the relation with her brother. At the beginning of her second year she often called her brother 'Daddy'; by then father had become the favourite. The delight in seeing him, the rapture when she heard his steps or his voice, the ways in which she mentioned him again and again in his absence, and many other expressions of her feelings towards him can only be described as being in love. The mother clearly recognized that at this stage the little girl was in some ways more fond of the father than of her. Here we have an instance of the early Oedipus situation which, in this case, was experienced first with the brother and then transferred to the father.

X

The depressive position, as I have argued in various connections, is an important part of normal emotional development, but the ways in which the child deals with these emotions and anxieties, and the defences he uses, are an indication of whether or not development is proceeding satisfactorily. (CH. N. 3.)

The fear of losing the mother makes parting from her, even for short periods, painful; and various forms of play both give expression to this anxiety and are a means of overcoming it. Freud's observation of the eighteen-month-old boy with his cotton-reel pointed in this direction.[1] As I see it, by means of this play the child was overcoming not only his feelings of loss but also his depressive anxiety.[2] There are various typical forms of play similar to that with the cotton-reel. Susan Isaacs mentioned a few instances in Chapter III and I shall now add some observations of this nature. Children, sometimes even before the second half of the first year, enjoy throwing things out of the pram again and again, and expect them back. I observed a further development of such play in G, an infant of ten months, who had recently begun to crawl. He never tired of throwing a toy away from himself and then getting hold of it by crawling towards it. I was told that he started this play about two months earlier when he made his first attempts to move himself forward. The infant E between six and seven months once noticed, while lying in his pram, that when he lifted his legs a toy which he had thrown aside rolled back to him, and he developed this into a game.

Already in the fifth or sixth month many infants respond with pleasure to 'peep-bo' (CH. N. 4); and I have seen babies playing this actively by pulling the blanket over the head and off again as early as seven months. The mother of the infant B made a bed-time habit of this game, thus leaving the child to go to sleep in a happy mood. It seems that the *repetition* of such experiences is an important factor in helping the infant to overcome his feelings of loss and grief. Another typical game which I found to be of great help and comfort to young children is to part from the child at bed-time saying 'bye-bye' and waving, leaving the room slowly, as it were disappearing gradually. The use of 'bye-bye' and waving, and later on saying 'back again', 'back soon' or similar words when the mother leaves the room, proves generally helpful or comforting. I know of some infants among whose first words were 'back' or 'again'.

To return to the infant girl B, with whom 'bye-bye' was one of the first words, I often noticed that when her mother was about to leave the room, a fleeting expression of sadness came

[1] *Beyond the Pleasure Principle* (1920). Cf. Chapter III where a description of this game is given.
[2] In 'The Observation of Infants in a Set Situation', D. W. Winnicott discussed in detail the game with the cotton-reel.

into the child's eyes, or she seemed near crying. But when the mother waved to her and said 'bye-bye', she appeared comforted and went on with her play activities. I saw her when she was between ten and eleven months practise the gesture of waving and I gained the impression that this had become a source not only of interest but of comfort.

The infant's growing capacity to perceive and understand the things around him increases his confidence in his own ability to deal with and even to control them, as well as his trust in the external world. His repeated experiences of the external reality become the most important means of overcoming his persecutory and depressive anxieties. This, in my view, is reality-testing and underlies the process in adults which Freud has described as part of the work of mourning.[1]

When an infant is able to sit up or to stand in his cot, he can look at people, and in some sense comes nearer to them; this happens to an even greater extent when he can crawl and walk. Such achievements imply not only a greater ability to come close to his object of his own will but also a greater independence from the object. For instance, the infant girl *B* (at about eleven months) thoroughly enjoyed crawling up and down a passage for hours on end and was quite contented by herself; but from time to time she crawled into the room where her mother was (the door had been left open), had a look at her or attempted to talk to her and returned to the passage.

The great psychological importance of standing, crawling and walking has been described by some psycho-analytic writers. My point here is that all these achievements are used by the infant as a means of regaining his lost objects as well as of finding new objects in their stead; all this helps the infant to overcome his depressive position. Speech development, beginning with the imitation of sounds, is another of those great achievements which bring the child nearer to the people he loves and also enables him to find new objects. In gaining gratifications of a new kind, the frustration and grievance relating to the earlier situations are lessened, which again makes for greater security. Another element in the progress achieved derives from the infant's attempts to control his

---

[1] 'Mourning and Melancholia' (1917).

objects, his external as well as his internal world. Every step in development is also used by the ego as a defence against anxiety, at this stage predominantly against depressive anxiety. This would contribute to the fact, which can often be observed, that, together with advances in development, such as walking or talking, children become happier and more lively. To put it from another angle, the ego's striving to overcome the depressive position furthers interests and activities, not only during the first year of life but throughout the early years of childhood.[1]

The following instance illustrates some of my conclusions regarding early emotional life. The infant boy D showed at the age of three months a very strong and personal relation to his toys, i.e. beads, wooden rings and rattle. He looked at them intently, touched them again and again, took them into his mouth and listened to the noise they made; he was angry with these toys and screamed when they were not in the position he wanted; he was pleased and liked them once more when they were fixed for him in the right position. His mother remarked, when he was four months old, that he worked off a good deal of anger on his toys; on the other hand, they were also a consolation to him in feelings of distress. At times he stopped crying when they were shown to him, and they also comforted him before going to sleep.

In his fifth month he clearly distinguished between father, mother and the maid; he showed this unmistakably in his look of recognition and in his expecting certain types of play from each of them. His personal relations were already very marked at that stage; he had also developed a particular attitude towards his bottle. For instance, when it was standing empty beside him on a table, he turned to it, making sounds, caressing it and from time to time sucking the teat. From his facial expression it could be gathered that he was behaving towards the bottle in the same way as towards a loved person. At the age of nine

---

[1] As I have pointed out in the previous chapter, although the crucial experiences of depressive feelings and the defences against them arise during the first year of life, it takes years for the child to overcome his persecutory and depressive anxieties. They are again and again activated and overcome in the course of the infantile neurosis. But these anxieties are never eradicated, and therefore are liable to be revived, though to a lesser extent, throughout life.

months he was observed looking at the bottle lovingly and talking to it, and apparently waiting for a reply. This relation to the bottle is all the more interesting since the little boy was never a good feeder, and showed no greed, in fact no particular pleasure in taking food. There had been difficulties in breast-feeding almost from the beginning, since the mother's milk gave out, and when a few weeks old he was entirely changed over to bottle-feeding. His appetite only began to develop in the second year, and even then largely depended on the pleasure of sharing his meal with his parents. We are reminded here of the fact that at nine months his main interest in the bottle seemed to be of an almost personal nature and did not relate only to the food it contained.

At ten months he became very fond of a humming top, being first attracted by its red knob, which he immediately sucked; this led to a great interest in the way it could be set to spin and the noise it made. He soon gave up his attempts to suck it, but his absorption in the top remained. When he was fifteen months old it happened that another humming top, of which he was also very fond, dropped on the floor while he was playing with it and the two halves came apart. The child's reaction to this incident was striking. He cried, was inconsolable and would not go back into the room where the incident had happened. When at last his mother succeeded in taking him there to show him that the top had been put together again, he refused to look at it and ran out of the room (even on the next day he did not want to go near the toy cupboard where the humming top was kept). Moreover, several hours after the incident, he refused to eat his tea. A little later on, however, it happened that his mother took up his toy dog and said: 'What a nice little doggie.' The boy brightened up, picked up the dog and kept on walking with it from one person to another expecting them to say, 'Nice little doggie'. It was clear that he identified himself with the toy dog, and therefore that the affection shown to it reassured him about the harm which he felt he had inflicted on the humming top.

It is significant that already at an earlier stage the child had shown outspoken anxiety about broken things. At about eight months, for instance, he cried when he dropped a glass—and another time a cup—and it broke. Soon he was so disturbed by the sight of broken things, irrespective of who had caused the damage, that his mother at once put them out of his sight. His distress on such occasions was an indication of both persecutory and depressive anxiety. This becomes clear if we link his behaviour at about eight months with the later incident of the humming top. My conclusion is that both bottle and humming top symbolically represented the mother's breast (we shall remember that at ten months he behaved towards the humming top as he did at nine months towards his bottle), and that when the humming top came apart this meant to him the destruction of the mother's breast and body. This would explain his emotions of anxiety, guilt and grief with regard to the broken humming top.

I have already linked the broken top with the broken cup and the bottle, but there is an earlier connection to be made. As we have seen, the child showed at times great anger towards his toys, which he treated in a very personal way. I would suggest that his anxiety and guilt observed at a later stage could be traced back to the aggression expressed towards the toys, particularly when they were not accessible. There is a still earlier link with the relation to his mother's breast which had not satisfied him and had been withdrawn. Accordingly, the anxiety over the broken cup or glass would be an expression of guilt about his anger and destructive impulses, primarily directed against his mother's breast. By symbol-formation, therefore, the child had displaced his interest on to a series of objects, from the breast to the toys: bottle—glass—cup—humming top, and transferred personal relations and emotions such as anger, hatred, persecutory and depressive anxieties and guilt on to these objects.[1]

Earlier in this chapter I described this child's anxiety relating to a stranger, and illustrated by that instance the splitting of the mother figure (here the grandmother figure) into a good and bad mother. The fear of the bad mother as well as love for the good one, which showed strongly in his personal relations, were marked. I suggest that both these aspects of personal relations entered into his attitude towards broken things.

[1] As regards the importance of symbol-formation for mental life cf. Chapter III, also my papers 'Infant Analysis' and 'The Importance of Symbol-Formation in the Development of the Ego'.

The mixture of persecutory and depressive anxieties which he manifested in the incident of the broken humming top, refusing to go into the room, and later even near the toy-cupboard, shows the fear of the object having turned into a dangerous object (persecutory anxiety) because it has been injured. There was no doubt, however, about the strong depressive feelings which were also operative on this occasion. All these anxieties were relieved when he became reassured by the fact that the little dog (standing for himself) was 'nice', *i.e.* good, and was still loved by his parents.

Conclusion

Our knowledge of constitutional factors and their interaction is still incomplete. In the chapters which I have contributed to this book I have touched upon some factors, which I shall now summarize. The innate capacity of the ego to tolerate anxiety may depend on a greater or lesser cohesiveness of the ego at birth; this in turn makes for a greater or lesser activity of schizoid mechanisms, and correspondingly for a greater or lesser capacity for integration. Other factors present from the beginning of post-natal life are the capacity for love, the strength of greed and the defences against greed.

I suggest that these interrelated factors are the expression of certain states of fusion between the life and death instincts. These states basically influence the dynamic processes by which destructive impulses are counteracted and mitigated by the libido, processes of great moment in moulding the infant's unconscious life. From the beginning of post-natal life constitutional factors are bound up with external ones, starting with the experience of birth and the earliest situations of being handled and fed.[1] Furthermore, as we have good grounds to assume, from early days onwards the mother's unconscious attitude strongly affects the infant's unconscious processes.

[1] Recent studies of pre-natal modes of behaviour, particularly as described and summarized by A. Gesell (*The Embryology of Behaviour*) provide food for thought about a rudimentary ego and the extent to which constitutional factors are already at work in the foetus. It is also an open question whether or not the mother's mental and physical state influences the foetus as regards the constitutional factors mentioned above.

We are, therefore, bound to conclude that constitutional factors cannot be considered apart from environmental ones and *vice versa*. They all go to form the earliest phantasies, anxieties and defences which, while falling into certain typical patterns, are infinitely variable. This is the soil from which springs the individual mind and personality.

I have endeavoured to show that by carefully observing young infants, we can gain some insight into their emotional life as well as indications for their future mental development. Such observations, within the limits mentioned above, to some extent support my findings about the earliest stages of development. These findings were arrived at in the psycho-analysis of children and adults, as I was able to trace their anxieties and defences back to babyhood. We may recall that Freud's discovery of the Oedipus complex in the unconscious of his adult patients led to a more enlightened observation of children, which in turn fully confirmed his theoretical conclusions. During the last few decades the conflicts inherent in the Oedipus complex have been more widely recognized and as a result the understanding of the child's emotional difficulties has increased; but this applies mainly to children in a more advanced stage of development. The very young infant's mental life is still a mystery to most adults. I venture to suggest that a closer observation of babies, stimulated by the increased knowledge of early mental processes which was derived from the psycho-analysis of young children, should in time to come lead to a better insight into the baby's emotional life.

It is my contention—put forward in some chapters of this book and in previous writings—that excessive persecutory and depressive anxieties in young infants are of crucial significance in the psychogenesis of mental disorders. In the present chapter I have repeatedly pointed out that an understanding mother may by her attitude diminish her baby's conflicts and thus in some measure help him to cope more effectively with his anxieties. A fuller and more general realization of the young infant's anxieties and emotional needs will therefore lessen suffering in infancy and so prepare the ground for greater happiness and stability in later life.

CHAPTER NOTES

CH. N. 1 (p. 243)

There is one fundamental aspect of this problem which I wish to mention. My psycho-analytic work has led me to conclude that the new-born infant unconsciously feels that an object of unique goodness exists, from which a maximal gratification could be obtained, and that this object is the mother's breast. I furthermore believe that this unconscious knowledge implies that the relation to the mother's breast and a feeling of possessing the breast develop even in children who are not being breast-fed. This would explain the fact referred to above that bottle-fed children, too, introject the mother's breast in both its good and bad aspects. How strong the capacity of a bottle-fed infant is to establish securely the good breast in his inner world depends on a variety of internal and external factors, among which the inherent capacity for love plays a vital part.

The fact that at the beginning of post-natal life an unconscious knowledge of the breast exists and that feelings towards the breast are experienced can only be conceived of as a phylogenetic inheritance.

To consider now the part ontogenetic factors play in these processes. We have good reason to assume that the infant's impulses bound up with the sensations of the mouth direct him towards the mother's breast, for the object of his first instinctual desires is the nipple and their aim is to suck the nipple. This would imply that the teat of the bottle cannot fully replace the desired nipple, nor the bottle the desired smell, warmth and softness of the mother's breast. Therefore, notwithstanding the fact that the infant may readily accept and enjoy bottle-feeding (particularly if a situation approximating to breast-feeding is established) he may still feel that he is not receiving the maximal gratification, and consequently experiences a deep longing for the unique object which could provide it.

The desire for unobtainable, ideal objects is a general feature in mental life, for it derives from the various frustrations the child undergoes in the course of his development, culminating in the necessity to renounce the Oedipus object. Feelings of frustration and grievance lead to phantasying backwards and often focus in retrospect on the privations suffered in relation to the mother's breast, even in people who have been satisfactorily breast-fed. I found, however, in a number of analyses that, in people who have not been breast-fed, the nature of the longing for an unobtainable object shows a particular intensity and quality, something so deep-rooted that its origin in the first feeding experience and first object-relation of the infant becomes apparent. Such emotions vary in strength between one individual and another, and have different effects on mental development. For instance, in some people the feeling of having been deprived of the breast may contribute to a strong sense of grievance and insecurity, with various implications for object-relations and the development of the personality. In other people the longing for a unique object which, although it has eluded them, is yet felt to exist somewhere may strongly stimulate certain lines of sublimations, such as the search for an ideal, or high standards for one's own attainments.

I will now compare these observations with a statement by Freud. Speaking of the fundamental importance of the infant's relation to the mother's breast and to the mother, Freud says:

'The phylogenetic foundation has so much the upper hand in all this over accidental personal experience that it makes no difference whether a child has really sucked at the breast or has been brought up on the bottle and never enjoyed the tenderness of a mother's care. His development takes the same path in both cases; *it may be that in the latter event his later longing is all the greater.*' (*An Outline of Psycho-Analysis*, p. 56.) (My italics.)

Here Freud attributes to the phylogenetic factor such over-riding importance that the actual feeding experience of the infant becomes relatively insignificant. This goes further than the conclusions to which my experience has led me. However, in the passage italicized by me, Freud seems to consider the possibility that having missed the experience of breast-feeding is felt as a deprivation, for otherwise we could not account for the longing for the mother's breast being 'all the greater'.

Ch. N. 2 (p. 252)

I have made it clear that the processes of integration, which express themselves in the infant's synthesizing his contrasting emotions towards the mother—and consequently the bringing together of the good and bad aspects of the object—underlie depressive anxiety and the depressive position. It is implied that these processes are from the outset related to the object. In the weaning experience it is the primary loved object which is felt to be lost and therefore the persecutory and depressive anxieties relating to it are reinforced. The beginning of weaning thus constitutes a major crisis in the infant's life and his conflicts come to another climax during the final stage of weaning. Every detail in the way weaning is carried out has a bearing on the intensity of the infant's depressive anxiety and may increase or diminish his capacity to work through the depressive position. Thus a careful and slow weaning is favourable while an abrupt weaning, by suddenly reinforcing his anxiety, may impair his emotional development. A number of pertinent questions arise here. For instance, what is the effect of a substitution of bottle-feeding for breast-feeding in the first weeks, or even months, of life? We have reason to assume that this situation differs from normal weaning, starting at about five months. Would this imply that, since in the first three months persecutory anxiety predominates, this form of anxiety is increased by early weaning, or does this experience produce an earlier onset of depressive anxiety in the infant? Which of these two outcomes will prevail may depend partly on external factors, such as the actual moment when weaning is begun and the way the mother handles the situation; partly on internal factors which could be broadly summarized as the strength of the inherent capacity for love and integration—which in turn implies also an inherent strength of the ego at the beginning of life. These factors, as I have repeatedly contended, underlie the infant's capacity to establish his good object securely, to some degree even when he has never had the experience of being fed by the breast.

Another question applies to the effect of late weaning, as is customary with primitive peoples and also in certain sections of civilized communities. I have not enough data on which to base an answer to this problem. I can, however, say that as far as I can judge from observation as well as from psycho-analytic experience, there is an optimum period for starting weaning at about the middle of the first year. For at this stage the infant is going through the depressive position, and weaning in some ways helps him to work through the inescapable depressive feelings. In this process he is supported by the increasing range of object-relations, interests, sublimations and defences which he develops at this stage.

As regards the completion of weaning—that is, the final change-over from sucking to drinking from a cup—it is more difficult to make a general suggestion as regards an optimum time. Here the needs of the individual child, which at this stage can be more easily gauged by observation, should be taken as the decisive criterion.

With some infants there is even a further stage in the process of weaning to be considered, and this is the giving up of thumb- or finger-sucking. Some infants give it up under pressure from the mother or nurse, but, according to my observation, even if infants seem to renounce finger-sucking of their own accord (and here, too, external influences cannot altogether be discounted) this entails conflict, anxiety and depressive feelings characteristic of weaning, in some cases with loss of appetite.

The question of weaning links up with the more general problem of frustration. Frustration, if not excessive (and we shall remember here that up to a point frustrations are inevitable), may even help the child to deal with his depressive feelings. For the very experience that frustration can be overcome tends to strengthen the ego and is part of the work of mourning which supports the infant in dealing with depression. More specifically, the mother's reappearance proves again and again that she has not been destroyed and has not been turned into the bad mother, which implies that the infant's aggression has not had the dreaded consequences. There is thus a delicate and individually variable balance between the harmful and helpful effects of frustration, a balance which is determined by a variety of internal and external factors.

Ch. N. 3 (p. 257)

It is my contention that both the paranoid-schizoid and the depressive position are part of normal development. My experience has led me to conclude that if persecutory and depressive anxieties in early infancy are excessive in proportion to the capacity of the ego to deal step by step with anxiety, this may result in the pathological development of the child. I have described in the previous chapter the division in the relation to the mother (the 'good' and the 'bad' mother), which is characteristic of an ego not yet sufficiently integrated, as well as of the splitting mechanisms which are at their height during the first three or four months of life. Normally, the fluctuations in the relation to the mother, and temporary states of withdrawal—influenced by splitting processes—cannot be easily gauged, since at that stage they are closely linked with the immature state of the ego. However, when development is not proceeding satisfactorily, we can get certain indications of this failure. In the present chapter I have referred to some typical difficulties which indicate that the paranoid-schizoid position is not being satisfactorily worked through. Though the picture differed in some points, all these instances had one important feature in common: a disturbance in the development of object-relations which can already be observed during the first three or four months of life.

Again, certain difficulties are part of the normal process of going through the depressive position, such as fretfulness, irritability, disturbed sleep, greater need for attention, and changes in the attitude towards the mother and food. If such disturbances are excessive and persist unduly, they may indicate a failure to work through the depressive position and may become the basis for manic-depressive illness in later life. The failure to work through the depressive position may, however, lead to a different outcome: certain symptoms, such as withdrawal from the mother and other people, may become stabilized instead of being transitory and partial. If together with this the infant becomes more apathetic, failing to develop the widening of interests and acceptance of substitutes which is normally present simultaneously with depressive symptoms, and is partly a way of overcoming them, we may surmise that the depressive position is not being successfully worked through; that a regression to the former position, the paranoid-schizoid position, has taken place—a regression to which we have to attribute great importance.

To repeat my conclusion expressed in earlier writings: persecutory and depressive anxieties, if excessive, may lead to severe mental illnesses and mental deficiency in childhood. These two forms of anxiety also provide the fixation-points for paranoic, schizophrenic and manic-depressive illnesses in adult life.

CH. N. 4 (p. 258)

Freud mentions the infant's pleasure in the game played with his mother when she hides her face and then reappears. (Freud does not say what stage of infancy he is referring to; but from the nature of the game one might assume that he is referring to infants in the middle or later months of the first year, as well as perhaps to older ones.) In this connection he states that the infant 'cannot as yet distinguish between temporary absence and permanent loss. As soon as he misses his mother he behaves as if he were never going to see her again; and repeated consolatory experiences to the contrary are necessary before he learns that her disappearance is usually followed by her reappearance.' (*Inhibitions, Symptoms and Anxiety*, p. 167.)

As regards further conclusions, the same difference of view exists on this point as in the interpretation of the cotton-reel game mentioned earlier. According to Freud, the anxiety which a young infant experiences when he misses his mother produces '. . . a traumatic situation if he happens at the time to be feeling a need which she is the one to gratify. It turns into a danger-situation if this need is not present at the moment. Thus the first determinant of anxiety which the ego itself introduces is loss of perception of the object (which is equated with loss of the object itself). There is as yet no question of loss of love. It is only later on that experience teaches the child that the object can be present but angry with him;

and then the loss of love on the part of the object becomes a new and much more enduring danger and determinant of anxiety'. (*Loc. cit.*, p. 168.) In my view, which I have stated in various connections and am briefly recapitulating here, the young infant experiences love as well as hatred towards his mother, and when he misses her and his needs are not satisfied her absence is felt to be the result of his destructive impulses; hence persecutory anxiety results (lest the good mother may have turned into the angry persecuting mother) and mourning, guilt and anxiety (lest the loved mother be destroyed by his aggression). These anxieties, constituting the depressive position, are again and again overcome, *e.g.* by play of a consolatory nature.

After having considered some differences of opinion as regards the emotional life and anxieties of the young infant, I would draw attention to a passage in the same context as the above quotation, where Freud seems to qualify his conclusions about the subject of mourning. He says, '. . . When does separation from an object produce anxiety, when does it produce mourning and when does it produce, it may be, only pain?   Let me say at once that there is no prospect of answering these questions at present. We must content ourselves with drawing certain distinctions and adumbrating certain possibilities.' (*Loc. cit.*, pp. 166-7.)

VIII

ON THE THEORY OF ANXIETY
AND GUILT[1]

By MELANIE KLEIN

MY conclusions regarding anxiety and guilt have evolved gradually over a number of years; it may be useful to retrace some of the steps by which I arrived at them.

I

Concerning the origins of anxiety, Freud put forward to begin with the hypothesis that anxiety arises out of a direct transformation of libido. In *Inhibitions, Symptoms and Anxiety* he reviewed his various theories on the origin of anxiety. As he put it: 'I propose to assemble, quite impartially, all the facts that we do know about anxiety and to give up the idea of making any immediate synthesis of them.'[2] He stated again that anxiety arises from direct transformation of libido but now seemed to attribute less importance to this 'economic' aspect of the origin of anxiety. He qualified this view in the following statements: 'The whole matter can be clarified, I think, if we commit ourselves to the definite statement that as a result of repression the intended course of the excitatory process in the id does not occur at all; the ego succeeds in inhibiting or deflecting it. If this is so the problem of "transformation of affect" under repression disappears.'[3] And: 'The problem of how anxiety arises in connection with repression may be no simple one; but we may legitimately maintain the opinion that the ego is the actual seat of anxiety and give up our earlier view that the cathectic energy of a repressed impulse is automatically turned into anxiety.'[4]

Regarding the manifestations of anxiety in young children, Freud said that anxiety is caused by the child 'missing someone who is loved and longed for'.[5] In connection with the girl's

---

[1] First published in *I.J.Ps-A.*, XXIX, 1948.
[2] *Loc. cit.*, p. 96.   [4] *Loc. cit.*, p. 23.
[3] *Loc. cit.*, p. 21.   [5] *Loc. cit.*, p. 105.

most fundamental anxiety, he described the infantile fear of loss of love in terms which in some measure seem to apply to infants of both sexes: 'If the mother is absent or has withdrawn her love from the child, it can no longer be certain that its needs will be satisfied and may be exposed to the most painful feelings of tension.'[1]

In the *New Introductory Lectures*, referring to the theory that anxiety arises from a transformation of unsatisfied libido, Freud said that it has 'found some support in certain almost universal phobias of small children. . . . Children's phobias and the anxious expectation in anxiety-neurosis serve as two examples of one way in which neurotic anxiety comes about; *i.e.* through direct transformation of libido.'[2]

Two conclusions, to which I shall return later on, can be drawn from these and similar passages: (*a*) in young children it is unsatisfied libidinal excitation which turns into anxiety; (*b*) the earliest *content* of anxiety is the infant's feeling of danger lest his need should not be satisfied because the mother is 'absent'.

II

As regards guilt, Freud held that it has its origin in the Oedipus complex and arises as a sequel to it. There are passages, however, in which Freud clearly referred to conflict and guilt arising at a much earlier stage of life. He wrote: '. . . guilt is the expression of the conflict of ambivalence, *the eternal struggle between Eros and the destructive or death instinct.*'[3] (My italics.) Also: '. . . an intensification of the sense of guilt—resulting from the *innate conflict of ambivalence*, from the eternal struggle between love and the death trends. . . .'[4] (My italics.)

Furthermore, speaking of the view propounded by some authors that frustration heightens the sense of guilt, he said: 'How then is it to be explained dynamically and economically that a heightening of the sense of guilt should appear in place of an unfulfilled erotic desire? This can surely only happen in a

---

[1] *New Introductory Lectures on Psycho-Analysis* (1932), p. 115.
[2] *Loc. cit.*, pp. 109–10.
[3] *Civilization and its Discontents* (1930), p. 121.
[4] *Loc. cit.*, pp. 121–2.

roundabout way: the thwarting of the erotic gratification provokes an access of aggressiveness against the person who interfered with the gratification, and then this tendency to aggression in its turn has itself to be suppressed. So then *it is, after all, only the aggression which is changed into guilt,* by being suppressed and made over to the super-ego. I am convinced that very many processes will admit of much simpler and clearer explanation if we restrict the findings of psycho-analysis in respect of the origin of the sense of guilt to the aggressive instincts.'[1] (My italics.)

Here Freud unequivocally stated that guilt derives from aggression and this, together with the sentences quoted above ('innate conflict of ambivalence') would point to guilt arising at a very early stage of development. Taking, however, Freud's views as a whole, as we find them summarized again in the *New Introductory Lectures on Psycho-Analysis*, it is clear that he maintained his hypothesis that guilt sets in as a sequel to the Oedipus complex.

Abraham, particularly in his study of the libidinal organization[2] threw much light on the earliest phases of development. His discoveries in the field of infantile sexuality were bound up with a new approach to the origin of anxiety and guilt. Abraham suggested that 'in the stage of narcissism with a cannibalistic sexual aim the first evidence of an instinctual inhibition appears in the shape of morbid anxiety. The process of overcoming the cannibalistic impulses is intimately associated with a sense of guilt which comes into the foreground as a typical inhibitory phenomenon belonging to the third (earlier anal-sadistic) stage'.[3]

Abraham thus contributed materially to our understanding of the origins of anxiety and guilt, since he was the first to point out the connection of anxiety and guilt with cannibalistic

---

[1] *Loc. cit.,* p. 131. In the same book (on p. 116) Freud accepted my hypothesis (expressed in my papers 'Early Stages of the Oedipus Conflict', 1928, and 'The Importance of Symbol-Formation in the Development of the Ego', 1930) that the severity of the super-ego to some extent results from the child's aggression which is projected on to the super-ego.

[2] 'A Short Study of the Development of the Libido, viewed in the Light of Mental Disorders.'

[3] *Loc. cit.,* p. 496.

desires. He compared his brief survey of the psycho-sexual development to a 'time-table of express trains in which only the larger stations at which they stop are given'. He suggested that the 'halting-places that lie between cannot be marked in a summary of this kind'.[1]

III

My own work not only corroborated Abraham's discoveries on anxiety and guilt and showed their importance in proper perspective, but also developed them further by bringing them together with a number of new facts discovered in the analyses of young children.

When I analysed infantile anxiety-situations, I recognized the fundamental importance of sadistic impulses and phantasies from all sources which converge and reach a climax in the earliest stages of development. I also came to see that the early processes of introjection and projection lead to establishing within the ego, side by side with extremely 'good' objects, extremely frightening and persecuting objects. These figures are conceived in the light of the infant's own aggressive impulses and phantasies, i.e. he projects his own aggression on to the internal figures which form part of his early super-ego. To anxiety from these sources is added the guilt derived from the infant's aggressive impulses against his first loved object, both external and internalized.[2]

In a later paper[3] I illustrated by an extreme case the pathological effects of the anxiety aroused in infants by their destructive impulses, and concluded that the earliest defences of the ego (in normal as well as in abnormal development) are directed against the anxiety aroused by aggressive impulses and phantasies.[4]

[1] Loc. cit., pp. 495–6.
[2] Cf. my paper, 'Early Stages of the Oedipus Conflict' (presented to the International Psycho-Analytical Congress, Innsbruck, 1927).
[3] 'The Importance of Symbol-Formation in the Development of the Ego' (presented to the International Psycho-Analytical Congress, Oxford, 1929).
[4] I have dealt with this problem more fully and from various angles in my book, The Psycho-Analysis of Children, Chapters 8 and 9.

Some years later, in my attempt to reach a fuller under-standing of infantile sadistic phantasies and their origin, I was led to apply Freud's hypothesis of the struggle between the life and death instincts to the clinical material gained in the analysis of young children. We remember that Freud stated: 'The activity of the dangerous death instincts within the individual organism is dealt with in various ways; in part they are rendered harmless by being fused with erotic components, in part they are diverted towards the external world in the form of aggression, while for the most part they undoubtedly continue their inner work unhindered.'[1]

Following this line of thought I put forward the hypothesis[2] that anxiety is aroused by the danger which threatens the organism from the death instinct; and I suggested that this is the primary cause of anxiety. Freud's description of the struggle between the life and death instincts (which leads to the deflec-tion of one portion of the death instinct outwards and to the fusion of the two instincts)[3] would point to the conclusion that anxiety has its origin in the fear of death.

In his paper on masochism[4] Freud drew some fundamental conclusions regarding the connections between masochism and the death instinct, and he considered in this light the various anxieties arising from the activity of the death instinct turned inwards.[5] Among these anxieties he does not, however, mention the fear of death.

In *Inhibitions, Symptoms and Anxiety* Freud discussed his reasons for not regarding the fear of death (or fear for life) as a primary anxiety. He based this view on his observation that 'the unconscious seems to contain nothing that would lend sub-stance to the concept of the annihilation of life' (p. 93). He also pointed out that nothing resembling death can ever have been experienced, except possibly fainting, and concluded that 'the

---

[1] *The Ego and the Id* (1923), p. 79.
[2] Cf. *The Psycho-Analysis of Children*, pp. 183–4.
[3] *The Ego and the Id*, p. 79.
[4] 'The Economic Problem in Masochism' (1924). In this paper Freud first applied the new classification of instincts to clinical problems. 'Moral masochism thus becomes the classical piece of evidence for the existence of "instinctual fusion" ' (p. 267).
[5] *Loc. cit.*, p. 261.

fear of death should be regarded as analogous to the fear of castration'.

I do not share this view because my analytic observations show that there is in the unconscious a fear of annihilation of life. I would also think that if we assume the existence of a death instinct, we must also assume that in the deepest layers of the mind there is a response to this instinct in the form of fear of annihilation of life. Thus in my view the danger arising from the inner working of the death instinct is the first cause of anxiety.[1] Since the struggle between the life and death instincts persists throughout life, this source of anxiety is never eliminated and enters as a perpetual factor into all anxiety-situations.

My contention that anxiety originates in the fear of annihilation derives from experience accumulated in the analyses of young children. When in such analyses the earliest anxiety-situations of the infant are revived and repeated, the inherent power of an instinct ultimately directed against the self can be detected in such strength that its existence appears beyond doubt. This remains true even when we allow for the part which frustration, internal and external, plays in the vicissitudes of destructive impulses. This is not the place for detailed evidence in support of my argument, but I shall quote by way of illustration one instance mentioned in my *Psycho-Analysis of Children* (p. 184). A five-year-old boy used to pretend that he had all sorts of wild animals, such as elephants, leopards, hyenas and wolves, to help him against his enemies. They represented dangerous objects—persecutors—which he had tamed and could use as protection against his enemies. But it appeared in the analysis that they also stood for his own sadism, each animal representing a specific source of sadism and the organs used in this connection. The elephants symbolized his muscular sadism, his impulses to trample and stamp. The tearing leopards represented his teeth and nails and their functions in his attacks. The wolves symbolized his excrements invested with destructive properties. He sometimes became very frightened that the wild animals he had tamed would turn

---

[1] See Chapter IX. In 1946 I arrived at the conclusion that this primary anxiety-situation plays an important part in schizophrenic illness.

against him and exterminate him. This fear expressed his sense of being threatened by his own destructiveness (as well as by internal persecutors).

As I have illustrated by this instance, the analysis of the anxieties arising in young children teaches us a good deal about the forms in which the fear of death exists in the unconscious, that is to say, about the part this fear plays in various anxiety-situations. I have already mentioned Freud's paper on the 'Economic Problem in Masochism', which was based on his new discovery of the death instinct. To take the first anxiety-situation he enumerated[1]: 'the fear of being devoured by the totem animal (father)'. This in my view is an undisguised expression of the fear of total annihilation of the self. The fear of being devoured by the father derives from the projection of the infant's impulses to devour his objects. In this way first the mother's breast (and the mother) becomes in the infant's mind a devouring object[2] and these fears soon extend to the father's penis and to the father. At the same time, since devouring implies from the beginning the internalization of the devoured object, the ego is felt to contain devoured and devouring objects. Thus the super-ego is built up from the devouring breast (mother) to which is added the devouring penis (father). These cruel and dangerous internal figures become the representatives of the death instinct. Simultaneously the other aspect of the early super-ego is formed first by the internalized good breast (to which is added the good penis of the father), which is felt as a feeding and helpful internal object, and as the representative of the life instinct. The fear of being annihilated includes the anxiety lest the internal good breast be destroyed, for this object is felt to be indispensable for the preservation of life. The threat to the self from the death instinct working within is bound up with the dangers apprehended from the internalized devouring mother and father, and amounts to fear of death.

According to this view, the fear of death enters from the

---

[1] *Loc. cit.*, p. 261.
[2] Cf. examples given in Chapter III: the boy who said his mother's breast had bitten him and the girl who thought her mother's shoe would eat her up.

beginning into the fear of the super-ego and is not, as Freud remarked, a 'final transformation' of the fear of the super-ego.[1]

Turning to another essential danger-situation which Freud mentioned in his paper on Masochism, *i.e.* the fear of castration, I would suggest that the fear of death enters into and reinforces castration fear and is not 'analogous' to it.[2] Since the genital is not only the source of the most intense libidinal gratification, but also the representative of Eros, and since reproduction is the essential way of counteracting death, the loss of the genital would mean the end of the creative power which preserves and continues life.

IV

If we try to visualize in concrete form the primary anxiety, the fear of annihilation, we must remember the helplessness of the infant in face of internal and external dangers. I suggest that the primary danger-situation arising from the activity of the death instinct within is felt by him as an overwhelming attack, as persecution. Let us first consider in this connection some of the processes which ensue from the deflection of the death instinct outwards and the ways in which they influence anxieties relating to external and internal situations. We may assume that the struggle between life and death instincts already operates during birth and accentuates the persecutory anxiety aroused by this painful experience. It would seem that this experience has the effect of making the external world, including the first external object, the mother's breast, appear hostile. To this contributes the fact that the ego turns the destructive impulses against this primary object. The young infant feels that frustration by the breast, which in fact implies danger to life, is the retaliation for his destructive impulses towards it and that the frustrating breast is persecuting him. In addition he projects his destructive impulses on to the breast, that is to say, deflects the death instinct outwards; and in these ways the

---

[1] *Inhibitions, Symptoms and Anxiety* (1926), pp. 111–12.

[2] For a detailed discussion of the sources of anxiety which interact with the fear of castration, see my paper 'The Oedipus Conflict in the Light of Early Anxieties'.

attacked breast becomes the external representative of the death instinct.[1] The 'bad' breast is also introjected, and this intensifies, as we may assume, the internal danger-situation, *i.e.* the fear of the activity of the death instinct within. For by the internalization of the 'bad' breast, the portion of the death instinct which had been deflected outwards, with all its associated dangers, is turned inwards again and the ego attaches its fear of its own destructive impulses to the internal bad object. These processes may well happen simultaneously and therefore my description of them is not to be taken as a chronological account. To summarize: the frustrating (bad) external breast becomes, owing to projection, the external representative of the death instinct; through introjection it reinforces the primary internal danger-situation; this leads to an increased urge on the part of the ego to deflect (project) internal dangers (primarily the activity of the death instinct) into the external world. There is therefore a constant fluctuation between the fear of internal and external bad objects, between the death instinct acting within and deflected outwards. Here we see one important aspect of the interaction—from the beginning of life —between projection and introjection. External dangers are experienced in the light of internal dangers and are therefore intensified; on the other hand, any danger threatening from outside intensifies the perpetual inner danger-situation. This interaction exists in some measure throughout life. The very fact that the struggle has, to some extent, been externalized relieves anxiety. Externalization of internal danger-situations is one of the ego's earliest methods of defence against anxiety and remains fundamental in development.

The activity of the death instinct deflected outwards, as well as its working within, cannot be considered apart from the simultaneous activity of the life instinct. Side by side with the deflection of the death instinct outwards, the life instinct—by

[1] In my *Psycho-Analysis of Children* (pp. 180 ff.) I suggested that the earliest feeding difficulties of infants are a manifestation of persecutory fears. (I was referring to those feeding difficulties which appear even though the mother's milk is plentiful and no external factors would seem to prevent a satisfactory feeding-situation.) I concluded that these persecutory fears, when excessive, lead to a far-reaching inhibition of libidinal desires. Cf. also Chapter VI of the present book.

means of the libido—attaches itself to the external object, the gratifying (good) breast, which becomes the external representative of the life instinct. The introjection of this good object reinforces the power of the life instinct within. The good internalized breast, which is felt to be the source of life, forms a vital part of the ego and its preservation becomes an imperative need. The introjection of this first loved object is therefore inextricably linked with all the processes engendered by the life instinct. The good internalized breast and the bad devouring breast form the core of the super-ego in its good and bad aspects; they are the representatives within the ego of the struggle between the life and death instincts.

The second important part-object to be introjected is the penis of the father to which also both good and bad qualities are attributed. These two dangerous objects—the bad breast and the bad penis—are the prototypes of internal and external persecutors. Experiences of a painful nature, frustrations from internal and external sources, which are felt as persecution, are primarily attributed to the external and internal persecuting objects. In all such experiences, persecutory anxiety and aggression reinforce each other. For while the infant's aggressive impulses through projection play a fundamental part in his building up of persecutory figures, these very figures increase his persecutory anxiety and in turn reinforce his aggressive impulses and phantasies against the external and internal objects felt to be dangerous.

Paranoid disturbances in adults are, in my view, based on the persecutory anxiety experienced in the first few months of life. In the paranoid patient the essence of his fears of persecution is the feeling that there is a hostile agency which is bent on inflicting on him suffering, damage and ultimately annihilation. This persecutory agency may be represented by one or many people or even by the forces of nature. There are innumerable and in every case specific forms which the dreaded attack may take; but the root of persecutory fear in the paranoid individual is, I believe, the fear of annihilation of the ego—ultimately by the death instinct.

V

T shall now discuss more specifically the relation between guilt and anxiety and in this connection shall first reconsider some of Freud's and Abraham's views regarding anxiety and guilt. Freud approached the problem of guilt from two main angles. On the one hand he left no doubt that anxiety and guilt are closely connected with each other. On the other hand he came to the conclusion that the term 'guilt' is only applicable in regard to manifestations of conscience which are the result of super-ego development. The super-ego, as we know, in his view comes into being as a sequel to the Oedipus complex. Therefore with children under about four to five years of age, the terms 'conscience' and 'guilt' in his view do not yet apply and anxiety in the first few years of life is distinct from guilt.[1]

According to Abraham[2] guilt arises in the overcoming of cannibalistic—*i.e.* aggressive—impulses during the earlier anal-sadistic stage (that is, at a much earlier age than Freud assumed); but he did not consider a differentiation between anxiety and guilt. Ferenczi, who was also not concerned with the distinction between anxiety and guilt, suggested that something in the nature of guilt arises during the anal stage. He concluded that there may be a kind of physiological precursor of the super-ego which he calls 'sphincter-morality'.[3]

---

[1] A significant reference to the connection between anxiety and guilt is contained in the following passage: 'Here perhaps is the place to remark that at bottom the sense of guilt is nothing but a topographical variety of anxiety' (*Civilization and its Discontents*, p. 125). On the other hand, Freud definitely distinguishes between anxiety and guilt. In discussing the development of the sense of guilt, he says in reference to the use of the term 'guilt' in regard to early manifestations of 'bad conscience': 'We call this state of mind a "bad conscience"; but actually it does not deserve this name, for at this stage the sense of guilt is obviously only the dread of losing love, "social" anxiety. In a little child it can never be anything else, but in many adults too it has only changed in so far as the larger human community takes the place of the father or of both parents. . . . A great change takes place as soon as the authority has been internalized by the development of a super-ego. The manifestations of conscience are then raised to a new level: to be accurate, one should not call them conscience and sense of guilt before this.' (*Loc. cit.*, pp. 107–8.)

[2] 'A Short Study of the Development of the Libido.'

[3] Ferenczi, 'Psycho-Analysis of Sexual Habits' (1925), p. 267.

Ernest Jones, in a paper published in 1929,[1] dealt with the interaction between hate, fear and guilt. He distinguished between two phases in the development of guilt and suggested for the first stage the term 'pre-nefarious' stage of guilt. This he connected with the sadistic pre-genital stages of super-ego development and stated that guilt is 'always and inevitably associated with the hate impulse'. The second stage is '. . . the stage of guilt proper, the function of which is to protect against the external dangers'.

In my paper 'A Contribution to the Psychogenesis of Manic-Depressive States' I differentiated between two main forms of anxiety—persecutory and depressive anxiety—but pointed out that the distinction between these two forms of anxiety is not by any means clear-cut. With this limitation in mind I think that a differentiation between the two forms of anxiety is valuable both from the theoretical and practical point of view. In the paper referred to above I came to the conclusion that persecutory anxiety relates predominantly to the annihilation of the ego; depressive anxiety is predominantly related to the harm done to internal and external loved objects by the subject's destructive impulses. Depressive anxiety has manifold contents, such as: the good object is injured, it is suffering, it is in a state of deterioration; it changes into a bad object; it is annihilated, lost and will never be there any more. I also concluded that depressive anxiety is closely bound up with guilt and with the tendency to make reparation.

When I first introduced my concept of the depressive position in the paper referred to above, I suggested that depressive anxiety and guilt arise with the introjection of the object as a whole. My further work on the paranoid-schizoid position,[2] which precedes the depressive position, has led me to the conclusion that though in the first stage destructive impulses and persecutory anxiety predominate, depressive anxiety and guilt already play some part in the infant's earliest object-relation, *i.e.* in his relation to his mother's breast.

During the paranoid-schizoid position, that is, during the first three to four months of life, splitting processes, involving the splitting of the first object (the breast) as well as of the feel-

---

[1] 'Fear, Guilt and Hate.'   [2] Cf. Chapter IX.

ings towards it, are at their height. Hatred and persecutory anxiety become attached to the frustrating (bad) breast, and love and reassurance to the gratifying (good) breast. However, even at this stage such splitting processes are never fully effective; for from the beginning of life the ego tends towards integrating itself and towards synthesizing the different aspects of the object. (This tendency can be regarded as an expression of the life instinct.) There appear to be transitory states of integration even in very young infants—becoming more frequent and lasting as development goes on—in which the cleavage between the good and bad breast is less marked.

In such states of integration, a measure of synthesis between love and hatred in relation to part-objects comes about, which according to my present view gives rise to depressive anxiety, guilt and the desire to make reparation to the injured loved object—first of all to the good breast.[1] That is to say that I now link the onset of depressive anxiety with the relation to part-objects. This modification is the result of further work on the earliest stages of the ego and of a fuller recognition of the gradual nature of the infant's emotional development. There is no change in my view that the basis of depressive anxiety is the synthesis between destructive impulses and feelings of love towards *one* object.

Let us next consider how far this modification influences the concept of the depressive position. I would now describe this position as follows: during the period from three to six months considerable progress in the integration of the ego comes about. Important changes take place in the nature of the infant's object-relations and of his introjection-processes. The infant perceives and introjects the mother increasingly as a complete person. This implies a fuller identification and a more stable relation with her. Although these processes are still primarily focussed on the mother, the infant's relation to the father (and other people in his environment) undergoes similar changes and the father too becomes established in his mind as a whole person. At the same time, splitting processes diminish in strength and

[1] We must remember, though, that even during this stage the mother's face and hands, and her whole bodily presence, increasingly enter into the gradual building up of the child's relation to her as a person.

are predominantly related to whole objects, while in the earlier stage they were mainly connected with part-objects.

The contrasting aspects of the objects and the conflicting feelings, impulses and phantasies towards it, come closer together in the infant's mind. Persecutory anxiety persists and plays its part in the depressive position, but it lessens in quantity and depressive anxiety gains the ascendancy over persecutory anxiety. Since it is a loved *person* (internalized and external) who is felt to be injured by aggressive impulses, the infant suffers from intensified depressive feelings, more lasting than the fleeting experiences of depressive anxiety and guilt in the earlier stage. The more integrated ego is now increasingly confronted with a very painful psychic reality—the complaints and reproaches emanating from the internalized injured mother and father who are now complete objects, persons— and feels compelled under the stress of greater suffering to deal with the painful psychic reality. This leads to an over-riding urge to preserve, repair or revive the loved objects: the tendency to make reparation. As an alternative method, very likely a simultaneous one, of dealing with these anxieties, the ego resorts strongly to the manic defence.[1]

The developments I have described imply not only important qualitative and quantitative changes in feelings of love, depressive anxiety and guilt but also a new combination of factors which constitute the depressive position.

It can be seen from the foregoing description that the modification of my views regarding the earlier onset of depressive anxiety and guilt have not in any essentials altered my concept of the depressive position.

At this point I wish to consider more specifically the processes by which depressive anxiety, guilt and the urge to make reparation come about. The basis of depressive anxiety is, as I described, the process by which the ego synthesizes destructive impulses and feelings of love towards one object. The feeling that the harm done to the loved object is caused by the subject's

---

[1] The concept of the manic defence and its wider application to mental life has been dealt with in some detail in my papers 'A Contribution to the Psychogenesis of Manic-Depressive States' and 'Mourning and its Relation to Manic-Depressive States'.

aggressive impulses I take to be the essence of guilt. (The infant's feeling of guilt may extend to every evil befalling the loved object—even the harm done by his persecutory objects.) The urge to undo or repair this harm results from the feeling that the subject has caused it, *i.e.* from guilt. The reparative tendency can, therefore, be considered as a consequence of the sense of guilt.

The question now arises: is guilt an element in depressive anxiety? Are they both aspects of the same process, or is one a result or a manifestation of the other? While I cannot at present give a definite answer to this question, I would suggest that depressive anxiety, guilt and the reparative urge are often experienced simultaneously.

It seems probable that depressive anxiety, guilt and the reparative tendency are only experienced when feelings of love for the object predominate over destructive impulses. In other words, we may assume that recurrent experiences of love surmounting hatred—ultimately of the life instinct surmounting the death instinct—are an essential condition for the ego's capacity to integrate itself and to synthesize the contrasting aspects of the object. In such states or moments the relation to the bad aspect of the object, including persecutory anxiety, has receded.

However, during the first three or four months of life, a stage at which (according to my present views) depressive anxiety and guilt arise, splitting processes and persecutory anxiety are at their height. Therefore persecutory anxiety very quickly interferes with progress in integration, and experiences of depressive anxiety, guilt and reparation can only be of a transitory nature. As a result, the loved injured object may very swiftly change into a persecutor, and the urge to repair or revive the loved object may turn into the need to pacify and propitiate a persecutor. But even during the next stage, the depressive position, in which the more integrated ego introjects and establishes increasingly the whole person, persecutory anxiety persists. During this period, as I described it, the infant experiences not only grief, depression and guilt, but also persecutory anxiety relating to the bad aspect of the super-ego; and defences against persecutory anxiety exist side by side with defences against depressive anxiety.

I have repeatedly pointed out that the differentiation between depressive and persecutory anxieties is based on a limiting concept. However, in psycho-analytic practice it has been found by a number of workers that the differentiation between persecutory and depressive anxiety is helpful in the understanding and unravelling of emotional situations. To give one instance of a typical picture which may confront us in the analysis of depressive patients: during a particular session a patient may suffer from strong feelings of guilt and despair about his incapacity to restore the damage which he feels he has caused. Then a complete change occurs: the patient suddenly brings up material of a persecutory kind. The analyst and analysis are accused of doing nothing but harm, grievances which lead back to early frustrations are voiced. The processes which underlie this change can be summarized as follows: persecutory anxiety has become dominant, the feeling of guilt has receded, and with it the love for the object seems to have disappeared. In this altered emotional situation, the object has turned bad, cannot be loved, and therefore destructive impulses towards it seem justified. This means that persecutory anxiety and defences *have been reinforced* in order to escape from the overwhelming burden of guilt and despair. In many cases, of course, the patient may show a good deal of persecutory anxiety together with guilt, and the change to a predominance of persecutory anxiety does not always appear as dramatically as I have here described it. But in every such case the differentiation between persecutory and depressive anxiety helps our understanding of the processes we are trying to analyse.

The conceptual distinction between depressive anxiety, guilt and reparation on the one hand, and persecutory anxiety and the defences against it on the other, not only proves helpful in analytic work but also has wider implications. It throws light on many problems connected with the study of human emotions and behaviour.[1] One particular field in which I have

---

[1] In his paper, 'Towards a Common Aim—a Psycho-Analytical Contribution to Ethics', R. E. Money-Kyrle applied the distinction between persecutory and depressive anxieties to attitudes towards ethics in general and towards political beliefs in particular, and has since expanded these views in his book *Psycho-Analysis and Politics*.

found this concept illuminating is the observation and understanding of children.

I will here briefly summarize the theoretical conclusion regarding the relation between anxicty and guilt which I have put forward in this section. Guilt is inextricably bound up with anxiety (more exactly, with a specific form of it, depressive anxiety); it leads to the reparative tendency and arises, during the first few months of life, in connection with the earliest stages of the super-ego.

VI

The inter-relation between the primary internal danger and the danger threatening from without throws light on the problem of 'objective' *versus* 'neurotic' anxiety. Freud defined the distinction between objective anxiety and neurotic anxiety as follows: 'Objective danger is a danger that is known, and objective anxiety is anxiety about a known danger of this sort. Neurotic anxiety is anxiety about an unknown danger. Neurotic danger is thus a danger that has still to be discovered. Analysis has shown that it is an instinctual danger.'[1] And, again: 'An objective danger is a danger which threatens a person from an external object, and a neurotic danger is one which threatens him from an instinctual demand.'[2]

In some connections, however, Freud referred to an interaction between these two sources of anxiety,[3] and general analytic experience has shown that the distinction between objective and neurotic anxiety cannot be sharply drawn.

I shall here return to Freud's statement that anxiety is caused by the child 'missing someone who is loved and longed for'.[4] In describing the infant's fundamental fear of loss, Freud said: 'He cannot as yet distinguish between temporary absence

---

[1] *Inhibitions, Symptoms and Anxiety* (1926), p. 159.

[2] *Loc. cit.*, p. 163.

[3] This interaction between anxiety derived from external and internal causes is referred to by Freud with regard to some cases of neurotic anxiety. 'The danger is known and objective but the anxiety in regard to it is overgreat, greater than seems proper . . . analysis shows that to the known objective danger is attached an unknown instinctual one.' (*Loc. cit.*, p. 160.)

[4] *Loc. cit.*, p. 105.

and permanent loss. *As soon as he misses his mother he behaves as if he were never going to see her again;* and repeated consolatory experiences to the contrary are necessary before he learns that her disappearance is usually followed by her reappearance.'[1] (My italics.)

In another passage describing the fear of loss of love he said that it is 'obviously a continuation of the fear of the infant at the breast when it misses its mother. You will understand what *objective danger-situation* is indicated by this kind of anxiety. If the mother is absent or has withdrawn her love from the child, it can no longer be certain that its needs will be satisfied, and may be exposed to the most painful feelings of tension.'[2] (My italics.)

However, a few pages earlier in the same book, Freud described this particular danger-situation from the point of view of neurotic anxiety, which seems to show that he approached this infantile-situation from both angles. In my view these two main sources of the infant's fear of loss can be described as follows: one is the child's complete dependence on the mother for the satisfaction of his needs and the relief of tension. The anxiety arising from this source could be called objective anxiety. The other main source of anxiety derives from the infant's apprehension that the loved mother has been destroyed by his sadistic impulses or is in danger of being destroyed, and this fear—which could be called 'neurotic anxiety'—relates to the mother as an indispensable external (and internal) good object and contributes to the infant's feeling that she will never return. There is from the beginning a constant interaction between these two sources of anxiety, that is to say, between objective and neurotic anxiety or, in other words, anxiety from external and internal sources.

Furthermore, if external danger is from the beginning linked with internal danger from the death instinct, no danger-situation arising from external sources could ever be experienced by the young child as a purely external and known danger. But it is not only the infant who cannot make such a clear dif-

[1] *Loc. cit.*, p. 167.
[2] *New Introductory Lectures on Psycho-Analysis* (1932), p. 115.

ferentiation: to some extent the interaction between external and internal danger-situations persists throughout life.[1]

This was clearly shown in the analyses carried out in war-time. It appeared that even with normal adults anxiety stirred up by air-raids, bombs, fire, etc.—*i.e.* by an 'objective' danger-situation—could only be reduced by analysing, over and above the impact of the actual situation, the various early anxieties which were aroused by it. In many people excessive anxiety from these sources led to a powerful denial (manic defence) of the objective danger-situation, which showed itself in an apparent lack of fear. This was a common observation with children and could not be explained only by their incomplete realization of the actual danger. Analysis revealed that the objective danger-situation had revived the child's early phantastic anxieties to such an extent that the objective danger-situation had to be denied. In other cases the relative stability of children in spite of war-time dangers was not determined so much by manic defences as by a more successful modification of early persecutory and depressive anxieties, resulting in a greater feeling of security regarding both the inner and the external world, and in a good relationship with their parents. With such children, even when the father was absent, the reassurance gained from the presence of the mother, and from home life, counteracted the fears stirred up by objective dangers.

These observations become understandable if we remember that the young child's perception of external reality and external objects is perpetually influenced and coloured by his phantasies, and that this in some measure continues throughout life. External experiences which rouse anxiety at once activate even in normal persons anxiety derived from intrapsychic sources. The interaction between objective anxiety and neurotic anxiety—or, to express it in other words, the inter-action between anxiety arising from external and from internal

[1] As I pointed out in my *Psycho-Analysis of Children*, p. 266: 'If a normal person is put under a severe internal or external strain, or if he falls ill or fails in some other way, we may observe in him the full and complete operation of his deepest anxiety-situations. Since, then, every healthy person *may* succumb to a neurotic illness, it follows that he can never have entirely given up his old anxiety-situations.'

sources—corresponds to the interaction between external reality and psychic reality.

In estimating whether anxiety is neurotic or not, we have to consider a point to which Freud repeatedly referred, the quantity of anxiety from inner sources. This factor is however linked with the ego's capacity of evolving adequate defences against anxiety, *i.e.* the proportion of the strength of anxiety to the strength of the ego.

VII

It was implicit in this presentation of my views that they developed from an approach to aggression which differed substantially from the main trend in psycho-analytic thought. The fact that Freud discovered aggression first as an element in the child's sexuality—as it were as an adjunct to libido (sadism)—had the effect that for a long time psycho-analytical interest centred on the libido and that aggression was more or less considered as an auxiliary to libido.[1] In 1920 came Freud's discovery of the death instinct manifesting itself in destructive impulses and operating in fusion with the life instinct, and in 1924 followed Abraham's deeper exploration of sadism in the young child. But even after these discoveries, as can be seen from the bulk of psycho-analytical literature, psycho-analytical thought has remained predominantly concerned with the libido and with the defences against libidinal impulses and has correspondingly underrated the importance of aggression and its implications.

From the beginning of my psycho-analytic work, my interest was focussed on anxiety and its causation, and this brought me nearer to the understanding of the relation between aggression and anxiety.[2] The analyses of young children, for which I evolved Play Technique, supported this angle of approach, for they revealed that anxiety in young children could only be alleviated by analysing their sadistic phantasies and impulses with a greater appreciation of the share aggression has in sadism and in the causation of anxiety. This fuller evaluation of the importance of aggression led me to certain

---

[1] Cf. Chapter X, in which Paula Heimann discusses this theoretical bias in favour of the libido and its influence on the development of theory.

[2] This strong emphasis on anxiety entered already into my first publications.

theoretical conclusions which I presented in my paper 'The Early Stages of the Oedipus Conflict' (1927). There I put forward the hypothesis that—both in the normal and pathological development of the child—anxiety and guilt arising during the first year of life are closely connected with processes of introjection and projection, with the first stages of the super-ego development and of the Oedipus complex; and that in these anxieties aggression and the defences against it are of paramount importance.

Further work on these lines was carried out in the British Psycho-Analytical Society from about 1927 onwards. In this Society, a number of psycho-analysts, working in close cooperation, made numerous contributions[1] to the understanding of the cardinal role of aggression in mental life; while, taking psycho-analytic thought in general, a change of view in this direction has appeared only in sporadic contributions during the last ten to fifteen years; these have, however, increased of late.

One of the results of the new work on aggression was the recognition of the major function of the reparative tendency, which is an expression of the life instinct in its struggle against the death instinct. Not only were the destructive impulses thereby seen in better perspective, but a fuller light was thrown on the interaction of the life and death instincts, and therefore also on the role of the libido in all mental and emotional processes.

Throughout this chapter I have made clear my contention that the death instinct (destructive impulses) is the primary factor in the causation of anxiety. It was, however, also implied, in my exposition of the processes leading to anxiety and guilt, that the primary object against which the destructive impulses are directed is the object of the libido, and that it is therefore the *interaction* between aggression and libido—ultimately the fusion as well as the polarity of the two instincts—which causes anxiety and guilt. Another aspect of this interaction is the mitigation of destructive impulses by libido. An optimum in the interaction between libido and aggression implies that the anxiety arising from the perpetual activity of the death instinct, though never eliminated, is counteracted and kept at bay by the power of the life instinct.

[1] Cf. the bibliography appended to Chapter II, p. 64.

NOTES ON SOME
SCHIZOID MECHANISMS[1]

By MELANIE KLEIN

INTRODUCTION

THE present chapter is concerned with the importance of early paranoid and schizoid anxieties and mechanisms. I have given much thought to this subject for a number of years, even before clarifying my views on the depressive processes in infancy. In the course of working out my concept of the infantile depressive position, however, the problems of the phase preceding it again forced themselves on my attention. I now wish to formulate some hypotheses at which I have arrived regarding the earlier anxieties and mechanisms.[2]

The hypotheses I shall put forward, which relate to very early stages of development, are derived by inference from material gained in the analyses of adults and children, and some of these hypotheses seem to tally with observations familiar in psychiatric work. To substantiate my contentions would require an accumulation of detailed case material for which there is no room in the frame of this paper, and I hope in further contributions to fill this gap.

At the outset it will be useful to summarize briefly the conclusions regarding the earliest phases of development which I have already put forward.[3]

In early infancy anxieties characteristic of psychosis arise which drive the ego to develop specific defence-mechanisms. In this period the fixation-points for all psychotic disorders are to be found. This hypothesis led some people to believe that I

---

[1] This paper was read before the British Psycho-Analytical Society on December 4, 1946, and has been left unchanged as then published, apart from a few slight alterations (in particular the addition of one paragraph and some footnotes).

[2] Before completing this paper I discussed its main aspects with Paula Heimann and am much indebted to her for stimulating suggestions in working out and formulating a number of the concepts presented here.

[3] Cf. my *Psycho-Analysis of Children*, and 'A Contribution to the Psychogenesis of Manic-Depressive States'.

regarded all infants as psychotic; but I have already dealt sufficiently with this misunderstanding on other occasions. The psychotic anxieties, mechanisms and ego-defences of infancy have a profound influence on development in all its aspects, including the development of the ego, super-ego and object-relations.

I have often expressed my view that object-relations exist from the beginning of life, the first object being the mother's breast which to the child becomes split into a good (gratifying) and bad (frustrating) breast; this splitting results in a severance of love and hate. I have further suggested that the relation to the first object implies its introjection and projection, and thus from the beginning object-relations are moulded by an interaction between introjection and projection, between internal and external objects and situations. These processes participate in the building up of the ego and super-ego and prepare the ground for the onset of the Oedipus complex in the second half of the first year.

From the beginning the destructive impulse is turned against the object and is first expressed in phantasied oral-sadistic attacks on the mother's breast, which soon develop into on-slaughts on her body by all sadistic means. The persecutory fears arising from the infant's oral-sadistic impulses to rob the mother's body of its good contents, and from the anal-sadistic impulses to put his excrements into her (including the desire to enter her body in order to control her from within) are of great importance for the development of paranoia and schizophrenia.

I enumerated various typical defences of the early ego, such as the mechanisms of splitting the object and the impulses, idealization, denial of inner and outer reality and the stifling of emotions. I also mentioned various anxiety-contents, including the fear of being poisoned and devoured. Most of these phenomena—prevalent in the first few months of life—are found in the later symptomatic picture of schizophrenia.

This early period (first described as the 'persecutory phase') I later termed 'paranoid position',[1] and held that it precedes

[1] When this paper was first published in 1946, I was using my term 'paranoid position' synonymously with W. R. D. Fairbairn's 'schizoid position'. On further deliberation I decided to combine Fairbairn's term with mine and throughout the present book I am using the expression 'paranoid-schizoid position'.

the depressive position. If persecutory fears are very strong, and for this reason (among others) the infant cannot work through the paranoid-schizoid position, the working through of the depressive position is in turn impeded. This failure may lead to a regressive reinforcing of persecutory fears and strengthen the fixation-points for severe psychoses (that is to say, the group of schizophrenias). Another outcome of serious difficulties arising during the period of the depressive position may be manic-depressive disorders in later life. I also concluded that in less severe disturbances of development the same factors strongly influence the choice of neurosis.

While I assumed that the outcome of the depressive position depends on the working through of the preceding phase, I nevertheless attributed to the depressive position a central role in the child's early development. For with the introjection of the object as a whole the infant's object-relation alters fundamentally. The synthesis between the loved and hated aspects of the complete object gives rise to feelings of mourning and guilt which imply vital advances in the infant's emotional and intellectual life. This is also a crucial juncture for the choice of neurosis or psychosis. To all these conclusions I still adhere.

Some Notes on Fairbairn's Recent Papers

In a number of recent papers[1] W. R. D. Fairbairn has given much attention to the subject-matter with which I am now dealing. I therefore find it helpful to clarify some essential points of agreement and disagreement between us. It will be seen that some of the conclusions which I shall present in this paper are in line with Fairbairn's conclusions, while others differ fundamentally. Fairbairn's approach was largely from the angle of ego-development in relation to objects, while mine was predominantly from the angle of anxieties and their vicissitudes. He called the earliest phase the 'schizoid position'; he stated that it forms part of normal development and is the basis for adult schizoid and schizophrenic illness. I agree with this contention and consider his description of developmental schizoid

---

[1] Cf. 'A Revised Psychopathology of the Psychoses and Neuroses', 'Endopsychic Structure Considered in Terms of Object-Relationships' and 'Object-Relationships and Dynamic Structure'.

phenomena as significant and revealing, and of great value for our understanding of schizoid behaviour and of schizophrenia. I also think that Fairbairn's view that the group of schizoid or schizophrenic disorders is much wider than has been acknowledged is correct and important; and the particular emphasis he laid on the inherent relation between hysteria and schizophrenia deserves full attention. His term 'schizoid position' would be appropriate if it is understood to cover both persecutory fear and schizoid mechanisms.

I disagree—to mention first the most basic issues—with his revision of the theory of mental structure and instincts. I also disagree with his view that to begin with only the bad object is internalized—a view which seems to me to contribute to the important differences between us regarding the development of object-relations as well as of ego-development. For I hold that the introjected good breast forms a vital part of the ego, exerts from the beginning a fundamental influence on the process of ego-development and affects both ego-structure and object-relations. I also differ from Fairbairn's view that 'the great problem of the schizoid individual is how to love without destroying by love, whereas the great problem of the depressive individual is how to love without destroying by hate'.[1] This conclusion is in line not only with his rejecting Freud's concept of primary instincts but also with his underrating the role which aggression and hatred play from the beginning of life. As a result of this approach, he does not give enough weight to the importance of early anxiety and conflict and their dynamic effects on development.

Certain Problems of the Early Ego

In the following discussion I shall single out one aspect of ego-development and I shall deliberately not attempt to link it with the problems of ego-development as a whole. Nor can I here touch on the relation of the ego to the id and super-ego.

So far we know little about the structure of the early ego. Some of the recent suggestions on this point have not convinced me: I have particularly in mind Glover's concept of ego nuclei

---

[1] Cf. 'A Revised Psychopathology' (1941).

and Fairbairn's theory of a central ego and two subsidiary egos. More helpful in my view is Winnicott's emphasis on the un-integration of the early ego.[1] I would also say that the early ego largely lacks cohesion, and a tendency towards integration alternates with a tendency towards disintegration, a falling into bits.[2] I believe that these fluctuations are characteristic of the first few months of life.

We are, I think, justified in assuming that some of the functions which we know from the later ego are there at the beginning. Prominent amongst these functions is that of dealing with anxiety. I hold that anxiety arises from the operation of the death instinct within the organism, is felt as fear of annihilation (death) and takes the form of fear of persecution. The fear of the destructive impulse seems to attach itself at once to an object— or rather it is experienced as the fear of an uncontrollable over-powering object. Other important sources of primary anxiety are the trauma of birth (separation anxiety) and frustration of bodily needs; and these experiences too are from the beginning felt as being caused by objects. Even if these objects are felt to be external, they become through introjection internal per-secutors and thus reinforce the fear of the destructive impulse within.

The vital need to deal with anxiety forces the early ego to develop fundamental mechanisms and defences. The destruc-tive impulse is partly projected outwards (deflection of the death instinct) and, I think, attaches itself to the first external ob-ject, the mother's breast. As Freud has pointed out, the remain-ing portion of the destructive impulse is to some extent bound by the libido within the organism. However, neither of these processes entirely fulfils its purpose, and therefore the anxiety of being destroyed from within remains active. It seems to me in keeping with the lack of cohesiveness that under the pressure

---

[1] Cf. D. W. Winnicott, 'Primitive Emotional Development' (1945). In this paper Winnicott also described the pathological outcome of states of un-integration, for instance the case of a woman patient who could not distin-guish between her twin sister and herself.

[2] The greater or lesser cohesiveness of the ego at the beginning of post-natal life should be considered in connection with the greater or lesser capacity of the ego to tolerate anxiety which, as I have previously contended (*Psycho-Analysis of Children*, particularly p. 83), is a constitutional factor.

of this threat the ego tends to fall to pieces.[1] This falling to pieces appears to underlie states of disintegration in schizophrenics.

The question arises whether some active splitting processes within the ego may not occur even at a very early stage. As we assume, the early ego splits the object and the relation to it in an active way, and this may imply some active splitting of the ego itself. In any case, the result of splitting is a dispersal of the destructive impulse which is felt as the source of danger. I suggest that the primary anxiety of being annihilated by a destructive force within, with the ego's specific response of falling to pieces or splitting itself, may be extremely important in all schizophrenic processes.

Splitting Processes in Relation to the Object

The destructive impulse projected outwards is first experienced as oral aggression. I believe that oral-sadistic impulses towards the mother's breast are active from the beginning of life, though with the onset of teething the cannibalistic impulses increase in strength—a factor stressed by Abraham.

In states of frustration and anxiety the oral-sadistic and cannibalistic desires are reinforced, and then the infant feels that he has taken in the nipple and the breast in bits. Therefore in addition to the divorce between a good and a bad breast in the young infant's phantasy, the frustrating breast—attacked in oral-sadistic phantasies—is felt to be in fragments; the gratifying breast, taken in under the dominance of the sucking libido, is felt to be complete. This first internal good object acts as a focal point in the ego. It counteracts the processes of splitting and dispersal, makes for cohesiveness and integration, and is instrumental in building up the ego.[2] The infant's feeling of having inside a good and complete breast may, however, be shaken by frustration and anxiety. As a result, the divorce

---

[1] Ferenczi in 'Notes and Fragments' (1930) suggests that most likely every living organism reacts to unpleasant stimuli by fragmentation, which might be an expression of the death instinct. Possibly, complicated mechanisms (living organisms) are only kept as an entity through the impact of external conditions. When these conditions become unfavourable the organism falls to pieces.

[2] D. W. Winnicott (loc. cit.) referred to the same process from another angle: he described how integration and adaptation to reality depend essentially on the infant's experience of the mother's love and care.

between the good and bad breast may be difficult to maintain, and the infant may feel that the good breast too is in pieces.

I believe that the ego is incapable of splitting the object—internal and external—without a corresponding splitting taking place within the ego. Therefore the phantasies and feelings about the state of the internal object vitally influence the structure of the ego. The more sadism prevails in the process of incorporating the object, and the more the object is felt to be in pieces, the more the ego is in danger of being split in relation to the internalized object fragments.

The processes I have described are, of course, bound up with the infant's phantasy-life; and the anxieties which stimulate the mechanism of splitting are also of a phantastic nature. It is in phantasy that the infant splits the object and the self, but the effect of this phantasy is a very real one, because it leads to feelings and relations (and later on thought-processes) being in fact cut off from one another.[1]

Splitting in Connection with Projection and Introjection

So far I have dealt particularly with the mechanism of splitting as one of the earliest ego-mechanisms and defences against anxiety. Introjection and projection are from the beginning of life also used in the service of this primary aim of the ego. Projection, as Freud described, originates from the deflection of the death instinct outwards and in my view it helps the ego to overcome anxiety by ridding it of danger and badness. Introjection of the good object is also used by the ego as a defence against anxiety.

Closely connected with projection and introjection are some other mechanisms. Here I am particularly concerned with the connection between splitting, idealization and denial. As regards splitting of the object, we have to remember that in states of gratification love-feelings turn towards the gratifying breast, while in states of frustration hatred and persecutory anxiety attach themselves to the frustrating breast.

[1] In the discussion following the reading of this paper Dr. W. C. M. Scott referred to another aspect of splitting. He stressed the importance of the breaks in continuity of experiences, which imply a splitting in time rather than in space. He referred as an instance to the alternation between states of being asleep and states of being awake. I fully agree with his point of view.

Idealization is bound up with the splitting of the object, for the good aspects of the breast are exaggerated as a safeguard against the fear of the persecuting breast. While idealization is thus the corollary of persecutory fear, it also springs from the power of the instinctual desires which aim at unlimited gratification and therefore create the picture of an inexhaustible and always bountiful breast—an ideal breast.

We find an instance of such a cleavage in infantile hallucinatory gratification. The main processes which come into play in idealization are also operative in hallucinatory gratification, namely, splitting of the object and denial both of frustration and of persecution. The frustrating and persecuting object is kept widely apart from the idealized object. However, the bad object is not only kept apart from the good one but its very existence is denied, as is the whole situation of frustration and the bad feelings (pain) to which frustration gives rise. This is bound up with denial of psychic reality. The denial of psychic reality becomes possible only through strong feelings of omnipotence—an essential characteristic of early mentality. Omnipotent denial of the existence of the bad object and of the painful situation is in the unconscious equal to annihilation by the destructive impulse. It is, however, not only a situation and an object that are denied and annihilated—*it is an object-relation* which suffers this fate; and therefore a part of the ego, from which the feelings towards the object emanate, is denied and annihilated as well.

In hallucinatory gratification, therefore, two interrelated processes take place: the omnipotent conjuring up of the ideal object and situation, and the equally omnipotent annihilation of the bad persecutory object and the painful situation. These processes are based on splitting both the object and the ego.

In passing I would mention that in this early phase splitting, denial and omnipotence play a role similar to that of repression at a later stage of ego-development. In considering the importance of the processes of denial and omnipotence at a stage which is characterized by persecutory fear and schizoid mechanisms, we may remember the delusions of both grandeur and of persecution in schizophrenia.

So far, in dealing with persecutory fear, I have singled out the oral element. However, while the oral libido still has the lead, libidinal and aggressive impulses and phantasies from other sources come to the fore and lead to a confluence of oral, urethral and anal desires, both libidinal and aggressive. Also the attacks on the mother's breast develop into attacks of a similar nature on her body, which comes to be felt as it were as an extension of the breast, even before the mother is conceived of as a complete person. The phantasied onslaughts on the mother follow two main lines: one is the predominantly oral impulse to suck dry, bite up, scoop out and rob the mother's body of its good contents. (I shall discuss the bearing of these impulses on the development of object-relations in connection with introjection.) The other line of attack derives from the anal and urethral impulses and implies expelling dangerous substances (excrements) out of the self and into the mother. Together with these harmful excrements, expelled in hatred, split-off parts of the ego are also projected on to the mother or, as I would rather call it, *into* the mother.[1] These excrements and bad parts of the self are meant not only to injure but also to control and to take possession of the object. In so far as the mother comes to contain the bad parts of the self, she is not felt to be a separate individual but is felt to be *the* bad self.

Much of the hatred against parts of the self is now directed towards the mother. This leads to a particular form of identification which establishes the prototype of an aggressive object-relation. I suggest for these processes the term 'projective identification'. When projection is mainly derived from the infant's impulse to harm or to control the mother,[2] he feels her

[1] The description of such primitive processes suffers from a great handicap, for these phantasies arise at a time when the infant has not yet begun to think in words. In this context, for instance, I am using the expression 'to project *into* another person' because this seems to me the only way of conveying the unconscious process I am trying to describe.

[2] M. G. Evans, in a short unpublished communication (read to the British Psycho-Analytical Society, January, 1946) gave some instances of patients in whom the following phenomena were marked: lack of sense of reality, a feeling of being divided and parts of the personality having entered the mother's body in order to rob and control her; as a consequence the mother and other people similarly attacked came to represent the patient. M. G. Evans related these processes to a very primitive stage of development.

to be a persecutor. In psychotic disorders this identification of an object with the hated parts of the self contributes to the intensity of the hatred directed against other people. As far as the ego is concerned the excessive splitting off and expelling into the outer world of parts of itself considerably weaken it. For the aggressive component of feelings and of the personality is intimately bound up in the mind with power, potency, strength, knowledge and many other desired qualities.

It is, however, not only the bad parts of the self which are expelled and projected, but also good parts of the self. Excrements then have the significance of gifts; and parts of the ego which, together with excrements, are expelled and projected into the other person represent the good, *i.e.* the loving parts of the self. The identification based on this type of projection again vitally influences object-relations. The projection of good feelings and good parts of the self into the mother is essential for the infant's ability to develop good object-relations and to integrate his ego. However, if this projective process is carried out excessively, good parts of the personality are felt to be lost, and in this way the mother becomes the ego-ideal; this process too results in weakening and impoverishing the ego. Very soon such processes extend to other people,[1] and the result may be an over-strong dependence on these external representatives of one's own good parts. Another consequence is a fear that the capacity to love has been lost because the loved object is felt to be loved predominantly as a representative of the self.

The processes of splitting off parts of the self and projecting them into objects are thus of vital importance for normal development as well as for abnormal object-relations.

The effect of introjection on object-relations is equally important. The introjection of the good object, first of all the mother's breast, is a precondition for normal development. I

---

[1] W. C. M. Scott in an unpublished paper, read to the British Psycho-Analytical Society a few years ago, described three inter-connected features which he came upon in a schizophrenic patient: a strong disturbance of her sense of reality, her feeling that the world round her was a cemetery, and the mechanism of putting all good parts of herself into another person—Greta Garbo—who came to stand for the patient.

have already described that it comes to form a focal point in the ego and makes for cohesiveness of the ego. One characteristic feature of the earliest relation to the good object—internal and external—is the tendency to idealize it. In states of frustration or increased anxiety, the infant is driven to take flight to his internal idealized object as a means of escaping from persecutors. From this mechanism various serious disturbances may result: when persecutory fear is too strong, the flight to the idealized object becomes excessive, and this severely hampers ego-development and disturbs object-relations. As a result the ego may be felt to be entirely subservient to and dependent on the internal object—only a shell for it. With an unassimilated idealized object there goes a feeling that the ego has no life and no value of its own.[1] I would suggest that the condition of flight to the unassimilated idealized object necessitates further splitting processes within the ego. For parts of the ego attempt to unite with the ideal object, while other parts strive to deal with the internal persecutors.

The various ways of splitting the ego and internal objects result in the feeling that the ego is in bits. This feeling amounts to a state of disintegration. In normal development, the states of disintegration which the infant experiences are transitory. Among other factors, gratification by the external good object[2] again and again helps to break through these schizoid states. The infant's capacity to overcome temporary schizoid states is in keeping with the strong elasticity and resilience of the

---

[1] Cf. 'A Contribution to the Problem of Sublimation and its Relation to the Processes of Internalization' (1942) where Paula Heimann described a condition in which the internal objects act as foreign bodies embedded in the self. Whilst this is more obvious with regard to the bad objects, it is true even for the good ones, if the ego is compulsively subordinated to their preservation. When the ego serves its good internal objects excessively, they are felt as a source of danger to the self and come close to exerting a persecuting influence. Paula Heimann introduced the concept of the assimilation of the internal objects and applied it specifically to sublimation. As regards ego-development, she pointed out that such assimilation is essential for the successful exercise of ego-functions and for the achievement of independence.

[2] Looked at in this light, the mother's love and understanding of the infant can be seen as the infant's greatest stand-by in overcoming states of disintegration and anxieties of a psychotic nature.

infantile mind. If states of splitting and therefore of disintegration, which the ego is unable to overcome, occur too frequently and go on for too long, then in my view they must be regarded as a sign of schizophrenic illness in the infant, and some indications of such illness may already be seen in the first few months of life. In adult patients, states of depersonalization and of schizophrenic dissociation seem to be a regression to these infantile states of disintegration.[1]

In my experience, excessive persecutory fears and schizoid mechanisms in early infancy may have a detrimental effect on intellectual development in its initial stages. Certain forms of mental deficiency would therefore have to be regarded as belonging to the group of schizophrenias. Accordingly, in considering mental deficiency in children at any age one should keep in mind the possibility of schizophrenic illness in early infancy.

I have so far described some effects of excessive introjection and projection on object-relations. I am not attempting to investigate here in any detail the various factors which in some cases make for a predominance of introjective and in other cases for a predominance of projective processes. As regards normal personality, it may be said that the course of ego-development and object-relations depends on the degree to which an optimal balance between introjection and projection in the early stages of development can be achieved. This in turn has a bearing on the integration of the ego and the assimilation of internal objects. Even if the balance is disturbed and one or the other of these processes is excessive, there is some interaction between introjection and projection. For instance, the projection of a predominantly hostile inner world which is ruled by persecutory fears leads to the introjection—a taking back—of

---

[1] Herbert Rosenfeld, in 'Analysis of a Schizophrenic State with Depersonalization' (1947), has presented case-material to illustrate how the splitting mechanisms which are bound up with projective identification were responsible both for a schizophrenic state and depersonalization. In his paper 'A Note on the Psychopathology of Confusional States in Chronic Schizophrenias' (1950) he also pointed out that a confusional state comes about if the subject loses the capacity to differentiate between good and bad objects, between aggressive and libidinal impulses, and so on. He suggested that in such states of confusion splitting mechanisms are frequently reinforced for defensive purposes.

a hostile external world; and *vice versa*, the introjection of a distorted and hostile external world reinforces the projection of a hostile inner world.

Another aspect of projective processes, as we have seen, concerns the forceful entry into the object and control of the object by parts of the self. As a consequence, introjection may then be felt as a forceful entry from the outside into the inside, in retribution for violent projection. This may lead to the fear that not only the body but also the mind is controlled by other people in a hostile way. As a result there may be a severe disturbance in introjecting good objects—a disturbance which would impede all ego-functions as well as sexual development and might lead to an excessive withdrawal to the inner world. This withdrawal is, however, caused not only by the fear of introjecting a dangerous external world but also by the fear of internal persecutors and an ensuing flight to the idealized internal object.

I have referred to the weakening and impoverishment of the ego resulting from excessive splitting and projective identification. This weakened ego, however, becomes also incapable of assimilating its internal objects, and this leads to the feeling that it is ruled by them. Again, such a weakened ego feels incapable of taking back into itself the parts which it projected into the external world. These various disturbances in the interplay between projection and introjection, which imply excessive splitting of the ego, have a detrimental effect on the relation to the inner and outer world and seem to be at the root of some forms of schizophrenia.

Projective identification is the basis of many anxiety-situations, of which I shall mention a few. The phantasy of forcefully entering the object gives rise to anxieties relating to the dangers threatening the subject from within the object. For instance, the impulses to control an object from within it stir up the fear of being controlled and persecuted inside it. By introjecting and re-introjecting the forcefully entered object, the subject's feelings of inner persecution are strongly reinforced; all the more since the re-introjected object is felt to contain the dangerous aspects of the self. The accumulation of anxieties of this nature, in which the ego is, as it were, caught between a variety of external and internal persecution-situations, is a basic element in paranoia.[1]

I have previously described[2] the infant's phantasies of attacking and sadistically entering the mother's body as giving rise to various anxiety-situations (particularly the fear of being imprisoned and persecuted within her) which are at the bottom of paranoia. I also showed that the fear of being imprisoned (and especially of the penis being attacked) inside the mother is an important factor in later disturbances of male potency (impotence) and also underlies claustrophobia.[3]

Schizoid Object-Relations

To summarize now some of the disturbed object-relations which are found in schizoid personalities: the violent splitting of the self and excessive projection have the effect that the person towards whom this process is directed is felt as a persecutor. Since the destructive and hated part of the self which is split off and projected is felt as a danger to the loved object and therefore gives rise to guilt, this process of projection in some

[1] Herbert Rosenfeld, in 'Analysis of a Schizophrenic State with Depersonalization' and 'Remarks on the Relation of Male Homosexuality to Paranoia' (1949), discussed the clinical importance of those paranoid anxieties which are connected with projective identification in psychotic patients. In the two schizophrenic cases he described, it became evident that the patients were dominated by the fear that the analyst was trying to force himself into the patient. When these fears were analysed in the transference-situation, improvement could take place. Rosenfeld has further connected projective identification (and the corresponding persecutory fears) with female sexual frigidity on the one hand and on the other with the frequent combination of homosexuality and paranoia in men.

[2] *Psycho-Analysis of Children*, Chapter 8, particularly p. 189, and Chapter 12, particularly p. 329.

[3] Joan Riviere, in an unpublished paper 'Paranoid Attitudes seen in Everyday Life and in Analysis' (read before the British Psycho-Analytical Society in 1948), reported a great deal of clinical material in which projective identification became apparent. Unconscious phantasies of forcing the whole self into the inside of the object (to obtain control and possession) led, through the fear of retaliation, to a variety of persecutory anxieties such as claustrophobia, or to such common phobias as of burglars, spiders, invasion in wartime. These fears are connected with the unconscious 'catastrophic' phantasies of being dismembered, disembowelled, torn to pieces and of total internal disruption of the body and personality and loss of identity—fears which are an elaboration of the fear of annihilation (death) and have the effect of reinforcing the mechanisms of splitting and the process of ego-disintegration as found in psychotics.

ways also implies a deflection of guilt from the self on to the other person. Guilt has, however, not been done away with, and the deflected guilt is felt as an unconscious responsibility for the people who have become representatives of the aggressive part of the self.

Another typical feature of schizoid object-relations is their narcissistic nature which derives from the infantile introjective and projective processes. For, as I suggested earlier, when the ego-ideal is projected into another person, this person becomes predominantly loved and admired because he contains the good parts of the self. Similarly, the relation to another person on the basis of projecting bad parts of the self into him is of a narcissistic nature, because in this case as well the object strongly represents one part of the self. Both these types of a narcissistic relation to an object often show strong obsessional features. The impulse to control other people is, as we know, an essential element in obsessional neurosis. The need to control others can to some extent be explained by a deflected drive to control parts of the self. When these parts have been projected excessively into another person, they can only be controlled by controlling the other person. One root of obsessional mechanisms may thus be found in the particular identification which results from infantile projective processes. This connection may also throw some light on the obsessional element which so often enters into the tendency for reparation. For it is not only an object about whom guilt is experienced but also parts of the self which the subject is driven to repair or restore.

All these factors may lead to a compulsive tie to certain objects or—another outcome—to a shrinking from people in order to prevent both a destructive intrusion into them and the danger of retaliation by them. The fear of such dangers may show itself in various negative attitudes in object-relations. For instance, one of my patients told me that he dislikes people who are too much influenced by him, for they seem to become too much like himself and therefore he gets tired of them.

Another characteristic of schizoid object-relations is a marked artificiality and lack of spontaneity. Side by side with this goes a severe disturbance of the feeling of the self or, as I would put it, of the relation to the self. This relation, too, appears to be artificial. In other words, psychic reality and the relation to external reality are equally disturbed.

The projection of split-off parts of the self into another person essentially influences object-relations, emotional life and the personality as a whole. To illustrate this contention I will select as an instance two universal phenomena which are interlinked: the feeling of loneliness and fear of parting. We know that one source of the depressive feelings accompanying parting from people can be found in the fear of the destruction of the object by the aggressive impulses directed against it. But it is more specifically the splitting and projective processes which underlie this fear. If aggressive elements in relation to the object are predominant and strongly aroused by the frustration of parting, the individual feels that the split-off components of his self, projected into the object, control this object in an aggressive and destructive way. At the same time the internal object is felt to be in the same danger of destruction as the external one in whom one part of the self is felt to be left. The result is an excessive weakening of the ego, a feeling that there is nothing to sustain it, and a corresponding feeling of loneliness. While this description applies to neurotic individuals, I think that in some degree it is a general phenomenon.

One need hardly elaborate the fact that some other features of schizoid object-relations, which I described earlier, can also be found in minor degrees and in a less striking form in normal people—for instance shyness, lack of spontaneity or, on the other hand, a particularly intense interest in people.

In similar ways normal disturbances in thought-processes link up with the developmental paranoid-schizoid position. For all of us are liable at times to a momentary impairment of logical thinking which amounts to thoughts and associations being cut off from one another and situations being split off from one another; in fact, the ego is temporarily split.

The Depressive Position in Relation to the Paranoid-Schizoid Position

I now wish to consider further steps in the infant's development. So far I have described the anxieties, mechanisms and defences which are characteristic of the first few months of life. With the introjection of the complete object in about the second quarter of the first year marked steps in integration are made. This implies important changes in the relation to objects. The loved and hated aspects of the mother are no longer felt to be so widely separated, and the result is an increased fear of loss, states akin to mourning and a strong feeling of guilt, because the aggressive impulses are felt to be directed against the loved object. The depressive position has come to the fore. The very experience of depressive feelings in turn has the effect of further integrating the ego, because it makes for an increased understanding of psychic reality and better perception of the external world, as well as for a greater synthesis between inner and external situations.

The drive to make reparation, which comes to the fore at this stage, can be regarded as a consequence of greater insight into psychic reality and of growing synthesis, for it shows a more realistic response to the feelings of grief, guilt and fear of loss resulting from the aggression against the loved object. Since the drive to repair or protect the injured object paves the way for more satisfactory object-relations and sublimations, it in turn increases synthesis and contributes to the integration of the ego.

During the second half of the first year the infant makes some fundamental steps towards working through the depressive position. However, schizoid mechanisms still remain in force, though in a modified form and to a lesser degree, and early anxiety-situations are again and again experienced in the process of modification. The working through of the persecutory and depressive positions extends over the first few years of childhood and plays an essential part in the infantile neurosis. In the course of this process, anxieties lose in strength, objects become both less idealized and less terrifying, and the ego becomes more unified. All this is interconnected with the growing perception of reality and adaptation to it.

If development during the paranoid-schizoid position has not proceeded normally and the infant cannot—for internal or external reasons—cope with the impact of depressive anxieties, a vicious circle arises. For if persecutory fear, and correspondingly schizoid mechanisms, are too strong, the ego is not capable of working through the depressive position. This forces

the ego to regress to the paranoid-schizoid position and reinforces the earlier persecutory fears and schizoid phenomena.
Thus the basis is established for various forms of schizophrenia
in later life; for when such a regression occurs, not only are
the fixation-points in the schizoid position reinforced, but
there is a danger of greater states of disintegration setting
in. Another outcome may be the strengthening of depressive
features.

External experiences are, of course, of great importance in
these developments. For instance, in the case of a patient who
showed depressive and schizoid features, the analysis brought
up with great vividness his early experiences in babyhood,
to such an extent that in some sessions physical sensations in
the throat or digestive organs occurred. The patient had been
weaned suddenly at four months of age because his mother fell
ill. In addition, he did not see his mother for four weeks. When
she returned, she found the child greatly changed. He had been
a lively baby, interested in his surroundings, and he seemed
to have lost this interest. He had become apathetic. He had
accepted the substitute food fairly easily and in fact never
refused food. But he did not thrive on it any more, lost weight
and had a good deal of digestive trouble. It was only at the
end of the first year, when other food was introduced, that he
again made good physical progress.

Much light was thrown in the analysis on the influence these
experiences had on his whole development. His outlook and
attitudes in adult life were based on the patterns established in
this early stage. For instance, we found again and again a
tendency to be influenced by other people in an unselective
way—in fact to take in greedily whatever was offered—together
with great distrust during the process of introjection. This
process was constantly disturbed by anxieties from various
sources, which also contributed to an increase of greed.

Taking the material of this analysis as a whole, I came to the
conclusion that at the time when the sudden loss of the breast
and of the mother occurred, the patient had already to some
extent established a relation to a complete good object. He had
no doubt already entered the depressive position but could not
work through it successfully and the paranoid-schizoid position

became regressively reinforced. This expressed itself in the 'apathy' which followed a period when the child had already shown a lively interest in his surroundings. The fact that he had reached the depressive position and had introjected a complete object showed in many ways in his personality. He had actually a strong capacity for love and a great longing for a good and complete object. A characteristic feature of his personality was the desire to love people and trust them, unconsciously to regain and build up again the good and complete breast which he had once possessed and lost.

Connection between Schizoid and Manic-Depressive Phenomena

Some fluctuations between the paranoid-schizoid and the depressive positions always occur and are part of normal development. No clear division between the two stages of development can therefore be drawn; moreover, modification is a gradual process and the phenomena of the two positions remain for some time to some extent intermingled and interacting. In abnormal development this interaction influences, I think, the clinical picture both of some forms of schizophrenia and of manic-depressive disorders.

To illustrate this connection I shall briefly refer to some case-material. I do not intend to present a case-history here and am therefore only selecting some parts of material relevant to my topic. The patient I have in mind was a pronounced manic-depressive case (diagnosed as such by more than one psychiatrist) with all the characteristics of that disorder: there was the alternation between depressive and manic states, strong suicidal tendencies leading repeatedly to suicidal attempts, and various other characteristic manic and depressive features. In the course of her analysis a stage was reached in which a real and great improvement was achieved. Not only did the cycle stop but there were fundamental changes in her personality and her object-relations. Productivity on various lines developed, as well as actual feelings of happiness (not of a manic type). Then, partly owing to external circumstances, another phase set in. During this last phase, which continued for several months, the patient co-operated in the analysis in a particular way. She came regularly to the analytic sessions, associated fairly freely, reported dreams and provided material for the analysis. There was, however, no emotional response to my interpretations and a good deal of contempt of them. There was very seldom any conscious confirmation of what I suggested. Yet the material by which she responded to the interpretations reflected their unconscious effect. The powerful resistance shown at this stage seemed to come from one part of the personality only, while at the same time another part responded to the analytic work. It was not only that parts of her personality did not co-operate with me; they did not seem to co-operate with each other, and at the time the analysis was unable to help the patient to achieve synthesis. During this stage she decided to bring the analysis to an end. External circumstances contributed strongly to this decision and she fixed a date for the last session.

On that particular date she reported the following dream: there was a blind man who was very worried about being blind; but he seemed to comfort himself by touching the patient's dress and finding out how it was fastened. The dress in the dream reminded her of one of her frocks which was buttoned high up to the throat. The patient gave two further associations to this dream. She said, with some resistance, that the blind man was herself; and when referring to the dress fastened up to the throat, she remarked that she had again gone into her 'hide'. I suggested to the patient that she unconsciously expressed in the dream that she was blind to her own difficulties, and that her decisions with regard to the analysis as well as to various circumstances in her life were not in accordance with her unconscious knowledge. This was also shown by her admitting that she had gone into her 'hide', meaning by it that she was shutting herself off, an attitude well known to her from previous stages in her analysis. Thus the unconscious insight, and even some co-operation on the conscious level (recognition that *she* was the blind man and that she had gone into her 'hide'), derived from isolated parts of her personality only. Actually, the interpretation of this dream did not produce any effect and did not alter the patient's decision to bring the analysis to an end in that particular hour.[1]

[1] I may mention that the analysis was resumed after a break.

The nature of certain difficulties encountered in this analysis as well as in others had revealed itself more clearly in the last few months before the patient broke off the treatment. It was the mixture of schizoid and manic-depressive features which determined the nature of her illness. For at times throughout her analysis—even in the early stage when depressive and manic states were at their height—depressive and schizoid mechanisms sometimes appeared simultaneously. There were, for instance, hours when the patient was obviously deeply depressed, full of self-reproaches and feelings of unworthiness; tears were running down her cheeks and her gestures expressed despair; and yet she said, when I interpreted these emotions, that she did not feel them at all. Whereupon she reproached herself for having no feelings at all, for being completely empty. In such sessions there was also a flight of ideas, the thoughts seemed to be broken up, and their expression was disjointed.

Following the interpretation of the unconscious reasons underlying such states, there were sometimes sessions in which the emotions and depressive anxieties came out fully, and at such times thoughts and speech were much more coherent.

This close connection between depressive and schizoid phenomena appeared, though in different forms, throughout her analysis but became very pronounced during the last stage preceding the break just described.

I have already referred to the developmental connection between the paranoid-schizoid and depressive positions. The question now arises whether this developmental connection is the basis for the mixture of these features in manic-depressive disorders and, as I would suggest, in schizophrenic disorders as well. If this tentative hypothesis could be proved, the conclusion would be that the groups of schizophrenic and manic-depressive disorders are more closely connected developmentally with one another than has been assumed. This would also account for the cases in which, I believe, the differential diagnosis between melancholia and schizophrenia is exceedingly difficult. I should be grateful if further light could be thrown on my hypothesis by colleagues who have had ample material for psychiatric observation.

Some Schizoid Defences

It is generally agreed that schizoid patients are more difficult to analyse than manic-depressive types. Their withdrawn, unemotional attitude, the narcissistic elements in their object-relations (to which I referred earlier), a kind of detached hostility which pervades the whole relation to the analyst create a very difficult type of resistance. I believe that it is largely the splitting processes which account for the patient's failure in contact with the analyst and for his lack of response to the analyst's interpretations. The patient himself feels estranged and far away, and this feeling corresponds to the analyst's impression that considerable parts of the patient's personality and of his emotions are not available. Patients with schizoid features may say: 'I hear what you are saying. You may be right, but it has no meaning for me.' Or again they say they feel they are not there. The expression 'no meaning' in such cases does not imply an active rejection of the interpretation but suggests that parts of the personality and of the emotions are split off. These patients can, therefore, not deal with the interpretation; they can neither accept it nor reject it.

I shall illustrate the processes underlying such states by a piece of material taken from the analysis of a man patient. The session I have in mind started with the patient's telling me that he felt anxiety and did not know why. He then made comparisons with people more successful and fortunate than himself. These remarks also had a reference to me. Very strong feelings of frustration, envy and grievance came to the fore. When I interpreted—to give here again only the gist of my interpretations—that these feelings were directed against the analyst and that he wanted to destroy me, his mood changed abruptly. The tone of his voice became flat, he spoke in a slow, expressionless way, and he said that he felt detached from the whole situation. He added that my interpretation seemed correct, but that it did not matter. In fact, he no longer had any wishes, and nothing was worth bothering about.

My next interpretations centred on the causes for this change of mood. I suggested that at the moment of my interpretation the danger of destroying me had become very real to him and the immediate consequence was the fear of losing me. Instead of feeling guilt and depression, which at certain stages of his analysis followed such interpretations, he now attempted to deal with these dangers by a particular method of splitting. As we know, under the pressure of ambivalence, conflict and guilt, the patient often splits the figure of the analyst; then the analyst may at certain moments be loved, at other moments hated. Or the relation to the analyst may be split in such a way that he remains the good (or bad) figure while somebody else becomes the opposite figure. But this was not the kind of splitting which occurred in this particular instance. The patient split off those parts of himself, *i.e.* of his ego, which he felt to be dangerous and hostile towards the analyst. He turned his destructive impulses from his object *towards his ego*, with the result that parts of his ego temporarily went out of existence. In unconscious phantasy this amounted to annihilation of part of his personality. The particular mechanism of turning the destructive impulse against one part of his personality, and the ensuing dispersal of emotions, kept his anxiety in a latent state.

My interpretation of these processes had the effect of again altering the patient's mood. He became emotional, said he felt like crying, was depressed, but felt more integrated; then he also expressed a feeling of hunger.[1]

The violent splitting off and destroying of one part of the personality under the pressure of anxiety and guilt is in my experience an important schizoid mechanism. To refer briefly to another instance: a woman patient had dreamed that she had to deal with a wicked girl child who was determined to murder somebody. The patient tried to influence or control the child

---

[1] The feeling of hunger indicated that the process of introjection had been set going again under the dominance of the libido. While to my first interpretation of his fear of destroying me by his aggression he had responded at once with the violent splitting off and annihilation of parts of his personality, he now experienced more fully the emotions of grief, guilt and fear of loss, as well as some relief of these depressive anxieties. The relief of anxiety resulted in the analyst again coming to stand for a good object which he could trust. Therefore the desire to introject me as a good object could come to the fore. If he could build up again the good breast inside himself, he would strengthen and integrate his ego, would be less afraid of his destructive impulses, in fact he could then preserve himself and the analyst.

and to extort a confession from her which would have been to the child's benefit; but she was unsuccessful. I also entered into the dream and the patient felt that I might help her in dealing with the child. Then the patient strung up the child on a tree in order to frighten her and also prevent her from doing harm. When the patient was about to pull the rope and kill the child, she woke. During this part of the dream the analyst was also present but again remained inactive.

I shall give here only the essence of the conclusions I arrived at from the analysis of this dream. In the dream the patient's personality was split into two parts: the wicked and uncontrollable child on the one hand, and on the other hand the person who tried to influence and control her. The child, of course, stood also for various figures in the past, but in this context she mainly represented one part of the patient's self. Another conclusion was that the analyst was the person whom the child was going to murder; and my role in the dream was partly to prevent this murder from taking place. Killing the child—to which the patient had to resort—represented the annihilation of one part of her personality.

The question arises how the schizoid mechanism of annihilating part of the self connects with repression which, as we know, is directed against dangerous impulses. This, however, is a problem with which I cannot deal here.

Changes of mood, of course, do not always appear as dramatically within a session as in the first instance I have given in this section. But I have repeatedly found that advances in synthesis are brought about by interpretations of the specific causes for splitting. Such interpretations must deal in detail with the transference-situation at that moment, including of course the connection with the past, and must contain a reference to the details of the anxiety-situations which drive the ego to regress to schizoid mechanisms. The synthesis resulting from interpretations on these lines goes along with depression and anxieties of various kinds. Gradually such waves of depression—followed by greater integration—lead to a lessening of schizoid phenomena and also to fundamental changes in object-relations.

Latent Anxiety in Schizoid Patients

I have already referred to the lack of emotion which makes schizoid patients unresponsive. This is accompanied by an absence of anxiety. An important support for the analytic work is therefore lacking. For with other types of patients who have strong manifest and latent anxiety, the relief of anxiety derived from analytic interpretation becomes an experience which furthers their capacity to co-operate in the analysis.

This lack of anxiety in schizoid patients is only apparent. For the schizoid mechanisms imply a dispersal of emotions including anxiety, but these dispersed elements still exist in the patient. Such patients have a certain form of latent anxiety; it is kept latent by the particular method of dispersal. The feeling of being disintegrated, of being unable to experience emotions, of losing one's objects, is in fact the equivalent of anxiety. This becomes clearer when advances in synthesis have been made. The great relief which a patient then experiences derives from a feeling that his inner and outer worlds have not only come more together but back to life again. At such moments it appears in retrospect that when emotions were lacking, relations were vague and uncertain and parts of the personality were felt to be lost, everything seemed to be dead. All this is the equivalent of anxiety of a very serious nature. This anxiety, kept latent by dispersal, is to some extent experienced all along, but its form differs from the latent anxiety which we can recognize in other types of cases.

Interpretations which tend towards synthesizing the split in the self, including the dispersal of emotions, make it possible for the anxiety gradually to be experienced as such, though for long stretches we may in fact only be able to bring the ideational contents together but not to elicit the emotions of anxiety.

I have also found that interpretations of schizoid states make particular demands on our capacity to put the interpretations in an intellectually clear form in which the links between the conscious, pre-conscious and unconscious are established. This is, of course, always one of our aims, but it is of special import-ance at times when the patient's emotions are not available and we seem to address ourselves only to his intellect, however much broken up.

It is possible that the few hints I have given may to some extent apply as well to the technique of analysing schizophrenic patients.

Summary of Conclusions

I will now summarize some of the conclusions presented in this paper. One of my main points was the suggestion that in the first few months of life anxiety is predominantly experienced as fear of persecution and that this contributes to certain mechanisms and defences which are significant for the paranoid-schizoid position. Outstanding among these defences are the mechanisms of splitting internal and external objects, emotions and the ego. These mechanisms and defences are part of normal development and at the same time form the basis for later schizophrenic illness. I described the processes underlying identification by projection as a combination of splitting off parts of the self and projecting them on to another person, and some of the effects this identification has on normal and schizoid object-relations. The onset of the depressive position is the juncture at which by regression schizoid mechanisms may be reinforced. I also suggested a close connection between the manic-depressive and schizoid disorders, based on the interaction between the infantile paranoid-schizoid and depressive positions.

IX

APPENDIX

FREUD's analysis of the Schreber case[1] contains a wealth of material which is very relevant to my topic but from which I shall here draw only a few conclusions.

Schreber described vividly the splitting of the soul of his physician Flechsig (his loved and persecuting figure). The 'Flechsig soul' at one time introduced the system of 'soul divisions', splitting into as many as forty to sixty sub-divisions.

[1] 'Psycho-Analytic Notes upon an Autobiographical Account of a Case of Paranoia (Dementia Paranoides)' (1911).

These souls having multiplied till they became a 'nuisance', God made a raid on them and as a result the Flechsig soul survived in 'only one or two shapes'. Another point which Schreber mentions is that the fragments of the Flechsig soul slowly lost both their intelligence and their power.

One of the conclusions Freud arrived at in his analysis of this case was that the persecutor was split into God and Flechsig, and also that God and Flechsig represented the patient's father and brother. In discussing the various forms of Schreber's delusion of the destruction of the world, Freud states: 'In any case the end of the world was the consequence of the conflict which had broken out between him, Schreber, and Flechsig, or, according to the aetiology adopted in the second phase of his delusion, of the indissoluble bond which had been formed between him and God. . . .' (*Loc. cit.*, pp. 455–6.)

I would suggest, in keeping with the hypotheses outlined in the present chapter, that the division of the Flechsig soul into many souls was not only a splitting of the object but also a projection of Schreber's feeling that his ego was split. I shall here only mention the connection of such splitting processes with processes of introjection. The conclusion suggests itself that God and Flechsig also represented parts of Schreber's self. The conflict between Schreber and Flechsig, to which Freud attributed a vital role in the world-destruction delusion, found expression in the raid by God on the Flechsig souls. In my view this raid represents the annihilation by one part of the self of the other parts—which, as I contend, is a schizoid mechanism. The anxieties and phantasies about inner destruction and ego-disintegration bound up with this mechanism are projected on to the external world and underlie the delusions of its destruction.

Regarding the processes which are at the bottom of the paranoic 'world catastrophe', Freud arrived at the following conclusions: 'The patient has withdrawn from the persons in his environment and from the external world generally the libidinal cathexis which he has hitherto directed on to them. Thus all things have become indifferent and irrelevant to him, and have to be explained by means of a secondary rationalization as being "miracled up, cursory contraptions". The end of the world is the projection of this internal catastrophe; for his subjective world has come to an end since he has withdrawn his love from it.' (*Loc. cit.*, pp. 456–7.) This explanation specifically concerns the disturbance in object-libido and the ensuing breakdown in relation to people and to the external world. But a little further on (pp. 461–2) Freud considered another aspect of these disturbances. He said: 'We can no more dismiss the possibility that disturbances of the libido may react upon the egoistic cathexes than we can overlook the *converse possibility*—namely, that *a secondary or induced disturbance of the libidinal processes may result from abnormal changes in the ego. Indeed, it is probable that processes of this kind constitute the distinctive characteristic of psychoses*' (my italics). It is particularly the possibility expressed in the last two sentences which provides the link between Freud's explanation of the 'world catastrophe' and my hypothesis. 'Abnormal changes in the ego' derive, as I have suggested in this chapter, from excessive splitting processes in the early ego. These processes are inextricably linked with instinctual development, and with the anxieties to which instinctual desires give rise. In the light of Freud's later theory of the life and death instincts, which replaced the concept of the egoistic and sexual instincts, disturbances in the distribution of the libido presuppose a defusion between the destructive impulse and the libido. The mechanism of one part of the ego annihilating other parts which, I suggest, underlies the 'world catastrophe' phantasy (the raid by God on the Flechsig souls) implies a preponderance of the destructive impulse over the libido. Any disturbance in the distribution of the narcissistic libido is in turn bound up with the relation to introjected objects which (according to my work) from the beginning come to form part of the ego. The interaction between narcissistic libido and object-libido corresponds thus to the interaction between the relation to introjected and external objects. If the ego and the internalized objects are felt to be in bits, an internal catastrophe is experienced by the infant which both extends to the external world and is projected on to it. Such anxiety-states relating to an internal catastrophe arise, according to the hypothesis discussed in the present chapter, during the period of the infantile paranoid-schizoid position and form the basis for later schizophrenia. In Freud's view the dispositional fixation to dementia praecox is found in a very early stage of development. Referring to dementia praecox, which Freud distinguished from paranoia, he said: 'The dispositional point of fixation must therefore be situated further back than in paranoia, and must lie somewhere at the beginning of the course of development from auto-erotism to object-love.' (*Loc. cit.* p. 464.)

I wish to draw one more conclusion from Freud's analysis of the Schreber case. I suggest that the raid, which ended in the Flechsig souls being reduced to one or two, was part of the attempt towards recovery. For the raid was to undo, one may say heal, the split in the ego by annihilating the split-off parts of the ego. As a result only one or two of the souls were left which, as we may assume, were meant to regain their intelligence and their power. This attempt towards recovery, however, was effected by very destructive means used by the ego against itself and its introjected objects.

Freud's approach to the problems of schizophrenia and paranoia has proved of fundamental importance. His Schreber paper (and here we also have to remember Abraham's paper[1] quoted by Freud) opened up the possibility of understanding psychosis and the processes underlying it.

---

[1] 'The Psycho-Sexual Differences between Hysteria and Dementia Praecox' (1908).

X

NOTES ON THE THEORY OF THE LIFE AND DEATH INSTINCTS

By PAULA HEIMANN

A NEW psychological era began with the discovery by Breuer and Freud[1] that the hysterical symptoms of their patient were caused by unsolved intra-psychic conflicts. Following the observations made in this particular case Freud continued to investigate his patients' emotional life, and his researches into the nature of conflict led him to the discovery of the Unconscious. From this point he proceeded to explore the dynamics and structure of the mind and to evolve his theories about mental illness and mental development. One might, therefore, call the systematic investigation of emotional conflict—up till then outside the sphere of medical science—the birth of psychoanalysis.

Freud traced emotional conflicts to the operation of basic forces with opposite aims, *i.e.* antagonistic instincts. Throughout his work he maintained a dualistic approach to psychological processes and stressed the necessity to understand the nature of the instincts. At first, following the generally accepted contrast between hunger and love, he saw the opposing instinctual forces in the self-preservative and sexual instincts, later he differentiated between ego instincts and sexual instincts and thought that this dualism was in keeping with the human being's double role of an individual and a representative of his species. But advances in his work did not corroborate this distinction, and ultimately he arrived at the conclusion that a life instinct and a death instinct are the prime movers of human behaviour.

It is interesting to see how Freud himself hesitated to give full recognition and status, as it were, to his last discovery about the instincts, and yet how he was driven on by its impelling truth to follow his notion of an antithesis as final and cardinal

[1] 'On the Psychical Mechanism of Hysterical Phenomena' (1893).

as that between a primary instinct of life and a primary instinct of death. He stressed the hypothetical nature of this theory, never regarded it as a shibboleth of psycho-analysis and merely confessed to a 'cool goodwill' for it. Yet his writings contain passages like the following which clearly show conviction in his theory: 'They [a group of instincts] are the actual life instincts; the fact that they run counter to the trend of the other instincts which lead towards death indicates a contradiction between them and the rest, one which the theory of the neuroses has recognized as full of significance. . . .'[1]

Freud once explained the hostile reception of his discoveries by the fact that, like those of Copernicus and Darwin, they wound man's narcissism.[2] Copernicus destroyed the cherished belief that man's earth is in the centre of the universe (the 'cosmological blow' to narcissism); from Darwin came the 'biological blow', when he showed that man has no privileged position in the scheme of creation; and psycho-analysis caused the 'psychological blow' by discovering that man is not master in his own inner world since there are unconscious mental processes beyond his control.

I would suggest that Freud's theory of the death instinct has much intensified this psychological blow. The resentment and anxiety roused by interference with man's narcissism are bound to be still greater when to the painful wound is added the fear that the forces of death are active in man himself.[3]

---

[1] *Beyond the Pleasure Principle* (1920), p. 50.

[2] 'One of the Difficulties of Psycho-Analysis' (1917).

[3] 'We suppose that there are two fundamentally different kinds of instincts, the sexual instincts in the widest sense of the word (Eros, if you prefer that name) and the aggressive instincts whose aim is destruction. When it is put like that, you will hardly think of it as anything new; it looks as though it were a theoretical glorification of the commonplace opposition between love and hate, which may perhaps coincide with the polarity of attraction and repulsion which physics postulates for the inorganic world. But it is remarkable that this hypothesis was nevertheless felt by many to be an innovation, and indeed a most undesirable one which ought to be got rid of as soon as possible. I think a strong emotional factor was responsible for this rejection. Why have we ourselves taken so long to bring ourselves to recognize the existence of an aggressive instinct? Why was there so much hesitation in using for our theory facts which lay ready to hand and were familiar to everyone? One would probably meet with but little opposition if one were to ascribe to animals an instinct with such an aim as this. But to introduce it into the human constitution seems impious; it contradicts

The theory of the death instinct is frowned upon and has been much disputed. One argument denies its legitimate origin from psychological considerations and asserts that Freud arrived at it exclusively by way of speculation and imaginings concerning biological events. In fact this is not so. In *Beyond the Pleasure Principle* Freud clearly starts with clinical material, *i.e.* the dreams of patients suffering from traumatic neuroses which, in contrast to the wish-fulfilling function of dreams, repeat the painful traumatic event; also the play of children re-enacting an unpleasant experience over and over again. While it is true that he breaks off the discussion of both these phenomena, it is clear that he does so only after showing the element of repetition which is the essential point. He goes on to describe the observation that patients in psycho-analytic treatment, instead of remembering repressed events, *repeat* them in their current lives, thus causing much pain to themselves. From clinical observations he comes to deduce the existence of the 'repetition-compulsion', a concept which has since fully proved its validity for psychological work, and shows that this compulsion is ubiquitous and not dictated by the pleasure-principle.

The fact is therefore that Freud proceeded from clinical observations when he embarked on the journey which led him to assume the death instinct and that on his way he discovered a most important psychological principle, viz. the repetition-compulsion; moreover, throughout he kept in contact with clinical facts.[1]

His biological speculations suggest that, when by an event which 'baffles conjecture' life was created from the inanimate, the tendency to return to the original condition came into being

too many religious prejudices and social conventions. No, man must be by nature good, or at least well-disposed. If he occasionally shows himself to be brutal, violent and cruel, these are only passing disturbances of his emotional life, mostly provoked, and perhaps only the consequence of the ill-adapted social system which he has so far made for himself.' (Freud, *New Introductory Lectures on Psycho-Analysis*, p. 134.)

[1] Cf. also: '. . . for it is not on account of the teaching of history and of our own experience in life that we maintain the hypothesis of a special instinct of aggression and destructiveness in man, but on account of general considerations, to which we were led in trying to estimate the importance of the phenomena of sadism and masochism.' (*New Introductory Lectures on Psycho-Analysis*, p. 135.)

as well. Together with the life instinct the death instinct began to operate in the animate being. We may leave it to the biologists to judge the value of Freud's biological considerations, but we have the right to use the psychological part—to use it without claiming that it solves all the mysteries of human life.

Psychological work does not show the operation of instinct directly. What we do see is impulses giving rise to emotions, hopes, fears, conflicts, behaviour and actions. We observe processes like the transformation of unconscious desire into conscious fear, or of unconscious hate into conscious exaggerated love.

Let us distinguish between impulses as clinically observable entities and instincts as the ultimate forces from which these impulses spring. Instinct is then a concept, an abstraction, consistent with a particular psychological approach. We can neither prove nor disprove it by direct observation. What we can do is to present an interpretation of the facts which we observe. Such interpretation will include some speculation, which, naturally, is open to doubt. Science cannot be pursued, however, by the mere collection of observable material. If we never leave the ground of facts, we give up scientific procedure, which arrives by means of abstraction and inference—speculation—at the discovery of the principles of which the observed facts are a manifestation. A non-analytical psychologist[1] said: 'Science extends the range of evidence beyond what is accessible to common sense.' The scientific worker must combine sober observation with imaginative interpretation. There are pitfalls. Imagination may lead astray if it moves too far from the facts observed, but such a flight of fantasy is not more fruitless than the mechanical listing of facts without any imaginative work on the data obtained.[2]

It has been said that Freud's theory of the instincts trespasses outside psychology into physiology and biology—but so does the subject matter of psychology, the human being. Psychologists,

---

[1] Stout, *The Groundwork of Psychology*, p. 26.

[2] Both failures, I would think, derive from a narcissistic attitude on the part of the worker, who remains aloof from the object of his research, in the one case by following only his own whims, in the other by withholding any contribution of his own to his observations. Such a narcissistic attitude is essentially uncreative.

psychiatrists and psycho-analysts—none of us deals with an isolated psyche. We are daily shown the extension of psychological forces into the physical sphere by processes like conversion symptoms and psycho-somatic disorders (and *vice versa*, the effect of physical processes on a person's psychological condition) and we cannot exclude physiological and biological considerations from our work.

The study of human behaviour compels us to recognize a dualistic source of forces in the depths of the personality. Moreover, our observations show us that there is no sharp cleavage between mind and body. This compels us to introduce a physical factor into our concept of the ultimate dualistic source. These requirements are fulfilled by Freud's concept of primary instincts pursuing the opposite aims of life and death.

According to Freud's theory the two basic instincts are always fused with one another. The nature of this fusion and the events which alter the proportions or the effectiveness of either instinct must be of the greatest significance, but as yet our knowledge does not take us that far. It may well be that it is the character of this instinctual blend which decides whether an attitude or an activity is healthy or morbid.

Though fused, the two basic instincts struggle against each other within the organism. The life instinct aims at union and drives one individual towards others, the death instinct aims at breaking up the organism and the union between individual organisms, or at preventing such union from being formed. The development from the unicellular to the multicellular individual, with its increasing differentiation through the formation of organs with specialized functions, would be the work of the life instinct; at the same time this development constitutes as many targets for the death instinct, since every step in union offers a potential disintegration.

The theory of the two basic instincts led to a new classification. Both the sexual and the self-preservative instincts are now considered the representatives of the life instinct. The former view that the two aims of human life are in conflict has been corrected. In essence they are complementary. Normally a person's feeling of being alive is supremely heightened in the act of procreation, and fulfilment of the individual coincides with that of the species. Psycho-analytic investigation has shown that, where there are conflicts between the two aims, they arise from disturbances in the individual's development, but they cannot be attributed to an inherent antithesis between these aims themselves.

The psychological expression of the life instinct is found in love, in constructive trends and co-operative behaviour, all of which essentially spring from the drive for union; the poetic phrase 'Eros as the force that binds' is often quoted in psycho-analytic literature. The death instinct is expressed by hate, destructiveness and negativistic trends, that is, all those modes of behaviour which are antagonistic towards making or maintaining connections, intra-psychically as well as socially.

Freud suggested that the main technique available to the life instinct in its fight against the death instinct is the deflection outward of the death instinct. He regarded this mechanism as the origin of projection and thought that the death instinct is 'mute' when it operates inside the organism and becomes manifest only in acts subsequent to deflection.

It is, however, a question whether the death instinct is so 'mute', when it attacks the self. There are ample opportunities for watching self-destructive behaviour, from small blunders which people commit obviously against their own interests to serious self-damage ('accident-proneness'), gross masochistic behaviour and suicide. Moreover, the existence of physical illness and deterioration as well as of difficulties in recovery should be attributed to the operation of the death instinct, which meets the external damaging agencies half-way and facilitates their influence.

The problem of projection of the dangerous forces within is also not simple. Not only destructive impulses are projected, a process which relieves the person from the pain of feeling dangerous urges raging within himself. Good, loving impulses and traits too are projected,[1] and such projection will prove

[1] Cf. Chapters IV and IX. In his paper 'On Narcissism: an Introduction' (1914) Freud discusses various attitudes towards the loved object which can be observed in men and women. He describes it as characteristic for the man to love according to the anaclitic type and to show a sexual overestimation of the loved object. 'Complete object-love of the anaclitic type is, properly speaking, characteristic of the man. It displays the marked

helpful or dangerous according to the character of the object chosen for it, and of the further relations with this object. The danger of projection lies in its obscuring reality; often indeed it leads to serious delusions. To project 'good' loving impulses on to a 'bad' object and thus turn it 'good' may be no less harmful than to project destructive, 'bad' impulses on to a loved object and so to lose it. On the other hand, projection of good impulses will prove beneficial if it strengthens the subject's attachment to a benevolent object and allows the subject to introject goodness from it. (Such introjection includes the subject's receiving again what was originally part of his own ego.)

The statement that love represents the life instinct and hate the death instinct needs some qualification. In sado-masochism love is intricately connected with the wishes to inflict and to suffer pain, tendencies derived from the death instinct. Yet these phenomena do not challenge the theory of the primary instincts. They are evidence for the fusion between them, which is part of the theory. The same consideration holds for hate, if directed against an assailant, and even for the killing of another person in self-defence. Destructive behaviour in the service of self-preservation indicates that the fusion between the basic instincts is in favour of the life instinct. This interpretation is supported by the observation that, when self-defence is the predominant motive, aggression is not deliberately cruel.

These examples, moreover, warn us against any attempt to oversimplify matters. We cannot draw a straight line from an event on the complex higher level of experience to one basic instinct. In the course of development from the latter to the former manifold vicissitudes of the primary instinctual aim take

sexual overestimation which is doubtless derived from the original narcissism of the child, now transferred to the sexual object. This sexual overestimation is the origin of the peculiar state of being in love, a state suggestive of a neurotic compulsion, which is thus traceable to an impoverishment of the ego in respect of libido in favour of the love-object.'

Closer investigation of the mechanisms used in what Freud here calls 'transference to the sexual object' has shown that parts of the ego are here split off and projected. Components of the ego-attitudes—traits, etc., and libido—are disowned by the self, split off from the ego and projected on to the object, which subsequently appears to possess highly appreciated qualities rendering it not only supremely lovable, but also exceedingly superior to the subject. (Cf. the concept of projective identification defined in Chapter IX.)

place, precisely as a result of the influence exerted by the antithetical instinct, the interaction between the basic instincts.

There are, however, certain observations which suggest that the basic instinctual fusion is capable of modification to such a degree as to allow either basic instinct to operate almost unalloyed. A kind of defusion seems to take place with either instinct reigning supreme. I have in mind examples of extreme self-sacrifice and devotion (without a masochistic pleasure-premium) on the one hand, and of wanton and excessive cruelty on the other.

I wish to discuss only the latter, since the former are not usually treated as a controversial psychological problem.

It is unnecessary to give instances. From time to time the world is shocked by reports of savagely cruel, 'bestial' murders committed by an individual or a group. Excessive cruelty is committed, either without any provocation or, if there was some provocation, the cruelty displayed clearly exceeded what could be considered necessary or expedient in response. Moreover, in such cases the cruel acts are so calculated and worked out in detail that nothing but an instinctual urge for savage cruelty can be regarded as the motive and purpose. The murderer needs a victim to satisfy his urge to inflict maximal suffering on someone, and he proceeds obviously without any inhibition arising from empathy, guilt or horror at what he is doing.

Strangely enough, such behaviour is usually regarded as perverse sexuality, and often such crimes are called 'sexual crimes'. It is true that sadism is a form of sexual perversion, but it is necessary to distinguish between sexual practices in which sadism (and masochism) have some share, and violent assaults in which cruelty is the predominant feature. In a strict sense of the term, sexual perversion should refer to such physical intimacies between adults in which fore-pleasure excels over end-pleasure, oral and excretory activities, voyeuristic and exhibitionistic aims exceed the urge for heterosexual intercourse, and also where bodily pleasure is derived from contact with a person of the same sex. Freud has shown that such perverse sexuality (which usually contains a small admixture of sadistic and masochistic elements) is due to a persistence of infantile sexuality, and represents ways in which a child experiences sexual gratification.

The murdered victim of the so-called sexual crime does not die from a sexual experience, however infantile it may be, but from the infliction of maximally cruel violence. The sexual aspect of the murderer's behaviour may possibly only be introduced in order to deceive the victim and so to provide the opportunity for the aim of the urge to cruelty. Possibly the murderer starts in a state of sexual excitement, which, however, soon subsides and merely serves to open the floodgates to the violent and destructive impulses. It seems that the investigators of these crimes are aware that only the elemental power of an instinct can be their cause, but can only concede to sexuality the character of such an instinctual force. I would suggest that Freud's theory of the two basic instincts in the struggle against one another, and of the deflection outward of the death instinct by the life instinct, gives us an idea of the forces concerned. I think the hypothesis is justified that in cases of wanton cruelty a kind of instinctual disaster takes place, that for some reason the fusion between the two primary instincts is broken up, and the death instinct stirs within the self to an extreme degree without any mitigation by the life instinct, so that the only defence by the latter is the most primitive, i.e. the crude deflection of the inner danger of cruel suffering and death on to a victim. I do not suggest that the murderer experiences his own threatening inner catastrophe in any way consciously, or that he acts in a state of conscious panic, but I think that his actions can only be understood by the assumption of his being seized by a frenzied urge to find a victim—as a substitute for himself. This assumption alone seems to me to explain the complete absence of any empathy with the victim's suffering, the need for as many savage details in the act of murdering as possible and of the satisfaction obtained (mistakenly thought to be sexual in nature) by the victim's agonies. Owing to some such process at the deepest level, which for want of more certain knowledge I call an instinctual catastrophe, the murderer must feel the raging of the force of death within himself to such an intense degree, because uncontrolled by the life instinct, that nothing but deflection outward could save him from it.

Freud's theory of the instincts of life and death as the ultimate source of motivations represents a most comprehensive co-ordination system for our clinical observations which clearly indicate that emotions and behaviour are the result of the impact of two opposed forces. The much discussed problem of the origin of anxiety, too, now appears in a clearer light.

In the main there are three theories concerning the origin of anxiety. The first is Freud's original theory which regards anxiety as the result of an 'automatic transformation' of repressed libidinal impulses. When a libidinal claim is repressed, anxiety appears in its place. Although Freud later[1] qualified this statement and pointed to the observation that anxiety often precedes repression, and even though at times he seemed to discard this theory, he yet did not in fact abandon it. It recurs frequently in his writings.

The second theory was put forward by Ernest Jones,[2] who started by considering what it is that enables human beings to feel fear at all. He concluded that there is an 'innate capacity of fearing', which he classified as the 'fear instinct'.

Melanie Klein[3] has produced the third theory. Anxiety arises in a direct line from the destructive impulses; the danger to the organism from the death instinct, the source of the destructive impulses, is the primary cause of anxiety. The libidinal factor, however, enters her theory, in that libidinal frustration by heightening aggression increases or liberates anxiety, whereas libidinal gratification diminishes or keeps anxiety at bay. In operation therefore it is the degree of fusion and the interplay between the primary instincts which are responsible for anxiety.

I think it is possible to define this interaction and to describe the share of either instinct in the production of anxiety. It will then be seen that these three theories, which seem to be greatly at variance between themselves, can be reconciled.

---

[1] *Inhibitions, Symptoms and Anxiety*, 1926, pp. 23, 112, *et al.*

[2] 'The Pathology of Morbid Anxiety' (1911), p. 423: 'Morbid anxiety is commonly described by Freudians as being derived from repressed sexuality. While this is clinically true, it is psychologically perhaps more accurate to describe it as a reaction against repressed sexuality, a reaction derived from the *instinct of fear*.' (My italics.)

[3] Cf. Chapter VIII; also *Psycho-Analysis of Children*, pp. 183-4.

There can be no doubt that the capacity of fearing is innate, as much so as the capacity of loving or hating. It forms part of the individual's psychological equipment. Anxiety may be regarded as the condition in which the capacity of fearing is actuated. It is subjectively felt as a state of painful tension which impels the individual to take steps towards its removal, and these steps imply defences against the danger. In this way anxiety serves a protective function[1] and must be ranged together with the self-preservative instincts. This would mean that it is the life instinct to which the innate capacity of fearing should be attributed, as well as its activation in the experience of anxiety.

The danger, on the other hand, against which the life instinct institutes and mobilizes the capacity of fearing originates in the operations of the death instinct, whose aims are antagonistic to life and health.[2]

Danger arising primarily within the organism provides the stimulus for the human being's innate capacity of fearing. This pattern may be regarded as the intra-psychic disposition for recognizing external dangers and using against them defences learnt originally in the response to internal danger.

These considerations obviously make full use of Melanie Klein's theory and of Ernest Jones's concept of an 'innate capacity of fearing', whilst they make it unnecessary to complicate the theory of the basic instincts by assuming a third primary instinct.

As regards Freud's original theory of an 'automatic transformation' of repressed libido, I would suggest that two factors have to be recognized. First, that the notion of an 'automatic' process in the production of anxiety implies an instinctual element, an event on the instinctual level; secondly, we have to consider the force which is responsible for the inhibition of a libidinal impulse. As we know, inhibition of a libidinal desire may lead to substitute-gratification, e.g. sublimation, and in such a case anxiety does not appear and no unfavourable condition of tension ensues. If the repression of a libidinal desire leads to an intolerable condition, it can be seen in analysis that

[1] Ernest Jones, loc. cit.
[2] Freud, *Beyond the Pleasure Principle*.

destructive impulses[1] enter into the libidinal wish, so that the gratification desired (and repressed) would have simultaneously allowed their expression as well (a deflection outwards of the death instinct). In such cases libidinal repression leads to anxiety, in response to the danger from the stirring of the death instinct within the self. The anxiety which is connected with certain types of repression is thus the response to a danger which arises from the activity of the death instinct. The notion of an 'automatic transformation' of repressed libido implies a struggle between the basic instincts in which the life instinct cannot enforce full victory (libidinal gratification or sublimation), but in face of the danger can bring about the anxiety response.

It may be useful to state explicitly that I have been concerned only with the origin of anxiety on the deepest, the instinctual level, and not with the complex processes on higher levels, which, however, are constructed according to the basic pattern.

One word may be added about the many instances in which anxiety fails in bringing about purposeful, protective behaviour. As we know, an excess of anxiety may paralyse the person and thus aggravate the danger against which it should protect. In such cases the struggle between the basic instincts issues in favour of the death instinct which has proved capable of interfering with the very defence, the mobilization of the capacity of fearing, which the life instinct brought about. A similar constellation of forces would account for the undue absence of anxiety and of protective behaviour in the face of danger.

*   *   *   *   *   *

Freud's final theory of primary instincts of life and death, clinically represented by the impulses of love, sexuality and self-preservation or of destructiveness and cruelty, has not yet been fully worked out and applied. In his work the libido-theory still stands in its original form, in which cruelty is treated as a 'component instinct' of the libido. Psycho-analytical theory has treated the two instincts in an unequal manner: the sexual instinct is the first-born and privileged child, the destructive

[1] Cf. Chapter V.

instinct is the late-comer, the stepchild. The first was recognized from the beginning and distinguished with a name, *libido*; it took much longer to recognize its adversary, which still has not been given a special name. (The term '*destrudo*' suggested by Edoardo Weiss[1] many years ago has not received civic rights in psycho-analytical terminology.)

One of the foundation-stones of psycho-analysis is the principle that the libido develops anaclitically, *i.e.* in dependence on the physiological functions. Although this principle, discovered by Freud, was readily enough accepted and its usefulness is established beyond doubt, its implications have not been worked out fully. All the familiar phenomena of oral, anal, muscular, etc., erotisms, as well as those of the libidinal ties formed with the object which satisfies the physiological needs, exemplify the attachment of the libido to bodily functions. Melanie Klein's work with young children,[2] her discovery of the intensely destructive phantasies connected with bodily functions, produced the data which led to the conclusion that the same principle applies to the operation of the destructive impulses. In the light of her findings it can be seen that Freud, in discovering that libido attaches to the great physiological functions, did more than describe a character of the libido: he stated a special case of a broader principle, which concerns the mode of operation of instinct in general, and which rests upon the fact that the human organism is a mind/body entity. The instincts are the source of the energies on which all the mind/body processes depend. They lie on the borderland between soma and psyche; Janus-faced, they turn one face to the bodily, the other to the mental components of the organism. Both instincts—the libido and the destructive instincts—seek to fulfil their aims in bodily activities, just as, conversely, mental functions derive from them both.[3] Mental experiences are bound to accompany the operation of the instincts in the body, and an emotional relationship must follow in the wake of the bodily activities with the object who satisfies or frustrates them, *i.e.* relations of both a libidinal and a destructive

---

[1] 'Todestrieb und Masochismus' (1935).
[2] See *Psycho-Analysis of Children* (1932).
[3] As Freud described in some detail in 'Negation'.

kind are formed with objects, beginning with the first. Conversely, the object's attitude in physical contact involves emotional elements as well. It goes without saying that the mother who feeds her child does not offer him *merely* a physical substance, nor has she herself merely a physical sensation.

Freud's view that the libido develops 'anaclitically' must be expanded to include also the development of relationships in which destructive impulses predominate. Frustration of physical needs paves the way for object-hostility. Early hate no less than early love is closely linked with bodily sensations. The terms 'oral-sadistic' and 'anal-sadistic' in fact describe the attachment of cruelty to bodily functions, although they were coined prior to the discovery that cruelty represents the death instinct, and is not part of the libido but fundamentally opposed to it.

There is another basic contention of the libido-theory which is derived from the attachment of the libido to the physiological functions, namely, that of the erotogenicity of virtually all organs. This too must be expanded on the basis of Melanie Klein's work. The organs capable of producing pleasurable sensations involving libidinal phantasies will also be the seat of sensations which accompany destructive instinctual impulses and cruel phantasies.[1]

All bodily and mental activities, based as they are on the primary instincts, are bound to serve two masters, the life instinct and the death instinct.

*   *   *   *   *   *

Does the theory of a death instinct advance our psychological understanding further than the more simple concept of an instinct of destructiveness or of inborn aggressiveness would do? It has been argued that the speculations bound up with the concept of a death instinct are unnecessary, since all clinical data of destructiveness and cruelty can be accounted for by the assumption that there is an instinct of destructiveness.

Against this I would suggest that, by rejecting the postulate of an ultimate source for a destructive instinct (or for inborn aggressiveness), the entire background of our theoretical

---

[1] Cf. Joan Riviere's description of the destructive charges of various organs. 'Limbs shall trample . . .', p. 50.

concepts and the total frame of reference for psychological work would be impoverished. The implications of the concept of a death instinct operating in antithesis to the life instinct are much richer than those of a destructive instinct. We should be in a similar situation to that in which we were with regard to sexual problems before the sexual instinct was recognized as derived from a greater entity, the life instinct. The imperative nature of the sexual impulses and the significance of pleasure for emotional life were only incompletely understood before Freud showed the derivation of the libido from the life instinct. There was an hiatus in the theoretical ordering of facts as long as the self-preservative instincts were seen in opposition to the sexual impulses. Many problems became more accessible when Freud united the sexual and the self-preservative instincts as varying expressions of the one superimposed force, the life instinct.

In a similar way cruelty and the whole system of motivations related to it can only be seen in true perspective if recognized as derived from a source as powerful and ultimate as the death instinct. Without this connection the destructive instinct hangs, so to say, in mid-air, it is like an ambassador without a country to account for his existence and function. Conversely, the theory of the life and death instincts, of an antithesis as final and cardinal as that between inherently conflicting primary instincts, offers us a bridge to the deepest aspects of human nature and simultaneously helps us to find our way through the confusing wealth of meanings (over-determination) and ambiguities of the surface expressions of the psychological processes. Over-determination is caused by the basic dualism and bears witness to the dynamic operations it engenders.

Again, acceptance of the theory of the death instinct changes our assessment of hostility and cruelty; so that since these are elements of the complex and interacting emotional network, our conception of the total personality is influenced. One sees the human mind by its very nature compelled to manipulate constantly between two basically opposed forces, from which all emotions, sensations, desires and activities derive. It can never escape conflict and can never be static, but must always go on, one way or another, must always employ devices to mediate for an equilibrium between its antithetical drives. It is the successful outcome of such devices which brings states of harmony and oneness, and these states are threatened by endogenous as well as exogenous factors. And since the instincts are inborn, we have to conclude that some form of conflict exists from the beginning of life.

We claim that the orientation towards psychological problems which follows from the acceptance of the primary instincts of life and death is of inestimable value in our work. Our evaluation of the conflicts in *social* relations is notably influenced when we approach them against the dynamic background of a perpetual *intra-psychic* struggle between life and death. We hear a great deal in our work about wrongs done to our patients by their parents, wives, husbands, partners in work and so on, and their complaints often seem truthful and in line with general observations. Yet analysis shows how much unhappy experiences are actively provoked or exploited by the sufferer. On account of the need to deflect hatred and destructiveness, ultimately the death instinct, from the self on to objects, 'bad' objects are needed and will be created, if not found to hand.

Closely linked with this problem is that of frustration (of bodily needs or of libidinal desires) which also appears in a different light when considered in relation to the operation of the life and death instincts. Since frustration acts as a lever for the deflection of hate and destructiveness from the self, it is sought after because an object which inflicts the pain of frustration may be more justifiably hated and annihilated. Thus frustration has its appointed place in the design of primitive defences. But precisely for this reason a frustrating environment, lack of understanding and love are so dangerous for the child. When the environment meets his primitive needs for the deflection of his destructive impulses half-way by coldness, rejection and hostility, a vicious circle is created. The child grows up in the expectation of badness and, when he finds his fears confirmed in the world outside, his own cruel and negativistic impulses are perpetuated and increased.

Our understanding of the individual becomes more poignant through our awareness of the deep biological sources from which his destructiveness, his defensive need for unhappiness and his anxieties spring, and our capacity to deal with such baffling technical problems as sado-masochism, delusions of persecution or negative therapeutic reactions will be greater through the light gained in our work from Freud's concept of the life and death instincts.

BIBLIOGRAPHY

(*N.B.—I.J.Ps-A.* = *International Journal of Psycho-Analysis.*)

ABRAHAM, K. (1908) 'The Psycho-Sexual Differences between Hysteria and Dementia Praecox', *Selected Papers on Psycho-Analysis.* Hogarth Press.

(1924) 'A Short Study of the Development of the Libido viewed in the Light of Mental Disorders', *Selected Papers on Psycho-Analysis.* Hogarth Press.

(1925) 'Character-Formation on the Genital Level of the Libido', *Selected Papers on Psycho-Analysis.* Hogarth Press.

BALDWIN, J. M. (1911) *Genetic Logic.* George Allen.

BALINT, M. (1948) 'Individual Differences in Early Infancy', *Journal of Genetic Psychology*, LXXIII.

(1949) 'Early Developmental Stages of the Ego: Primary Object-Love', *I.J.Ps-A.*, XXX.

BAYLEY, N. (1936) *The California Infant Scale of Motor Development.* University of California Press.

BERNFELD, S. (1929) *Psychology of the Infant.* Kegan Paul.

BRIERLEY, M. (1932) 'Some Problems of Integration in Women', *I.J.Ps-A.*, XIII.

(1944) 'Notes on Metapsychology as Process Theory', *I.J.Ps-A.*, XXV.

FAIRBAIRN, W. R. D. (1941) 'A Revised Psychopathology of the Psychoses and Neuroses', *I.J.Ps-A.*, XXII.

(1944) 'Endopsychic Structure Considered in Terms of Object-Relationships', *I.J.Ps-A.*, XXV.

(1946) 'Object-Relationships and Dynamic Structure', *I.J.Ps-A.*, XXVII.

FERENCZI, S. (1909) 'Introjection and Transference', in *Sex in Psycho-Analysis.* Basic Books, New York, 1950.

(1924) 'Thalassa: a Theory of Genitality', *The Psycho-Analytic Quarterly.* New York, 1938.

(1925) 'Psycho-Analysis of Sexual Habits', *Further Contributions to the Theory and Technique of Psycho-Analysis.* Hogarth Press.

(1930) 'Notes and Fragments', *I.J.Ps-A.*, XXX.

FREUD, S. (and BREUER J.) (1893) 'On the Psychical Mechanism of Hysterical Phenomena', in Freud, *Collected Papers*, Vol. I. Hogarth Press.

FREUD, S. (1896) 'Heredity and the Aetiology of the Neuroses', *Collected Papers*, Vol. I. Hogarth Press.

(1896) 'The Aetiology of Hysteria', *Collected Papers*, Vol. I. Hogarth Press.

(1900) *The Interpretation of Dreams.* Revised English Translation. George Allen and Unwin, 1932.

(1905) *Three Essays on the Theory of Sexuality.* Imago Publishing Co., 1949.

(1905) 'My Views on the Part played by Sexuality in the Aetiology of the Neuroses', *Collected Papers*, Vol. I. Hogarth Press.

(1908) 'Hysterical Phantasies and their Relation to Bisexuality', *Collected Papers*, Vol. II. Hogarth Press.

(1909) 'The Origin and Development of Psycho-Analysis.' (Five lectures delivered at Clark University.) *American Journal of Psychology*, 21, 1910.

(1909) 'Analysis of a Phobia in a Five-Year-Old Boy', *Collected Papers*, Vol. III. Hogarth Press.

(1911) 'Formulations Regarding the Two Principles in Mental Functioning', *Collected Papers*, Vol. IV. Hogarth Press.

(1911) 'Psycho-Analytic Notes upon an Autobiographical Account of a Case of Paranoia (Dementia Paranoides)', *Collected Papers*, Vol. III. Hogarth Press.

(1912) 'Types of Neurotic Nosogenesis', *Collected Papers*, Vol. II. Hogarth Press.

(1912–13) *Totem and Taboo.* Routledge, 1950.

(1914) 'On Narcissism: an Introduction', *Collected Papers*, Vol. IV. Hogarth Press.

(1915) 'Instincts and Their Vicissitudes', *Collected Papers*, Vol. IV. Hogarth Press.

(1915) 'The Unconscious', *Collected Papers*, Vol. IV. Hogarth Press.

(1915) 'Some Character-Types met with in Psycho-Analytic Work', *Collected Papers*, Vol. IV. Hogarth Press.

(1916–17) *Introductory Lectures on Psycho-Analysis.* George Allen and Unwin.

(1917) 'One of the Difficulties of Psycho-Analysis', *Collected Papers*, Vol. IV. Hogarth Press.

(1917) 'Mourning and Melancholia', *Collected Papers*, Vol. IV. Hogarth Press.

(1918) 'From the History of an Infantile Neurosis', *Collected Papers*, Vol. III. Hogarth Press.

(1920) *Beyond the Pleasure Principle.* The International Psycho-Analytical Press, 1922.

(1922) 'Two Encyclopaedia Articles', *Collected Papers*, Vol. V. Hogarth Press, 1950.

(1923) *The Ego and the Id*. Hogarth Press.

(1924) 'The Economic Problem in Masochism', *Collected Papers*, Vol. II. Hogarth Press.

(1925) *An Autobiographical Study*. Hogarth Press.

(1925) 'Negation', *Collected Papers*, Vol. V. Hogarth Press.

(1926) *Inhibitions, Symptoms and Anxiety*. Hogarth Press, 1936.

(1928) 'Humour', *Collected Papers*, Vol. V. Hogarth Press.

(1930) *Civilization and its Discontents*. Hogarth Press.

(1931) ' Female Sexuality', *Collected Papers*, Vol. V. Hogarth Press.

(1932) *New Introductory Lectures*. Hogarth Press.

(1940) *Outline of Psycho-Analysis*. Hogarth Press.

GESELL, A. (1928) *Infancy and Human Growth*. Macmillan.

(1939) *Biographies of Child Development*. Hamish Hamilton.

(1940) *The First Five Years of Life*. Methuen.

(1946) *The Embryology of Behaviour*. Hamish Hamilton.

GOODENOUGH, F. (1931) *Anger in Young Children*. University of Minnesota Press.

HAZLITT, V. (1930) 'Children's Thinking', *British Journal of Psychology*, XX.

(1933) *The Psychology of Infancy*. Methuen.

HEIMANN, P. (1942) 'Sublimation and its Relation to Processes of Internalization', *I.J.Ps-A.*, XXIII.

ISAACS, S. (1929) 'Privation and Guilt', *I.J.Ps-A.*, X.

(1930) *Intellectual Growth in Young Children*. Routledge and Kegan Paul.

(1933) *Social Development of Young Children*. Routledge and Kegan Paul.

JONES, E. (1911) 'The Pathology of Morbid Anxiety', *Papers on Psycho-Analysis*. Fourth edition. Bailliere, Tindall and Cox.

(1916) 'The Theory of Symbolism', *Papers on Psycho-Analysis*. Fifth edition. Bailliere, Tindall and Cox.

(1927) 'The Early Development of Female Sexuality', *Papers on Psycho-Analysis*. Fifth edition.

(1929) 'Fear, Guilt and Hate', *Papers on Psycho-Analysis*. Fifth edition.

(1935) 'Early Female Sexuality', *Papers on Psycho-Analysis*. Fifth edition.

KLEIN, M. (1926) 'Infant Analysis', *Contributions to Psycho-Analysis*. Hogarth Press, 1948.

(1928) 'Early Stages of the Oedipus Conflict', *Contributions to Psycho-Analysis*. Hogarth Press.

(1930) 'The Importance of Symbol-Formation in the Development of the Ego', *Contributions to Psycho-Analysis*. Hogarth Press.
(1932) *The Psycho-Analysis of Children*. Hogarth Press.
(1935) 'A Contribution to the Psychogenesis of Manic-Depressive States', *Contributions to Psycho-Analysis*. Hogarth Press.
(1940) 'Mourning and its Relation to Manic-Depressive States', *Contributions to Psycho-Analysis*. Hogarth Press.
(1945) 'The Oedipus Complex in the Light of Early Anxieties, *Contributions to Psycho-Analysis*. Hogarth Press.
(1948) *Contributions to Psycho-Analysis*, 1921–45. Hogarth Press.
LEWIS, M. M. (1936) *Infant Speech*. Kegan Paul.
(1937) 'The Beginning of Reference to Past and Future in a Child's Speech', *British Journal of Educational Psychology*, VII.
(1938) 'The Beginning and Early Functions of Questions in a Child's Speech', *British Journal of Educational Psychology*, VIII.
MACK-BRUNSWICK, R. (1928) 'Die Analyse eines Eifersuchtswahnes', *Intern. Zeitschrift für Psychoanalyse*, Bd. XIV.
MIDDLEMORE, M. P. (1941) *The Nursing Couple*. Hamish Hamilton.
MONEY-KYRLE, R. E. (1945) 'Towards a Common Aim: a Psycho-Analytical Contribution to Ethics', *British Journal of Medical Psychology*, XX.
(1951) *Psychoanalysis and Politics*. Gerald Duckworth and Co. Ltd.
MURPHY, L. B. (1937) *Social Behavior and Child Personality*, Columbia University Press.
PRATT, KARL CHAPMAN, and others. (1930) 'The Behavior of the Newborn Infant'. *Ohio State Univ. Studies*, Contrib. Psych. No. 10.
RADÓ, S. (1928) 'The Problem of Melancholia', *I.J.Ps-A.*, IX.
RIBBLE, M. A. (1944) 'Infantile Experience in Relation to Personality Development', *Personality and the Behavior Disorders*, Vol. II, Chapter 20. Ronald Press Company.
ROSENFELD, H. (1947) 'Analysis of a Schizophrenic State with Depersonalization', *I.J.Ps-A.*, XXVIII.
(1949) 'Remarks on the Relation of Male Homosexuality to Paranoia, Paranoid Anxiety and Narcissism', *I.J.Ps-A.*, XXX.
(1950) 'A Note on the Psychopathology of Confusional States in Chronic Schizophrenias', *I.J.Ps-A.*, XXXI.
SCHMIDEBERG, M. (1933) 'Some Unconscious Mechanisms in Pathological Sexuality', *I.J.Ps-A.*, XIV.
SEARL, M. N. (1933) 'The Psychology of Screaming', *I.J.Ps-A.*, XIV.

SHARPE, E. F. (1935) 'Similar and Divergent Unconscious Determinants Underlying the Sublimations of Pure Art and Pure Science', *I.J.Ps-A.*, XVI.

SHIRLEY, M. (1933) *The First Two Years*, Vols. I, II, III. University of Minnesota Press. (A study of the development of twenty-five normal children.)

STOUT, G. F. (1920) *The Groundwork of Psychology*. Kegan Paul.

VALENTINE, C. W. (1930) 'The Innate Bases of Fear', *Journal of Genetic Psychology*, XXXVII.

WALLER, H. K. (1921) 'Breast Feeding', *The Practitioner's Encyclopaedia of Midwifery and the Diseases of Women*.

WEISS, E. (1935) 'Todestrieb und Masochismus', *Imago*, XXI.

WINNICOTT, D. W. (1931) *Disorders of Childhood*. Heinemann.
(1941) 'The Observation of Infants in a Set Situation', *I.J.Ps-A.*, XXII.
(1945) 'Primitive Emotional Development', *I.J.Ps-A.*, XXVI.

INDEX

INDEX

347